# The Community of the Renewed Covenant

Christianity and Judaism in Antiquity Series
Gregory E. Sterling, Series Editor

Volume 10

*The University of Notre Dame Press gratefully acknowledges
the generous support of Jack and Joan Conroy of Naples,
Florida, in the publication of titles in this series.*

# The Community of the Renewed Covenant

The Notre Dame Symposium
on the
Dead Sea Scrolls

Edited by

EUGENE ULRICH
and
JAMES VANDERKAM

University of Notre Dame Press
Notre Dame • Indiana

Copyright © 1994 by University of Notre Dame
Notre Dame, IN 46556
www.undpress.nd.edu
All Rights Reserved

Manufactured in the United States of America

Paperback published in 1996; reprinted in 2004, 2009

*Library of Congress Cataloging-in-Publication Data*

Notre Dame Symposium on the Dead Sea Scrolls (1993: University of Notre Dame)
    The Community of the renewed covenant : the Notre Dame Symposium on the Dead Sea Scrolls / edited by Eugene Ulrich and James VanderKam.
        p.  cm. — (Christianity and Judaism in antiquity : v.10)
    Includes index.
    ISBN 0-268-00802-7 (cl. alk. paper)
    ISBN 13: 978-0-268-00816-1 (pb. alk. paper)
    ISBN 10: 0-268-00816-7 (pb. alk. paper)
    1. Dead Sea scrolls—Congresses. 2. Qumran community—Congresses. 1. Ulrich, Eugene Charles (1938– ).  II. VanderKam, James C. III. Title. IV. Series. / BM487.N65  1993
296.1'55—dc20                                                     94-29484
                                                                                   CIP

∞ *This book is printed on acid-free paper.*

*For*
*Lester and Renée Crown*
*Newton and Jo Minow*
*whose vision and generosity have contributed greatly*
*to Jewish-Christian understanding*
*and for*
*Paul M. and Barbara Henkels*
*whose quest for excellence has brought*
*these distinguished lecturers*
*to the Notre Dame Campus*

# Christianity and Judaism in Antiquity Series (CJAS)

The Christianity and Judaism in Antiquity Program at the University of Notre Dame came into existence during the afterglow of the Second Vatican Council. The doctoral program combines the distinct academic disciplines of the Hebrew Bible, Judaism, the New Testament, and the Early Church in an effort to explore the religion of the ancient Hebrews, the diverse forms of Second Temple Judaism, and its offspring in the religions of Rabbinic Judaism and the multiple incarnations of early Christianity. While the scope of the program thus extends from the late Bronze and Early Iron Ages to the late antique world, the fulcrum lies in the Second Temple and Early Christian periods. Each religion is explored in its own right, although the program cultivates a History-of-Religions approach that examines their reciprocally illuminating interrelationships and their place in the larger context of the ancient world.

During the seventies a monograph series was launched to reflect and promote the orientation of the program. Initially known as Studies in Judaism and Christianity in Antiquity, the series was published under the auspices of the Center for the Study of Judaism and Christianity in Antiquity. Six volumes appeared from 1975–86. In 1988 the series name became Christianity and Judaism in Antiquity as the editorship passed to Charles Kannengiesser, who oversaw the release of nine volumes. Professor Kannengiesser's departure from Notre Dame necessitated the appointment of a new editor. At the same time, the historic connection between the series and the CJA doctoral program was strengthened by the appointment of all CJA faculty to the editorial board. Throughout these institutional permutations, the purpose of the series has continued to be the promotion of research into the origins of Judaism and Christianity with the hope that a better grasp of the common ancestry and relationship of two of the world's religions will not only illuminate the ancient world but the modern world as well.

Gregory E. Sterling<br>
Series Editor<br>
30 June 1994

# CONTENTS

**Abbreviations**     x

**Introduction**
JAMES VANDERKAM AND EUGENE ULRICH     xiii

## The Identity of the Community

SHEMARYAHU TALMON
    The Community of the Renewed Covenant:
        Between Judaism and Christianity     3

## The Community and Its Religious Law

JOSEPH M. BAUMGARTEN
    Sadducean Elements in Qumran Law     27

LAWRENCE H. SCHIFFMAN
    The *Temple Scroll* and the Nature of Its Law:
        The Status of the Question     37

JOHN STRUGNELL
    MMT: Second Thoughts on a Forthcoming Edition     57

## The Scriptures at Qumran

EUGENE ULRICH
    The Bible in the Making: The Scriptures at Qumran     77

JULIO TREBOLLE BARRERA
    The Authoritative Functions of Scriptural Works at Qumran     95

EMANUEL TOV
    Biblical Texts as Reworked in Some Qumran Manuscripts
        with Special Attention to 4QRP and 4QParaGen-Exod    111

## Wisdom and Prayer

DANIEL J. HARRINGTON, S.J.
    Wisdom at Qumran    137

EILEEN M. SCHULLER, O.S.U.
    Prayer, Hymnic, and Liturgical Texts from Qumran    153

## Apocalypticism, Messianism, and Eschatology

DEVORAH DIMANT
    Apocalyptic Texts at Qumran    175

JOHN J. COLLINS
    Teacher and Messiah? The One Who Will Teach
        Righteousness at the End of Days    193

JAMES VANDERKAM
    Messianism in the Scrolls    211

ÉMILE PUECH
    Messianism, Resurrection, and Eschatology at
        Qumran and in the New Testament    235

## Indexes

Biblical Passages    259

Ancient Literature    270

Subjects    275

Modern Authors    286

# Abbreviations

| | |
|---|---|
| AB | Anchor Bible |
| *ALUOS* | *Annual of Leeds University Oriental Society* |
| *ANRW* | *Aufstieg und Niedergang der römischen Welt* |
| ATDan | Acta theologica danica |
| *BA* | *Biblical Archaeologist* |
| *BAR* | *Biblical Archaeology Review* |
| BASOR | Bulletin of the American Schools of Oriental Research |
| BETL | Bibliotheca ephemeridum theologicarum lovaniensium |
| *Bib* | *Biblica* |
| *BibLeb* | *Bibel und Leben* |
| BIOSCS | Bulletin of the International Organization for Septuagint and Cognate Studies |
| BJS | Brown Judaica Studies |
| *BO* | *Bibliotheca orientalis* |
| *BZ* | *Biblische Zeitschrift* |
| CahRB | Cahiers de la Revue biblique |
| *CBQ* | *Catholic Biblical Quarterly* |
| CBQMS | Catholic Biblical Quarterly, Monograph Series |
| ConB | Coniectanea biblica |
| CRINT | Compendia rerum iudaicarum ad novum testamentum |
| *DBSup* | *Dictionnaire de la Bible, Supplément* |
| DJD | Discoveries in the Judaean Desert |
| *DSD* | *Dead Sea Discoveries* |
| Ebib | Etudes bibliques |
| ErIsr | Eretz Israel |
| *EstBib* | *Estudios bíblicos* |
| ETL | Ephemerides theologicae lovanienses |
| HAR | Hebrew Annual Review |
| HDR | Harvard Dissertations in Religion |
| *HeyJ* | *Heythrop Journal* |
| HSM | Harvard Semitic Monographs |
| HSS | Harvard Semitic Studies |

| | |
|---|---|
| *HTR* | *Harvard Theological Review* |
| HTS | Harvard Theological Studies |
| *HUCA* | *Hebrew Union College Annual* |
| HUCM | Monographs of the Hebrew Union College |
| *IEJ* | *Israel Exploration Journal* |
| *JBL* | *Journal of Biblical Literature* |
| *JJS* | *Journal of Jewish Studies* |
| *JNES* | *Journal of Near Eastern Studies* |
| *JQR* | *Jewish Quarterly Review* |
| *JSJ* | *Journal for the Study of Judaism in the Persian, Hellenistic and Roman Period* |
| *JSNT* | *Journal for the Study of the New Testament* |
| JSNTSup | Journal for the Study of the New Testament, Supplement Series |
| *JSOT* | *Journal for the Study of the Old Testament* |
| JSOTSup | Journal for the Study of the Old Testament, Supplement Series |
| *JSP* | *Journal for the Study of the Pseudepigrapha* |
| JSPSup | Journal for the Study of the Pseudepigrapha, Supplement Series |
| *JSS* | *Journal of Semitic Studies* |
| NRSV | New Revised Standard Version |
| *NTS* | *New Testament Studies* |
| OBO | Orbis biblicus et orientalis |
| *PAAJR* | *Proceedings of the American Academy of Jewish Research* |
| *RB* | *Revue biblique* |
| *RevQ* | *Revue de Qumrân* |
| *RHR* | *Revue de l'histoire des religions* |
| SBLASP | SBL Abstracts and Seminar Papers |
| SBLDS | SBL Dissertation Series |
| SBLMS | SBL Monograph Series |
| SBLRBS | SBL Resources for Biblical Study |
| SBLSCS | SBL Septuagint and Cognate Studies |
| SBLSP | SBl Seminar Papers |
| SBT | Studies in Biblical Theology |
| SJLA | Studies in Judaism in Late Antiquity |
| SPB | Studia postbiblica |
| STDJ | Studies on the Texts of the Desert of Judah |
| SUNT | Studien zur Umwelt des Neuen Testaments |

| | |
|---|---|
| *TDNT* | G. Kittel and G. Friedrich (eds.), *Theological Dictionary of the New Testament* |
| *VT* | *Vetus Testamentum* |
| VTSup | Vetus Testamentum, Supplements |
| *WZKM* | *Wiener Zeitschrift für die Kunde des Morgenlandes* |
| *ZKT* | *Zeitschrift für katholische Theologie* |

# Introduction

*James VanderKam and Eugene Ulrich*

The last few years have witnessed profound changes in the field of Dead Sea Scrolls research. The most visible differences have been the full publication of all photographs of the scrolls, the appearance of a number of volumes of *Discoveries in the Judaean Desert*, the transformation and, more importantly, the great expansion of the international team that has been assigned to edit the remaining unpublished texts, so that the work can be handled more expeditiously. A greater amount of labor is being expended on the scrolls today than had been done for decades, new fragments are appearing constantly, and the texts and the community behind them have again become major newsmakers, as they were when the discoveries were made in the 1940's and 1950's.

In light of the bewildering flurry of activity in recent years, it seemed worthwhile to gather a small group of scholars who are deeply involved in the process of editing unpublished manuscripts and to ask them to assess the present state of the field in the areas in which they concentrate. The editors applied for and received a grant from the Paul M. and Barbara Henkels Visiting Scholars Series, administered through the Institute for Scholarship in the Liberal Arts at the University of Notre Dame. Professor Lawrence S. Cunningham, chair of the Department of Theology at Notre Dame, also made available to us monies from the Crown–Minow Fund of the department. We are most grateful to these generous benefactors for the support which made the conference a reality. The financial support allowed us to invite eleven world-renowned Qumran scholar-editors to the Notre Dame campus for a conference entitled "The Dead Sea Scrolls: State of the Question" that took place from April 25 to April 27, 1993. There before an enthusiastic audience of participants, other scholars, and students, the experts presented the papers that are here published. The firm of E. J. Brill elected to use the conference as the setting in which they made the first public presentation of *The Dead Sea Scrolls on Microfiche: A Comprehensive Facsimile Edition of the Texts from the Judaean Desert* (ed. E. Tov)—a landmark event in making the scrolls accessible to all interested parties.

The papers were prepared especially for the conference, and their final form is conditioned by the discussions that followed the oral presentations. The participants revised their manuscripts after the conference and submitted them in final form during the past summer. The papers by Ulrich and VanderKam, though not read at the conference, are also new essays which had been delivered only days before at a symposium on the Dead Sea Scrolls (April 21–22, 1993), held in connection with the opening of the Library of Congress's exhibition of the Dead Sea Scrolls. We are grateful for permission to print these two papers in the present volume.

The first essay—"The Community of the Renewed Covenant: Between Judaism and Christianity"—is the opening address delivered by one of the deans of Qumran scholarship, Shemaryahu Talmon of the Hebrew University of Jerusalem. In his wide-ranging paper he presents his understanding of the scrolls and the community associated with them. Talmon urges that the primary route to identifying the community be through the texts themselves and cautions against too readily laying the Essene template over the scrolls. His address provides the title for the book *The Community of the Renewed Covenant*, that is, a community which felt itself part of the ancient covenant between God and his people but a community that was likewise convinced the covenant had been made anew with them in a more intense fashion.

On the days following Talmon's opening address, the conference was divided into four sessions that centered about four topics. Those same four topics constitute the sections of this volume. Joseph Baumgarten of the Baltimore Hebrew University, whose publications on Qumran texts began in the 1950's, addresses the topic of "Saducean Elements in Qumran Law." Baumgarten is, of course, the scholar who first drew attention (in 1980) to the fact that some of the purity laws in the *Temple Scroll* and the so-called "Halakhic Letter" (4QMMT) matched positions which in the Mishnah are attributed to the Sadducees. He reviews the history of study of the *Damascus Document* or Zadokite Fragments and the discovery of "Sadducean" elements in Qumran law, but he also notes that the Sadducees described by Josephus embraced theological positions diametrically opposed to those of the Qumran texts. He discusses another similarity between the Sadduceees and the residents of Qumran—their approaches to tradition. These points of agreement do not, however, permit one to identify the Qumranites as Sadducees, as there are many areas for which we have no evidence of agreement between them.

Professor Lawrence Schiffman of New York University deals with "The *Temple Scroll* and the Nature of Its Law: The Status of the Question." In his paper he proceeds, as he says, in somewhat encyclopedic fashion. First he treats introductory issues such as the manuscripts, their condition and dates. Next he turns to a summary of the contents which follow the pentateuchal order, although the editor frequently digresses and stops to collect other pertinent material from elsewhere in the Torah. Through his exegetical techniques the compiler weaves all the data together into a unified whole. He used a number of sources but has in almost all cases carefully unified them through a consistent exegetical method and according to his theological views. The sources "stem from the Sadducean heritage of those who founded the sect." The section giving the law of the king is the key to dating the scroll to a time no earlier than the second half of John Hyrcanus's reign. It was then that the editor called for the reforms articulated in the scroll. For the writer the revealed pentateuchal law required interpreting so that the reader could arrive at the true meaning of this single revelation. The sources of the *Temple Scroll* go back to the time of the sect's origin; the founders brought them with them to Qumran.

Professor John Strugnell of Harvard Divinity School writes on the topic "MMT: Second Thoughts on a Forthcoming Edition." He reviews the history of work on the "Halakhic Letter" which he and E. Qimron have edited, but deals particularly with various points on which he feels their edition (which appeared in late May 1994) could be improved. He argues that the calendar, found in only one of the copies, is uncertainly related to the other sections of the work. Section B of the text, the legal paragraphs, is introduced in a manner reminiscent of the Deuteronomic law code. The laws included in it raise questions about the purpose for their selection, their character and affiliation. The second section should not, however, be termed a treatise as it is in the edition. The third and final section of the text is hortatory, another indication that it is not really a letter but more like Deuteronomy. Strugnell not only opposes characterizing the work as a letter but also finds in it no specific evidence that the Teacher of Righteousness wrote it or that the recipient was the Wicked Priest. 4QMMT appears to be pre-Qumranic.

Eugene Ulrich of the University of Notre Dame reviews the evidence of the many biblical manuscripts from Qumran, examining both the external shape of the collections of Scripture and the internal shape of individual books in the Jewish community at the close of the Second Temple period. Externally, there was a "Bible in the making" but not yet a "Bible" as such; there was an inner core of the commonly accepted Law and the Prophets, but no common agreement on the extent, the order, or the classification of the books nearer the periphery of the collection. Internally, the textual forms of many books display multiple literary editions of the individual books, indicative of the progressive manner in which the books were composed over the centuries.

Julio Trebolle Barrera of the Universidad Complutense of Madrid reflects on the authoritative functions of scriptural works at Qumran. Against the theoretical background of sociological analysis, he discusses conscious and unconscious textual factors and their social influence. He illustrates how those conscious and unconscious factors relate to both specific textual examples and broader examples of the Greek recensions and, behind them, successive Hebrew editions of biblical books. From there he moves to harmonistic or paraphrastic "rewritten" texts which helped open the path to new theological developments in Samaritan and Christian traditions.

Emanuel Tov of the Hebrew University of Jerusalem examines a wide-spread phenomenon exemplified in many genres and many degrees in the Qumran manuscripts: varied forms of creative reworking, expanding, and rephrasing of biblical texts. After discussing the *Temple Scroll* and a variety of works which exhibit paraphrastic retellings of biblical narratives, he provides an extended treatment of the work entitled the "Reworked Pentateuch," preserved in five different manuscripts. He describes the contents, character, and arrangement of the work, giving detailed examples of its exegetical additions and omissions.

Daniel Harrington of the Weston School of Theology discusses a large, previously unknown wisdom composition found at Qumran in the context of other wisdom texts already known at Qumran as well as wider Jewish and Christian wisdom materials. Briefly describing the strategy that he and John Strugnell have adopted in arranging and analyzing the numerous fragments, he describes the contents in some detail and then offers reflections on the nature of the work, observations about distinctive words and ideas, and the text's relationship to other works. He concludes by comparing it at length with the roughly contemporary Book of Sirach.

Professor Eileen Schuller of McMaster University provides a survey of the large and diverse corpus of hymns, prayers, and liturgical texts found at Qumran. She probes the problematic area of terminology, the nature and system of liturgical practice, and the attempt to distinguish between texts whose authorship displays the specific views and practices of the Qumran community and those whose authorship reflects common Jewish views and practices.

Professor Devorah Dimant from the University of Haifa presents a paper on "Apocalyptic Texts at Qumran." The apocalypses (in her broad sense of the term) found there do not employ the distinctive terminology of the sectarian texts, and most of them are written in Aramaic. It appears that the Qumran community itself did not author apocalypses. About twenty-five Aramaic works have been identified at Qumran, ten of which are apocalypses, nine are testaments, and six are aggadic narratives. Aramaic court tales, a number of which have been identified in the corpus, are closely related to the apocalypses and are a source for them. The Aramaic works are attached to antediluvian characters such as Enoch or to a patriarch, display a general pietistic atmosphere, and offer historical sketches. She also deals with Hebrew apocalyptic texts, which are few and different from the Aramaic ones. They include no court tales or aggadic narratives in general, almost no testaments, and they are attributed, not to Enoch, but to Moses and Ezekiel and work more closely with biblical material. The primary use of Aramaic and the kind of material with which it is linked may point not only to a Babylonian-Persian phase but also to an Aramaic stage in the development of apocalyptic literature.

Professor John J. Collins of the University of Chicago deals with the subject "Teacher and Messiah? The One Who Will Teach Righteousness at the End of Days." The latter part of his title comes from the sixth column of the *Damascus Document* (CD VI 11). In his study Collins examines uses of the phrase אחרית הימים in various Qumran documents and shows that the expression does not mean the end of history although it does point to a future time. CD VI 11 does not look for a return of the historical Teacher of Righteousnes but to an eschatological figure who will have prophetic and priestly qualities (like the historical Teacher) and who will teach righteousness at that time.

James VanderKam of the University of Notre Dame examines the information about messiahs at Qumran in "Messianism in the Scrolls." The scrolls reveal a consistent pattern of a davidic messiah accompanied by a priest who is also termed a messiah in 1QS IX 11 and in the *Damascus Document*. The titles used for each member of the messianic dyarchy are assembled. The former is called messiah, branch of David, and prince of the congregation, while the latter is named messiah, interpreter of the law, and (chief) priest. The functions ascribed to both are summarized.

Professor Émile Puech of the École Biblique et Archéologique Française in Jerusalem analyzes "Messianism, Resurrection, and Eschatology at Qumran and in the New Testament." He first surveys the references to the two messiahs, priestly and davidic, in a variety of texts from different times in the group's history—a dyarchy based on biblical models—and also the evidence in the scrolls for the expectation that a prophet (a new Elijah) would be a forerunner of the messiahs. In the New Testament Jesus is presented as a davidic and priestly messiah, and the prior coming of Elijah is well attested in the gospels. Puech also treats the evidence for a belief about the resurrection of the righteous at the messianic time (and the destruction of the wicked) and finds it taught, whether implicitly or explicitly, in diverse scrolls from different historical periods. There are strong similarities with these views, too, in the New Testament.

We wish to acknowledge the generous assistance we have received from several individuals both in organizing the conference and in preparing the volume. Harriet Baldwin and her staff at the Center for Continuing Education at Notre Dame were of immeasurable help in handling the preparations for and running of the conference. To them we express hearty thanks for all they did to make the occasion memorable and smooth. We are grateful to Dr. John Wright (Ph.D., Notre Dame, 1989) who contributed to the editorial process by reading a number of the papers and offering suggestions for improvement. Dr. Daniel Harlow (Ph.D., Notre Dame, 1994) has labored long and carefully in bringing the text of the book into final form. To him we offer our thanks for work very well done. Monica Walsh and Les Walck, Ph.D. students in the CJA program at Notre Dame, also deserve our hearty thanks for their excellent work with computers and with the indexes.

# The Identity of the Community

# The Community of the Renewed Covenant: Between Judaism and Christianity

## Shemaryahu Talmon

The very title of my presentation indicates that, like the overwhelming majority of scholars engaged in Qumran research, I date the community whose members deposited the scrolls in the caves between ca. 200 BCE and 100 CE. In that span of time, the Jewish people was embroiled in an unprecedented process of internal diversification that after the turn of the era would climax in the consolidation of Pharisaic or 'normative' Judaism on the one hand, and of Christianity on the other hand.

I propose to show that the heuristic value of the Qumran finds does not lie in their offering the student significant data relating to actual historical events. Rather, their importance inheres: (1) in the light—indeed only dim—which they throw on the quite opaque social history and the history of ideas of Judaism in the late Second Temple period, and (2) in the information which can be elicited from them pertaining to the conceptual universe of Judaism, in an era in which Christianity progressively emerges as the most powerful force in the ancient world.

Let me enlarge somewhat on this summary statement:[1]

I conceive of the 'Community of the Renewed Covenant,'[2] יחד באי הברית החדשה, in short *yaḥad*, as standing at a three-point junc-

---

This paper was written during the period of my fellowship at the Annenberg Research Institute in Philadelphia. I wish to thank the director of the Institute and the entire staff for providing excellent library facilities and research conditions in a most congenial atmosphere.

[1] I shall keep the bibliographical apparatus to a minimum, since the pertinent publications are adequately recorded in up-to-date surveys, such as J. A. Fitzmyer, *The Dead Sea Scrolls: Major Publications and Tools for Study* (rev. ed.; Atlanta: Scholars Press, 1990).

[2] I shall explain below my insistence on using this designation.

ture in the history of Judaism and Christianity: (1) Its existence coincided with the last phase in the history of biblical Israel. At that time, the latest biblical writings, such as the book of Daniel, were authored or completed. (2) Somewhat later, the collection of authoritative books came effectively to a close, and there emerged what is known as the 'Canon of Hebrew Scriptures' or the 'Old Testament.'[3] (3) Concurrently, those days were marked by the onset of a process that at the height of the period would culminate in the crystallization of 'normative,'[4] or more precisely, Pharisaic Judaism that was to become the predominant factor in the ensuing history of the Jewish people and in the development of its religion.

It follows that the Community of the Renewed Covenant straddled, as it were, two significant stages in Jewish history. Its spiritual universe was stressed between the waning biblical age and the incipient era of the Sages. Close to the apex of the period in question, the curtain rises on nascent Christianity. Therefore, those times concomitantly constitute the backdrop before which unfolds the history of the primitive Church that is to become Judaism's rival claimant to the biblical heritage.

Viewed against this background, the scrolls promise to give some help for partly inscribing the proverbial blank page between the Hebrew Bible and the Mishnah on the one hand, and between the Hebrew Bible and the New Testament on the other hand.[5]

---

[3] For my reticence to use these designations and my view of the progressive emergence of the collection of Hebrew Scriptures, see: "Heiliges Schrifttum und kanonische Bücher aus jüdischer Sicht: Überlegungen zur Ausbildung der Grösse 'Die Schrift' im Judentum," *Mitte der Schrift? Ein jüdisch-christliches Gespräch: Texte des Berner Symposions vom 6.–12. Januar 1985* (ed. M. Klopfenstein, U. Luz, S. Talmon and E. Tov; Judaica et Christiana 11; Bern: Lang, 1987) 45–79.

[4] G. F. Moore introduced the term 'normative Judaism' in reference to *Judaism in the First Centuries of the Christian Era: The Age of the Tannaim* (2 vols.; Oxford: Clarendon, 1927) 1.3. It is often mistakenly applied as a demarcation of Judaism in pre-Christian times.

[5] See my "Between the Bible and the Mishnah," *The World of Qumran From Within: Collected Studies* (Jerusalem: Magnes; Leiden: Brill, 1989) 11–52.

# I. Methods and Terminology

## A. Investigative Methods

From the very inception of Qumran studies, I have sounded a caveat against all attempts to equate the Community of the Renewed Covenant with any one socio-religious group, movement, sect, or philosophy of Judaism at the turn of the era mentioned in classical sources:

1. Considerations of proper methodology require that a new phenomenon, like the Covenanters' community, should first be investigated from within, viz., by an analysis of its own literature, before any attempt is made to compare it, much less equate it, with any other contemporary socio-religious phenomenon.

2. When comparisons are later applied, one should steer clear of a nugget-picking atomization, and avoid pitting isolated features identified in one cultural phenomenon against their presumed counterparts in another. Rather, the comparison should be informed by a holistic approach which takes into account the relative importance of the features compared in the overall socio-religious web of the entities under review.[6]

3. We must further keep in mind a general sociological principle. Comparable traits in the posture of discrete religious or, for that matter, political groups are wont to arise from analogous societal conditions and credal tenets which were operative in the initial stages of their formation. The very confrontation with established religious or political authorities will often produce surprising similarities of conceptual thought and organization in widely divergent opposition parties, foremost in dissident factions which are in the same historical stream.

4. It may be considered axiomatic that a comparison of societal and religious traits which mark various groups in Judaism at the end of the Second Temple period will bring to the fore telling similarities. All these factions derive their basic beliefs and concepts from the bib-

---

[6] See my remarks in "The Comparative Method in Biblical Interpretation," *Congress Volume: Göttingen, 1977* (ed. J. E. Emerton; VTSup 29; Leiden: Brill, 1978) 320–52.

lical tradition common to all.⁷ Pierre Benoit's "warning against an imprudent tendency to accept as immediate contacts arising from direct influence what in fact may be no more than independent manifestations of a common trend of the time" is as appropriate today as it was thirty years ago.⁸ The specific spiritual profile of each faction is ultimately determined by its discordant interpretation of the shared fund of religious tenets and credal values.⁹ A disregard of discrepancies in the search for similarities obfuscates the individuality of discrete socio-religious entities, and runs the danger of producing parallelomania.¹⁰ Therefore, when one comes to compare diverse divisions of Judaism at the turn of the era, more weight should be accorded to discordancies than to analogies. In the last count, the particular cultural profile of a societal organism is edged by peculiar signifiers which set it off from other groups, and not by characteristics which it shares with them.

5. The disjointed comparison of the Covenanters in each instance with only one socio-religious entity of contemporary Judaism produces a slanted picture of a presumably pronounced affinity of their community with one or the other group and veils the intricate web of overlapping analogies and divergences in which all are enmeshed. What is needed is a synoptic overview which will enable scholars to define, as accurately as possible, the place which the Community of the Renewed Covenant occupied in the overall composition of the Jewish people at the time.

6. For the above reasons, I insist on viewing the Community of the Renewed Covenant as a socio-religious phenomenon *sui generis* of Judaism at the height of the Second Temple period. A study of this group from within heightens the recognition of the internal multiformity which characterized Judaism in those days, showing it to have been more diversified than is suggested by the sources which were at our disposal prior to the Qumran discoveries. The Covenanters' community is another tessera in the mosaic-like composition of the Jewish

---

⁷ See S. Talmon, "The Emergence of Jewish Sectarianism in the Early Second Temple Period," *King, Cult and Calendar in Ancient Israel: Collected Studies* (Jerusalem: Magnes; Leiden: Brill, 1986) 165–201.

⁸ P. Benoit, "Qumran and the New Testament," *NTS* 7 (1960–61) 276–96.

⁹ I have illustrated this 'diversity within commonality' in "Types of Messianic Expectation at the Turn of the Era," *King, Cult and Calendar*, 202–24.

¹⁰ S. Sandmel, "Parallelomania," *JBL* 81 (1962) 1–13.

people at the turn of the era, in addition to Samaritans, Hasidim, Sadducees, Boethusians, Zealots, Essenes, Pharisees, and nascent Christianity, to name only the more prominent factions.

## B. *The Importance of Adequate Terminology*

The geographical location of the Qumran settlement in the Desert of Judah close to the shores of the Dead Sea, and characteristic features of communal organization recorded in the scrolls, induced from the very outset the hypothesis that the newly discovered 'Qumranians' were none but the enigmatic Essenes, concisely described by Josephus, Philo, and Pliny the Elder.[11] The 'Essene Sect' faded from the historical horizon in the first century CE. Therefore, it was considered probable that its last members were absorbed into the early Christian community. In consequence, the 'Qumranians equaling Essenes' hypothesis was sometimes fused with the initially distinct proposition to identify the group whose 'library'[12] had been discovered in the Qumran caves with nascent Christianity.

Scholars who were engaged in the decipherment and interpretation of the Qumran documents in the early stages of the discovery applied to the description and analysis of these altogether unknown materials designations and technical terms which mirrored their own *Sitz im Leben*. The retreat of an evidently small band of males to an isolated site in the uninhabitable wilderness, on the eve of the emergence of nascent Christianity, occasioned already in the early stages of research the introduction of a vocabulary appropriated from Christian monasticism.[13] For its part, this pregnant vocabulary *nolens volens* enhanced the tendency to identify that previously unknown community with the early Jesus movement.

---

[11] For a variety of reasons, I have consistently argued against this premature identification.

[12] For my reticence to apply this technical term to the agglomeration of scrolls in the caves, see "The Essential Community of the Renewed Covenant: How Should Qumran Studies Proceed?" *Papers of the Library of Congress Qumran Symposium, April 21–22, 1993* (forthcoming).

[13] I am fully convinced that scholars adopted this specific terminology intuitively. It does not evidence a premeditated intent to give Qumran research a Christian orientation, as some suspicion-prone and publicity-hunting writers have argued.

In the study of the Community of the Renewed Covenant, I consider it imperative to purge from the discussion expressions which affect, or outright predicate, the group's characterization. The problem can be subsumed under 'What's in a Name?' It is illustrated by the following examples of prevalent terms:

1. The designation 'Qumran Community' creates the misleading impression that the socio-religious entity under review was exclusively comprised of the small contingent of not more than 200–300 male members who lived as a 'commune' in and/or around the communal center, extensive remains of which were excavated on the site.[14] This commune, however, only constituted the spearhead of the much wider Community of the Renewed Covenant.[15]

Equally, the epithet 'Qumran Sect' should be avoided.[16] Sociologists of religion are still debating the unequivocal definition of 'sect' vis-à-vis other socio-religious configurations. In addition, a characterization of the *yaḥad* which would be methodologically defensible labors under the lack of contemporary sources providing first-hand information on other structured factions in Judaism at the height of the Second Temple period from which it seceded. At that time it was still an open question which faction would win the upper hand, and which others would then be relegated to the status of 'dissenters' or 'sects.'

Even less commendable is the name 'Qumran Essenes.' It presupposes the hypothetical identity of the Covenanters with the Essenes—*quod erat demonstrandum*.

---

[14] I fully concur with the commonly accepted identification of the site as the Covenanters' community center. Other interpretations of the erstwhile function of the ruins, like the 'Roman Villa'-theory, or the 'Fortress'-hypothesis entertained by N. Golb, are almost universally rejected. See N. Golb, "Who Hid the Dead Sea Scrolls," *BA* 48 (1985) 68–82; idem, "The Dead Sea Scrolls: A New Perspective," *American Scholar* 58 (1989) 177–207; idem, "Die Entdeckungen in der Wüste Judäas—Neue Erklärungs-versuche," *Qumran. Ein Symposion* (ed. J. H. Bauer, J. Fink and H. D. Galter; *Grazer Theologische Studien* 15 [1993]) 87–116.

[15] For my differentiation between 'commune' and 'community,' see "The Essential Community."

[16] In contrast, only 'Qumran' should be used in sigla which identify scrolls and fragments which were actually found in caves adjacent to the site. The designation 'Qumran Scrolls' is certainly preferable to the commonly employed misnomer 'Dead Sea Scrolls.' It hardly needs stressing that if those manuscripts would have been lying for two millennia in the Dead Sea, they would certainly not have been found.

2. Celibacy. We do not find in the Covenanters' literature a single text which proscribes sexual intercourse or explicitly advocates 'celibacy' as a permanent mode of life.[17] Quite to the contrary. References to wives and children abound in writings, such as 1QS, 1QS$^a$, CD and 11QT, and laws pertaining to marital relations are developed beyond those recorded in the biblical legal corpora.

Furthermore, unpublished fragments of wisdom writings from Qumran join biblical literature in extolling family life and procreation. These texts pertain indeed to the life of community members in their 'camps' all over the country. But also the 'commune'—the settlement at Qumran—was certainly not a 'monastery' in the established signification of this term. It is incorrect to depict as 'monks'[18] the Covenanters who abstained from sexual intercourse and family life for an unspecified number of years of their residence there.[19] During that circumscribed period of abstention, all sexual intercourse, including marital relations, was considered an offense. A member caught *in flagranti* was expelled from the Commune. I thus interpret a truncated line in a fragmentary copy of the Zadokite Document (4QD$^e$ = 4Q270): ואשר יקר[ב] לזנות לאשתו אשר לא במשפט ויצא ולא ישוב עוד, "(a member of the commune) who approaches his wife[20] to whore (with her) against the rule, will (be forced to) leave (the commune), and will never return (to it)."[21]

It follows that a member's temporary abstention from sexual intercourse[22] can in no way be equated with the lifelong celibacy which

---

[17] J. Baumgarten, "The Qumran-Essene Restraints on Marriage," *Archaeology and History in the Dead Sea Scrolls: The New York University Conference in Memory of Yigael Yadin* (ed. L. H. Schiffman; JSOT/ASOR Monographs 2; JSPSup 8; Sheffield: JSOT Press, 1990) 13 underlines "the continuing uncertainty as to whether celibacy was in fact practiced at Qumran," but does not resolve the problem.

[18] See, e.g., E. F. Sutcliffe, *The Monks of Qumran as Depicted in the Dead Sea Scrolls* (London: Burns & Oates; Westminster, MD: Newman, 1960); idem, "The Pre-Christian Monks of Qumran," *The Month* N.S. 17 (London 1–6.1957) 101–10.

[19] There is room for conjecturing that that span of time as a rule amounted to 10 years, except for men who became members of the community's 'governing council' and who may have stayed there until the mandatory retirement age of 60.

[20] Cf. 1QS$^a$ I 9–10; CD V 8–9; et al.

[21] The text is quoted here courtesy of its editor, Prof. J. Baumgarten.

[22] To establish a comparison with Paul's chapter on 'women' in 1 Corinthians 7, suggested to me by Drs. Sidnie White and George Brooke, would require a painstaking analysis, beyond the framework of this paper.

Josephus ascribes to the Essenes,[23] or with that which typifies Christian monasticism.

3. There is no basis for equating the 'immersion' in water which a Covenanter practiced at the end of every work-day with one-time Christian 'baptism.'[24] Immersion was an indispensable act by which a member purified himself from latent ritual uncleanness incurred in the course of the day, and a prerequisite for his participation in the *yaḥad*'s communal meal.

The Covenanters' routinely recurring immersion differs phenomenologically from Christian initiation-baptism, which marks the entrance of the baptized into the community of believers. Moreover, the fundamental dissimilarity is further underscored by the absence of any water-connected ritual from a novice's induction ceremony into the Community of the Renewed Covenant (1QS I 16–II 25),[25] in which also a veteran's membership was reconfirmed.

In sum: We should avoid applying a vocabulary to the description of the Community of the Renewed Covenant which tends to obfuscate its specific identity and which is prone to predetermine the conclusions of the proposed analysis.

---

[23] E. Qimron introduces a differentiation between a class of non-marrying *yaḥad* members and other Covenanters who did marry. See his "Celibacy in the Dead Sea Scrolls and the Two Kinds of Sectarians," *The Madrid Qumran Congress: Proceedings of the International Congress on the Dead Sea Scrolls Madrid 18–21 March, 1991* (2 vols.; ed. J. Trebolle Barrera and L. Vegas Montaner; STDJ 11; Leiden: Brill; Madrid: Editorial Complutense, 1992) 1.287–94. This hypothesis parallels the differentiation between marrying and non-marrying Essenes, proposed in the past. But it cannot be substantiated by evidence from the Covenanters' literature.

[24] The difference between 'immersion' and 'baptism' was often pointed out in the past, but their equation is still proposed by some scholars. The issue is discussed in numerous publications. See, e.g., E. F. Sutcliffe, "Baptism and Baptismal Rites at Qumran," *HeyJ* 1 (1960) 69–101; J. Gnilka, "Die essenischen Tauchbäder und die Johannestaufe," *RevQ* 3 (1961–62) 186–207; idem, "Der Täufer Johannes und der Ursprung der christlichen Taufe," *BibLeb* 4 (1963) 39–49; G. Vermes, "Biblical Studies and the Dead Sea Scrolls," *JSOT* 39 (1987) 113–28.

[25] I fail to find any basis for H. C. Kee's assertion that at Qumran "The initiation into the community through baptism [*sic!*] is to be followed by instruction and guidance by the sons of Aaron and the Levites." See his "Membership in the Covenant People at Qumran and in the Teaching of Jesus," *Jesus and the Dead Sea Scrolls* (ed. J. H. Charlesworth; New York: Doubleday, 1992) 118.

## II. The Community of the Renewed Covenant: Between Rabbinic Judaism and Nascent Christianity

Let me now turn to a concise examination of the *yaḥad*'s singular position in the overall framework of Judaism at the turn of the era. In the present context, I can dwell only on some facets of the required comprehensive endeavor. It would seem that these facets have not received adequate attention in Qumran research. While taking note of conceptual and organizational analogies of the *yaḥad* and other entities in contemporary Judaism, I shall underscore fundamental differences which set the Community of the Renewed Covenant apart from all other streams, underscoring especially non-conformities with respect to emerging Pharisaism and to primitive Christianity.

I propose to highlight the peculiar profile of the Covenanters' community by tracing basic features of its world-view from within and sketching fundamentals of its societal structure. The prerequisite building stones for this undertaking derive first and foremost from the 'Foundation Documents':[26] the *Community Rule* (1QS) and the *Rule of the Congregation* or the *Messianic Rule* (1QSª), in conjunction with the *Damascus Document* (CD);[27] the *Pesher on Habakkuk* (1QpHab); the *War Scroll* (1QM); to some extent, the *Hôda2yôt Scroll* (1QH); and the *Temple Scroll* (11QT). All but the last were found in Cave 1, painstakingly secured in covered jars which had been made airtight by the application of bitumen to the gaps between the vessel and its lid. These Foundation Documents directly address the membership of the community, detail at length the main tenets of the *yaḥad*'s theology, and reveal the Covenanters' self-understanding. Other writings, among them items of halakhic import, such as the polemical epistle *miqṣat maʿaśê hat-tôrâ* (4QMMT),[28] calendrical fragments, *et sim.*, do not qual-

---

[26] This term was independently introduced into the discussion by H. C. Kee, "Membership," 199–121.

[27] As is well known, parts of two medieval copies of this work were found at the end of last century in the Genizah of the Ezra Synagogue in Old Cairo. Fragments of over ten copies discovered in the caves conclusively prove its original association with the Covenanters' community.

[28] The writer of that piece enumerates some twenty-odd legal matters on whose interpretation he and his adherents differ from the addressee and his followers. I suggest that scholars are setting too much store on this work.

ify as Foundation Documents and can furnish only supplementary information.

## A. The Self-implantation of the Community of the Renewed Covenant in the History of Early Post-exilic Israel [29]

The Covenanters identify their community as the sole legitimate representative of biblical Israel. An intense Bible-orientation certainly also informed Rabbinic Judaism and Christianity. But the Covenanters' self-identification with ancient Israel, their *Eigenbegrifflichkeit*,[30] was quite different, indeed singular. It can be best appreciated by a juxtaposition with Rabbinical traditions which encapsulate the 'normative' posture with respect to the biblical world.[31]

1. The Concept of 'Renewed Covenant.' The designation "(Community of) those who entered into the Renewed Covenant," יחד באי הברית החדשה (CD VI 19) or אשר באו בברית החדשה (CD VIII 29),[32] which the Covenanters apply to themselves—significantly only in Foundation Documents[33]—underscores the intended self-implantation in the world of biblical Israel. The prophet Jeremiah employed the ha-

---

[29] I developed this point at some length in "Between the Bible and the Mishnah," 25–52; see further, "Die Bedeutung der Qumranfunde für die jüdische Religionsgeschichte," *Qumran. Ein Symposion,* 146–70.

[30] Cf. B. Landsberger, "Die Eigenbegrifflichkeit der Babylonischen Welt," *Islamica* 2 (1926) 355–72.

[31] The required in-depth analysis of this issue cannot be given in the present framework. The selected facets discussed below only illustrate the point.

[32] See A. Jaubert, *La notion d'alliance dans le Judaïsme aux abords l'ère chrétienne* (Patristica Sorbonensia 6; Paris: Seul, 1963), esp. 211–95; further R. F. Collins, "The Berith-Notion of the Cairo Damascus Covenant and its Comparison with the New Testament," *ETL* 39 (1963) 555–94; A. S. Kapelrud, "Der Bund in den Qumranschriften," *Bibel und Qumran: Beiträge zur Erforschung der Beziehungen zwischen Bibel- und Qumranwissenschaft. Hans Bardtke zum 22.9.1966* (Berlin: Evangelische Haupt-Bibelgesellschaft, 1968) 137–49; N. Ilg, "Überlegungen zum Verständnis von *Berît* in den Qumrantexten," *Qumrân. Sa piété, sa théologie et son milieu* (ed. M. Delcor; BETL 46; Paris: Duculot; Leuven: University Press, 1978) 257–64.

[33] To the best of my knowledge, this title has not turned up in any unpublished document.

*pax legomenon* ברית חדשה (Jer 31:31), "renewed covenant,"[34] in a prophecy set in a series of consolatory oracles (Jer 31:1–14, 23–30, 31–34, 35–40). He invokes God's promise to renew in the future the ancient covenant which he had established with the Exodus generation (Jer 31:32), and which had been suspended in the wake of the destruction of Jerusalem and the ensuing exile (Jer 31:15–22). Biblical historiographers and prophets of the post-exilic period viewed their return from the Babylonian exile as the realization of Jeremiah's prophecy that 70 years after the fall of Jerusalem the Judean kingdom would be reconstituted (Jer 25:11–12; 29:10; Zech 1:12–17; 7:5; Dan 9:24; Ezra 2:3; 2 Chron 36:20–22).

In contrast, the Covenanters evidently disregarded Jeremiah's prophecy. They set their hopes instead upon Ezekiel's symbolic act signifying doom (Ezek 4:4–6) in the face of the Babylonians' siege on Jerusalem, by investing it with an implied promise of a future restoration, which they see as being fulfilled in the foundation of their community (CD I 1–8). They view the *yaḥad* as the latest link in a chain of recurring reaffirmations of the covenant to which the Bible gives witness (CD II 14–III 20). God had originally established his covenant with Adam. He renewed it after each critical juncture in the history of the world and of Israel: after the flood, with Noah, the 'Second Adam'; then with the patriarchs; again with the entire people at Sinai; with the priestly house of Aaron; and ensuingly, after the monarchic system had taken root in Israel, with the royal house of David. In their own days, the days of the present generation, בדור אחרון, "he raised for himself" from among all the evildoers "men called by name, that a remnant might be left in the land, and that the earth might be filled with their offspring" (CD II 11–12). The thread of Israel's historical past, which had snapped when Jerusalem and the temple were destroyed, is retied with the establishment of the *yaḥad*'s 'renewed covenant.'

The intrinsic *community*-signification of ברית comes to the fore in the induction rite of novices into the *yaḥad*, when also the membership of veterans was presumably reaffirmed. This annually repeated ritual is palpably molded upon the 'Blessing and Curse' ceremony, which the Pentateuchal tradition reports to have been enacted by Moses

---

[34] The term is picked up in the καινὴ διαθήκη of the NT. See J. Behm, *Der Begriff Διαθήκη im Neuen Testament* (Leipzig: Deichert, 1912); G. Quell and J. Behm, "διαθήκη," *TDNT* 2.106–34.

prior to Israel's enrootment in the Land of Canaan (Deuteronomy 27–28).[35] Subsequently, that ceremony was again performed by Joshua (Josh 8:30–35; cf. 23:1–26) as a *de iure* covenantal underpinning of the *de facto* conquest of the land. The *yaḥad* members perceived the reenactment of the biblical ceremony in their induction ritual as the confirmation of their community's claim to be the only legitimate heir to biblical Israel.

The Covenanters' understanding of ברית points up a fundamental variance between their posture vis-à-vis biblical Israel and the stance maintained by the Rabbinic faction. The *yaḥad*'s community-centered conception of ברית is totally absent from the Rabbinic universe of thought.[36] The Rabbis understood their existential situation to differ fundamentally from that of biblical Israel. Consequently, they did not develop the notion that in their days, and with their community, God had renewed his covenant of old with the people of Israel. In contrast to the pointed *communal* thrust of the Covenanters' concept of ברית and specifically of ברית חדשה the noun ברית, *per se* and in diverse word combinations, connotes in the Rabbinic vocabulary exclusively the act of circumcision.[37] On the strength of this rite, every male infant is *individually* accepted into ברית אברהם אבינו, God's ancient covenant with the ancestors, which foreshadowed the covenant with all Israel.[38] To the best of my knowledge, this specific technical connotation of ברית is not documented in *yaḥad* literature. On the other hand, the *communal* dimension of ברית which attaches to the concept

---

[35] N. Lohfink, "Der Bundesschluss im Lande Moab: Redaktionsgeschichtliches zu Dtn 28, 69–32, 47," *BZ* 6 (1962) 32–56.

[36] For a contrasting view see A. Segal, "Covenant in Rabbinic Writings," *The Other Judaisms of Late Antiquity* (BJS 127; Atlanta: Scholars Press, 1987) 147–65.

[37] See Ch. J. Kasowski, *Thesaurus Talmudis. Concordantiae Verborum Quae in Talmude Babylonico Reperiuntur* (Jerusalem: Ministry of Education of Israel; New York: JTS, 1960) 8.812-814; M. D. Gross, אוצר האגדה מהמשנה והתוספתא התלמודים והמדרשים וספרי הזהר (Jerusalem: Harav Kuk, 1942) 1.137-138.

[38] It is of interest to note that the term ברית is not present in the tale of Jacob's daughter Dinah, in reference to the Shechemites' circumcision (Genesis 34). It is equally absent from the retold version of this incident in the *Testament of Levi*. See J. C. Greenfield and M. E. Stone, "Remarks on the Aramaic Testament of Levi From the Geniza," *RB* 86 (1979) 214–20; this text is a "medieval copy of a text similar to that which was found at Qumran," (ibid., 215) published by J. T. Milik, *DJD* 1.87–91. See further Milik, "Le Testament de Lévi en araméen," *RB* 62 (1956) 398–406; idem, *The Books of Enoch: Aramaic Fragments of Qumrân Cave 4* (Oxford: Clarendon, 1976) 23–25.

of 'covenant renewal' in the Covenanters' theology, as reflected in the Foundation Documents, appears to be altogether absent from the Rabbinic world of thought.

2. The Sages conceived of the biblical era as a closed chapter, and of their own times as an intrinsically new phase in the history of Israel. In consequence, they drew a clear line between the biblical books—termed תורה שבכתב, 'written law'—and their own writings—designated תורה שבעל פה, 'oral law.' These collocations are rather late. They are first used in post-Mishnah sources and their actual signification remains opaque:

> The mythic category of 'Oral Torah' makes its appearance . . . only with the [Talmud] Yerushalmi and not in any document closed prior to that time, although a notion of a revelation over and above Scripture—not called 'Oral Torah' to be sure—comes to expression in [Tractate] Avot. Implicitly, moreover, certain sayings of the Mishnah itself, e.g., concerning rulings of the Torah and rulings of the Sages, may contain the notion of a secondary tradition, beyond revelation. But that tradition is not called 'the oral Torah'. . . . Even in the [Talmud] Yerushalmi the mythic statement of the matter . . . is lacking. It is only in the [Talmud] Bavli, e.g., in the famous story of Hillel and Shammai and the convert at b.Shab. 30b-31a, that the matter is fully explicit.[39]

Both collections were held holy and authoritative. But their respective holiness and authority were of a quite distinct character. A third category consisted of 'extraneous books,' ספרים חיצונים, which could not be subsumed under either תורה שבכתב or תורה שבעל פה. It included compositions which normative Jewish tradition did not hand down. They were preserved in varying compilations of apocrypha or pseudepigrapha in the Old Testament canon of the Church, in Greek, Latin, and Ethiopic translation. Hebrew and/or Aramaic originals of several such works, as well as of hitherto unknown writings of the same genre, have turned up among the Qumran finds: *1 Enoch, Jubilees,* Tobit, the *Testaments of the Patriarchs,* and the Proverbs of Ben

---

[39] J. Neusner, "The Meaning of Oral Torah," *Early Rabbinic Judaism: Historical Studies in Religion, Literature and Art* (SJLA 13; Leiden: Brill, 1975) 1-33; idem, *Oral Tradition in Judaism: The Case of the Mishnah* (New York: Garland, 1987).

Sira.⁴⁰ In addition, we find in Rabbinic literature scattered references to sundry works which did not belong with any of these three classes and seem to be devoid of a common denominator: translations of biblical books into Aramaic, prayer collections, compositions of a presumably foreign origin, such as the rather nebulous ספרי המירם (*m. Yad.* 4:6), and possibly also writings of a heretical character.⁴¹

3. Books of the תורה שבכתב category were said to be מטמאים את הידים, to "render the hands unclean." This characterization did not apply to books subsumed under תורה שבעל פה, *viz.*, the Sages' own literature, nor to the ספרים חיצונים, and obviously not to the above-mentioned, altogether undefined, fourth type of writings.

The English renditions of all these Hebrew terms, like their translations into other modern languages, are etymologically correct but do not capture their specific technical signification. מטמאים את הידים cannot be taken to indicate actual 'defilement' incurred by handling holy books, כתבי הקדש, the prominent designation of biblical books which sets them apart from all other writings. Moreover, Rabbinic sources never mention a specific case of defilement actually incurred through the handling of holy books. Nor do they register any purification ritual requisite for the removal of such defilement.

Also the collocations תורה שבכתב and תורה שבעל פה cannot be understood as references to specifically different technical modes of handing down diverse categories of binding credal teachings and ritual ordinances, one to be transmitted only in writing, the other only orally. We must assume, on the one hand, that an undefinable part of biblical legislation was actually passed on from generation to generation without ever being committed to writing. On the other hand, Rabbinic 'oral law' soon was as much transmitted in writing as was the 'written torah.' Consequently, a possibly ancillary differentiation between two exclusive modes of transmissions should have become obsolete. But against expectation the designations תורה שבכתב and תורה שבעל פה remained in force. This fact indicated that they are

---

⁴⁰ Fragments of Ben Sira's Proverbs were also discovered on Masada. See Y. Yadin, *The Ben Sira Scroll From Masada* (Jerusalem: Israel Exploration Society/Shrine of the Book, 1965).

⁴¹ See S. Talmon, "Oral and Written Transmission, or the Heard and the Seen Word in Judaism of the Second Temple Period," *Jesus and the Oral Gospel Tradition* (ed. H. Wansbrough; JSNTSup 64; Sheffield: JSOT Press, 1991) 132–148.

catchphrases which have a much wider connotation than the presumed purely technical one which is usually ascribed to them.

It follows that the actual signification of the collocations מטמא (אינו מטמא) את הידים, and תורה שבעל פה, תורה שבכתב cannot be established by etymological derivation. Rather, they are *Kunstausdrücke* whose connotation must be empirically established by having recourse to their actual use in Rabbinic literature. They give expression to the Sages' fundamental differentiation between the authoritative corpus of biblical books, the Hebrew Canon, and the equally authoritative, but nevertheless characteristically different, collectanea of Rabbinic writings: From one nothing can be abstracted, and nothing can be added to it; the other remained open-ended and was never explicitly closed.

4. Books subsumed under תורה שבכתב which 'defile the hands' were considered to have been authored under divine inspiration, ברוח הקדש, before a given point in time. All others were written after that caesura, rather loosely designated מכאן ואילך, 'from now on.' Some Rabbinic sayings reflect an attempt to define this cut-off date more precisely by identifying 'divine' with 'prophetic' inspiration: "after the demise of the last prophets—Haggai, Zechariah and Malachi, the holy spirit lapsed or was taken from Israel," משמת(ו) נביאים אחרונים חגי זכריה ומלאכי פסקה רוח הקדש מישראל.[42]

In the last count, these pronouncements too were intended to establish and safeguard the singularity of the biblical books vis-à-vis all other literature then in circulation, whether oral or written. At the same time, they disclose an attempt to define 'chronologically' the closing of the biblical canon.

## B. The Covenanters' Living Bible

1. The *yaḥad* literature conveys a totally different picture. We may assume that, like the Sages, the Covenanters also invested certain writings with various grades of authority and holiness, and considered others to be altogether profane and not binding. However, I do not know of any explicit statement which evidences the Covenanters' clear-cut differentiation between books of the Hebrew Bible, on the one hand, and, on the other hand, extra-biblical writings, like the evi-

---

[42] *T. Soṭa* 6:2 (ed. Zuckermandel 318, 21-22); *b. Soṭa* 48b; *b. Sanh.* 11a; *b. Yoma* 9b.

dently highly appreciated *sefer hagu/i*, ספר הגו/י (CD X 6; XIII 2; XIV 7–8; 1QS I 6–7) and the Foundation Documents, or the book of *Jubilees*, which the author of the *Damascus Document* juxtaposes to Moses' Torah (CD XVI 1–4). The Rabbinic counterpositioning of תורה שבכתב versus תורה שבעל פה is nowhere documented in the Covenanters' writings. Living conceptually in the world of the Bible, as said above, they appear to have viewed the biblical books as constituent parts of a yet expandable corpus of sacred literature and did not develop at all the notion of a 'closed biblical canon.' In fact, the very use of the term canon and the pursuance of 'canon research' in the context of Qumran may be considered an anachronism.

Altogether, the compass of the Hebrew Bible as Holy Scripture can serve as an important touchstone for the discernment of discrete socio-religious factions in Second Temple Judaism: The Samaritans accepted as their Bible only the Torah, viz. the five books of the Pentateuch.[43] Pharisaic Judaism sanctified a closed corpus of 24 books, the Hebrew Bible.[44] The Covenanters probably acclaimed as Holy Scriptures the same basic collection, but left open ended its constituent third part, the collection of *paraleipomena*.[45] The Christian Bible is most comprehensive, being constituted of three major components: the 24 books of the Hebrew Bible; a cluster of biblical apocrypha, which together with the books of the Hebrew Bible are subsumed under Old Testament; and the Gospels and Epistles as the New Testament.

2. The exceeding textual variability evident in the biblical scrolls found at Qumran indicates that the Covenanters had not established a fixed text tradition.[46] I suggest that Rabbinic Judaism established a

---

[43] They accorded sanctity also to medieval compilations, such as their Book of Joshua, to historical accounts of the *Tolidah* genre, *et al.*, but they kept them clearly apart from the Torah.

[44] In the present context, we do not need to consider the question whether or not Josephus and other sources attest to the onetime existence of a yet differently constituted corpus of biblical books.

[45] The absence of Esther, and of even a single explicit quotation from the book in the Covenanters' literature, remains unexplained, also after J. T. Milik's publication of fragments of a presumed Aramaic proto-Esther text. See his "Les modèles araméens du Livre d'Esther dans la grotte 4 de Qumrân," *Mémorial Jean Starcky* (*RevQ* 15 [1992]) 321–99.

[46] See S. Talmon, "Aspects of the Textual Transmission of the Bible in the Light of Qumran Manuscripts," *Textus* 4 (1964) 94–135, repr. in F. M. Cross and S. Talmon, eds., *Qumran and the History of the Biblical Text* (Cambridge, MA: Harvard University

*textus receptus* when the recitation of selected Bible texts became an integral component of the synagogue service, probably after 70 CE. A close scrutiny of pertinent Qumran sources proves that in the Covenanters' assemblies and convocations only prayers were offered. There are no references to a concomitant reading of Bible texts.[47]

Like the Chronicler, and in distinction from the Sages, *yaḥad*-authors and scribes injected their personalities into the biblical materials which they transmitted, adapting wordings to their own needs, rephrasing, expanding, and contracting. This was obviously done within a legitimate latitude of variation which, however, yet needs to be defined. Scholarly editions of the biblical scrolls and fragments from the caves, and the collation of variant readings in a reasoned apparatus, are indispensable for such an undertaking. But the prevalent 'Text and Version' approach, which informs modern text-criticism and is predominantly anchored in an investigation of medieval manuscripts, overshadows a more fundamental issue which pertains to the study of the biblical scrolls from Qumran. We must realize that in this context it does not suffice to collate variants and ensuingly align one Qumran manuscript with the MT or a proto-massoretic tradition, others with the Samaritan, the Septuagint, Theodotion, proto-Theodotion, καίγε, etc. The scrolls afford us a glimpse of the late stages of Hebrew literary creativity, when biblical literature was yet alive and malleable.[48] Before this background, I would also deem an anachronism the designation 'Reworked Bible,' which has become current coinage in the characterization of a specific type of biblical manuscripts from Qumran.

3. The Sages intentionally abandoned the use of typical biblical literary *Gattungen*—historiography, psalmody, and the prophetic genre. In their stead, they initiated or developed altogether new literary modes, such as *midrash*. Further, their legal terminology, early exemplified by the Mishnah, differs perceptibly from the phraseology and the syntactical structure of biblical legislative literature.

---

Press, 1975) 226–63 and in *World of Qumran*, 71–116; idem, "The Old Testament Text," *The Cambridge History of the Bible. Volume One: From the Beginnings to Jerome* (ed. P. R. Ackroyd and C. F. Evans; Cambridge: Cambridge University Press, 1970) 155–95.

[47] See S. Talmon, "The Emergence of Institutionalized Prayer in Israel," in *World of Qumran*, 200–43, esp. pp. 241–43.

[48] See S. Talmon, "The Textual Study of the Bible—A New Outlook," *Qumran and the History of the Biblical Text*, 321–400.

In contrast, *yaḥad* authors continued to spin out typical biblical literary genres. We find among the scrolls copies of works of a historiographical character which offer a wide-ranging survey of past events, encompass current occurrences, and proleptically refer to situations expected to come about in a future time. Equally, there has turned up an impressive corpus of extra-canonical compositions of the psalmodic genre which were not preserved in the Rabbinic tradition. These writings are often couched in a vocabulary and composed in a style which resemble biblical prototypes or exhibit evident affinities with biblical language and literature.[49]

In sum: the investigation of 'The Bible at Qumran' needs to be amplified by a study of 'Qumran and the Bible.' An in-depth probe of the Covenanters' 'Living Bible' is bound to illuminate their understanding of the biblical past, which differs significantly from normative Judaism's appreciation of the Hebrew Bible, and at the same time differs also from the status which Christian tradition accords to the Old Testament.

## C. Prophetic Inspiration

As said above, the realization that the biblical period had ended produced in the intellectual world of the Sages the idea that after the demise of the last biblical prophets, divine inspiration was withdrawn from Israel:[50] A later source dates the withdrawal of divine (prophetic) inspiration to the days of Alexander the Macedonian. From that time on, the community and the individual were enjoined to abide by Rabbinic precepts: מכאן ואלך הט אזנך ושמע דברי חכמים "from now on incline your ear and hearken to the instructions of the Sages."[51] Rabbinic Judaism shelved prophetic inspiration and progressively developed a rationalist stance.[52] Teaching, rooted in expert knowledge, replaced

---

[49] See, *int. al.*, Y. Thorion, "Die Sprache der Tempelrolle und die Chronikbücher," *RevQ* 43 (1983) 423–26; idem, "Neuere Bemerkungen zur Sprache der Qumranliteratur," *RB* 44 (1984) 579–82.

[50] See E. E. Urbach, "When did Prophecy Cease," *Tarbiz* 17 (1945) 1–11 (in Hebrew); F. E. Greenspahn, "Why Prophecy Ceased?" *JBL* 108 (1989) 37–49.

[51] S. ʿOlam Rab. 6 (ed. Ratner, 2).

[52] M. Weber speaks of a "Rationalisierungsprozess" which unfolded already in the biblical era and differentiated Israelite religion from paganism. I suggest that this process came to full fruition in the world of the Sages. See S. Talmon, "The Emergence

pronouncements which drew their legitimization from the unfathomable divine spirit.⁵³ The place of personal inspiration, which can be neither learned nor transmitted, was now taken by interpretation, based on an ever expanding set of objective rules, מידות שבהן התורה נדרשת. Their proper application can be acquired through diligent study. Majority decisions, arrived at by rational investigation, and finely honed exegesis, took the place of prophetically inspired dicta which cannot be questioned.

By contrast, the *yaḥad* embraced unreservedly the Bible's high appreciation of prophetic teaching and continued to subject the life of the individual and the community to the guidance of personalities who were possessed of the divine spirit, first and foremost to the guidance of the מורה (ה)צדק, the 'Legitimate Teacher.'⁵⁴ Being prophetically inspired, the Teacher's decisions were beyond debate and unconditionally binding.

In this respect, the Covenanters and nascent Christianity are on the same wave length. The acceptance of inspiration as the paramount principle of individual and communal life informs also the followers of Jesus. Like the Teacher's instructions, Jesus' pronouncements are authoritative, indisputable, and absolutely final. We should, however, highlight some significant differences:⁵⁵ Like the biblical prophets, and unlike Jesus, the Teacher is confined to the parameters of actual history. He is never accredited with performing miracles or superterrestrial acts. While indeed divinely inspired, he is not imbued with messianic propensities, nor is he ever portrayed as transcending the unbridgeable boundaries of his humanness.

---

of Jewish Sectarianism in the Early Second Temple Period," *Ancient Israelite Religion: Essays in Honor of Frank Moore Cross* (ed. P. D. Miller Jr., P. D. Hanson, and S. D. McBride; Philadelphia: Fortesss, 1987) 487–516, repr. *King, Cult, and Calendar*, 165–201.

⁵³ See Talmon, *World of Qumran*, 29–31.

⁵⁴ This is S. Ivry's felicitous rendition of the Hebrew term. Others translate 'Righteous Teacher,' 'Teacher of Righteousness,' *et sim*.

⁵⁵ See the most recent collection of essays edited by J. H. Charlesworth, *Jesus and the Dead Sea Scrolls* (New York: Doubleday, 1992), in which diverse aspects of this issue are discussed in detail, esp. J. H. Charlesworth, "The Dead Sea Scrolls and the Historical Jesus," 1–74.

## III. The Yaḥad's History and Pre-History

The *yaḥad*'s final dissent from the emerging brand of Pharisaic Judaism at the turn of the era constitutes the climax of the lengthy confrontation of these two streams. The climactic event is captured in words like נבנתה הגדר רחק החוק, "The wall is built, the boundary far removed" (CD IV 12; cf. Mic 7:11), פרשנו מרב העם, "We separated from the majority (?) of the people" (4QMMT), and אין עוד להשתפח לבית יהודה כי אם לעמוד איש על מצודו, "There shall be no more joining the house of Judah, but each man shall stand upon his watchtower" (CD IV 11–12).[56] This event can serve as the starting point for the attempt to sketch preceding stages in the development of the Covenanters' community.

It is my thesis that the Community of the Renewed Covenant should be viewed as the third- or second-century crystallization of a major socio-religious movement which arose in early post-exilic Judaism. The movement was prophetically inspired and inclined to apocalypticism. It perpetuated a spiritual trend whose origins can be traced to the prophets of the First Temple period—foremost Isaiah, Jeremiah and Ezekiel—and to the post-exilic prophets Haggai and Zechariah.[57] The development of the movement runs parallel to that of the competing rationalist stream which first surfaces in the book of Ezra, and especially in the book of Nehemiah, and will ultimately crystallize in Rabbinic or normative Judaism.

It follows that the roots of the *yaḥad*'s prophetically inspired belief-system, as that of the nascent rationalist stream, reach down into the period of the Return from the Babylonian Exile, *viz.*, into the fifth, possibly even into the sixth century BCE. At that time a bifurcation in the Jewish body politic appears to have set in. Led by rival priestly houses,[58] two major strands emerged which were divided on a variety

---

[56] E. Qimron (*The Damascus Document Reconsidered* [Jerusalem: Israel Exploration Society/Shrine of the Book, 1992] 17) suggests reading מצורו, as in 4Q177 10–11 6, instead of מצודו.

[57] The divergent views of Haggai and Zechariah, who were active contemporaneously in the last decades of the 6th century BCE, seem to be reflected in successive stages of the *yaḥad*'s redemption hopes.

[58] My proposition is not identical with H. Stegemann's debatable hypothesis, put forward in *Die Enstehung der Qumrangemeinde* (Rheinische Friedrich-Wilhelms-Universität; Bonn, 1971) that the 'Legitimate Teacher' once served as highpriest in the Temple, and was ousted from there by the 'Wicked Priest.' The hypothesis was questioned by,

of tenets pertaining to belief and ritual. In the course of their subsequent development, both movements experienced internal diversifications of their respective interpretations of the biblical tradition. In both movements this diversification generated new schismatic groups. At the turn of the era, the process culminated in the distinct pluriformity of Judaism, to which the classical sources give witness.

I submit that we can discern two main phases in the historical development of the prophetic strand: The 'primitive' stage of the unstructured 'movement' is only sparsely documented. By contrast, Qumran literature provides ample documentation of the second stage, when the 'movement' took on the form of the structured 'Community of the Renewed Covenant.'

From its inception, the 'prophetic movement' attracted followers in many Palestinian localities on a countrywide scale. In their urban habitations members lived a regular family life, conforming to the exceedingly familial stance which biblical society puts on a pedestal. We cannot accurately assess the size of the membership. But it was presumably so substantial that this movement could vie with other groups for supremacy in the Jewish body politic, foremost with the emerging rationalist stream, which experienced a parallel consolidation.

The movement crystallized progressively in the fourth and third century BCE. In the late third or early second century it hardened into the structured Community of the Renewed Covenant. Consequently, the life-span of this spiritual-ritual strand, in the diverse stages of its development, extends from some time after the destruction of the First Temple in 586 BCE to the destruction of the Second Temple in 70 CE.

The sector living at Qumran was the spearhead of the 'Community.' It was constituted as a 'Commune' of exclusively male members who resided there for a specified number of years. In preparation for the final war of cosmic dimensions, expected to erupt at an uncharted future point in time, they organized themselves in paramilitary divisions. During the period of service at Qumran, and only

---

*int. al.*, J. H. Charlesworth, "The Origin and Subsequent History of the Authors of the Dead Sea Scrolls: Four Transitional Phases Among the Qumran Essenes," *RevQ* 10 (1979–1980) 213–33, and more recently by J. J. Collins, "The Origin of the Qumran Community: A Review of the Evidence," *To Touch the Text: Biblical and Related Studies in Honor of Joseph A. Fitzmyer, S.J.* (ed. M. P. Horgan and P. J. Kobelski; New York: Crossroad, 1989) 159–78.

then, commune-members refrained from sexual intercourse and from family life. Qumran was the site of a permanent settlement with a periodically changing celibate population of not more than 200–250 males at a time.

The existence of the Movement/Community of the Renewed Covenant over a considerable length of time stands in the way of fully gauging its essential character. The diversity of ideological contents and literary genres which marks Qumran literature may reflect discrete stages of a spiritual development which affected the entire membership. But it may also have resulted from disagreements concerning theological and organizational matters which arose among the members in the span of half a millennium.

## Conclusion

The Community of the Renewed Covenant is a socio-religious phenomenon *sui generis* which should not be identified with any subdivision of Second Temple Judaism of which the classical sources speak. Analogies or similarities of the *yaḥad*'s ritual laws with Sadducean *halakhah*, of its communal structure with that of the Essenes, of their hyper-nomistic outlook with that of the Samaritans, or of a religious vocabulary which at times overlaps with the credal terminology of nascent Christianity, spring from common traditions rooted in the Hebrew Bible, in which all configurations of Judaism at the turn of the era had a share.

The Covenanters' theology was stressed between a utopian vision of an imminent restoration of biblical Israel's glorified history, and the palpably different reality of Jewish life in the Greco-Roman period. In their world of ideas wishful thinking coalesced indiscriminately with historical actuality. No other faction of Judaism at the turn of the era, or for that matter early Christianity, bears upon itself the stamp of facts welded with fancy, and of a hyper-nomism wedded with a fervent messianism.

The Community and Its Religious Law

# Sadducean Elements in Qumran Law

*Joseph M. Baumgarten*

It has become an almost universal scholarly convention to begin discussions about the Sadducees by bemoaning the fact that we do not have any of their writings. All we know about them comes from their opponents: Josephus, who relates that at the age of nineteen he began to govern his life by the rules of the Pharisees;[1] the New Testament writers and the Church fathers, who had little sympathy for those who denied the belief in resurrection; and the Rabbis, who had this and many other reasons for not wishing to preserve Sadducean literature. The Pharisees, it seems, fared better, for although, with minor exceptions,[2] we do not have any of their writings either, this may have been by their own choice, the result of their predilection for employing oral tradition (παράδοσις τῶν πρεσβυτέρων) as their characteristic medium for disseminating their doctrines. Besides, they were succeeded by the Rabbis of the Talmud, who ultimately ended up writing down a good deal of what they had received from the Pharisees. The Sadducees, alas, had no ideological posterity, unless with Abraham Geiger we consider the medieval Karaites as a kind of Sadducean reincarnation.

The accuracy of this sad picture of Sadducean fortunes can no longer be taken for granted. The first glimmer of a possible exception to the non-survival of Sadducean writings came at the beginning of this century from the dusty folios of Jewish sectaries which Solomon Schechter brought to light in the Cairo Genizah. It is ironic that nowadays one needs reminders to recall that two of the most important manuscripts of the Genizah were published by Schechter under the title *Fragments of a Zadokite Work*. Within a few years after this epochal publication in 1910, of what we today recognize as a

---

[1] Josephus, *Life* 1.2 §12.
[2] See for example *Megillat Taʿanit*.

key composition of the Dead Sea Scroll community, the work was born again and renamed the *Damascus Document* (CD). The meaning of "Damascus," whether geographical or symbolic, is still much debated, while the Zadokite character of the laws and ideology of the Sons of Zadok appears now to be relatively secure. Suffice it to observe that Schechter's term *Zadokite* was based on the prominence in the *Fragments* of Zadok as the rediscoverer of the Law and the designation of those who followed the true interpretation of the laws as Sons of Zadok. Schechter also took note of Qirqisani's seventh-century description of the Zadokites, in which there were a number of approximations of laws found in the *Fragments*; among them the prohibition of niece marriages and of remarriage after divorce and the use of a calendar with months of thirty days.

In a way, Schechter himself contributed to the obfuscation of the term *Zadokite*, for although he was aware that "the term Zadokites naturally suggests the Sadducees," he felt that "the present state of knowledge of the latter's doctrines and practices does not offer enough points of resemblance to justify the identification of them with our Sect."[3] Instead he sought to identify the Sect with the Dositheans, a Samaritan sect whose history is largely obscure, but whose origin the chronicler Abul-Fath pushes back as far as the time of Alexander the Great. The Dosithean identification has not, to my knowledge, found any substantial support and was in any case overshadowed by other theories about the laws found in CD.

Louis Ginzberg's erudite evaluation of the laws in CD from the perspective of rabbinic halakha, although entitled *Eine unbekannte jüdische Sekte*, led him to the conclusion that the sect should be identified as Pharisaic.[4] However, in order to maintain this thesis, he resorted to a good deal of textual emendation and particularly was constrained to excise the references to the calendar of *Jubilees* (CD XVI 3) as well as the ban on uncle-niece marriages as later interpolations. Chaim Rabin ventured in 1957 to revive Ginzberg's identification with the Pharisees by elaborating the parallels between the rules of the *yaḥad* and the *ḥaburah*, first noted by Saul

---

[3] S. Schechter, "Introduction," *Documents of Jewish Sectaries. Volume 1: Fragments of a Zadokite Work* (Library of Biblical Studies; ed. H. M. Orlinsky; New York: KTAV, 1970) xxi.

[4] L. Ginzberg, *Eine unbekannte jüdische Sekte* (New York: privately published, 1922; rpt. Hildesheim: Olms, 1972. English translation: *An Unknown Jewish Sect* [Moreshet 1; New York: Jewish Theological Seminary, 1976]).

Lieberman, but again this identification can no longer be maintained.[5]

Despite their differing identifications, Schechter and Ginzberg at least agreed that CD must be considered a product of the Second Temple period, but this premise was soon rejected by A. Büchler and other critics who maintained that the work stemmed from the Karaites of the Middle Ages. The links with Karaite literature were cited by Solomon Zeitlin in his quixotic crusade in the 1950's and 1960's against the antiquity of the scrolls, although in fairness we should recognize that Zeitlin served a valuable purpose by drawing attention to the likelihood that the medieval Karaites indeed had access to and were influenced by ancient Qumran writings.[6]

The Sadducean theory in its current form had its origin after Yadin's publication of the *Temple Scroll*, and as a long time proponent of the Essene hypothesis,[7] I must confess that I had something to do with lending it impetus. In a 1980 paper I pointed out that in three controversies between Pharisees and צדוקים concerning purity recorded in the Mishnah the positions taken in Qumran texts coincide with those of the צדוקים.[8] Two of these are found in the *Temple Scroll*, which insists (1) that purification for ritual purposes cannot be accomplished by immersion alone without waiting for sundown (In *m. Par.* 3:7 we are told that the Pharisees deliberately used to defile the priest before he burned the red cow and then had him immersed to counter the צדוקים who insisted that the ritual could be performed only by one whose purification was followed by sundown); and (2) that the bones, hides, and nails of the carcasses of unclean animals are as defiling as their flesh. The third is found in a citation from the letter now known as MMT, already reported by Milik in 1962, in which the writer insists that when liquids are poured from a pure source into an impure receptacle the source is contaminated by the connecting stream, called נצוק in *m.Yad.* 4:7. There the צדוקים say:

---

[5] C. Rabin, *Qumran Studies* (Oxford: Oxford University Press, 1957). Cf. this writer's review article, "Qumran Studies," *JBL* 77 (1958) 249–57.

[6] Cf. N. Wieder, *The Judean Scrolls and Karaism* (London: East and West Library, 1962); Y. Erder, "When did the Encounter of Qaraism with Apocryphal Literature close to the Dead Sea Scroll Literature Begin?" *Cathedra* 41–44 (1986–87) 54–68 (in Hebrew); H. Ben Shammai, "Methodological Notes concerning Research on the Relationship between the Qaraites and Ancient Jewish Sects," *Cathedra* 41–44 (1986–87) 69–86.

[7] Cf. J. Baumgarten, "The Covenant Sect and the Essenes" (Dissertation, Johns Hopkins University, 1954).

[8] J. Baumgarten, "The Pharisaic-Sadducean Controversies about Purity and the Qumran Texts," *JJS* 31 (1980) 157–70.

"We protest against you, O Pharisees, for you declare the נצוק clean."

These parallels, now confirmed by the description of the forthcoming text of MMT provided by Elisha Qimron and John Strugnell,[9] its editors, led me in the aforementioned paper to consider the possibility "that the צדוקים, who are portrayed in the Mishnah as complaining about Pharisaic laxities in the sphere of purity, were not the aristocratic Sadducees but heterodox rigorists of the 'Zadokite' type."[10] However, I noted that according to tannaitic sources Sadducean high priests did in fact perform the red cow ritual in accordance with the purity standards set forth in Qumran texts. I therefore concluded rather conservatively that the Sadducees and the Qumran exegetes, though distinct, followed similar and more stringent approaches in the area of purity.[11]

In the wake of the description of the halakhic contents of MMT, some scholars are now inclined to go much farther. One hypothesis, distancing itself from the long-held Essene identification, seeks to prove that "the earliest members of the sect must have been Sadducees . . . who protested the following of Pharisaic views in the Jerusalem Temple under the Hasmonean priests."[12] When their efforts to "win over the Hasmoneans and the remaining Jerusalem, Sadducees" failed, the Qumran Zadokites developed over time a more radicalized sectarian mentality. This approach raises some historical questions: (1) How reliable is the evidence that the early Hasmoneans were specifically committed to Pharisaic traditions? (2) Since the Hasmoneans under John Hyrcanus and more so during the reign of Alexander Jannaeus did abandon the Pharisaic regulations (νόμινα) and aligned themselves with the Sadducees (*Ant.* 13.10.6 §§ 293-298), would this not have inclined the Zadokites toward rapprochement with the establishment rather than radical-

---

[9] E. Qimron and J. Strugnell, "An Unpublished Halakhic Letter from Qumran," *Biblical Archaeology Today: Proceedings of the International Congress on Biblical Archaeology, Jerusalem April 1984* (ed. J. Amitai; Jerusalem: Israel Exploration Society, 1985) 400–07.

[10] Baumgarten, "Pharisaic-Sadducean Controversies,"167.

[11] Cf. now the evaluation of Albert Baumgarten, who prefers the supposition that the Rabbis were no longer aware of the distinction between the Qumran Zadokites and the Sadducees. See his article "Qumran and Jewish Sectarianism during the Second Temple Period," *The Scrolls of the Judaean Desert: Forty Years of Research* (ed. M. Broshi, S. Japhet, D. Schwartz, and S. Talmon; Jerusalem: Bialik Institute and Israel Exploration Society, 1992) 139–51 (in Hebrew).

[12] L. Schiffman, "The New Halakhic Letter (4QMMT) and the Origins of the Dead Sea Sect," *BA* 53/2 (June 1990) 69.

ized isolation? Moreover, in the sphere of theology, the deterministic doctrines set forth in the *Serekh ha-Yaḥad* and the *Hôdāyôt* appear diametrically opposite to what Josephus tells us about the Sadducees:

> The Sadducees . . . do away with Fate (εἱμαρμένη) altogether . . . They maintain that man has the free choice of good or evil, and that it rests with each man's will whether he follows the one or the other. As for the persistence of the soul after death, penalties in the underworld, and rewards, they will have none of them. (*J.W.* 2.8.14 §§164-165 [LCL]).

By contrast, there is now a Cave 4 text, 4Q521, which catalogues God's providential actions[13] and reads in part:

> כי יכבד את חסידים על כסא מלכות עד . . .
> ופר[י מעש]ה טוב לאיש לוא יתאחר . . . כי ירפא חללים ומתים יחיה

> For he will grant honor to the pious on the throne of eternal royalty . . . and the fruit of a man's good action shall not be delayed . . . for he will heal the pierced and resurrect the dead.

Allowing for the possibility that this text may come from a Pharisaic source which happened to be preserved in the Qumran library, it would still be a formidable task to reconcile the Epicurean outlook of the Sadducees with the abundant allusions to eschatological retribution in the Qumran literature. Moreover, the developed angelology and receptivity for apocalyptic writings at Qumran seem out of character for conservative "establishment" Sadducees.

Professor Sussman, who has provided us with a most valuable assessment of MMT from the perspective of the history of halakha, is inclined to discount the importance of theology as a determinant of sectarian identity:

> What distinguishes them [the sect] and what concerns them in the inter-sectarian polemics are matters of halakha, not beliefs and opinions, not theology, and not national or political ques-

---

[13] É. Puech, "Une apocalypse messianique (4Q521)," *RevQ* 15 (1992) 485.

tions. Certainly there were also controversies in these areas, but the tangible subject about which the writer [of MMT] is concerned and turns to his opponents, 'that it may be good with you and your people, so that you may rejoice at the end of time', is the halakha.[14]

This is a welcome corrective to the neglect of halakha in much of the contemporary scholarship on the scrolls,[15] but it should not lead us to belittle the significance of religious doctrines as components of the character of the major Second Temple movements. Even in rabbinic sources the doctrinal aspects of Sadducean teaching are not overlooked, such as the denial of resurrection and the sarcastic depiction of the Pharisees who "afflict themselves in this world and have nothing in the world to come."[16]

Interestingly, Sussman is of the opinion that there is no tangible evidence in early rabbinic sources for any controversy between the sects concerning the fundamental question of the validity of the Oral Law.[17] He has perhaps legitimate doubts about the originality of the interpretation found in the scholion to *Megillat Ta'anit*, which alludes to the opposition of the Sages to the Sadducean Book of Decrees, which was "written and deposited."[18] But it is not clear why he would dismiss the ideological implications of the antique *baraita* (*b. Kidd.* 66a) which depicts a Sadducean plotter telling King Yannai to kill the Sages and not worry about the fate of the Torah, for it is "wrapped up and deposited" for anyone to read. This response was seen by Urbach as reflecting the Sadducean rejection of oral tradition as the vital element in the continuity of Torah, and here Josephus provides significant corroboration:

> The Pharisees had passed on to the people certain ordinances handed down by the fathers and not written in the Laws of

---

[14] Y. Sussman, "The Study of the History of Halakha and the Dead Sea Scrolls: Initial Talmudic Reflections in the light of MMT," *Tarbiz* 59 (1989–90) 36 (in Hebrew).

[15] See my evaluation in "The Laws of the Damascus Document in Current Research," *The Damascus Document Reconsidered* (ed. M. Broshi; Jerusalem: Israel Exploration Society/Shrine of the Book, Israel Museum, 1992) 51–62.

[16] *B. Sanh.* 90b and *'Abot R. Nat.* [A] 5.

[17] Sussman, "History of Halakha," 57.

[18] Cf. J. N. Epstein, *Introduction to Tannaitic Literature* (Jerusalem: Magnes, 1957 695 (in Hebrew); E. Urbach, "The Derasha as a Basis of Halakha," *Tarbiz* 27 (1957–58) 181 (in Hebrew); and S. Lieberman, *Greek and Hellenism in the Land of Israel* (Jerusalem: Bialik, 1962) 215 (Hebrew translation).

Moses, for which reason they are rejected by the sect of Sadducees, who hold that only those ordinances should be considered valid which were written down, and those which had been handed down by the fathers need not be observed (*Ant.* 13.10.5 §297 [LCL]).

We have elsewhere argued that there is implied here a Pharisaic avoidance of writing down their ordinances, although some have taken issue with this inference.[19] However, there can hardly be any doubt that, at the very least, we have here a fundamental Pharisaic–Sadducean dispute about the authority of ordinances which derived from transmitted traditions, ἐκ πατέρων διαδοχῆς, rather than canonical texts.[20] We should therefore pose the question as to where the Qumranites stood on this crucial issue.

Let us try to provide a tentative answer. The *Damascus Document*, still the central source for the sect's concept of the historical context of their covenant, is emphatically negative about the contemporary generation and that of their predecessors. The covenanters saw themselves as a remnant living in a "period of wrath" which began with the destruction of the Temple when God "hid his face from Israel" and which lasted down to their very own days.[21] During this period "all Israel had gone astray"; they were "guilty men" because they lacked the proper understanding of the Sabbaths, the holidays, and other "hidden things" of the Law. Thus repentance for the Covenanters could hardly take form of a return to the "tradition of the fathers." Even David did not fully know the Torah, because it was hidden since the days of Joshua and the elders (CD V 2–3). It is hardly accidental that in the Qumran corpus of laws, now augmented by Cave 4 materials, there is never any mention of authoritative tradents from the past. Yose ben Yoʿezer, Yehoshua ben Perachyah, Shimʿon ben Shetach, to whom rabbinic sources attribute important early Pharisaic rulings, have no Qumran counterparts. The righteous teacher is a contemporary figure to

---

[19] J. Baumgarten, "The Unwritten Law in the Pre-Rabbinic Period," *JSJ* 3 (1972) 7–29. Cf. Seth Schwartz, *Josephus and Judean Politics* (SPB 39; Leiden: Brill, 1990) and Steve Mason, *Flavius Josephus on the Pharisees: A Compostion-Historical Study* (Columbia Studies in the Classical Tradition 18; Leiden: Brill, 1991).

[20] Cf. Albert Baumgarten, "The Pharisaic Paradox," *HTR* 80 (1987) 63–77.

[21] See now D. Dimant, "New Light from Qumran on the Jewish Pseudepigrapha—4Q390," *The Madrid Qumran Congress: Proceedings of the International Congress on the Dead Sea Scrolls, Madrid 18–21 March, 1991* (2 vols.; ed. J. Trebolle Barrera and L. Vegas Montaner; STDJ 11; Leiden: Brill; Madrid: Editorial Complutense, 1992) 2.405–47.

whom have been revealed "hidden things" unknown to Israel, and his followers continue to search the Scriptures in the hope that "from time to time" they, too, may be granted revealed, though nontraditional, illuminations. In MMT their legal interpretations are characteristically introduced with the formula אנחנו אומרים, "We say." This contrasts markedly with the extended chains of named tradents which often precede halakhic traditions in the Talmud. In short, the covenanters had a rich library, but they did not accept a מסורת, they did not rely on παράδοσις.

This lack of esteem for tradition may also have been characteristic of the Sadducees. "The Sadducees," Josephus says, "own no observance of any sort apart from the laws; in fact, they reckon it a virtue to dispute with the teachers of the path of wisdom that they pursue" (Ant. 18.1.4 §16 [LCL]). M. Kister takes this to be the result of their reliance on their own exegesis of the Bible, which invariably entails innovation, without taking any human authority or tradition into account.[22]

Does this congruity between the Sadducee and Qumran exegetes and their agreements on the rigorous interpretation of the laws of purity suffice to establish their common origin? We do not believe so. We have already noted the diametrically opposite theological views, and their different socioeconomic orientations are well known. Even in the sphere of halakha, the congruities which we have found are confined to the areas of purity and ritual. Sussman's recent enumeration of halakhic controversies with Sadducees and Boethusians found in tannaitic sources includes twelve subjects other than those three questions of purity concerning which we pointed out agreements with Qumran. On these twelve we lack any evidence of agreement between Qumran and the Sadducees. This lack of congruity applies likewise to the significant sphere of the calendar.

The Sadducees did agree with Qumran and other sectarian exegetes in taking "on the morrow of the Sabbath" (Lev 23:11, 15) to mean Sunday, but according to the Talmud, they set the Omer offering on the Sunday following the Sabbath which occurred *during* the week of Passover, not the Sabbath (25/I) which came *after* Passover.[23] Moreover, there is no substantial evidence that they fol-

---

[22] M. Kister, "Some Aspects of Qumranic Halakha," *The Madrid Qumran Congress*, 2.571–88.

[23] B. *Menaḥ* 66a reads: ממחרת השבת שבתוך הפסח. Sussman prefers the reading found in manuscripts of *Siphra*, ממחרת שבת הפסח, but even the latter can hardly signify the Sabbath *after* Passover.

lowed the schematic solar calendar found in *Jubilees* and the Qumran writings.[24] Parenthetically, the theory that the *Jubilees*-Qumran calendar preserves the ancient priestly biblical chronology is now considerably weakened by the emendation of the chronology of the Flood found in 4Q252.[25] According to Gen 8:3–4 the Flood lasted 150 days, from the 17th of the second month to the 17th of the seventh month. The writer of 4Q252, however, realized that in the Qumran solar calendar the interval really has 152 days. He therefore introduced two days between the end of the mighty waters and the resting of the ark.

Abraham Geiger often maintained that the Sadducees were the guardians of the "old halakha," while the Pharisees were more progressive and introduced innovations found in rabbinic law.[26] In principle, this view may be valid with regard to the Pharisaic ordinances referred to by Josephus, which may perhaps be identified with rabbinic enactments (*takkanot*). However, MMT now shows that the rabbinic interpretation of Temple and purity laws was already known and well enough established to become the target of sectarian polemics in the Hasmonean period.

This is a remarkable illustration of the relevance of rabbinic sources, despite their later editing, for the religious history of the Second Temple period. We trust that the demonstration of the antiquity of such rabbinic traditions will lead to a change in the rather negative stance of some scholars on the importance of the Talmud for the understanding of pre-Christian literature.[27] On the other hand, it should not lead us to discount the information concerning religious practice which may be gleaned from such earlier sources as Philo, Josephus, and the New Testament.

We have noted elsewhere that seven details of Essene halakha which Josephus thought worthy of notice are now explicitly confirmed in Qumran texts.[28] Sussman has recently revived the

---

[24] Cf., however, Sussman, "History of Halakha," 30–31.

[25] See Timothy H. Lim, "The Chronology of the Flood Story in a Qumran Text (4Q252)," *JJS* 43 (1992) 288–98.

[26] See his latest formulation in *Gesammelte Abhandlungen* (ed. Samuel Poznanski; Warsaw, 1910) 116–26 (in Hebrew).

[27] See for example J. Fitzmyer, *Responses to 101 Questions on the Dead Sea Scrolls* (New York: Paulist, 1992) 46–47.

[28] J. Baumgarten, "The Disqualifications of Priests in 4Q Fragments of the 'Damascus Document,' a Specimen of the Recovery of pre-Rabbinic Halakha," *The Madrid Qumran Congress*, 2.503–14.

hypothesis, first proposed by Azariah de Rossi in the sixteenth century, that the Essenes may be identified with the Boethusians, who appear in rabbinic sources in conjunction with the Sadducees. This remains a complex literary and historical question.

In sum, we have not yet found compelling reasons to go beyond our rather conservative 1980 assessment of the similarities between Sadducean and Qumran rigorous interpretations of the laws of purity. One may speculate that they are perhaps the result of the convergence of two different approaches: the Sadducean approach, which limited the application of purity to the Temple and its rituals; and the Qumran approach, which applied purity within the isolated sphere of a community which separated itself from the multitude of the people and was therefore unconcerned about the difficulties of maintaining its rigid standards. But we must not forget that substantial areas of religious practice were commonly shared by most Jews of the Second Temple period, regardless of their ideological affiliations.

Such inconclusive assessments are not likely to satisfy those who expect scholarship to produce immediate and decisive identifications for all the literary remnants of the past. For those who would rather ride upon the swift steeds of unproven theory, we cite Isaiah 30:15: בשובה ונחת תושעון בהשקט ובבטחה תהיה גבורתכם, "In returning and rest you shall be saved; in quietness and in trust shall be your strength" [NRSV].

# The *Temple Scroll* and the Nature of Its Law:
# The Status of the Question

## Lawrence H. Schiffman

To assess the current state of research on a document known to the scholarly world for less than thirty years is at best a daunting challenge. One lacks the perspective of time to make possible a realistic and fair evaluation of where matters stand. To do so when the document is 60 columns long and has attracted so much well deserved attention is doubly difficult. To do so fairly when one is himself the author of so large a part of the research to be summarized may make this task virtually impossible.[1] Nonetheless, a serious attempt will be made here to present a sense of where research on this scroll has been going, taking into account the studies of the many scholars working on this important text.

In many ways this discussion will proceed in encyclopedic fashion, beginning with text and manuscripts, then moving to contents, sources, dating, theology of law, connection with other scrolls and finally historical significance. Along the way, I hope to trace the debate that has ensued since the exciting announcement of the recovery of this scroll in the aftermath of the Six Day War in 1967.[2] For me, research on this document has occupied much of the intervening years, and I hope to convey at least some sense of what it is that has

---

[1] For bibliography see F. García Martínez, "El Rollo del Templo (11 Q Temple): Bibliografia sistemática," *RevQ* 12 (1986) 425–40; idem, "The Temple Scroll: A Systematic Bibliography 1985–1991," *The Madrid Qumran Congress: Proceedings of the International Congress on the Dead Sea Scrolls, Madrid 18–21 March 1991* (ed. J. Trebolle Barrera and L. Vegas Montaner; STDJ 11; Leiden: Brill; Madrid: Editorial Complutense, 1992) 2.393–403.

[2] Initial impressions are conveyed in Y. Yadin, "The Temple Scroll," *BA* 30 (1967) 135–39; idem, "The Temple Scroll," *New Directions in Biblical Archaeology* (ed. D. N. Freedman and J. C. Greenfield; Garden City, NY: Doubleday, 1967) 139–48.

led me to devote so much energy to what Yadin has termed "the hidden law of the Dead Sea Sect."[3]

The *Zohar* tells us that הכל תלוי במזל אפילו ספר תורה בהיכל, "everything is dependent on fortune, even a Torah scroll in the ark."[4] It was the good fortune of this Torah scroll, known to us as *Megillat Ha-Miqdash*, the *Temple Scroll*, to have come into the hands of the late Yigael Yadin, Israel's leading scholar of Judean Desert documents. It was his dogged determination to marshal all the forces at his disposal to produce the finest possible edition and commentary on this scroll that provided the launching pad for all later research.[5] There can be no question that we are all indebted to his great work, even where, as we will see, scholarship continues to proceed in new directions.[6]

## Text and Manuscripts

The *Temple Scroll* (11QT<sup>a</sup>) was first brought to the attention of Yadin in 1960 by Joseph Uhrig, a Virginia minister, who claimed to negotiate on behalf of a Jordanian antiquities dealer.[7] After two years of negotiations and a loss of $10,000, Yadin had little more to show than a small fragment proffered as a sample, and he gave up hope of recovering the scroll. Some of us recently heard Frank M. Cross relate that he traveled to Beirut in early 1967 where the well known scrolls dealer Kando, who recently passed away, involved him in preliminary negotiations for the purchase of what later turned out to be the *Temple Scroll*. In the aftermath of the Six Day

---

[3] This is the subtitle of a popular volume by Y. Yadin, *The Temple Scroll: The Hidden Law of the Dead Sea Sect* (London: Weidenfeld and Nicholson, 1985).

[4] *Zohar* 3.134a. The actual meaning of this statement, as opposed to the popular usage which led us to include it here, is that everything is dependent for its sanctity on the flow (from the root *nzl*) of divine effulgence from above, even the Torah scroll which only derives its holiness from that divine emanation.

[5] Y. Yadin, *Megillat Ha-Miqdash*, (3 vols. and Supplementary Plates; Jerusalem: Israel Exploration Society, 1977); idem, *The Temple Scroll* (3 vols. and Supplementary Plates; Jerusalem: Israel Exploration Society, 1983).

[6] Cf. my review in *BA* 48 (1985) 122–26 in which I surveyed the outlines of the debate as it had then taken shape.

[7] H. Shanks, "Intrigue and the Scroll: Behind the Scenes of Israel's Acquisition of the Temple Scroll," *BAR* 13/6 (1987) 23–27.

War in 1967, Yadin located Kando and the scroll, and it was eventually purchased for the Shrine of the Book in Jerusalem for $105,000.[8]

The scroll was in poor condition when it reached Yadin. It had been kept under the floor of the antiquities dealer's home in a shoe box. In addition, other fragments were in a cigar box and some had been hidden elsewhere. The task of unrolling the scroll and placing the fragments in order was made even more difficult because the writing of some columns was preserved only on the back of the preceding column. The upper edge had been severely damaged by dampness, either in antiquity or while in the possession of the antiquities dealer.

The scroll consists of nineteen sheets, mostly of 3–4 columns each. Adding space for the damaged beginning, the entire scroll would have been approximately 8.75 m, making it the longest of the preserved scrolls (1QIsa$^a$ is 7.34 m). It is written in two hands, one scribe writing columns I–V and another (with some overlap of text) the remainder of the scroll. Yadin suggests that the scribe of the first part of the scroll repaired the scroll by rewriting the first part which had become worn through use.[9] The scribal techniques and script are typical of the other Qumran manuscripts.

E. Tov associates the language of the manuscript with the Qumran scribal practice.[10] While the language of the scroll does indeed have much in common with the dialect in which the sectarian compositions from Qumran are written, in certain linguistic features and in its legal terminology, it exhibits more affinities to Rabbinic Hebrew than do most of the sectarian scrolls.[11]

The editing of 11QT$^a$ posed particular problems. Because the scroll had been closely rolled, as is clear from the photograph published by Yadin,[12] writing had left impressions on the back of the adjacent columns, even at points where that text was not preserved on the front. Yadin produced mirror photos of this writing and used it to supplement the text available on the front of the manuscript.

---

[8] Yadin, *Temple Scroll*, 1.1–5.

[9] Ibid., 12.

[10] E. Tov, "The Orthography and Language of the Hebrew Scrolls Found at Qumran and the Origins of the Scrolls," *Textus* 13 (1986) 55.

[11] L. H. Schiffman, "The Temple Scroll in Literary and Philological Perspective," *Approaches to Ancient Judaism II* (ed. W. S. Green; BJS 11; Chico, CA: Scholars Press, 1980) 143–58.

[12] Yadin, *Temple Scroll*, vol. 3, plate 6, nos. 1–2.

Immediately with the publication of the text, Elisha Qimron began to reexamine the readings in Yadin's edition. By the time Yadin published his English version some six years later, he had already accepted some of Qimron's readings.[13] Numerous differences in reading or identification of letters which Yadin was unable to read have been suggested in published articles by Qimron.[14]

The techniques used by Yadin were developed further in the last few years. Bruce and Kenneth Zuckerman rephotographed the scroll in color with high resolution and special lighting techniques, thereby providing some additional readings. Elisha Qimron used these along with the older photos to read even more text which will appear in a new edition of the scroll which he is preparing. Qimron and Zuckerman are utilizing computerized techniques to rejoin the partial readings on the fronts and backs of often more than one column in order to confirm the accuracy of the readings Qimron has reconstructed. It is hoped that this edition will serve as the basis for the extensive commentary which I am preparing.

In Yadin's view, the *Temple Scroll* is extant in two other fragmentary Qumran manuscripts which he used in restoring parts of the text. In dealing with the date of the 11QT scroll, he identified the script of the two scribes of 11QT$^a$ as Herodian, dating to around the turn of the eras.[15] He then discussed what he considered to be two fragmentary manuscripts, dating Rockefeller 43.975 to the Herodian period but 43.366 to the Hasmonean, from the end of the second century BCE. Here Yadin was making use of the designations of the Palestine Archaeological Museum (PAM) photograph numbers for large fragments to identify manuscripts scattered on a number of plates. As it turns out, 43.975 is indeed another manuscript of the *Temple Scroll* from cave 11 and is now designated 11QT$^b$. The entire corpus of surviving fragments of this text has been published in an

---

[13] Yadin, "Addenda and Corrigenda," in *Temple Scroll*, 1.405–19; 2.passim.

[14] See E. Qimron, "The Text of the Temple Scroll," *Leshonenu* 42 (1978) 136–45; idem, "New Readings in the Temple Scroll," *IEJ* 28 (1978) 161–72; idem, "Three Notes on the Text of the Temple Scroll," *Tarbiz* 51 (1981–82) 135–37; idem, "Textual Notes on the Temple Scroll," *Tarbiz* 53 (1983) 139–41; idem, "Further New Readings in the Temple Scroll," *IEJ* 37 (1987) 31–35; idem, "Column 14 of the Temple Scroll," *IEJ* 38 (1988) 44–46 and plate 11; idem, "The Need for a Comprehensive Critical Edition of the Dead Sea Scrolls," *Archaeology and History in the Dead Sea Scrolls: The New York Conference in Memory of Yigael Yadin* (ed. L. H. Schiffman; JSPSup 8; Sheffield: JSOT Press, 1990) 121–31.

[15] Yadin, *Temple Scroll*, 1.17.

edition by B. Z. Wacholder[16] and the official editor of these fragments, F. García Martínez, recently presented his edition in the Madrid conference volume.[17]

The Hasmonean manuscript, PAM 43.366, was determined by J. Strugnell to belong not to a manuscript of the *Temple Scroll* but rather to a Pentateuch with supplementary materials. Further, Strugnell called attention to a group of cave 4 fragments which quote the *Temple Scroll* or one of its sources and which he dated to no later than about 150 BCE.[18]

We now know this expanded Pentateuch to be the Pentateuchal Paraphrase, or Rewritten Pentateuch, being prepared for the publication by E. Tov and S. White.[19] Of the manuscripts of this document or documents, one of these, 4Q365, is in the exact same hand as these supposed *Temple Scroll* fragments, and it was to this material which Strugnell alluded. Recent examination by White makes possible greater understanding of the problem, but leaves matters undecided. Briefly, the passages in question are found in 4Q365, among fragments of the reworked Pentateuch. They stand out for their different style, and they overlap in part with passages from the *Temple Scroll*. Yet the presence there of material not found in the *Temple Scroll* (as presently preserved) as well as the textual differences between this material and the scroll make it impossible to say that these fragments simply come from another copy of the scroll copied by the scribe of 4Q365. So we are in the position which the Mishnah calls חמר גמל,[20] driving a donkey while dragging along a camel, i.e. pulled from both sides. We have the incongruity of this material with 4Q365 arguing that it is not part of that text, and the differences between it and 11QT$^a$ arguing that it is not simply a copy of the *Temple Scroll*. Accordingly, it has been designated by Tov and

---

[16] B. Z. Wacholder with M. Abegg, "The Fragmentary Remains of 11QTorah (Temple Scroll): 11QTorah$^b$ and 11QTorah$^c$ plus 4QparaTorah Integrated with 11QTorah$^a$," *HUCA* 62 (1991) 1–116.

[17] F. García Martínez, "11QTemple$^b$: A Preliminary Publication," *Madrid Qumran Congress*, 2.363–91.

[18] Letter from J. Strugnell, published in B. Z. Wacholder, *The Dawn of Qumran: The Sectarian Torah of the Teacher of Righteousness* (HUCM 8; Cincinnati: Hebrew Union College Press, 1983) 250–56.

[19] S. A. White, "4Q364 & 365: A Preliminary Report," *Madrid Qumran Congress*, 1.217–28; E. Tov, "The Textual Status of 4Q364–367 (4QPP)," *Madrid Qumran Congress*, 1.43–82.

[20] M. ʿErub. 3:4; 4:10.

White as 4Q365a. In any case, the date and the character of this material must lead to the conclusion that either it itself, or 4Q365 as a whole, served as a source for the *Temple Scroll* as suggested by Strugnell, or that it is closely related to the scroll in some other way.

Accordingly, we can summarize that there are two manuscripts of the text of the scroll preserved in cave 11 and some cave 4 fragments which overlap sufficiently to indicate the existence of either sources for our document or closely related texts.

In addition, this discussion has ramifications for the question of dating. The manuscript of 11QT$^a$ was written first by a Herodian period scribe and then repaired with some columns replaced by a second scribe in the same period. It has been carbon dated to 97 BCE–1 CE.[21] 11QT$^b$ was also copied in the Herodian period. Although I continue to agree with Yadin's dating of the composition of the document to the Hasmonean period,[22] as I will explain below, it must be remembered that the manuscript Yadin took as a Hasmonean period text of the *Temple Scroll* is that known to be 4Q365a, or parts of it. Therefore, there remains no actual manuscript of the scroll from earlier than the Herodian period.

## Contents

The scroll presents itself as a rewritten Torah which begins with the renewal of the Sinaitic covenant of Exodus 34 and then turns to the building of the tabernacle in Exodus 35. From this point, the scroll continues in the order of the canonical Torah. The author began by discussing the structure, furnishings and equipment of the Temple according to the order of the Torah, but constantly digressed to discuss the relevant offerings that utilized these structures or equipment, only to return to the Scriptural order. In the process, he treated the architecture of the Temple and its precincts, laws of sacrifice, priestly dues and tithes, the ritual calendar, festival offerings, ritual purity and impurity, sanctity of the Temple, laws of the king and the army, prophecy, foreign worship, witnesses, laws of war, and various marriage and sex laws. He dealt first with the cult and rit-

---

[21] G. Bonnani, M. Broshi, I. Carmy, S. Ivy, J. Strugnell, W. Wölfi, "Radiocarbon Dating of the Dead Sea Scrolls," ʾAtiqot 20 (1991) 27–32.

[22] Yadin, *Temple Scroll*, 1.386–90; L. H. Schiffman, "The King, his Guard and the Royal Council in the *Temple Scroll*," *PAAJR* 54 (1987) 257–58.

ual and only then moved on to discuss various prescriptions culled from Deuteronomy 18–22. The author apparently worked through the Pentateuch in order, at the same time bringing in the relevant materials from the rest of the biblical corpus, so creating his composition.[23] Yadin maintains that the author and the members of the sect regarded the Temple Scroll as "a veritable Torah of the Lord."[24] He supports this assertion by pointing out that the divine name is written in the same square script in which the rest of the scroll is written, a characteristic of the "canonical" books at Qumran.

This "new Torah" nevertheless does not purport to be messianic. The author tells us explicitly that the scroll describes the Temple in which Israel will worship *before* the end of days (11QT XXIX 2–10).[25] It is an ideal Temple, built upon the principles of Scriptural exegesis and the beliefs of the author or authors. This Temple, it was expected, would be replaced in the end of days with a divinely created sanctuary. Until then, the author/redactor saw his scroll as representing the correct way in which the Temple was to be built and operated.

The scroll does not simply recapitulate the prescriptions of Exodus, Leviticus, Numbers and Deuteronomy. It collects together the various Pentateuchal (and sometimes prophetic) material relevant to the issue at hand and weaves together a unified, consistent text. In this respect it can be said that the text reredacts the Torah, combining all materials on the topic together.

Yet the scroll goes farther. It uses a distinct form of exegesis, in some ways similar to the *midrash* of the later Rabbis, to reconcile the differences between the various Pentateuchal texts so as to create a unified and consistent whole. At times, it makes minor additions to clarify its legal stance. In a few places, extensive passages appear which are not based on our canonical Scriptures. In this way the scroll propounds its own views on the major issues of Jewish law relating to Temple, cult, government, and sanctity.[26] It is this exegetical and legal approach which makes the *Temple Scroll* so central for the history of Jewish law and midrashic exegesis. In addition, the scroll contains allusions to contemporary events and sheds light on the sects of the Second Temple period.

---

[23] Cf. J. Milgrom, "The Temple Scroll," *BA* 41 (1978) 105–20.

[24] Yadin, *Temple Scroll*, 1.392.

[25] Cf. M. O. Wise, "The Covenant of the Temple Scroll XXIX, 3–10," *RevQ* 14 (1989) 49–60.

[26] Cf. Yadin, *Temple Scroll*, 1.71–88.

We should note that by and large the manuscript is built on a Penteuchal text of the canonical Torah. In other words, there is no question that the authors of the various sources, and the author/redactor of the finished product, made use of the canonical Torah.

Yet as is to be expected, the Torah which served as the textual substratum for the scroll was not in all respects identical to that of the Masoretic text. Innumerable minor variants existed in the substratum.[27] These must be carefully distinguished from the intentional modifications made by the author or the sources in order to convey their halakhic or exegetical views.[28]

Yadin devoted considerable attention to the all-important question of the manner in which the scroll was composed and edited in antiquity. He states that the editing took several forms: drafting the text in the first person to indicate that God himself gave these commands, unifying duplicate commands including those which are contradictory, modifying and adding to commands to indicate halakhic rulings, and adding entirely new sections. Yadin notes the author's modification of Pentateuchal verses to dispel any doubt that it is God who is speaking. On the other hand, entire sections retain the Torah's phrasing with no such adaptations. Yadin maintains that the author sought to claim that the law had been handed down directly by God without the intermediacy of Moses. Hence, the author of the *Temple Scroll* modified the commands of Deuteronomy, in which God speaks through Moses, while preserving the language of Exodus, Leviticus and Numbers in which God is mentioned explicitly in the Pentateuchal text.

The author gathered together all material on each subject from the Five Books of Moses, and merged it into a unitary text. Whenever the various Pentateuchal texts presented apparent contradictions, the author harmonized these in accordance with his own brand of halakhic interpretation and drafted his version of the law of the Pentateuch to indicate his ruling. Often words are inserted or passages are otherwise modified to clarify matters ambiguous in the Torah in accord with the views of the author of our scroll. The au-

---

[27] E. Tov, "The *Temple Scroll* and Old Testament Textual Criticism," ERIsr 16 (1982) 100–11 (in Hebrew).

[28] See L. H. Schiffman, "The Septuagint and the Temple Scroll: Shared 'Halakhic Variants'," *Septuagint, Scrolls and Cognate Writings: International Symposium on the Septuagint and Its Relations to the Dead Sea Scrolls and Other Writings* (ed. G. J. Brooke and B. Lindars; SBLSCS 33; Atlanta: Scholars Press, 1992) 277–97.

thor's use of the first person, according to Yadin, also marks the additional material not based on the Pentateuch as the word of God.[29]

Yadin notes that the existence of a Temple plan is alluded to in 1 Chron 28:11–19 and that it served the author as the "starting point for his composition of the scroll." This passage provided the basis for the supplementary sections as the "authority for their existence in the biblical text itself."[30] For the Statues of the King (11QT LVI–LIX), the author based himself on an exegesis of Deut 17:18 and 1 Sam 10:25 from which he inferred the existence of a compilation of statutes. The detailed laws of festivals stem from the allusions to such prescriptions in the incomplete codes of the Torah. The laws of purity are an adaptation of the Pentateuchal legislation concerning the desert Tabernacle to the later circumstances of the Temple in Jerusalem. Yadin did not distinguish composite sources within the scroll. Many unique features distinguish the *Temple Scroll* from other biblical or Second Temple literature. The architecture of the Temple proposed here differs from biblical accounts, on which the author claims to base himself, as well as from descriptions of the Second Temple in Josephus and the Mishnah. Most interesting is the extension of the *temenos* (the "Temple City") by the addition of a third courtyard, so large that it would have encompassed most of what was then Jerusalem.[31] The courtyards and their gates represented the Israelite encampment in the wilderness. The entire Temple plan was intended to recreate the experience of the desert period in which sanctity was understood to radiate to all Israel from the sanctuary at its epicenter.[32] Unique approaches appear here for the construction of the Temple furnishings.[33]

The sacrificial festival calendar includes a number of festivals not part of the biblical or Rabbinic cycle. A second new year festival is to be celebrated on the first of Nisan, in the spring, followed by

---

[29] Yadin, *Temple Scroll*, 1.71–73.

[30] Ibid., 1.83.

[31] L. H. Schiffman, "Exclusion from the Sanctuary and the City of the Sanctuary," HAR 9 (1985) 317; M. Broshi, "The Gigantic Dimensions of the Visionary Temple in the Temple Scroll," *BAR* 13 (1987) 36–37.

[32] L. H. Schiffman, "Architecture and Law, The Temple and its Courtyards in the Temple Scroll," *From Ancient Israel to Modern Judaism, Intellect in Quest of Understanding: Essays in Honor of Marvin Fox* (ed. J. Neusner, E. R. Frerichs, N. M. Sarna; BJS 159; Atlanta: Scholars Press, 1989) 1.267–84.

[33] Cf. Yadin, *Temple Scroll*, 1.177–200; L. H. Schiffman, "The Furnishings of the Temple according to the Temple Scroll," *Madrid Qumran Congress*, 2.621–34.

annual celebration of the eight days of priestly ordination. Besides the Omer festival for the barley harvest (the second day of Passover) and the first fruits of wheat (*Shabûʿôt*), the scroll adds two more first fruits festivals, each at fifty day intervals, for oil and wine. The wood offering is also celebrated as an annual festival in the summer.[34] Extensive laws deal with the sacrificial procedure and ritual purity and impurity.[35] Here we see a general tendency to provide additional ways to protect the sanctuary from impurity. This brief survey does not even begin to represent the rich nature of the scroll's exegesis and the many details of Jewish law in which the text diverges from the views of other sectarian documents or Rabbinic literature.

## Sources

Even in its present form, it is not difficult to discern that the *Temple Scroll* has been redacted from a number of sources by an author/redactor who is himself the creator of the Deuteronomic paraphrase at the end (11QT LI 11—LVI 21; LX 1–LXVI 17). His sources most certainly included the sacrificial festival calendar (XIII 9–XXIX 1) and the law of the king and army (LVI 12–LIX 21). It has been suggested as well that the description of the Temple precincts and furnishings (II 1–XLVII 18, passim) and the laws of purity (XLVIII 1–LI 10) also constituted separate sources.[36]

The author/redactor sought to compose a complete Torah which would expound his views of the sanctity of the Temple, land and people, as well as of the ideal government and society. He worked through the Torah, arranging all the pertinent material around the first occurrence of a topic. In this way he reedited and reredacted the Pentateuchal legislation. At the appropriate places

---

[34] Yadin, *Temple Scroll*, 1.89–136; L. H. Schiffman, "The Sacrificial System of the *Temple Scroll* and the Book of Jubilees," SBLASP 24 (1985) 217–33.

[35] Cf. Yadin, *Temple Scroll*, 1.321–43; L. H. Schiffman, "Impurity of the Dead in the Temple Scroll," *Archaeology and History*, 135–56; J. Milgrom, "The Scriptural Foundations and Derivations of the Laws of Purity of the Temple Scroll," *Archaeology and History*, 83–99.

[36] A. M. Wilson and L. Wills, "Literary Sources in the Temple Scroll," *HTR* 75 (1982) 275–88; M. O. Wise, *A Critical Study of the Temple Scroll from Qumran Cave 11* (Studies in Ancient Oriental Civilization 49; Chicago: Oriental Institute, 1990) 195–98; F. García Martínez, "Sources et rédaction du *Rouleau du Temple*," *Henoch* 13 (1991) 219–32.

he inserted the preexistent collections at his disposal. To give the impression that his Torah was a complete Law, he appended at the end a selection of laws from Deuteronomy, some of which deal only tangentially with the theme of his scroll. This collection is not simply a paraphrase of Scripture. Rather, it includes numerous halakhic and exegetical modifications, as well as full blown midrashic interpretations.[37] Stegemann suggested that the Deuteronomic paraphrase may itself stem from an "expanded Torah scroll" or Deuteronomic scroll,[38] a proposal which we do not accept since from our literary studies we have discovered that the paraphrase is based more or less on our canonical Torah.

Yet this final author/redactor was not just a collector of scattered traditions. On the contrary, despite a few lapses, such as his redundant treatment of the laws of war from Deuteronomy 20 in both the Law of the King (11QT XLVIII 3–21) and in the Deuteronomic paraphrase (11QT LXI 12–LXII 16),[39] the redactor is both organized and consistent. He has carefully integrated his sources into his own composition. He presents materials which embody a consistent method of biblical exegesis, itself based on a particular "theology" of law, as well as a consistent view of holiness and sanctity.[40] Further, his subtle polemic runs like a thread throughout the entire composition. This consistency of approach means that we can examine his final product to determine what circumstances would have led him to include various materials in his work, just as we may ask what conditions may have led the authors of these sections to have composed them. It goes without saying that we may ask similar questions regarding those portions of the scroll which are the compositions of the author/redactor.

In view of the parallels between the *Temple Scroll* and the *Miqṣat Ma'ăśēh Hat-tôrâ*, and between both of these and descriptions of the Sadducees in tannaitic literature, it is most likely that the sources we are discussing here stem from the Sadducean heritage

---

[37] L. H. Schiffman, "The Deuteronomic Paraphrase of the Temple Scroll," *RevQ* 15 (1992) 543–67.

[38] H. Stegemann, "Is the Temple Scroll a Sixth Book of the Torah Lost for 2500 years?" *BAR* 13/6 (1987) 28–35; idem, "The Origins of the Temple Scroll," *Congress Volume Jerusalem* (ed. J. A. Emerton; VTSup 40; Leiden: Brill, 1988) 248–49.

[39] L. H. Schiffman, "The Laws of War in the *Temple Scroll*," *RevQ* 13 (1988) 299–311.

[40] L. H. Schiffman, "The Theology of the *Temple Scroll*," *Proceedings of the Annenberg Conference* (forthcoming).

of those who founded the sect. In these sources, therefore, we may begin to discover the nature of the approach to biblical exegesis of this group.

## Dating

Rockefeller 43.366 (4Q365a), taken by Yadin as the earliest manuscript of the Temple Scroll, was one of the factors which led him to date the composition of the scroll to no later than the reign of John Hyrcanus (134–104 BCE) or slightly earlier.[41] Yet, as already noted, this fragment cannot definitely be established as a manuscript of our scroll. It does prove the existence of elements of the scroll in similar or even the same form in that period, but it says nothing about the document in its entirety as preserved in 11QT$^a$.

All sources now included in the scroll presuppose the existence of a canonical Torah differing from MT only in minor details. Only a few legal rulings can be shown to derive from variant biblical texts. For this reason the scroll had to have been completed after the period of the return from exile in Babylonia, *circa* late sixth to midfifth centuries BCE. As we have mentioned, all manuscripts of the *Temple Scroll* identified thus far are of Herodian date. It is within these parameters that we must seek both a dating and a *Sitz im Leben* for the scroll.

The language of the scroll indicated to Yadin that the text could not have been composed before the Hasmonean period. For Yadin, "the blatantly Qumran-sectarian nature of several laws"[42] was further evidence for this dating. Indeed, the contents of the scroll, emphasizing the sacrificial Temple and ritual, the laws of the king and the death penalty regulations, would call for a Hasmonean dating, in Yadin's view. Based on the law describing the use of rings for holding sacrificial animals, Yadin concludes that "the scroll—or its doctrine—was already known in the time of John Hyrcanus"[43] and that this view influenced him to install such rings, as related in Rabbinic sources.[44] He further argues that the Law of the

---

[41] Yadin, *Temple Scroll*, 1.390; cf. 1.20.

[42] Ibid., 1.387.

[43] Ibid., 1.388.

[44] Cf. S. Lieberman, *Hellenism in Jewish Palestine* (New York: Jewish Theological Seminary of America, 1962) 139–43.

King and laws of conscription (11QT LVI–LIX) are most appropriate to the reign of John Hyrcanus against whose practices the scroll polemicizes. Yadin concludes that the scroll must have been composed by the time of John Hyrcanus or slightly earlier. This dating, he notes, accords with the archeological finds at Qumran which indicate that the sectarian settlement there was founded in the second half of the second century BCE.[45]

The key to the dating of the *Temple Scroll* as a whole must indeed be the Law of the King (11QT LVI 12–LIX 21). This section represents the most sustained example of original composition, as opposed to the rewriting of Scripture, in the entire document. The Law of the King was previously composed as a unit which was then transferred into the *Temple Scroll* by its author/redactor. Here are found the clearest references to specific historical events.

The Law of the King emphasizes the separation of roles of the high priest and king and the need to constitute the *gerousia*, the "council of elders," consisting of twelve each of priests, Levites and Israelites. It argues against the hiring of mercenaries which were used extensively by John Hyrcanus. The *Temple Scroll* requires that the king have a special palace guard to protect him against kidnapping. Here we have an allusion to the perfidious kidnapping and murder of Jonathan the Hasmonean in 143 BCE (1 Macc 13:24). The text further polemicizes against campaigns such as those of John Hyrcanus and Alexander Jannaeus when it prohibits wars with Egypt for the sake of accumulating wealth.[46]

Elsewhere, in a detailed study of the Law of the King, we concluded that both the legal and historical aspects of this material all point to a Hasmonean dating.[47] At this time, the author of the Law of the King sought a complete reformation of the existing structures of the governmental system. Both extant copies of the *Temple Scroll* are Herodian. We must, of course, allow time for composition. Since the text reflects the historical experience of the Hasmoneans Jonathan (160–143 BCE) and John Hyrcanus (134–104 BCE), we must see the composition of the Law of the King as taking place no earlier than the second half of the reign of John Hyrcanus. He is the first of the Hasmoneans to have consolidated a stable empire.

---

[45] Yadin, *Temple Scroll*, 1.390.

[46] Cf. M. Weinfeld, "'Temple Scroll' or 'Kings Law'," *Shnaton* 3 (1978) 214–37; idem, "The Royal Guard according to the Temple Scroll," *RB* 87 (1980) 394–96.

[47] See above, n. 22.

Since the Law of the King is incorporated into the fully redacted scroll, it is therefore appropriate to date the scroll as a whole to no earlier than the second half of the reign of John Hyrcanus.[48] At this time, the author/redactor called for a thoroughgoing revision of the existing Hasmonean order, desiring to replace it with a Temple, sacrificial system, and government which was the embodiment of the legislation of the Torah according to his view.

B. Z. Wacholder has adopted Yadin's basic theory that the scroll was a second Torah. Arguing that the scroll ought to be named 11Q Torah, Wacholder propounded an extremely unlikely thesis to the effect that this text was part of what was intended to be a messianic, second Torah written by none other than the Teacher of Righteousness. Wacholder took the view, in accord with Yadin's suggestion,[49] that the teacher was named Zadok as described in the *Zadokite Fragments*, and further claimed that this was the same Zadok whose grave was mentioned in the *Copper Scroll*. Wacholder claimed that the *Temple Scroll* was the second part of a two-part text of which the first part was the book of *Jubilees*. This second Torah was the messianic Torah which was to replace the current Torah at the dawn of the eschaton. He claimed that these were understood to be the two Torahs given to Israel at Sinai, and found supposed allusions to this tradition in other Jewish works. According to Wacholder, the *Temple Scroll* was to be dated to approximately 200 BCE.[50]

Wacholder's views, where they diverge from those advanced earlier by Yadin, are highly speculative. On most matters, the work of Yadin easily withstands his challenge. Wacholder's date of 196 BCE is simply too early in view of the provenance of the Law of the King. The *Temple Scroll* explicitly states (XXIX 2–10) that it describes the laws of the sacrificial ritual to be practiced until the time of the messianic era (עד יום הברכה or, in the widely accepted reading of Qimron, עד יום הבריאה). The scroll is certainly not a description of an eschatological temple and its ritual; it is pre-messianic. It intends to describe the way in which the rituals should be practiced in the present age. *Jubilees*, while sharing certain motifs

---

[48] The scroll is dated to 103–88 BCE by M. Hengel, J. H. Charlesworth, D. Mendels, "The Polemical Character of 'On Kingship' in the Temple Scroll: An Attempt at Dating 11QTemple," *JJS* 37 (1986) 28–38.

[49] Yadin, *Temple Scroll*, 1.395 and 1.395–96 n. 18.

[50] Wacholder, *Dawn of Qumran*, 202–12.

with the Qumran scrolls, as already observed by Yadin, and while manuscripts of it were found in the Dead Sea caves, is not part of the same text as the *Temple Scroll*. Its style, Hebrew orthography, and theme are completely different from those of the *Temple Scroll*. The details of its ritual calendar and sacrificial laws differ as well. Zadok is most probably a symbolic name and not that of the Teacher of Righteousness (even Yadin was very tentative on this point), and we do not even know for sure if the *Copper Scroll* is part of the sect's literature. In our view, it is unrealistic for any scholar to expect to determine the name of the teacher or his exact dates, or to identify the author of any given scroll definitively. Such precision is beyond the limits of the evidence available to us.

It is worth pausing to explain a common mistake in dating the *Temple Scroll*. From the beginning of research on this scroll scholars have attempted to find a period in which in some way the Temple architecture or the laws of the scroll would have been practiced. The assumption here was that the *Temple Scroll* described some kind of a reality which could actually be located somewhere in the history of the Land of Israel in the Second Temple period. But, in fact, the text is a polemic against the existing order, calling for radical change in the order of the day, putting forward reforms in areas of cultic, religious and political life. So the true *Sitz im Leben* of the scroll is precisely one in which the circumstances of real life are the opposite of those called for by the author.

## Theology of Law

One of the fundamental issues in Second Temple Judaism was that of how to incorporate extra-biblical traditions and teachings into the Jewish legal system and how to justify them theologically. Despite the fact that in antiquity and late antiquity there was little theoretical theological inquiry in Judaism (except in the Hellenistic Diaspora), issues of theology were of central importance and often lie behind other more clearly expressed disputes.

All Jewish groups in the Second Temple period endeavored to assimilate extra-biblical teachings into their way of life. Our detailed examination of the writings of the Dead Sea sect has led us to determine that they did so through the concept of the נגלה

("revealed") and נסתר ("hidden").⁵¹ That which was revealed was the simple meaning of Scripture and the commandments which were readily apparent from it. These were known to all Jews. Only the sect possessed the hidden knowledge, discovered through what it saw as inspired biblical exegesis, regularly conducted by members of the sect. Tradition was regarded as having no authority, since all Israel had gone astray and the true way had only been rediscovered by the sect's teacher. The laws which emerged from this interpretation were eventually composed in *serakhim*, lists of sectarian laws. These were then redacted into such collections as the *Zadokite Fragments* (*Damascus Document*) or the less organized "Ordinances" (4Q159, 513, 514). These rules and the interpretations upon which they were based served to make clear the application of the law of the Torah to the life of the sect in the present, pre-messianic age.⁵²

Although we do not have Pharisaic texts from this period, we can suggest the general lines of the approach of this group based on later accounts in the New Testament, on the writings of Josephus and on the reports in the even later tannaitic corpus. Apparently, the Pharisees possessed traditions "handed down by the fathers" and "unwritten laws." These included various legal traditions of great antiquity as well as interpretations of the biblical texts. Indeed, the Pharisees were known as expounders of the Torah and seem to have excelled in the application of the laws of the Pentateuch to their own circumstances and times. Somewhat later, the successors to the Pharisees, the tannaim (teachers of the Mishnah) would stress the notion that these traditions had been revealed by God to Moses on Sinai as a second Torah. Thus, the Rabbis asserted, God had given two Torahs to Israel, the written and the oral. For the Rabbis, this view essentially elevated the oral Torah to a sanctity and authority equal to that of the written. Yet evidence does not point to such an assertion on the part of the Pharisees themselves, although our sources do not allow us to be certain.⁵³

---

[51] L. H. Schiffman, *Halakhah at Qumran* (Leiden: Brill, 1975) 22–32; idem, *Halakhah, Halikhah U-Meshihiyut be-Khat Midbar Yehudah* (Jerusalem: Merkaz Zalman Shazar, 1993) 45–53.

[52] Cf. S. Fraade, "Interpretive Authority in the Studying Community at Qumran," *JJS* 44 (1993) 46–69.

[53] Cf. L. H. Schiffman, "Pharisees and Sadducees in *Pesher Nahum*," *Minhah le-Nahum: Biblical and Other Studies Presented to Nahum N. Sarna in Honor of his 70th Birthday* (ed. M. Brettler and M. Fishbane; Sheffield: JSOT Press, 1993) 274–84.

The Sadducean approach has yet to be properly investigated. The general claim that the Sadducees were strict literalists represents a misunderstanding of their approach, to a great extent predicated on late Rabbinic sources and on a parallel misunderstanding of the medieval Karaite movement. In any case, we should note that the Sadducees apparently saw only the written law as authoritative, although they admitted the need to interpret it. Their interpretations attempted to adhere as closely as possible to the plain meaning (what the Rabbis later called *peshaṭ*[54]) of Scripture.

Against this background, we can now understand the approach of the author/redactor of the *Temple Scroll*. He seeks to assimilate extra-biblical traditions by the contention that his new, rewritten Torah properly expresses the will of God as revealed in the original document. He asserts that the correct meaning of the divine revelation at Sinai, apparently left vague in the canonical Torah, is to be found in the *Temple Scroll*. This means that like those at Qumran, he has no dual Torah concept such as that of the tannaim. Neither does he accept the notion of the Qumran sectarian documents of a continuous, inspired revelation through biblical exegesis. He maintains only a one-time revelation at Sinai of a single Torah, the true contents of which are expressed in the scroll he authored and redacted.

## The Scroll and the Qumran Corpus

In his initial study of the *Temple Scroll*, Yadin assumed that it was part of the Qumran sectarian corpus and that it represented a text of Essene provenance. Accordingly, he interpreted the scroll to agree with the previously known Dead Sea sectarian texts and the descriptions of the Essenes of Philo and Josephus. Many scholars have followed this lead. Others have pointed to the absence of the usual Qumran polemical language and distinctive terminology, and the lack of some characteristic linguistic features in these texts.[55]

---

[54] Cf. D. W. Halivni, *Peshat and Derash* (Oxford/New York: Oxford University Press, 1991) 52–79.

[55] B. A. Levine, "The Temple Scroll: Aspects of its Historical Provenance and Literary Character," *BASOR* 232 (1978) 5–23; J. Milgrom, "'Sabbath' and 'Temple City' in the Temple Scroll," *BASOR* 232 (1978) 25–27; Y. Yadin, "Is the Temple Scroll a Sectarian Document?" *Humanizing America's Iconic Book* (Biblical Scholarship in North America 6; ed. G. M. Tucker and D. A. Knight; Chico, CA: Scholars Press, 1980) 153–69; Stegemann, "Origins of the Temple Scroll," 237–46; Schiffman, *Sectarian Law*, 13–17.

Further, this text has a different view of the origins, authority and derivation of Jewish law. Some recent scholarship has seen the *Temple Scroll* as emerging from a related group which was either contemporary with or earlier than the Qumran sect. Others have sought to place it much earlier,[56] in our view confusing elements of the source material with the completed scroll.

From the earliest analysis of the scroll by Yadin, it has been apparent that there was a certain commonality between law in this scroll and the law in the *Zadokite Fragments*. With the release of the Qumran manuscripts of the *Zadokite Fragments*, these affinities have become even more apparent. Yet at the same time we should call attention to examples of total incongruity between these texts, such as that which we found in our investigations of the laws of idolatry or oaths and vows.[57] These incongruities, along with other evidence, led us to conclude that the *Temple Scroll* could not simply be identified as a document of the Qumran sect.

Yet this view certainly must be modified in light of the even closer link between the *Temple Scroll* and 4QMMT. This "halakhic letter," to be published by J. Strugnell and E. Qimron, describes a series of some twenty-two laws about which the authors disputed with the established authorities of the Jerusalem priesthood. Due to this disagreement, 4QMMT claims, its authors left Jerusalem and forswore worship in its Temple.[58] It is most likely that this letter dates to the origin of the Qumran community.[59] In general, 4QMMT takes positions equivalent to those of the Sadducees in Rabbinic literature and ascribes to the Jerusalem priests views identified as

---

[56] Stegemann, "Origins of the Temple Scroll," 246-56. Cf. his "The Institutions of Israel in the Temple Scroll," *The Dead Sea Scrolls: Forty Years of Research* (ed. D. Dimant and U. Rappoport; STDJ 10; Leiden: Brill; Jerusalem: Magnes/Yad Ben-Zvi, 1992) 156-85.

[57] L. H. Schiffman, "The Law of Vows and Oaths (Num. 30, 3-16) in the Zadokite Documents and the Temple Scroll," *Mémorial Jean Starcky* (*RevQ* 15 [1991]) 199-213. Contrast also the texts discussed in L. H. Schiffman, "Legislation Concerning Relations with Non-Jews in the Zadokite Fragments and in Tannaitic Literature," *RevQ* 11 (1983) 379-89 with those treated in my "The Laws of Idolatry in the Temple Scroll," *H. N. Richardson Memorial Volume* (Winona Lake, IN: Eisenbrauns, forthcoming).

[58] E. Qimron and J. Strugnell, "An Unpublished Halakhic Letter from Qumran," *Biblical Archaeology Today: Proceedings of the International Congress on Biblical Archaeology, Jerusalem, April 1984* (ed. J. Amitai; Jerusalem: Israel Exploration Society, 1985) 400-07; cf. another article by the same name, *Israel Museum Journal* 4 (1985) 9-12.

[59] Cf. L. H. Schiffman, "The New 'Halakhic Letter' and the Origins of the Dead Sea Sect," *BA* 53 (1990) 64-73.

Pharisaic in Rabbinic literature.[60] In many cases, the rulings of this text agree with those of the *Temple Scroll*. This new evidence suggests that the sources of the *Temple Scroll* stem from forerunners of the sect who shared Sadducean rulings on many matters.

If this is the case, we can reconstruct a variety of Saducean laws not previously available to us. Further, if the polemics of the *Temple Scroll* are indeed directed against the views of the Pharisees, as Yadin has suggested over and over in his commentary, it would confirm the early dating of many Pharisaic-Rabbinic laws known otherwise only from the later Rabbinic corpus.

## Significance

This scroll is the largest of the Dead Sea Scrolls and for this reason alone it vastly enriches the textual heritage of Second Temple Judaism. Further, it shows that the exegesis of Scripture for the derivation of Jewish law, the activity which the later Rabbis called *midrash*, was already a central part of the Judaism of some groups in the Hasmonean period. This exegesis served as the basis of highly developed legal teachings which are evidence that among some groups of Second Temple Jews strict adherence to a living and developing tradition of Jewish law was the norm. Further, some of these Jews objected strenuously to the conduct of the Hasmoneans in the religious, political and military spheres. These opponents were at the forefront of the movement represented by the Qumran sect. Among the texts they brought with them to Qumran were the sources of the *Temple Scroll*.

Since these sources probably reflected Sadducean views and exegesis, it now seems that from the *Temple Scroll* we will be able to increase substantially our knowledge of this hitherto elusive group which played so important a role in Second Temple Judaism. Further, it may allow us to reconstruct as well a variety of Pharisaic teachings from the Second Temple period. All in all, the study of the *Temple Scroll* promises to enrich many aspects of our knowledge of the richness of Second Temple Judaism.

---

[60] M. R. Lehmann, "The Temple Scroll as a Source of Sectarian Halakhah," *RevQ* 9 (1978) 579; J. M. Baumgarten, "The Pharisaic-Sadducean Controversies about Purity and the Qumran Texts," *JJS* 31 (1980) 157–70; Y. Sussman, "The Study of the History of Halakha and the Dead Sea Scrolls: Initial Talmudic Reflections in the light of MMT," *Tarbiz* 59 (1989/90) 11–76 (in Hebrew).

# MMT: Second Thoughts on a Forthcoming Edition

*John Strugnell*

I have been recently looking over Elisha Qimron's latest draft of our joint critical edition of 4Q *Miqṣat Maʿăśēh Hat-tôrâ* (4QMMT)—now in its final redaction, or so we hope—and it seemed it would be useful if I offered for this conference some comments on parts of that book. A short history of the work on MMT and of the collaboration between myself and Qimron might explain how I could offer critical comments on certain parts of a book of which we are joint authors. We use on the title page the formula of joint authorship. The fact that Qimron's name precedes mine implies nothing about the greater or lesser significance of the contribution of each; we are merely listed in alphabetic order. Since the patterns of our collaboration changed over the years, it would perhaps have been appropriate to find for the title page a formula that showed how Qimron's part kept becoming larger and mine smaller, but such an appropriate and exact formula was hard to find. Perhaps an exposition of the history of the work will at the same time indicate the extent of our individual contributions and explain in what way one contributor can put forward second thoughts, or even retractations, on what is still at least partially his own work.

## The History of the Project

My work on the fragments of MMT started in the same way as that on any other of the 4Q manuscripts for which I was responsible, and the initial work on them was done principally by me, with substantial help from J. T. Milik: first came the identification of the fragments, then a start at the hypothetical reconstruction and ordering of these fragments in their several manuscripts, and finally some attempt at understanding the whole. The stage I had reached by

1959 is attested by the handwritten provisional concordance that we had drawn up at that time for the private use of the editors. By then the identification of the fragments had been done almost completely, and the reconstruction and ordering of the manuscripts were substantially advanced.

Over the next twenty years progress was continuous but slow. Many reasons can be adduced for the delay. I had to work at the same time on the edition of over 100 other 4Q manuscripts and only once was I able to devote a sustained period of time to working on the commentary on MMT. Then again there were financial and political difficulties in the way of the 4Q edition in general. And finally I was misled by a false hypothesis that the laws in the work were angelic laws (as in the *Book of Jubilees*) rather than legal pronouncements of a human group. It was not until 1979 that an encounter with Qimron got the edition definitively underway again. I was visiting Jerusalem at the time, to arrange for a sabbatical year at the Institute for Advanced Studies of the Hebrew University. One rainy afternoon a young historian of the Hebrew language, called appropriately Qimron, sought me out in my room at the École Biblique, to discuss with me matters of Qumrân Hebrew, and to show me his recent Ph.D. thesis on the subject. Our conversation moved on to MMT, of which a few samples had been published and which intrigued him professionally. I showed him the rest of the fragments of the work and explained to him what was blocking progress. He asked if at least his linguistic skills could be of use, and we quickly agreed that he could usefully contribute, not so much by making the translation more exact as especially by drawing up a grammar of the work—there his special training could be of great help. At that time then, 1979, I was envisaging a work still primarily my own, but with at least a major excursus by Qimron on the grammar. I also sustained collaboration with him on the reconstruction and translation of the text.

It was not until 1981–82, however, that Qimron and I were able to spend a year together in Jerusalem doing substantial work on Qumrân grammar, on the special grammar of MMT, and on the reconstruction of the manuscripts into a hypothetical composite text of the whole. By the end of that year, it became clear that I would need more help, especially in the area of the legal background of one part of the work. In the other subject matters, the calendaric and the homiletic material, I felt at home, but for the legal I was inadequately skilled. Qimron, feeling that this matter was beyond his competence also, offered to look around among the younger generation of scholars in Jerusalem to see if he could find an appropriate co-editor for the legal area. Although he found several of his contemporaries willing to discuss legal problems in the text and to make scattered contributions, no one was willing to take on responsibility for the legal area as a whole, especially for the redaction of a major commentary on it, in the same way that he himself would be doing for the linguistic area. Accordingly Qimron, though with hesitations, volunteered to take over that area too. Although he was not trained for it—he was, after all, primarily a linguist—he felt confident that he would continue to receive help from friends with stronger halakhic competences. As we continued our work, various possible supplements to the text were suggested by the study of the legal background and, contrariwise, the damaged text suggested various reconstructions according to one or other of the several historical and legal contexts possible.

For the next eight years we worked together when we could, apart when necessary. I was in Jerusalem for the next three summers, and then Qimron spent a sabbatical at Harvard, working also on the problems of the historical background of the text and consulting with numerous authorities as he lectured widely across the U.S.A. In the next years I began regularly to spend half-years in Jerusalem, which gave us longer periods of work together. But he was in Beersheba and I in Jerusalem, where I was much occupied also with the general problems of the edition of the 4Q manuscripts. So there were still obstacles to our collaboration.

By the fall of 1990 it was time to fill in the missing sections of the whole edition, and for one of us to go to the SBL meeting at New Orleans for a discussion with Scholars Press on the material problems in preparing a camera-ready copy. By then Qimron had finished the two large chapters on the grammar and the legal background. I had also finished the material presentation of four of the six manuscripts, and by the end of that year I could promise to have ready the presentation of the other two manuscripts. We agreed that Qimron was to reduce our years of discussion on the text and its supplements, on which by this time we were both virtually in agreement, into the form of a running commentary on the composite text. At the same time he would finish a final polishing of that composite text itself. At that time we foresaw handing in our camera-ready copy in the spring of 1991. Objectively this was not an unrealistic estimate, but then came my lengthy bout with sickness. I could no longer contribute actively, and Qimron took over the general editorial responsibilities for the whole, revising all the available contributions of others. He himself finished the commmentary on the composite text. Some further appendices that had been foreseen on various topics were put to one side. The remaining work that had been planned for completion in six monsths stretched out for two-and-a-half years. But all is now in the last stage of being prepared for the printer.

This account of the slow gestation of our edition—which at the start was to be an *editio princeps* but must now be called only an *editio major*—will also show how in our joint undertaking the proportions of the contributions of each of us have changed from time to time. I suppose that by the time of Qimron's final redaction of the contributions of all of us, my part will finally be reduced to twenty five percent or so and his increased to sixty five or seventy percent. Each of us, of course, has also made many contributions now found in chapters redacted by the other. All too frequently in scholarship the form of the joint work is used to put the work of a junior scholar under the umbrella of a senior who has effectively contributed little. The case has occurred in many fields of scholarship; even in the field of Qumrânology it is not unknown. But truth gets known, and the recompense is in the end embarrassing. I think, for instance, of the public bracketing of the names of such false authors. The great rabbinic commentary to the New Testament is now cited only under the name of Billerbeck, and Strack's name, if it still is mentioned, is put in Coventry, marked off by brackets which embarrassingly perpetuate the memory of a bluff that has been discovered. Qimron's part was to increase and mine to decrease, and perhaps we should have used the phrases of our title page to spell this out in greater detail. But at least I have a good conscience of not having been a Strack!

In what follows I will not offer a review, point by point, of the forthcoming *editio major* but rather will draw attention to a few features in the text or commentary that seem to me to need notice or improvement. You will, I hope, note how nimbly I step around the pitfalls of criticizing opinions that I myself originated or of abandoning an opinion of Qimron that I have hitherto supported. However, second thoughts may be better.

## Section A: The Calendaric Section

Most writers divide MMT into three sections: a calendaric one, a legal one, and a final hortatory one. Each of these presents difficulties that have not yet been completely explained in the discussion.

The calendar implied in the first section is the 364-day calendar familiar to scholars from the *Book of Jubilees*, the *Temple Scroll*, and several Qumrân texts: its listing of Sabbaths is easy to understand and reconstruct; its listing of feasts is also easy to understand, though the choice of the feasts that it makes is irregular and much harder to understand. The principal question is whether this list belongs to the same work as is composed by sections B, and C, i.e. to MMT. The legal and hortatory parts of MMT are addressed by one group to another, and have a notably polemic tendency to them. The calendar, however, is clearly only a list, not addressed to anyone, and with no internal indicators of polemical intent. (It would be rash to try to postulate a missing incipit to this list that would convert it into a polemic document. That it could have had its own incipit is not impossible, but to postulate one with precisely such a polemical tendency would be highly unlikely!)

This calendar, then, is hard to relate to the rest of the work, whether form-critically or even in terms of subject matter. What is more, there are further material indicators that render it problematical whether the section belongs to MMT at all. In manuscript 4Q394 the presence of the 364-day calendar-list is certain since it is preserved directly before the first line of section B (the legal section). However, in the second manuscript of the work, 4Q395, which also gives the start of section B, enough uninscribed leather is preserved before section B to make it highly probable that no text ever stood before it; section A thus becomes attested only in half of those manuscripts where we should have found it. To this argument we can add another that, if one were to reconstruct the whole calendar in 4Q394, it would be hard to postulate before it anything except an incipit of a calendar—scarcely a general title for the whole work (whether this whole work would have been cast in the form of a letter or some other genre) and certainly no room for one, two, or more separate sections of the work (in whatever subject matter or form) would have preceded. That much one can tell by reconstructions, in the style of Professor Stegemann, of the diminishing widths of the layers in manuscript A. There was no space for any greater length of scroll at the beginning.

The hesitant consequence of these ambiguous observations is that it is far from certain that the calendar, as found here, belonged to any letter at all or that it formed any part of the document MMT$^{B+C}$. At the most, it should be conceived as a list of another genre, prefixed in 4Q394 for uncertain reasons to sections B and C. The calendar in it may simply have been a noncontroversial list, a non-polemic mnemonic like our "30 days has September." It was addressed to no "opponents" and formed no part of MMT's loftier polemic or hortatory themes.

## Section B: The Legal Section

As for the legal section, which gives us a score of pronouncements on topics that at first seem very varied, I think that you will find Qimron's translation and legal commentary generally satisfactory, although there may still be space for improvement in detail.

The beginning of the legal section does not provide a sentence easy to supplement completely; the incipit that would have told us so much about the form of this work and its purpose stays at least half unreconstructed. At the start of a new paragraph (B 1–3), the text runs, eliminating supplements which are possible but uncertain,

```
אלה מקצת דברינו [ ]ל שהם מ[ ]               [
המעשים שא א[נ]ח[נ]נו**ים וכו]לם על]           [
                                   וטהרת [ ]הר...
```

Next comes the first law.

The phrases at the end of this damaged section—"the precepts which we *recommend*," "all of them concerning," and then, at the end, "purity"—make, formally and materially, plausible parts of an incipit to a collection of purity laws. Form-critically, the first words look extremely unlikely to belong to the incipit *of a letter* (though they could conceivably be the beginning of a section inside a letter); in fact, however, they look very like the incipit of a *collection of laws*—indeed, there is a very close parallel to them in another incipit of a collection of laws, the first verse of Deuteronomy: "These are the words that Moses spoke to all Israel." Syntactically, the indefinite phrase "some of our words" could be, in the language of MMT, a variant for Deuteronomy's "the words"; and the next damaged word in MMT could well corresponded to the word "Israel" that comes next also in the verse from Deuteronomy.

There is no obvious supplement for the fragmentary words that follow. The lacunae could be filled in several ways. Qimron's supplements are all plausible, but none of the supplements so far proposed for the beginning brings that feeling of conviction which we expect from a palmary conjecture and which might be confirmed by a good literary parallel. Despite these difficulties of reconstruction, we can say that this sentence is scarcely likely to be an incipit of a letter but more likely to introduce a collection of laws, pronouncements, or the like—that is, after all, the function of the possible parallel in Deuteronomy.

It is hard to maintain that these laws were chosen because of their structural importance for this legal topos. Banal though it may seem at first, a literal translation of the incipit, "these are *some* of our precepts," makes a suitable introduction for the following subject matter. Such an indefinite title for a collection or a treatise seems formally attested also in Hellenistic book titles and not merely in the rare Oriental parallels that can be found. For the moment, then, the formal indications are that this is just an introduction to a collection of some laws, however chosen. In working on our edition, I had tried to suggest to Qimron another formal possibility, which would also explain the presence in Section B of the same mixture of personal pronouns as in the following Section C, each having also the same reference. I had wondered whether sections B and C, rather than a letter, could instead be a *treatise*. Yet the treatise is, at least in Hellenistic literature, a very ill-defined genre, and such a distribution of the personal pronouns could be expected in many other literary contexts too. So the suggestion, which you will find mentioned in the *editio major*, that this was a treatise, rather than a letter, should be withdrawn. In its place, I now suggest that we have in these lines a free-standing introduction to a collection of laws, perhaps consciously modelled on the opening of Deuteronomy.

I will speak later on the jurisprudential basis and topical coherence of these laws, and on why they were collected. Before I do so, I should warn you that in MMT, even when a law is wholly or largely preserved, the translation and interpretation of it are difficult. For instance, it can often only be decided by examination of the details of legal tradition whether a subordinate clause in this dialect is temporal, concessive, conditional, or the like. Again, one notes the occurrence of rulings whose text seems complete, with no material loss of text, but where the legislator seems to have failed to express the operative sentence of the law. One can find this in other legal collections too, though rarely. In those cases, moreover, the phenomenon is probably accidental, and scribal omission could be suspected of being the cause. Here, though, we have at least three cases in about twenty laws. Is this significant?

Some scattered marks of the type of the laws can also be noticed:

A frequent feature is the justification of a legal position by a quotation, even though these quotations are never of biblical law, but at most of established principles, as it would seem. The biblical text, however, clearly influences the verbal formulation of the MMT cases.

Another characteristic is that the laws are a written collection of pronouncements ascribed to the "we"–community, not to God or to the angels nor even Moses as its source.

There is nothing very special about the technique of exegesis. It probably surpasses our knowledge to say what their intentions in hermeneutics were. To ascribe to them historical-critical motives or to see them as searching, like some modern jurists, for the "intention of the legislator" would probably be foreign to them.

Let us pass over many other problems of translation or of legal detail and, instead, ask some profounder questions about the collection of laws in general—though perhaps the evidence in MMT will in the end turn out to be inadequate for resolving such problems. I refer to such problems as the following:

1) What is the principle by which such laws belong together or were selected? Can we look for a formal or material principle in this code? Most of these laws relate to the sanctuary, to things done there, to the priesthood, and to related questions of purity touching on priestly marriage, leprosy, etc. (With such a definition only one law seems alien to the interests of the code.) This collection, however, would not represent an exhaustive or systematic presentation of the laws concerning such topics. We should probably best understand it as a selection from the laws on such topics. However. it is not yet apparent what polemic made this choice of subjects controversial or intellectually coherent.

2) What is the significance of the fact that these laws have parallels, few but ineluctable, with the legal discussions that under-

lie the *Temple Scroll*, and with other works that I would regard as pre-Qumrânic in date, such as the legal section of the *Damascus Document*?

3) What is the significance of the fact that they coincide with some later Rabbinic attestations of Sadducean positions in certain disputes between Sadducee and Pharisee? Whether we can advance to a conclusion that the writers of MMT, and perhaps also their Qumrânite descendants, should be called Sadducees at least *juxta modum*, is too long a question to be handled here. In antiquity historians used the titles Sadducee, Hasid, and also Essene in a changing and fluid way. When we limit ourselves to the legal evidence, it is hard to separate this new corpus of law in MMT from that of some of the later Sadducees. It is also hard to separate it from the law of other texts related to the early Qumrân sect or its predecessors. One should not forget that, in the early days of the study of the Qumrân sect, several scholars ascribed their texts to the Sadducees, rather than to the Essenes, and vainly tried to draw attention to the fact that the sect's self-appellation בני צדוק really was the same as "Zadokite" or "Sadducee." Perhaps that part of their argument deserves to be revived.

Such questions of nomenclature tend to be of lesser importance than those concerning the nature of law; they only provide us with information that is accidental and of a historical kind. But if we look at the legal corpus itself, we find some very significant characteristics. Though the names used for the law were generally biblical, with no special meaning, the absence of one may be more than accidental. Modern scholars describe this material as הלכה, and in Rabbinic language that is perfectly correct. But MMT fails consistently to use this description for its own laws, using instead more general terminology such as חוק, משפט, תורה, etc. We may suspect that this is not without significance. Also in all the other Qumrân texts, both the proto-Qumrânic ones and the later Qumrânic ones also, the word הלכה is avoided. Indeed, there is only one possible allusion to it, and that in a stock phrase, דורשי חלקות, "seekers after smooth things." There it is associated clearly with the legal teaching of the sect's opponents. In this punning phrase, the Qumrânite authors seem to tease another group, probably the Pharisees, and to mock their use of הלכה. Could the absence in MMT of the word preferred by their opponents be insignificant and due to chance? After all the legal section of MMT is fairly brief. This, however, is not likely, since the same word הלכה is absent also from those other works we have defined as pre-Qumrânic and close to MMT, and indeed absent from the whole Qumrân corpus.

However, even if the word was consciously avoided, we have no means strictly of guessing why. What understanding of the law is expressed in MMT's formulation of these laws? What understanding of the word הלכה as used in its opponents' positions was rejected by MMT? The significance of a linguistic observation about the absence of the word may be hard to define, but to neglect it, and to call these rulings הלכה when the authors carefully avoid doing so, risks seeing the rules and the controversy through the eyes of their opponents and introducing an anachronism into our understanding of these laws. I tried to persuade Qimron to substitute another word for הלכה in his legal chapter, but to change a term so frequently used throughout so long a chapter seemed to him too great an effort, for a point that was minor and not likely to create misunderstanding. I, however, fear that leaving it may be fraught with greater consequences. Despite the obscurities, the question should be interesting to pursue.

The incompleteness of this code also prevents us from answering some important questions about the history of this legal tradition, as well as questions of jurisprudence regarding the structure and basis of this code and of the legal understanding of its framers, both the scholars who redacted it and the priestly classes in general that transmitted it.

There are other ways in which we can look at a corpus of laws. Does it defend and express the socio-economic interests of its legislators? Does it express a specific jurisprudential view of law— e.g., realism or nominalism? One should note in the Proceedings of the 1988 Haifa Congress, the interesting defense by D. R. Schwartz of the proposition that much of the priestly legislation, here, in the *Temple Scroll*, and in the *Damascus Code* can be characterized as systematically realist, while the positions opposed to these laws, often but not necessarily Pharisaic propositions, are nominalist.[1] This distinction may be made about many a legal system, ancient or modern, but if it was being made here, one must ask in what language it would have been understood or expressed by the lawyers of MMT. Certainly

---

[1] D. R. Schwartz, "Law and Truth: On Qumran–Sadducean and Rabbinic Views of Law," *The Dead Sea Scrolls: Forty Years of Research* (ed. D. Dimant and U. Rappaport; STDJ 10; Leiden: Brill; Jerusalem: Magnes Press/Yad Izhak ben-Zvi, 1992) 229–40.

other jurisprudential categories might also be examined to see which best justifies the opposition between the principles of Pharisaic law and those of Sadducean law.

## Section C: The Hortatory Epilogue

Clearly the subject matter of the final section is very different from that of the collection of laws. The damage to the text and the loss of over twenty complete lines at the beginning make it difficult to establish the point where the text changes from one section and subject-matter, i.e., that of section B, to another. It also makes it difficult to establish whether there was any formal marker of that shift. There could have been a brief, formal incipit of the new section or an imperceptible glide from the one to the other.

Qimron sees this as a homiletic closure to his epistle, after its preceding sections. You will remember how I have frequently questioned the use of the term "epistle" for the earlier sections, finding it inappropriate on form-critical grounds. The same uneasiness confronts me as I turn to section C. The beginning, it is true, is completely missing, but the bulk of the section, and especially the end which is completely preserved, would be formally unlike any letter's conclusion. Admittedly, many forms can be found in the conclusion of a letter, but this passage seems rather an exhortation on the observance of the previously mentioned laws. Like the legal section, this contained a "we" for the writers and a "you" identical to the addressee of the legal section. In section C the "you" group is split up into a "thou" and "thy people Israel," which suggests the mention of a singular leader or sovereign of Israel. Whoever that may be, the *dramatis personae* of Section C would not be inconsistent with those of Section B. We would not expect formally such a conclusion in a legal letter, but one might suggest that such a hortatory conclusion (putting it broadly, a benediction) would well fit at the end of a legal code as it does in covenant formulae. Deuteronomy would thus provide a parallel for the ending of this work just as it did for the beginning.

You will not find in our edition a chapter on the theology and tradition-history of section C, a counterpart perhaps to Qimron's lengthy treatment of the legal background of the laws. The *editio major* contains a running commentary on some details in section C but not a thoroughgoing attempt to understand the relations between the language and theological traditions of this section and those of works that we expect to be, chronologically and in thought, near it, i.e., Daniel, *1 Enoch*, the *Dibrê Ham-mĕʾôrôt*, the *Damascus Document*, and the *Temple Scroll*. The lack of such a major chapter is to be laid to my fault. I had prepared notes for it, but when I fell sick, so much still needed to be done to polish them that Qimron decided that such a chapter should be left over for the definitive major edition which we were then planning to put out a few years after the preliminary edition. Now that "preliminary edition" has become our present *editio major*, and we no longer plan any further definitive edition, although one could have been very useful, to incorporate the improvements we expect from other scholars after they have digested our preliminary edition. Like many other things in Qumrân studies, certain departures from our first plans have become necessary, and that chapter is now left for others among you to write.

One notices that, although the grammar of Section C is similar to that of Section B, with its numerous ש- relative clauses and participles, there is very little in the somewhat biblicizing and commonplace language and thought that we feel characteristic of the Qumrân sect, of its writings, of its organization, and of its special theology—e.g., its Two-Spirit doctrine. This was true of the far longer *Temple Scroll* as well, where the apparent difference cannot be due to chance alone. One might object that the phrase in MMT, והרחיק ממך מחשבת רעה ועצת בליעל (C 29) shows some of the Two-Spirit dualism typical of Qumrân; but, first of all, its meaning is ambiguous and, secondly, not all somewhat dualistic expressions must be considered specifically Qumrânic. From Second Isaiah onward many expressions that might be called dualistic have been quite at home in Judaism. Before Qumrân dualism, there were many less developed antecedent stages. In general, the absence from all of MMT of Qumrânic sectarian language, organizational or theological, requires some explanation, especially in the light of the similarity of the legal part of MMT to the legal traditions of the Qumrân sect. One will best explain this by making a distinction between MMT and the standard Qumrân texts. MMT could have been earlier than they or stood on another branch of the Sadducean family tree.

The language of this section is somewhat ordinarily biblical, and its intellectual contents rather amorphous. Accordingly, the precise nature of the exhortation is hard to follow, even if it can be generally translated where the text is complete. It should be especially noticed that some seven lines, relatively well preserved, could be placed at either one or the other of two different places. Lines 18 through 24 Qimron prefers to place at that point, but they could at least as plausibly be placed some 20 lines earlier, before line 1—on grounds of context and, preferably, on consideration of the material shape of the manuscript (so in the opinion of both myself and Professor Stegemann).

The disputed paragraph runs roughly as follows:

> ... in the days of Solomon the son of David. And the curses that have befallen from the days of Jeroboam the son of Nebat and up to when Jerusalem and Zedekiah king of Judah went into captivity. ... And we know that some of the blessings and the curses have been fulfilled as was written in the book of Moses. And this is the end of days when *they will return* to Israel. ... Think of the kings of Israel and contemplate their deeds, how whoever among them who feared the Tôrâ was delivered from troubles. They were seekers of Tôrâ. ...

All this would, it is true, fit thematically well after lines 15ff., where we find a quotation of Deuteronomy's text "and it shall come to pass, when all these things befall thee in the end of days, the blessing and the curse, then thou shall take it to heart and return to Him with all thy heart and soul at the end of days, then . . .", followed by further damaged phrases "it is written in the Book of Moses and in the Book of the Prophets, that there will come . . . the blessings . . . ." These phrases would lead smoothly on to the reference, at the start of our fragment, to further blessings in the days of *incerti loci* Solomon the son of David, and to blessings and curses throughout Israel's history up to the end of days. Such a sequence would certainly be conceivable in its thought even if not clear in all its details. Materially, however, this placing of the fragment would be difficult. One could make as good a case for placing it in the text missing before line 1, though the poor state of the text in lines 1ff. hinders us from seeing how appropriate the sequence of thought would be.

I refrain from discussing the arguments on either side but merely point out that, when we are unable to establish where a complete paragraph belongs, then we may not yet have reached too precise an understanding of the document. In any case, I suspect that this problem will not be solved until the missing chapter on the theological background of section C is written, perhaps to give us an answer to this major difficulty.

## Historical Conclusions

After coming to the end of this rapid presentation of certain significant points in the text of MMT, I will conclude by trying to suggest briefly where this new text is to be located in history and what significance it has for our knowledge of those times. Editors of a new text frequently try to find in it the solution for all the problems that it touches upon, and in the *editio major* you will find a long chapter from my own pen that works out our common postulates on the historical setting of MMT and that then, squeezing the evidence as hard as can be done, gives a maximalist presentation of all the historical details that we might win from it. Here instead I will give a minimalist statement. Even if some of our guesses, however plausible, are left to one side, are not the minimalist consequences that can still be drawn significant enough?

Minimalist and maximalist would agree that the work must have been written at some time between the reign of King Zedekiah, which gives us a *terminus a quo*, and the End of Days, the *terminus ad quem* for the authors! Other possible allusions to biblical passages may point us to the later part of the Post-Exilic Period. The earliest surviving manuscript should be dated about 50 BCE. The date half a century earlier that I proposed for a semi-cursive manuscript of the work must yield to a date between 50 to 1 BCE, as Mrs. Ada Yardeni has shown in a contribution she has made to the *editio major*.

Qimron's thesis, which in general I followed in the *editio major*, was that we had in MMT a letter addressed by the "we" group, a priestly group led by the Teacher of Righteousness, to a "you" group, a group broken up into "thee" and "thy people Israel." This Qimron understands as a priestly group, led by the "Wicked Priest" who is familiar to us from the *Pesharim*. The "they" group are legal opponents of the "we" group; the "you" group is warned against the practices of the first.

This is indeed maximalist. I have criticized the literary description of MMT as a letter, and I find nothing in the text suggesting the presence of the specific *dramatis personae* (e.g., Wicked Priest, Teacher of Righteousness) known from the other Qumrân texts. Especially, we have no evidence that there was any leader at all of the "we" group, let alone that he was to be identified with the Teacher of Righteousness. Further, although the leader of the "you" group was the head of his people Israel and therefore probably a High Priest, he is in no way depicted as wicked. In fact, his legal knowledge and prudence are singled out for praise; he is exhorted to hold fast to this code of laws that has just been sent to him. We would then have to describe MMT as addressed to a not-yet-Wicked Priest, though the difference is perhaps not important, in that one of the features clearly attested of the Qumrânite Wicked Priest was that he started off well but became evil. There were distinct periods in his life.

We will find no small differences if we try to identify the beliefs and practices of the protagonists here and those in the Qumrân corpus. Scholarship has usually situated the quarrel between the Wicked Priest and the Teacher of Righteousness around the question which of them had the right to be High Priest of Israel. That detail is certainly present in several of the *Pesharim*, but the MMT is silent on any such quarrel.

Another internal difference is also important. The language used to describe the later sect and the language that shows its sectarian, dualistic, and apocalyptic nature is missing in MMT. For instance, the "we" group is not called *yaḥad*, and we do not find theological characterizations of it like *běnê 'ôr*. I find it hard to explain all this from the difference of genre. In the third section, at least, some of these theological characterizations would be perfectly at home, while the legal sections seem to be concerned with what should be done by all the sons of Aaron, not by any narrower sectarian group. If we are right to associate MMT with the Qumrân sect—and note that it was frequently copied among them and even held nearly canonical rank—then typology will suggest that MMT reflects an earlier form of the sect, or even an antecedent of the sect, before many of the influences peculiar to the Qumrân community and its texts had been felt. The terminology of organization and theological assessment that we often ascribe to the Teacher of Righteousness leaves no trace in MMT. Instead, the work shows a mixture of primitive features, organizational and theological, such as we find also in the *Temple Scroll*, for which approximately the same date might perhaps be proposed.

There is, however, one passage, in a pesher on Psalm 37 that suggests to Qimron an association of MMT with the sect's founding crisis, the Wicked Priest, and the Teacher of Righteousness. It runs as follows:

> its interpretation concerns the Wicked Priest who spied on the Teacher of Righteousness, and tried to put him to death because of the Statute and the Law which he (i.e., the Teacher of Righteousness) had sent to him (i.e., the Wicked Priest).

Now is this association historically reliable? If so, it would formally ascribe MMT to the Teacher of Righteousness, a fact not attested by the text of MMT itself and implausible on grounds of its primitive theology. Nor would an attempt at executing the Teacher of Righteousness be a proportionate response to this eirenic writing! This looks rather very much like an affabulation in the later *Pesharim* of a legend about a venerable work circulating in the sect, ascribing it to one of the better known figures of the sect's beginnings. The creation of such pseudonymous settings for anonymous writings can, of course, be found in the titles of the Psalms and often elsewhere.

To summarize these perhaps discordant observations: The minimalist will call MMT not a letter but a legal proclamation sent to an accepted ruler, probably a High Priest of Israel (and possibly even the one who was later to turn to proto-Pharisaic positions and to become the Wicked Priest of the Commentaries). It was sent by a priestly faction that was later to evolve, under the influence of the Teacher of Righteousness, into the Qumrân sect. Further, it was sent to keep the then High Priest of Israel faithful to those Sadducean priestly laws that were shared at that time by him and them. It was only later, in the *Psalms Commentary*, that MMT was given the historical setting it lacked, by anachronistic projection into the later conflict over the authority of the Wicked Priest and the Teacher of Righteousness.

Nothing, in fact, is implied by MMT about a possible claim by the Teacher of Righteousness to the High Priesthood, but since neither the Teacher nor that controversy are mentioned at all in it, it would be rash to draw any consequences from this apparent discrepancy. The many other discrepancies between the theological description of the "we" group and the Qumrân sect are certainly there, but they suggest an early stage in the history or prehistory of the same sect rather than a completely different setting.

Comfortingly, though, all these historical and form-critical modifications leave Qimron's basic understanding of the Laws and the Exhortation themselves very little affected.

#  The Scriptures at Qumran

# The Bible in the Making: The Scriptures at Qumran

*Eugene Ulrich*

The first statement to make about the Bible at Qumran is that we should probably not think of a "Bible" in the first century BCE or the first century CE, at Qumran or elsewhere. There were collections of Sacred Scripture, of course, but no Bible in our developed sense of the term. Then, just as now, the precise list of books which were considered "Scripture" varied from group to group. When we say the word "Bible," there are at least three shapes to the idea—presuming that Christians would add a number of books (the New Testament) that Jews would not, and presuming that Catholics would add a number of books (the Apocrypha or Deutero-Canonicals) that Protestants would not, and Greek Orthodox would add more.

In this paper I will attempt to offer a sharper and more accurate understanding of the Scriptures at Qumran, or our Bible in the shape it had during the Qumran period, from two perspectives. The first is the external shape of the collection, or collections, of Scripture in the late Second Temple period in Judaism, at the time of the birth of Christianity. What did the collection of the unrolled books of the Scriptures look like? The second is an internal perspective: once the scrolls are unrolled and read, what do we learn from their contents? What are the results—as we can see them now—of the analysis that my colleagues and I have done on the biblical scrolls so far? I will then conclude with some reflections upon the significance of these new data for a sharper view of our Bible today.

I must preface this discussion with a few preliminary remarks. First, here I am speaking primarily as a historian. I hasten to add that I think that all that follows is also easily compatible religiously. But the attempt here is to describe the nature of the Bible as it was in this crucial period of religious history—as seen through the ancient window, and bathed in the new light, provided from Qumran.

Secondly, some of what follows could be interpreted as less than respectful to the traditional *textus receptus* of the Hebrew Bible, called the Massoretic Text (MT). Let me assure you, that is not my intent. I have high respect for this most important of witnesses to the ancient Hebrew Bible. But the evidence from the ancient world—and not just that of the scrolls, but also that of the Samaritan Pentateuch (SP) and the Septuagint (LXX, i.e., the Greek translation of the Hebrew)—makes us see things a bit more clearly than we used to, and I have found that sometimes this new knowledge comes at the cost of some uneasiness or defensiveness concerning our time-honored views, whether those views are entirely accurate or not.

Thirdly, it is important to stick to our coign of vantage: to look at the evidence concerning the Scriptures that we actually find at Qumran, at times aided by evidence from the New Testament and the Mishnah and Talmud. But to look with first-century eyes, not retrojecting later perspectives without warrant back onto first-century reality.

## I. The Scrolls and the External Shape of the Collection(s) of Scripture

### The Corpus of Scrolls of Scripture Found at Qumran

From the 11 caves at Qumran fragments from roughly 800 MSS were recovered.[1] Of these about 200, or 25%, were scriptural MSS.

---

[1] For principal publications and lists of the MSS, see: M. Burrows, ed., *The Dead Sea Scrolls of St. Mark's Monastery*, vol. 1 (New Haven: American Schools of Oriental Research, 1950). F. M. Cross et al., *Scrolls from Qumrân Cave I: The Great Isaiah Scroll, the Order of the Community, the Pesher to Habakkuk*; from photographs by John C. Trever (Jerusalem: Albright Institute of Archaeological Research and the Shrine of the Book, 1972). E. L. Sukenik, *The Dead Sea Scrolls of the Hebrew University* (Jerusalem: Hebrew University and Magnes Press, 1955). D. Barthélemy and J. T. Milik, *Qumrân Cave 1* (DJD 1; Oxford: Clarendon, 1955). P. Benoit, J. T. Milik, and R. de Vaux, *Les Grottes de Murabba'at. 1. Texte. 2. Planches* (DJD 2; Oxford: Clarendon, 1961). M. Baillet, J. T. Milik, and R. de Vaux, *Les 'Petites Grottes' de Qumrân. 1. Texte. 2. Planches* (DJD 3; Oxford: Clarendon, 1962). J. A. Sanders, *The Psalms Scroll of Qumrân Cave 11 (11QPs$^a$)* (DJD 4; Oxford: Clarendon, 1965). M. Baillet, *Qumrân Grotte 4, III* (DJD 7; Oxford: Clarendon, 1982). E. Tov in collaboration with R. A. Kraft, *The Seiyâl Collection Volume 1: The Greek Minor Prophets Scroll from Naḥal Ḥever (8ḤevXII gr)* (DJD 8; Oxford: Clarendon, 1989). P. W. Skehan, E. Ulrich, and J. E. Sanderson, *Qumran Cave 4, IV: Palaeo-Hebrew and Greek Biblical Manuscripts* (DJD 9; Oxford, Clarendon, 1992). E. Tov, ed., *The Dead Sea Scrolls on Microfiche: A Comprehensive Facsimile Edition of the Texts from the Judean Desert, Companion Volume* (Leiden: E. J. Brill, 1993). F. García Martínez, "Lista de MSS procedentes de Qumran," *Henoch* 11 (1989) 149–232. J. A. Fitzmyer, *The Dead Sea Scrolls: Major Publica-*

Cave 4 was by far the richest cave, with some 575 of those 800 MSS. Of the 575 MSS from Cave 4, roughly 127 were classified as "biblical," though as usual that designation needs some fine-print distinctions.[2] About 65 biblical MSS were recovered from the other 10 caves combined. At least one copy of each of the books of the traditional Hebrew canon, except for Esther and Nehemiah, was found at Qumran, as were some of the books of the wider canon.[3] The three books represented by the most MSS were the Psalms (39 total from all the caves, including 22 MSS from Cave 4), Deuteronomy (32 total, including 21 MSS from Cave 4), and Isaiah (22 total, including 18 MSS from Cave 4). It is interesting, but not surprising, that these three books are also the most frequently quoted in the NT.

## The Collection of Books of Scripture

The Qumran scrolls tell us many new and exciting things about the Scriptures. Why do I say Scriptures and not Bible? What is the difference? The Scriptures are a collection of sacred works that are considered authoritative for belief and practice within a religious community. The term "Bible," in the singular, adds the extra factor—linked with the idea of a "canon"—of inclusivity and exclusivity: these books are *in*, those books are *out*. From a visual perspective, the Bible is a single book which has a front cover and a back cover, and a definite table of contents.

During the Qumran period, however, and more broadly during the closing centuries of the Second Temple period in Judaism, there were "volumes" not "books." Literary works were written on scrolls, not in codices. Our word "volume" comes from the Latin word *volumen* "a rolled thing," from *volvo*, "to turn or roll." The codex, a stack of leaves or pages bound together, did not become the normal format for literary works until the third or fourth century.[4] Our early large

---

*tions and Tools for Study* (rev. ed.; SBLRBS 20; Atlanta: Scholars Press, 1990). E. Tov, "The Unpublished Qumran Texts from Caves 4 and 11," *BA* 55 (1992) 94–104.

[2] For a list and description of the biblical MSS from Cave 4, see E. Ulrich, "The Biblical Scrolls from Qumran Cave 4: An Overview and a Progress Report on their Publication," *RevQ* 14 (1989) 207–28. See also idem, "An Index of Passages in the Biblical Manuscripts from the Judean Desert (Genesis-Kings)," *DSD* 1 (1994) 113–29.

[3] E.g., Sirach, Tobit, *Jubilees, Enoch*, the Epistle of Jeremiah, etc.

[4] Edward M. Thompson, *An Introduction to Greek and Latin Palaeography* (Oxford: Clarendon, 1912) 51–53.

manuscripts of the Greek Bible, for example, dating from the fourth and fifth centuries of the common era, are codices.[5]

Thus, during the period of the Dead Sea Scrolls, the late Second Temple period, the time of Hillel and Christ, and several centuries beyond, our visual imaginations must conjure up books of the Scriptures inscribed on individual scrolls. When the pious community of the Covenant at Qumran studied the Scriptures, they unrolled individual scrolls. When Jesus stood up in the synagogue at Nazareth, the Gospel According to Luke narrates (4:16–20) that he unrolled a scroll of Isaiah—a scroll perhaps not too different from the Great Isaiah Scroll, found entirely intact in Cave 1 at Qumran and on display at the Shrine of the Book in Jerusalem. Although the entire Bible can be printed within a single book, it was impossible to copy all the Scriptures on a single scroll. Thus, we must imagine a collection of scrolls.

Exactly how many scrolls would have been included in this collection? It may help to envision a large jar of scrolls or a shelf of scrolls. Then, just as now, the precise list of books which were considered "Scripture" varied from group to group within Judaism. Which scrolls belonged in the jar? Which were relegated to outside the jar? Which scrolls were to be shelved on the main shelf of "Scripture," as opposed to the lower shelf marked (proleptically) "Apocrypha and Pseudepigrapha"? We have no clear evidence that anyone was explicitly asking these questions yet. To be sure, the Samaritans seem to have settled conservatively on the five Books of Moses alone as their authoritative Scriptures.[6] But what appears to have been the dominant view—shared by the Pharisees, the Qumran community, and the early Christians—included the Prophets as well.

1. So we come to our first conclusion: there was *no canon* as yet, no clearly agreed-upon list of which books were "Scripture" and which were not. This was the situation at least up to the fall of the Second Temple in 70, probably as late as the end of the first century, and arguably even up to the First Revolt against Rome in 132–135, since we find Rabbi Aqiba having to argue strenuously that, yes, The Song of Songs is in fact Scripture.

---

[5] The Septuagint MSS from Qumran, however, are scrolls, not codices; see DJD 3 and 9.

[6] Some would conclude, on the basis of Josephus, the same position for the Sadducees. But James VanderKam ("Revealed Literature in the Second-Temple Period" [in press]) argues that Josephus' statement must be interpreted "in a context in which he is distinguishing sources of authority for practice...."

2. But the *order* of the books was also unclear. This was usually no problem as long as the Scriptures are written on discrete scrolls. To be sure, the five Books of Moses had achieved a recognized order; of the few manuscripts in which we find more than one book written on a single scroll, only one may possibly preserve the physical connection between two books of the Torah, and it appears to be in the traditional order.[7] Their fixed order, however, is partly set by the chronological structure of the story from creation down to Moses.

But it was a different matter for the Prophets. I am unaware of any scroll that contains more than one prophetic book,[8] and so our evidence at Qumran is limited. Nonetheless, the Former Prophets (Joshua–Judges–Samuel–Kings) most likely maintained that fixed order, since, as for the Torah, the order is primarily determined by the chronological structure of the story that the books narrate. For the Latter Prophets, however, Jewish and Christian lists[9] from antiquity display varying orders, and as late as the Talmud (4th–5th century), the Rabbis tell us "the order of the Prophets is . . . Jeremiah, Ezekiel, Isaiah. . . ."[10]

3. What is more important is that it was unclear *which books* were included among the Prophets. One of the primary names for the Scriptures both at Qumran and in the New Testament is "The Law and the Prophets."[11] The *Rule of the Community* from Cave 1 at Qumran begins with the goal "that they may seek God with a whole heart and soul, and do what is good and right before Him as He commanded by the hand of Moses and all His servants the Prophets. . . ."[12] But which books were considered among the Prophets? Was Daniel? Were the Psalms? The *Florilegium* specifically mentions the "Book of the prophet Daniel,"[13] and the Gospel According to Matthew calls Daniel a

---

[7] 4QpaleoGen-Exod$^l$ probably contains the end of Genesis, plus one partly blank and three fully blank lines, then the beginning of Exodus. The physical join between the end of one book and the beginning of the next is not preserved on 4QGen-Exod$^a$, 4QExod-Lev$^f$, or 4QLev-Num$^a$.

[8] The Twelve Minor Prophets evidently were considered to comprise one book.

[9] A number of lists are reproduced in H. B. Swete, *An Introduction to the Old Testament in Greek* (rev. ed. by R. R. Ottley; New York: Ktav, 1968) 198–214.

[10] *B. B. Bat.* 14b.

[11] See, e.g., Luke 16:16, 29, 31; 24:27; Acts 26:22; 28:23.

[12] 1QS I 1–3; trans. G. Vermes, *The Dead Sea Scrolls in English* (3d ed.; London: Penguin, 1987) 62.

[13] 4Q174 II 3 (DJD 5.54).

prophet.[14] Moreover, Josephus and Melito also think of him as a prophet, and in fact the first written evidence that places Daniel not among the prophets but among the Ketubim or Writings is the much later Talmud. So Daniel was among the prophets in Judaism generally in the first century.

Similarly, with respect to the Psalms, the Qumran community produced *pesharim*, or commentaries, evidently only on prophetic books; but there turn up a few *pesharim* on the Psalms,[15] and 11QPs$^a$ speaks of David as having composed the Psalms through prophecy.[16] If we find ourselves hesitating here, we can again look at the New Testament which also interprets the Psalms prophetically.

4. What is more, apparently the category of "Prophets" was gradually perceived as being *stretched too far*. Though "the Law and the Prophets" (or "Moses and the Prophets") was a frequent designation for the Scriptures at Qumran and in the NT, 4QMMT at one point speaks of Moses, the Prophets, and David, parallel to Luke's speaking of "the Law and the Prophets and Psalms" (24:44). So the Book of Psalms, which had been counted among the Prophets began to establish a new category which eventually would be called the Ketubim or the Hagiographa. Other books as well, such as *Jubilees, Enoch,* Sirach, and a number of the other Apocrypha or Deutero-canonical works, were also being quoted or alluded to both at Qumran and in the New Testament in the same manner and the same contexts as other scriptural works.[17] And these, or some of these, became the Ketubim or the Hagiographa.

In short, though the books constituting the inner core of the collection, viz., the Torah and the main prophets, were clearly considered authoritative works of Scripture, and their order was largely but not fully set, works nearer the periphery were still finding their place.

---

[14] Matt 24:15; see also Mark 13:14.

[15] 1Q16, 4Q171, 4Q173; 4Q172?

[16] כול אלה דבר בנבואה אשר נתן לו מלפני העליון, 11QPs$^a$ XXVII 11 (DJD 4.48 + pl. XVI).

[17] *Jub.* 23:11 is quoted as authoritative in CD X 8–10 and its exact title, "The Book of the Divisions of the Times in their Jubilees and Weeks," occurs in CD XVI 3–4. In addition, allusions to *Enoch* occur fourteen times in the NT.

## II. The Individual Books of Scripture as Seen from Qumran

### *The Text Encountered in the Individual Scrolls*

What do the books of Scripture look like from within? When the individual books were unrolled in antiquity, did they look exactly like the text of the Hebrew Bible that we read or translate today? A healthy presumption is that no two MSS of any book in antiquity were ever exactly alike. Before the invention of the printing press in the 15th century and more recent photographic and electronic means of mass production of books, every copy of every book was indeed a copy, made individually by a more or less careful, but fallible, human being. But let's dismiss the individual minor variants and errors which populate every text. Let's also note but not get distracted by the differing systems or practices of orthography or spelling; much as in Elizabethan England, where spelling seems more a creative art than a linguistic science, so too in the scrolls we find a variety of orthographic styles. These two categories of variation between MSS—individual minor variants and orthographic differences—usually do not make much of a difference in meaning. But there has emerged a third category that teaches us much about the composition and transmission of the ancient biblical text, namely, multiple literary editions of biblical books and passages.

### *Multiple Literary Editions of Biblical Books and Passages*

Although in the traditional, pious, and popular imagination, the Books of Scripture were composed by single holy men from earliest times (Moses and Isaiah, for example), critical study of the text of Scripture demonstrates that the books are the result of a long literary development, whereby traditional material was faithfully retold and handed on from generation to generation, but also creatively expanded and reshaped to fit the new circumstances and new needs that the successive communities experienced through the vicissitudes of history. So the process of the composition of the Scriptures was organic, developmental, with successive layers of tradition. Ezekiel (3:1–3) was commanded to eat a scroll and found that it was sweet as honey. So perhaps I can be allowed to use the image of baklava for the composition of scriptural texts: many layers laid on top of one another by successive generations over the centuries, as the traditions were handed on faithfully but creatively adapted, and formed into a unity by the honey—sometimes heated—of the lived experience of the community over time.

At Qumran as in wider Judaism, we can see the scribes and their predecessors at work along two lines. Often the books of the Scriptures were simply copied as exactly as possible. But sometimes the scribes intentionally incorporated new material which helped interpret or bring home to their contemporary congregation in a new situation the relevance of the traditional text. These creative biblical scribes were actively handing on the tradition, but they were adding to it, enriching it, making it adaptable, up-to-date, relevant, multivalent. We must assume that by and large they knew explicitly what they were doing. Insofar as the scribes were handing on the tradition, they became part of the canonical process: handing on the tradition is a constitutive factor of the canonical process. James Sanders refers to this aspect as "repetition."[18] The repetition, in a sense, works like a hammer, pounding home again and again that this material is important. The texts were authoritative texts, and through the traditioning process they were being made more authoritative.

But the scribes were also updating the tradition, contemporizing it, making it relevant. That is, sometimes when the tradition was not adaptable, these scribes *made* it adaptable, thus giving it another of its canonical characteristics, a complementary factor that Sanders terms "resignification." That is, the tradition, important in its original setting, and important in itself beyond its importance for that original concrete situation, is found also to be important to me here and now in my present situation. The tradition proves adaptable, capable of having new significance in this new particular situation. The resignification—insofar as the tradition has proved useful or true—shows that indeed the tradition is *important in itself* (thus genuinely in the category of "tradition") and that it is *important to me* (thus genuinely in the category of "adaptable tradition"). The "authority" of such tradition is not an extraneous characteristic (authority imposed) but is intrinsic (the community recognizes the life-giving power of the tradition).[19]

---

[18] James A. Sanders, *Canon and Community: A Guide to Canonical Criticism* (Philadelphia: Fortress, 1984) 22.

[19] E. Ulrich, "The Canonical Process, Textual Criticism, and Latter Stages in the Composition of the Bible," *Sha'arei Talmon: Studies in the Bible, Qumran, and the Ancient*

Thus, we have gained a new window illuminating the ancient world and the biblical text in the making. The Qumran manuscripts and the versions document the creativity of religious leaders and scribes who produced revised literary editions of many of the books of Scripture. But, as is often the case with new knowledge, this new illumination brings complications. If this was the way the Scriptures were composed, how do we isolate "the original text"? What level do we translate in our modern Bible translations? We will touch on those problems later. Here, let us simply note that such *composition-by-stages* is the method by which the Scriptures were produced from the beginning, and that for some of the latter stages we now have manuscript evidence documenting two or more literary editions of some of the biblical books. We will describe these as we review the books at Qumran one by one.

*A Review of Individual Books*

The text of *Genesis* starts us off slowly and gently, like the beginning of a roller-coaster or ferris-wheel ride, though the ride will become more textually interesting soon. It appears that the text of Genesis had become basically stable by the late Second Temple period. All our MSS exhibit basically the same text type; most of the variants are only minor or unintentional.[20]

The Book of *Exodus*, however, provides a clear example of two editions of a biblical book. The different edition preserved in the Samaritan Pentateuch has been known since the seventeenth century, but its significance was capable of being dismissed, because the major differences were considered the work of the marginalized Samaritans. With the discovery of 4QpaleoExod$^m$,[21] however, we see that the Book

---

*Near East Presented to Shemaryahu Talmon* (ed. M. Fishbane and E. Tov with W. W. Fields; Winona Lake, IN: Eisenbrauns, 1992) 267–91, esp. pp. 288–89.

[20] A possible exception is the chronological system. For editions of the Cave 4 MSS, see James R. Davila, "Unpublished Pentateuchal Manuscripts from Cave IV, Qumran: 4QGenEx$^a$, 4QGen$^{b-h,j-k}$" (Dissertation, Harvard University, 1988).

[21] For the publication of 4QpaleoExod$^m$ see P. W. Skehan, E. Ulrich, and J. E. Sanderson, DJD 9.53–130. For preliminary publication and analyses see P. W. Skehan, "Exodus in the Samaritan Recension from Qumran," *JBL* 74 (1955) 182–87; idem, "Qumran and the Present State of Old Testament Text Studies: The Masoretic Text," *JBL* 78 (1959) 21–25, esp. p. 25; J. E. Sanderson, *An Exodus Scroll from Qumran: 4QpaleoExod$^m$ and the Samaritan Tradition* (HSS 30; Atlanta: Scholars Press, 1986); eadem, "The Contributions of 4QpaleoExod$^m$ to Textual Criticism," *Mémorial Jean Carmignac = RevQ*

of Exodus circulated in Judaism in two editions. One was the form traditionally found in the MT and translated in the LXX, and the other an intentionally expanded version with most of the features characteristic of the Samaritan version except the two *specifically* Samaritan features (namely, the addition of an eleventh commandment to build an altar on Mt. Gerizim, and the systematic use of the past, and not the future, of the verb in the formula "the place that the Lord has chosen" [not "will choose"]).[22]

The Book of *Leviticus*, perhaps because it was a work containing specific cultic regulations, also seems to have stabilized early, and to my knowledge, we have only one major textual tradition.[23]

The Book of *Numbers* again exhibits variant editions. 4QNum$^b$, edited by Nathan Jastram, shows a number of expansions shared by the Samaritan text of Numbers, but it is not specifically Samaritan.[24] Again, it seems that there were at least two editions of Exodus and Numbers that circulated within Judaism in the Second Temple period, and the Samaritans simply took one of those (the expanded version) and used that as their Torah, making only a few changes in accord with their beliefs.

The Book of *Deuteronomy* is one of the three most popular books at Qumran, just as it is in the New Testament.[25] It is too early to be

---

13 (1988) 547–60; eadem, "The Old Greek of Exodus in the Light of 4QpaleoExod$^m$," *Textus* 14 (1988) 87–104.

[22] Cf. Exod 20:17, and Deut 12:5, 11, 14, 18, etc.

[23] For the publication of 4QLev$^c$, see E. Tov in *Festschrift Milgrom* (in press). For 4QLev$^d$, see E. Tov, "4QLev$^d$ (4Q26)," *The Scriptures and the Scrolls: Studies in Honour of A. S. van der Woude on the Occasion of his 65th Birthday* (ed. F. García Martínez et al.; VTSup 49; Leiden: Brill, 1992) 1–5 + pls. 1–2.

[24] N. Jastram, "The Book of Numbers from Qumrân, Cave IV (4QNum$^b$)" (Dissertation, Harvard University, 1990).

[25] For editions of the Deuteronomy MSS see: Sidnie Ann White, "A Critical Edition of Seven Manuscripts of Deuteronomy: 4QDt$^a$, 4QDt$^c$, 4QDt$^d$, 4QDt$^f$, 4QDt$^g$, 4QDt$^i$, and 4QDt$^n$" (Dissertation, Harvard University, 1988); eadem, "The All Souls Deuteronomy and the Decalogue," *JBL* 109 (1990) 193–206; eadem, "Three Deuteronomy Manuscripts from Cave 4, Qumran," *JBL* 112 (1993) 23–42. Julie Ann Duncan, "A Critical Edition of Deuteronomy Manuscripts from Qumran, Cave IV: 4QDt$^b$, 4QDt$^e$, 4QDt$^h$, 4QDt$^j$, 4QDt$^k$, 4QDt$^l$" (Dissertation, Harvard University, 1989). Esther Eshel, "4QDeut$^n$—A Text That Has Undergone Harmonistic Editing," *HUCA* 62 (1991) 117–54. P. W. Skehan, "The Structure of the Song of Moses in Deuteronomy (Dt 32:1-43)," *CBQ* 13 (1951) 153–63; repr. P. W. Skehan, *Studies in Israelite Poetry and Wisdom* (CBQMS 1; Washington: Catholic Biblical Association of America, 1971) 67–77; idem, "A Fragment

able to give a definitive account of the textual nature of Deuteronomy, but there is a wide variety of textual variants preserved in the MSS from Qumran, and some MSS which preserve text that is totally from scripture were apparently not *biblical* MSS but MSS of biblical excerpts used for liturgical purposes.[26]

Once past the Book of Deuteronomy, the number of scrolls preserved for each book diminishes. For some books, either such a small percentage survives at Qumran, or the analyses are so recent, that it is hazardous to proffer judgments about them, since such judgments would undoubtedly be quoted and passed on as "the assured results of scholarship" in settings that would only cause disinformation. For the Book of Esther, for example, nothing survives (if the book had been there at all). Nothing survives of the Book of Nehemiah, unless Nehemiah was—this early—always considered as part of a single Book of Ezra–Nehemiah. From the following books only small amounts survive, and judgment—beyond that given in the preliminary editions—should be held in abeyance until sufficient analysis has been completed: the Books of *Judges*,[27] *Kings*,[28] *Ruth, Canticles, Qoheleth*,[29] *Lamentations*,[30] *Ezra*,[31] *Chronicles*.[32] The Book of *Ezekiel* survives

---

of the 'Song of Moses' (Deut. 32) from Qumran," *BASOR* 136 (1954) 12–15. Skehan, Ulrich, and Sanderson, DJD 9.131–54.

[26] E.g., 4QDeut$^j$ and 4QDeut$^n$.

[27] J. Trebolle Barrera, "Textual Variants in 4QJudg$^a$ and the Textual and Editorial History of the Book of Judges (1)," *RevQ* 14 (1989) 229–45.

[28] J. Trebolle Barrera, "A Preliminary Edition of 4QKings (4Q54)," *The Madrid Qumran Congress: Proceedings of the International Congress on the Dead Sea Scrolls, Madrid 18–21 March, 1991* (2 vols.; ed. J. Trebolle Barrera and L. Vegas Montaner; STDJ 11; Leiden: Brill; Madrid: Editorial Complutense, 1992) 1.229–46. Trebolle has developed a methodology for recovering an alternate edition of the Books of Kings; see his "Redaction, Recension, and Midrash in the Books of Kings," *BIOSCS* 15 (1982) 12–35.

[29] E. Ulrich, "Ezra and Qoheleth Manuscripts from Qumran (4QEzra, 4QQoh$^{a,b}$)," *Priests, Prophets, and Scribes: Essays on the Formation and Heritage of Second Temple Judaism in Honour of Joseph Blenkinsopp* (ed. E. Ulrich et al.; JSOTSup 149; Sheffield: JSOT Press, 1992) 139–57.

[30] F. M. Cross, "Studies in the Structure of Hebrew Verse: The Prosody of Lamentations 1:1–22," *The Word of the Lord Shall Go Forth: Essays in Honor of David Noel Freedman in Celebration of His Sixtieth Birthday* (ed. Carol L. Meyers and M. O'Connor: Winona Lake, IN: ASOR/Eisenbrauns, 1983) 129–55.

[31] Ulrich, "Ezra and Qoheleth Manuscripts."

[32] J. Trebolle Barrera, "Édition préliminaire de 4QChroniques," *RevQ* 15 (1992) 423–29.

in only three small MSS,³³ the Book of *Job* in only three,³⁴ and *Proverbs* in only two;³⁵ the text in these MSS appears to be generally similar to that of the traditional *textus receptus*.

The text of *Joshua* survives in only two MSS that are clearly the Book of Joshua. An edition of 4QJoshᵃ is in press at the moment, and 4QJoshᵇ has been published.³⁶ In addition, 4QpaleoParaJoshua (4Q123) is a MS with only four fragments surviving. They are so small that the work is difficult to identify, but the text is more reminiscent of the Book of Joshua than of any other known work, and it is conceivable that it is simply a variant textual form of the biblical book.³⁷ Furthermore, 4QJoshᵃ appears to present a variant edition of the text of that book. Though not fully certain, it is probable that the scroll contained an intentionally different order of the narrative in a highly significant matter—the building of the first altar in the newly-entered promised land. The passage that occurs at the end of chap. 8 in the traditional MT (though suspiciously after 9:2 in the LXX) is placed before chap. 5 in 4QJoshᵃ. What is more, one of our earliest witnesses to the biblical text, Josephus, similarly attests that Joshua built an altar at Gilgal immediately after crossing the Jordan and entering the Land.³⁸ The placement of the passage in the MT is admittedly odd, entailing the curious detour up to the otherwise insignificant Mt. Ebal. It is quite possible that 4QJoshᵃ and Josephus retain the original story and that it has been changed in the MT tradition due to anti-Samaritan polemic.

The Book of *Samuel* is somewhat more complex.³⁹ There do not appear to have been two separate editions of the entire book (or pair

---

³³ See the provisional transcription of 4QEzekᵃ and 4QEzekᵇ by Johan Lust, "Ezekiel Manuscripts in Qumran: Preliminary Edition of 4Q Eza and b," *Ezekiel and His Book: Textual and Literary Criticism and their Interrelation* (ed. J. Lust; Leuven: Leuven University Press, 1986) 90–100.

³⁴ For 4QpaleoJobᶜ, see DJD 9.155–57.

³⁵ See P. W. Skehan, "Qumran and Old Testament Criticism," 163.

³⁶ E. Ulrich, "4QJoshᵃ and the First Altar in the Promised Land," IOQS Paris Volume (in press). E. Tov, "4QJoshᵇ," *Intertestamental Essays in Honour of Józef Tadeusz Milik* (ed. Z. J. Kapera; Kraków: Enigma Press, 1992) 205–12 + pl. I.

³⁷ E. Ulrich, DJD 9.201–203.

³⁸ Josephus, *Ant.* 5 §20

³⁹ For 4QSamᵃ, see F. M. Cross, "A New Qumran Biblical Fragment Related to the Original Hebrew Underlying the Septuagint," *BASOR* 132 (1953) 15–26; idem, "The Ammonite Oppression of the Tribes of Gad and Reuben: Missing Verses from 1 Samuel 11 Found in 4QSamᵃ," *The Hebrew and Greek Texts of Samuel: 1980 Proceedings IOSCS—*

of books), but there are variant editions of certain passages. Insofar as Stanley Walters' analysis of 1 Samuel 1 is accepted, the argument can be made for a second, intentionally developed and changed edition of that narrative, perhaps due to theological and misogynist factors.[40] For the David–Goliath narrative in 1 Samuel 17–18 there are also two quite contrasting variant editions.[41]

The Book of *Isaiah* is one of the three most richly attested books at Qumran.[42] The textual character of the book and its many MS witnesses from Qumran is too complex for adequate summary here. The scrolls do not seem to preserve evidence of different editions, but the

---

*Vienna* (ed. E. Tov; Jerusalem: Academon, 1980) 105–19. E. Ulrich, *The Qumran Text of Samuel and Josephus* (HSM 19; Missoula, MT: Scholars Press, 1978); a list of contents of the MS is given on p. 271. See also E. Tov, "The Textual Affiliations of 4QSam^a," *JSOT* 14 (1979) 37–53; repr. in *The Hebrew and Greek Texts of Samuel* (ed. E. Tov; Jerusalem: Academon, 1980) 189–205; J. Trebolle Barrera, "El estudio de 4Q Sam^a: Implicaciones exegéticas e históricas," *Estudios bíblicos* 39 (1981) 5–18; and A. van der Kooij, "De tekst van Samuel en het tekstkritisch onderzoek," *Nederlands Theologisch Tijdschrift* 36 (1982) 177–204.

For 4QSam^b, see F. M. Cross, "The Oldest Manuscripts from Qumran," *JBL* 74 (1955) 147–72; and for 4QSam^c, see E. Ulrich, "4QSam^c: A Fragmentary Manuscript of 2 Samuel 14–15 from the Scribe of the *Serek Hay-yaḥad* (1QS)," *BASOR* 235 (1979) 1–25; repr. in *The Hebrew and Greek Texts of Samuel* (ed. E. Tov; Jerusalem: Academon, 1980) 166–88.

[40] Stanley D. Walters, "Hannah and Anna: The Greek and Hebrew Texts of 1 Samuel 1," *JBL* 107 (1988) 385–412.

[41] For the detailed characteristics of the two editions, see D. Barthélemy, D. W. Gooding, J. Lust, and E. Tov, *The Story of David and Goliath: Textual and Literary Criticism: Papers of a Joint Research Venture* (OBO 73; Fribourg, Suisse: Éditions Universitaires; Göttingen: Vandenhoeck & Ruprecht, 1986). I agree with the position of Tov and Lust and disagree with that of Barthélemy and Gooding. The correctness of either position, however, should not distract one from the main point that there are two editions of the biblical text.

[42] M. Burrows, ed., *The Dead Sea Scrolls of St. Mark's Monastery*, vol. 1 (New Haven: American Schools of Oriental Research, 1950). F. M. Cross et al., *Scrolls from Qumrân Cave I: The Great Isaiah Scroll, the Order of the Community, the Pesher to Habbakuk*; from photographs by John C. Trever (Jerusalem: Albright Institute of Archaeological Research and the Shrine of the Book, 1972). E. L. Sukenik, *The Dead Sea Scrolls of the Hebrew University* (Jerusalem: Hebrew University and Magnes Press, 1955), supplemented by D. Barthélemy and J. T. Milik, DJD 1.66–68. J. Muilenburg, "Fragments of Another Qumran Isaiah Scroll," *BASOR* 135 (1954) 28–32. P. W. Skehan, "Qumrân et découvertes au désert de Juda: IV. Littérature de Qumrân. — A. Textes bibliques. B. Apocryphes de l'Ancien Testament," *DBSup* 9 (1979) cols. 805–28; esp. cols. 811–12. See also P. W. Skehan, "The Text of Isaias at Qumrân," *CBQ* 17 (1955) 158–63. Francis J. Morrow, Jr., "The Text of Isaiah at Qumran" (Dissertation, The Catholic University of America, 1973).

multivalent poetic text shows at a number of points that the LXX faithfully translated an existing Hebrew text and was not "free," if free means tendentious or inventive.[43]

The Book of *Jeremiah*, however, does provide evidence of two literary editions,[44] and this appears to be widely recognized. The LXX preserves the earlier, shorter edition, documented in Hebrew in 4QJer$^b$, and the MT a subsequent, longer edition, with rearranged text.

The Hebrew MSS of the *Twelve Minor Prophets* do not offer strong signs of significantly diverse textual traditions,[45] but the Greek scroll from Naḥal Ḥever displays a systematic revision of the Old Greek translation toward the Hebrew text of the proto-Rabbinic tradition (MT).[46]

The Book of *Psalms* is again rich but difficult to summarize. More MSS of this book are preserved both at Qumran and in the Judean Desert generally than of any other work.[47] 11QPs$^a$ is an extensively preserved manuscript. It both includes nine compositions not found in the MT edition and exhibits an order partly identical with the traditional order of the MT but also significantly at variance with it. One of the additional compositions is drawn from another Davidic section of the Hebrew Bible, four were psalms preserved in the Greek and Syriac Bibles, and the remaining four were hitherto unknown. But significantly, all (except "David's Compositions") are composed like other biblical Psalms; they stand in marked contrast to the *Hôdāyôt* which

---

[43] See, e.g., P. W. Flint, "The Septuagint Version of Isaiah 23:1-14 and the Massoretic Text," *BIOSCS* 21 (1988) 35–54.

[44] E. Tov, "The Jeremiah Scrolls from Qumran," *RevQ* 14 (1989) 189–206; idem, "Three Fragments of Jeremiah from Qumran Cave 4," *RevQ* 15 (1992) 531–41; idem, "The Literary History of the Book of Jeremiah in the Light of Its Textual History," *Empirical Models for Biblical Criticism* (ed. J. H. Tigay; Philadelphia: University of Pennsylvania, 1985) 213–37; J. Gerald Janzen, *Studies in the Text of Jeremiah* (HSM 6; Cambridge, MA: Harvard University Press, 1973) 173–84; F. M. Cross, *Ancient Library*, 186–87 and nn. 37–38.

[45] R. E. Fuller, "The Minor Prophets Manuscripts from Qumrân, Cave IV" (Dissertation, Harvard University, 1988), esp. pp. 152–54.

[46] E. Tov, DJD 8.

[47] P. W. Skehan, "A Psalm Manuscript from Qumran (4QPs$^b$)" *CBQ* 26 (1964) 313–22; "Qumrân et découvertes," *DBSup* 9 (1979) cols. 805–28, esp. cols. 815–16; J. T. Milik, "Deux documents inédits du désert de Juda," *Biblica* 38 (1957) 245–68, esp. pp. 245–55. For analyses, see Gerald H. Wilson, *The Editing of the Hebrew Psalter* (SBLDS 76; Chico, CA: Scholars Press, 1985); and Peter W. Flint, "The Psalters at Qumran and the Book of Psalms" (Dissertation, University of Notre Dame, 1993).

sound post-biblical and reflect the theology of the Qumran commune. In "David's Compositions" a clear claim for the revelatory, and thus scriptural, character of the work is made by proclaiming that David composed all these psalms through God-given prophecy, as mentioned in part I above.

I am very close to being convinced that there are (at least) two major editions of the Psalter. One is that found in the MT and more or less reflected in the LXX, though there are numerous minor variants as well as the single major variant that the LXX includes Psalm 151, whereas the MT ends with Psalm 150. A second Psalter—a second edition of the scriptural Book of Psalms—is partly preserved in 11QPs$^a$; this assertion is supported by the fact that a second MS (11QPs$^b$) and perhaps a third (4QPs$^e$) also seem to exhibit this edition, whereas there is "only one scroll from Masada (MasPs$^b$), and none from Qumran, whose order *unambiguously* supports the Received Psalter against the 11QPs$^a$ arrangement."[48] It should also be noted that 11QPs$^a$ ends with Psalm 151, as does the LXX.

Finally, the eight MSS of the Book of *Daniel* from Qumran teach us a great deal about the text, language, and orthography of the book.[49] Though the scrolls themselves do not, the Old Greek in comparison with the MT does exemplify variant literary editions of Daniel.[50]

---

[48] Flint, "The Psalters," 147.

[49] See the editions of 1QDan$^a$ and 1QDan$^b$ by D. Barthélemy in DJD 1.50–52, and that of pap6QDan by M. Baillet in DJD 3.114–15 and pl. 23. For 4QDan$^{a,b,c}$, see E. Ulrich, "Daniel Manuscripts from Qumran. Part 1: A Preliminarly Edition of 4QDan$^a$," *BASOR* 267 (1987) 17–37; idem, "Daniel Manuscripts from Qumran. Part 2: Preliminarly Editions of 4QDan$^b$ and 4QDan$^c$," *BASOR* 274 (1989) 3–26. See also Ulrich, "Orthography and Text in 4QDan$^a$ and 4QDan$^b$ and in the Received Masoretic Text," *Of Scribes and Scrolls: Studies on the Hebrew Bible, Intertestamental Judaism, and Christian Origins presented to John Strugnell on the Occasion of His Sixtieth Birthday* (ed. H. W. Attridge, J. J. Collins, and T. H. Tobin; College Theology Society Resources in Religion 5; Lanham, MD: University Press of America, 1990) 29–42.

[50] D. O. Wenthe, "The Old Greek Translation of Daniel 1–6" (Dissertation, University of Notre Dame, 1991) demonstrates that the edition of the book in the MT is the earliest complete edition available, but not the first edition of the biblical Book of Daniel, and that the MT and LXX exhibit variant editions.

## Conclusions

1. Fifty years ago we had the Massoretic Text, the Samaritan Pentateuch, and the Septuagint, and our predecessors wrote "the history of the biblical text" on the basis of that evidence. Today we have a great deal of new information about the shape of the Bible before 135 CE. From a general perspective one could say that not much on the grand scale has changed, but when the focus is sharpened, some serious advances can be seen. Lines that were once obscure or perceived incorrectly are now noticeably clearer, though we could wish for yet greater clarity. Our knowledge has advanced, and so concomitant changes in our explanations will soon have to filter down.

2. The Scriptures were pluriform (as was Judaism and Christianity) until at least 70 CE, probably until 100, and quite possibly as late as 135 or beyond. Thus, we must revise our imaginations and our explanations. Neither the external shape nor the internal shape of the Scriptures has changed, but our knowledge of them has. We can now know significantly more, and know it more precisely. Externally, we know more about which books were "in" and which "out," and which books were in which category. Internally, we can now see more clearly that there were multiple literary editions of many of the biblical books. And we can understand that, e.g., the Book of Jeremiah or Daniel was considered among the books of Scripture, but the specific textual form was not a consideration. The process of the composition of the Scriptures was layered; some of the latter stages of that process—multiple literary editions of the books of Scripture—are demonstrated by our new extant evidence. [51]

3. Because the text of each book was produced organically, in multiple layers, determining "the original text" is a difficult, complex task; and theologically it may not even be the correct goal. How do we decide which of the many layers that could claim to be the "original reading" to select? Often the richer religious meanings in a text are those which entered the text at a relatively late or developed stage; do we choose the earlier, less rich reading or the later, more profound reading? In contrast, if a profound religious insight in an early stage of

---

[51] I have not yet studied 4Q364–367 in detail, but in light of this documented pluriformity of the developing text of the Scriptures, it may turn out that such works are more properly classified as "biblical" (i.e., scriptural) works rather than "paraphrases" or "reworked" biblical texts.

the text is toned down later by a standard formula or even a vapid platitude, which do we select? And must we not be consistent in choosing the early or the later edition or reading?

4. The Samaritans, the Jews, and the Christians ended up with three texts (not text types) and three collections of books because they each survived with a certain set of texts. Though their list of books was due to their religious principles and beliefs, the specific textual form of the individual books was accidental.

5. The MT, as the Samaritan, and the Septuagint, is not a univocal term or entity, but a collection of disparate texts, from different periods, of differing nature, of differing textual value, etc. There is no reason to think of the Massoretic collection as a *unit* (a codex, a "Bible"), or as a *unity*. The collection is like the Septuagint, a collection of varied forms of the various books.

6. Thus, finally, the situation has changed concerning translations of "The Holy Bible." The *New Revised Standard Version* now contains a number of improved readings based on the biblical MSS from Qumran. It can even claim to be the first Bible to contain a paragraph missing from all Bibles for 2000 years! It contains between chapters ten and eleven in 1 Samuel a paragraph found at Qumran and attested by Josephus, but absent from all other Bibles over the past two millennia.

But we still need to revise our approach toward translating the Bible. On the one hand, I have argued elsewhere that it is legitimate for a specific religious community or a specific scholarly project to produce a translation of a specific collection of texts as received within a faith tradition (e.g., the MT, the LXX, or the Samaritan Pentateuch).[52] On the other hand, a Bible translation that claims to be a scholarly or academically sound translation of the Hebrew Bible must be based on a critically established text, not just a diplomatic text (such as the MT or the LXX). While saying this, I must note that this is a statement of principle; it is very difficult in practice, and we are just getting to the point of being able to articulate the need; we may not yet be at the point of implementing it.

Qumran has begun to teach us a great deal about the Bible and the history of its text. There is a great deal still ahead to be learned.

---

[52] E. Ulrich, "Double Literary Editions of Biblical Narratives and Reflections on Determining the Form to be Translated," *Perspectives on the Hebrew Bible: Essays in Honor of Walter J. Harrelson* (ed. J. L. Crenshaw; Macon, GA: Mercer University Press, 1988) 101–16, esp. pp. 111–13.

# The Authoritative Functions of Scriptural Works at Qumran

*Julio Trebolle Barrera*

## I. Theoretical Framework

A theoretical basis for studying a very broad subject, the authoritative functions of scriptural works at Qumran, could be provided by the functional sociology of the Durkheim school.[1] Accordingly we should first identify the models of society that are applicable to the analysis of the Qumran community and then discuss the authoritative functions that the Scriptures could perform in the social group of Qumran and in other Jewish groups. We should determine, for example, if the model of rural *versus* urban society—which has been applied to Isralite origins with some success—applies in the case of the Essenes.[2] The Essenes, after all, expanded in rural areas, whereas the Pharisees and Sadducees were concentrated in urban centers. The function of the Scriptures is not the same for an elite group of experts as it is for an illiterate public (revised text *versus* vulgar text), nor the same for a majority group as it is for a sect of dissidents, "apocalyptic" in this case (canonical *versus* apocryphal; authorized text *versus* sectarian text).

In studies of "Ancient Judaism" the models of sociological analysis of the Max Weber school have found greater acceptance than those of the Durkheim school.[3] Weber analyzes the conflicts between three ideal types of authority: the legal, the traditional, and the charismatic. Thus we could analyze the authoritative functions of the biblical works in relation to these three types of authority as

---

[1] E. Durkheim, *The Elementary Forms of the Religious Life* (London: Allen & Unwin, 1915).

[2] S. Frick, *The Formation of the State in Ancient Israel: a Survey of Models and Theories* (Sheffield: JSOT Press, 1985).

[3] M. Weber, *Ancient Judaism* (New York: Free Press, 1952).

reflected in the Qumran literature and, particularly, in the three main genres of Qumran exegesis: legal, midrashic, and prophetic or apocalyptic. M. Fishbane has collected a great amount of relevant material in his work *Biblical Interpretation in Ancient Israel*.[4]

My contribution here concentrates on the first and main function of the Scriptures and of the biblical texts: the authoritative function, that is to say, the authorized function that the Scriptures perform on their own internal development and, as a consequence, on the development of the religious group and subgroups that appeal to the authority of those Scriptures.

Every religious society has to fix the minimum and maximum limits in which it will further develop. Holy Scriptures accomplish the function of establishing these limits. But in order to do that, the Scriptures themselves must have their own limits—their minimums and maximums of internal development—established, with respect to both the *collection* of Holy Books (the so-called biblical "Canon") and the *textual form* of each biblical book: shorter texts, intermediate texts and longer or paraphrastic texts such as those recently published.

Textual criticism cannot avoid resorting to two terms derived from social psychology: "conscious" vs. "unconscious." The dichotomy "intentional" vs. "unintentional" is decisive not only for the evaluation of textual variants ("unconscious" mistakes vs. readings "intentionally" created by scribes) but also for discussion about the authority of biblical texts. In an article published in 1977, Albrektson demolished "the current idea that the emergence of the standard text must have been the result of *a conscious and deliberated* text-critical activity with the purpose of creating a normative recension." According to Albrektson, the Rabbinic text "came to supplant other texts because the Pharisees supplanted other religious groups."[5] Talmon had already pointed out the relation between text and society: of the biblical textual traditions existing in Qumran times (more numerous than supposed by Cross), only those survived on which a religious group (Jewish, Samaritan, or Christian) conferred authority.[6]

---

[4] M. Fishbane, *Biblical Interpretation in Ancient Israel* (Oxford: Clarendon, 1985).

[5] B. Albrektson, "Reflections on the Emergence of a Standard Text of the Hebrew Bible," VTSup 29 (1978) 50, 63.

[6] S. Talmon, "The Old Testament Text," *The Cambridge History of the Bible* (ed. P. R. Ackroyd and C. F. Evans; Cambridge: Cambridge University Press, 1970) 1.159–99.

The theoretical discussions on the history of the biblical text by Cross, Tov, and Ulrich also exclude any conscious activity whose aim was to establish an authorized text. On the one hand, Cross explains the plurality of text-types as "the product of natural growth or development in the process of scribal transmission, not of conscious or controlled textual recension."[7] Tov, on the other hand, denies that the textual witnesses may be characterized as either recensions or text-types, which he defines as "a conscious effort to change an earlier text systematically in a certain direction."[8] According to Ulrich, "the choice of text type appears to be accidental in nature." However, "religious groups probably did develop the text intentionally. But most of the observable variation does not seem to be confessional or based on distinctive ideas associated with particular groups." Ulrich, therefore, calls upon researchers "to find evidence documenting which groups did what, where, and when? Did the various socio-religious groups intentionally or ideologically shape their specific forms of the text, and how did they do so?"[9]

To answer these questions it is necessary to examine activities that imply a conscious and deliberate change of the text of the biblical books. Such activities include new editions (as in the case of the book of Jeremiah), and recensions or systematic revisions. Both activities are the first and most important step in the process of diversification of the biblical text and, at the same time, of selection of the textual tradition from which an authorized text will later be issued. Now these activities—new (or second) editions and systematic revisions—are prior to the socio-religious diversification of Judaism that occurred around the Hellenistic crisis and previous to the appearance of any "triumphant" group. As a consequence, the questions stated before probably have no answer, at least if we try to answer them from

---

[7] F. M. Cross, "The Contribution of the Qumran Discoveries to the Study of the Biblical Text," *IEJ* 16 (1966) 85, n. 21.

[8] E. Tov, *Textual Criticism of the Hebrew Bible* (Minneapolis: Fortress; Assen/Maastricht: Van Gorcum, 1992) 160–61. Tov insists on recognizing the specific character of each text, to the point of challenging the existence and concept of textual "types." However, "within this variety, a few groups of closely related texts are discernible and there is even one group which bears exclusive typological features, namely, the Samaritan Pentateuch together with the pre-Samaritan texts" (163).

[9] E. Ulrich, "Pluriformity in the Biblical Text, Text Groups, and Questions of Canon," *The Madrid Qumran Congress: Proceedings of the International Congress on the Dead Sea Scrolls, Madrid 18–21 March, 1991* (2 vols.; ed. Julio Trebolle Barrera and Luis Vegas Montaner; STDJ 11; Leiden: Brill; Madrid: Editorial Complutense, 1992) 1.28–29.

the perspective chosen in this paper, that of the study of the history of the biblical text. For that purpose further investigation is needed, for example, in the field of comparative *halakah*.

What I would like to stress in this paper is that, if social groups exercise an influence on the formation of an authorized text, then it is the text in formation itself that exerts a social influence and a juridical and religious authority. In this respect I am following a model of analysis inspired by current trends in sociology, which restore the individual to society and leave more space to individual action in the context of a social and cultural system. Individuals have both conscious and unconscious motives for their actions, and the latter as well as the former have social consequences.[10]

## II. Conscious and Unconscious Textual Factors and Their Social Influence

Along the process of edition, recension and transmission of texts, conscious revision changes into unconscious mechanisms. Both factors, conscious and unconscious, contribute to the formation of a text that gradually gains greater authoritative weight.

For example, in the historical books or Former Prophets, numerous textual variants affect the terms "people" and "Israel." It is well known that there is a tendency, particularly in the Book of Judges, to make "Israel" the protagonist of stories that originally referred only to a tribe or a group of tribes. This tendency is present also at the textual level, which we can establish after the analysis of four series of variants:

1. "People" (עם, often "the troops") is replaced by "Israel."
Josh 7:11: חטא ישראל, ἡμάρτησεν ὁ λαός OG (B+L, OL Arm)
Josh 7:16: ויקרב את ישראל, καὶ προσήγαγην τὸν λαόν OG (B+L)
Josh 7:24: וכל ישראל עמו, καὶ πᾶς ὁ λαὸς μετ' αὐτοῦ (B)
Judg 2:7: ויעבדו העם//Josh 24:31: ויעבד ישראל
Judg 20:25: בבני ישראל, ἐκ τοῦ λαοῦ L, ἀπὸ υἱῶν Ισραηλ B
1 Sam 14:24: MT omits, καὶ πᾶς ὁ λαός B, καὶ Ισραηλ L
1 Sam 14:27: את העם, τὸν λαόν B, τοὺς υἱοὺς Ισραηλ L
1 Sam 14:38: פנות העם, τὰς φυλὰς τοῦ λαοῦ L, τὰς γωνίας τοῦ Ισραηλ B

---

[10] A. Giddens, *Social Theory and Modern Sociology* (Oxford: Blackwell, 1987).

# AUTHORITATIVE FUNCTIONS OF SCRIPTURAL WORKS 99

1 Kgs 1:20: עיני כל ישראל עליך, οἱ ὀφθαλμοὶ παντὸς Ισραηλ πρὸς σέ B, οἱ ὀφθαλμοὶ παντὸς τοῦ λαοῦ πρὸς σέ L

1 Kgs 8:5 (2 Chron 2:6): וכל עדת ישראל, καὶ πᾶς Ισραηλ B, καὶ πᾶς ὁ λαός L

1 Kgs 8:62: וכל ישראל עמו (= LXX) // 2 Chron 10:16 וכל העם

1 Kgs 12:15–16: וירא כל ישראל, καὶ εἶδον πᾶς Ισραηλ B, καὶ εἶδον πᾶς ὁ λαός

1 Kgs 16:16b–17: וימלכו כל ישראל, καὶ ἐβασίλευσαν ἐν Ισραηλ B, καὶ ἐβασίλευσεν ὁ λαός L

2. "Israel" is added to "the people" to form the expression "the people of Israel."

Josh 8:33: "in order to bless the people of Israel" (לברך את העם ישראל בראשנה), B (OL Arm) εὐλογῆσαι τὸν λαὸν ἐν πρώτοις.

1 Sam 2:14: MT and LXX have "Israel"; OL *populi Israel*. In the story of 1 Sam 2:11–26 (MT and LXX), all references are to the "people" (vv. 13, 23, 24, with oscillations in v. 22).

1 Sam 11:7: MT העם, B τὸν λαὸν Ισραηλ (OL *populum Israel*). In the literary unit 1 Sam 10:27b–11:15, the word "people" is used eight times ( MT and LXX vv. 11:4[bis], 5, 7 [L "Israel"] 11, 12, 14, 15).

1 Sam 14:18–23: MT and LXX "(sons of) Israel"; OL *populum Israel*. "People" is employed seven times in the story (13:16, 22; 14:2[bis], 3, 17, 20).

2 Sam 3:21: MT "all Israel", B πάντα Ισραηλ, L πάντα τὸν λαὸν Ισραηλ. 1 Kgs 12:1, 3 (2 Chron 10:1): MT LXX "all Israel." The OL reading, *omnis populus Israel*, is probably secondary, but "people" is the word in the context (12:5, 6, 7, 9, 10, 12, 13, 15, 16).

1 Kgs 16:21a: MT העם ישראל is incorrect, the older reading being possibly העם, "the people."

3. "Israel" is added in apposition to "people" ("My people, Israel," עמי ישראל).

Judg 20:2: MT "all the leaders of the people [and] all the tribes of Israel" (כל העם כל שבטי ישראל); πᾶσαι αἱ φυλαὶ τοῦ Ισραηλ B.

1 Sam 9:16: MT "of my people, Israel"; the word "people" is used two more times in this verse, not followed by "Israel" (cf. also 1 Sam 10:1b).

1 Sam 15:30: MT L "in the presence of the elders of my people and in the presence of Israel"; B "in the presence of the elders of Israel and in the presence of my people." The shorter reading "in the presence of my people" could be the older one.

2 Sam 3:18b: MT L "I will deliver my people Israel"; B "I will deliver Israel".

2 Sam 3:37: MT "all the troops (העם) and all Israel." In the preceding context (v. 36), only the troops (העם) are mentioned.

2 Sam 5:2: MT "ruler of Israel." The parallel passage in 1 Chron 11:2 has "ruler of my people, Israel."

In the following cases the repetition of את, על, or ב- ("for," "over," "of") may indicate that the word "Israel" has been juxtaposed to a previous reading "people." Modern translations often omit the repetition in order to create an easier reading.

1 Sam 27:12: MT בעמו בישראל, "*of* his own people, *of* Israel."

1 Sam 15:1: MT "*over* his people, *over* Israel" (על עמו על ישראל); L "*over* Israel, *over* his people"; B knows only the reading "over Israel" and the Lucianic ms. o "over his people."

2 Sam 6:21: MT נגיד על עם יהוה על ישראל, "ruler *over* the Lord's people, *over* Israel"; LXX "over his people, over Israel."

2 Sam 7:7: MT את עמי את ישראל, "to care *for* my people, *for* Israel." The parallel text 1 Chron 17:6 has only "to care for my people" (but NJPST "for my people + Israel"!). This shorter reading could be the older one.

2 Sam 7:8: MT "ruler *of* my people, *of* Israel" (על עמי על ישראל).

2 Sam 7:10: MT "*for* my people Israel, *for* Israel (... ל ... ל). LXX, the Hebrew text of 1 Chron 17:9 omits the repetition of ל, which could betray the juxtaposition of "Israel."

4. "Israel" is added without any relation to "people."

Josh 7:13: חרם בקרבך ישראל, τὸ ἀνάθεμα ἐστιν ἐν ὑμῖν B–L (omits MT ישראל).

Josh 8:10: "Joshua mustered the troops; then he and the elders of Israel (וזקני ישראל) marched upon Ai"; LXX–B omits "of Israel" (καὶ οἱ πρεσβύτεροι κατὰ πρόσωπον . . .).

Josh 8:34: MT אל המחנה הגלגלה; LXX εἰς τὴν παρεμβολήν Ισραηλ εἰς Γαλγαλα (LXX adds "Israel").

Josh 24:28: "Joshua then dismissed *the people* to their allotted portions" (וישלח יהושע איש לנחלתו)//Judg 2:6: "When Joshua dismissed the *people,* the *Israelites* went to their allotted territories (וישלח יהושע את העם וילכו בני ישראל איש לנחלתו); LXX has in both cases "dismissed the people and went (each) to . . ." (καὶ ἦλθεν/ἐπορεύθησαν ἀνήρ/ἕκαστος εἰς . . .). The longer text of Judges seems to be secondary.

Judg 10:10: "Then the Israelites cried out to the Lord" (ויזעקו בני ישראל אל יהוה); the Lucianic mss. d n p and the Hebrew text of the parallel passage 1 Sam 12:10 omit "the Israelites."
1 Kgs 20:15b: "Then he mustered all the troops, all the Israelites" (פקד את כל העם כל בני ישראל); instead of "all the Israelites" LXX has πᾶν υἱὸν δυνάμεως.

The most significant cases are those in which two parallel Hebrew texts offer two different readings, as in 1 Kgs 8:62 ("Israel") //2 Chron 10:16 ("people") (cf. also Judg 2:7//Josh 24:31; Judg 2:6// Josh 24:28; 2 Sam 5:2//1 Chron 11:2). More common are the cases in which the Septuagint is at variance with the MT. An analysis of the items listed above leads to the conclusion that the oldest form of the text is often that which preserves the reading "people," whereas the most recent form replaces, adds, or juxtaposes the term "Israel."[11] These changes, due to a deliberate tendency, become an unconscious mechanism as time goes on. This kind of Freudian *lapsus* is found also in modern versions, even in the *New Jewish Publication Society Translation* (1 Chron 17:6 "for My people" + "Israel").

The tendency to add the word "Israel," conscious in many cases, particularly at the literary and editorial levels, and unconscious in others, has a bearing of social character: the "Israelitization" of the text tries to enhance the national consciousness of the Israelites. As the text develops, it insists more and more on the message that for a Jew "there is no salvation outside of Israel" (*extra Israel nulla salus*), so that, *pace* Max Weber, the concepts of "peoplehood" (nation) and "chosen people" (Israel) are inseparable.[12] For future dissident groups—Samaritans, Qumranites, or Judeo-Christians—the only way to legitimate their claims was to arrogate for themselves the title "true Israel."

---

[11] These observations need to be taken into account in every kind of lexicographic, literary and historic analysis in which the terms "people" and "Israel" are involved. Cf. L. Rost, "Die Verzeichnungen für Land und Volk im Alten Testament," *Das kleine Credo und andere Studien zum Alten Testament* (Heidelberg: Quelle & Meyer, 1965) 76–101; N. Lohfink, "Beobachtungen zur Geschichte des Ausdrucks עם יהוה," *Probleme biblischer Theologie: Gerhard von Rad zum 70. Geburtstag* (ed. H. W. Wolff; München: Kaiser, 1971) 275–305.

[12] S. Talmon, "The Emergence of Jewish Sectarianism in the Early Second Temple Period," *Ancient Israelite Religion: Essays in Honor of F. M. Cross* (ed P. D. Miller, Jr., P. D. Hanson, and S. D. McBride; Philadelphia: Fortress, 1987) 598.

## III. Revisions and Recensions: Their Authoritative Function

We proceed now to consider the case of more systematic revisions or recensions. The mere existence of such an early revision of the Greek text as the so-called *kaige* recension (beginning of the first century BCE) proves that the first authoritative function of the biblical text is to control its own development, particulary the Scriptural character of the text of the versions. In an article titled "Greek Words and Hebrew Meanings," E. Tov has analyzed "a few words which carry some senses which have been determined by the Hebrew," among them the word δικαίωμα.[13] However, this was not the term employed in the Old Greek to translate the Hebrew חוק. The word δικαίωμα was instead chosen by the *kaige* recensor of Kings to substitute for the term πρόσταγμα of the Septuagint version.[14] The recensor chose a Greek word susceptible of a semantic content closer to the Hebrew חק/חקה, enriching it with a technical and Scriptural or authorized character, equivalent to that proper to the Hebrew term.[15]

---

[13] E. Tov, "Greek Words and Hebrew Meanings," *Melbourne Symposium on Septuagint Lexicography* (ed. T. Muraoka; Atlanta: Scholars Press, 1990) 83.

[14] The Old Greek translates חק/חקה by πρόσταγμα eight times in the non-*kaige* section: 1 Kgs 3:3; 3:14; 8:58; 8:61; 9:4; 9:6; 11:11; 11:38. The term πρόσταγμα is replaced by δικαίωμα in the *kaige* section: 1 Kgs 2:3; 2 Kgs 17:13; 17:19; 17:34; 17:37; 23:3. The proto-Lucianic text has preserved the Old Greek πρόσταγμα in 1 Kgs 2:3 and 2 Kgs 23:3; also in 2 Sam 22:23, in a *kaige* section, the B text offers δικαίωμα, whereas the proto-Lucianic text preserves the term πρόσταγμα. It is equally significant that a Hexaplaric addition in 1 Kgs 11:34 presents the recensional term δικαίωμα. In another Hexaplaric addition, 1 Kgs 11:33, the term employed is διακριβεῖας. The term משפט is differently translated in the non-*kaige* section (δικαίωμα) and in the *kaige* section (κρίσις). This phenomenon is easily observed in the books of Samuel: in the non-*kaige* section, משפט = δικαίωμα, 1 Sam 2:13; 8:3; 8:9; 8:11; 10:25; 27:11; 30:25; in the *kaige* section, משפט = κρίσις, 2 Sam 15:2; 15:4; 15:6; κρίμα in 2 Sam 8:15 and 22:23. 1 Kings alternates: κρίμα (2:3 *kaige*; 3:11; 3:28; 6:12; 10:9) and δικαίωμα (3:28; 8:45; 8:59) together with other correspondences (σύνταξις, παράταξις, κριτήριον, κρίσις, ἔθισμον, ἐνέδρα).

[15] The revision of the Greek text proceeded in various stages: Aquila's predecessors revised some of the OG translation techniques, Aquila translated the passages of the Hebrew wanting in the Septuagint (e.g., 1 Kgs 14:1-20) and, finally, the Hexaplaric and Lucianic recensions conflated the Hebrew and Greek traditions by incorporating the additions by Aquila and Theodotion into the Septuagint text. The text of Josephus possibly represents a kind of middle stage or a mixed text: while employing an Old

The point I want to stress here is that the recensions of the Greek text and consequently of the Old versions respond to a prior and parallel process of recension or revision of the Hebrew text. This path of research has hardly been explored. Between the fields of literary criticism (formation of the text) and textual criticism (transmission of the text) extends a kind of buffer zone that belongs to the field of what I called in my first publications "recensional criticism": the study of the process of recension and of the more or less systematic revisions of the biblical text.[16] Let us consider two examples that involve terms also belonging to the semantic field of "(biblical) authority": תורה and דרש.

The term תורה is not found in the Hebrew text corresponding to the non-*kaige* section 1 Kgs 2:12–21:43. It appears, however, eleven times in the text corresponding to the *kaige* sections 1 Kgs 1:1–2:11 and 1 Kgs 22:1–2 Kgs 25:30:[17]

| | |
|---|---|
| 1 Kgs 2:3 | ככתוב בתורת משה |
| 2 Kgs 10:31 | ללכת בתורת יהוה |
| 2 Kgs 14:6 | ככתוב בספר תורת משה |
| 2 Kgs 17:13 | ככל התורה אשר צויתי |
| 2 Kgs 17:34 | וכתורה וכמצוה אשר צוה יהוה |
| 2 Kgs 17:37 | והתורה והמצוה אשר כתב |
| 2 Kgs 21:8 | ולכל התורה אשר צוה |
| 2 Kgs 22:8 | ספר התורה מצאתי בבית יהוה |
| 2 Kgs 22:11 | את דברי ספר התורה |
| 2 Kgs 23:24 | את דברי התורה |
| 2 Kgs 23:25 | ככל תורת משה |

This becomes more evident if we observe that the terms in the plural, משפטים, חקות/חוקים and מצות, are very frequent in the non-*kaige* section 1 Kgs 2:12—1 Kgs 21:43 (eleven, four, and nine times respectively), in which the word תורה is not found.[18] They are less fre-

---

Greek (proto-Lucianic) text, it follows a Hebrew (proto-Massoretic) text in the passages missing in the Greek (for example, 1 Kgs 14:1-20, cf. *Ant.* 8.11.1).

[16] J. Trebolle Barrera, "Crítica recensional aplicada a LXX *IV Reges* 25:18-19," *EstBib* 36 (1977) 91–94.

[17] The only case present in 1–2 Samuel, 2 Sam 7:19, is not to be considered.

[18] חקות/חוקים: 1 Kgs 3:3; 3:14; 6:12; 8:58; 8:61; 9:4; 9:6; 11:11; 11:33; 11:34; 11:38. משפטים: 1 Kgs 6:12; 6:58; 9:4; 11:33 (the cases of משפט in the singular are not taken into account). מצות: 1 Kgs 3:14; 6:12; 8:58; 8:61; 9:6; 11:34; 11:38; 14:8; 18:18 (> LXX):

| | |
|---|---|
| 1 Kgs 3:3 | ללכת בחקות דוד |
| 1 Kgs 3:14 | לשמר חקי ומצותי |

quent in the *kaige* sections (six, one, and five times respectively),[19] in which תורה is used eleven times. It becomes evident that 1 Kings (which originally began at 1 Kgs 2:12) used the terms "laws and precepts," while 2 Kings employs already the word תורה as a technical term to refer to the five books of "the Law."

The word דרש is a characteristic term of the emergent Rabbinic hermeneutic. The verb דרש + את/-ב (בבעל, את יהוה) is employed twelve times in 2 Kings (*kaige* section). It replaces the verb שעל + ב- (באלוהים, ביהוה), employed eleven times in 1 Kings (non-*kaige* sec-

| | |
|---|---|
| 1 Kgs 6:12 | אם תלך בחקתי ואת משפטי תעשה ושמרת את כל מצותי |
| 1 Kgs 8:58 | ולשמר מצותיו וחקיו ומשפטיו |
| 1 Kgs 8:61 | ללכת בחקיו ולשמר מצותיו |
| 1 Kgs 9:4 | חקי ומשפטי תשמר |
| 1 Kgs 9:6 | ולא תשמרו מצותי חקתי |
| 1 Kgs 11:11 | ולא שמרת בריתי וחקתי |
| 1 Kgs 11:33 | לעשות הישר בעיני וחקתי ומשפטי |
| 1 Kgs 11:34 | שמר מצותי וחקתי |
| 1 Kgs 11:38 | לשמר חקותי ומצותי |
| 1 Kgs 14:8 | אשר שמר מצותי |
| 1 Kgs 18:18 | בעזבכם את מצות יהוה |

[19] חקות/חוקים: 1 Kgs 2:3; 2 Kgs 17:13; 17:15; 17:34; 17:37; 23:3; משפטים: 2 Kgs 17:37; מצות: 2 Kgs 17:13; 17:16; 17:19; 18:6; 23:3 (17:34 and 17:37 in singular):

| | |
|---|---|
| 1 Kgs 2:3 | לשמר חקתיו מצותיו ומשפטיו |
| 2 Kgs 17:13 | ושמרו מצותי חקותי |
| 2 Kgs 17:15 | וימאסו את חקיו |
| 2 Kgs 17:16 | ויעזבו את כל מצות יהוה |
| 2 Kgs 17:19 | לא שמר את מצות יהוה |
| 2 Kgs 17:19 | וילכו בחקות ישראל |
| 2 Kgs 17:34 | עשים כחקתם |
| 2 Kgs 17:37 | ואת החקים ואת המשפטים |
| 2 Kgs 18:6 | וישמר מצותיו אשר צוה יהוה |
| 2 Kgs 23:3 | ולשמר מצותי ואת עדותיו ואת חקתיו |

The Old Greek version ignores some passages (1 Kgs 6:12; 11:33 and 11:34) and is more regular in the use of the pair of words חוקים ומשפט/משפטים (1 Kgs 3:14; 8:58; 8:61; 9:4; 9:6; 11:11; 11:38). Cf. N. Lohfink, "Die ḥuqqîm ûmišpāṭîm im Buch Deuteronomium und ihre Neubegrenzung durch Dtn 12,1," Studien zum Deuteronomium und zur deuteronomistischen Literatur II (Stuttgart biblische Aufsatzbände Altes Testament 12; Stuttgart: Katholisches Bibelwerk, 1991) 241.

tion). The substitution of שעל + ב- by דרש reflects the social transition from the prophetic to the scribal function and from the oracular to the scriptural inquiry.[20]

The tendency to add the term "Israel" and to make explicit reference to the "Torah" along with other tendencies—such as that of adding oracular formulas (כה אמר יהוה) and references to the Prophets (in particular, to "Jeremiah the Prophet" in the Book of Jeremiah and in Chronicles)[21]—gives to the biblical text an increasing weight of authority or "canonicity."[22]

We may safely conclude that 2 Kings has a textual history different from that of 1 Kings. It passed through a recensional activity which did not affect 1 Kings. There is also a relation between the books affected by the *kaige* recension and those from which two editions or two different textual forms have been preserved: these books are *grosso modo* those of the Former Prophets (Joshua, Judges, Samuel–Kings) and the Later Prophets, except the book of Isaiah. It seems that the edition of the nomistic and priestly literature (the Torah, Chronicles–Ezra–Nehemiah, and the book of Isaiah among the Prophets) had acquired very early a stable textual form that did not need revision. By contrast, the historical and prophetic literature, affected by the deuteronomistic redaction, later passed through a complex process of re-edition and recension.

The model used to explain the recensional history of the versions is also to be applied to the history of the Hebrew text. The re-

---

[20] דרש (את יהוה or בבעל): 1 Kgs 22:5; 22:7; 22:8; 2 Kgs 1:2; 1:3; 1:6; 1:16; 1:16; 3:11; 8:8; 22:13; 22:18. The only case in which דרש appears in the non-*kaige* section, 1 Kgs 14:5, is the exception that confirms the rule. The whole passage of 1 Kgs 14:1-20 did not belong to the Hebrew *Vorlage* of the Septuagint. The text of 1–2 Samuel employs the verb שאל, except in 1 Sam 9:9, where the use of the verb דרש corresponds to an added gloss.

[21] R. Then, "*Gibt es denn keinen mehr unter den Propheten?*": *Zum Fortgang der alttestamentlichen Prophetie in frühjüdischer Zeit* (Beiträge zur Erforschung des Alten Testaments und des antiken Judentums 22; Frankfurt: Lang, 1990).

[22] 2 Kgs 17:13 is possibly the oldest biblical reference to the combined authority of "the Law and the Prophet": "Observe My commandments and My laws, according to all the *Torah* that I commanded your fathers and that I transmitted to you (to them, LXX) through My servants the *Prophets*." Similarly, two appendices at the end of the Book of Malachi have a joint reference to the Law and the Prophets, serving as the colophon of the book and, at the same time, of the collection of the Twelve Prophets and of the prophetic books. Cf. B. S. Childs, "The Canonical Shape of the Prophetic Literature," *Int* 32 (1978) 46–55; J. Blenkinsopp, *Prophecy and Canon: A Contribution to the Study of Jewish Origins* (Notre Dame: University of Notre Dame Press, 1977) 122–23.

censions of the Septuagint version correspond to a previous editorial and recensional process of the Hebrew text. The differences between the Old Greek text and the text of the recensions—the Hexaplaric, in particular—or between the Old Latin and the Vulgate correspond to differences between an Old Hebrew text and a revised Hebrew text, which is basically preserved in the often precisely called "Massoretic recension." This is the methodolical schema underlying the analysis carried out in the examples of part II above. It shows that the process of selection of an authorized text had old antecedents. In the final process of establishing an authorized text, unconscious factors of a scribal and social character seem to have played a major role: the texts were selected not after a critical scrutiny but only because they were the texts of the Pharisees (Albrektson, Ulrich). In the initial process the dominant factors were those of a conscious nature: the texts of the Pharisees were those corresponding to second or revised editions.

## IV. Harmonistic or Paraphrastic Texts: Authoritative Developments

The publication in recent years of new Qumran manuscripts characterized as frontier, expansionistic, harmonistic, parabiblical or paraphrastic (11Q*Temple Scroll*, 4QpaleoExod$^m$, 4QDeut$^n$ and 4QDeut$^j$, 4QNum$^b$, 4Q364–367 or 4QRP, and 4Q158, a copy of the previous work) has oriented the interest of research towards the study of the "long" texts. These new manuscripts present what seems to be a surplus, an excess of text in the frontier between the biblical and the parabiblical, the canonical and the apocryphal. Whereas the *Damascus Document* interprets the Scripture by making direct reference to the biblical text, the *Temple Scroll* introduces the interpretative elements into the text of the Torah, thereby producing a new Torah. 4QDeut$^n$ and 4QDeut$^j$ present additions taken from *halakhic* traditions not known by the biblical texts, and 4QNum$^b$ collects *halakhic* texts taken from other canonical books.[23] 4Q364–367, "Reworked Pen-

---

[23] S. A. White, "4QDt$^n$: Biblical Manuscript or Excerpted Text?," *Of Scribes and Scrolls: Studies on the Hebrew Bible, Intertestamental Judaism, and Christian Origins presented to John Strugnell on the Occasion of His Sixtieth Birthday* (ed. H. W. Attridge, J. J. Collins, and T. H. Tobin; Lanham, MD: University Press of America, 1990) 13–20; J. A. Duncan, "Considerations of 4QDt$^j$ in Light of the 'All Souls Deuteronomy' and Cave 4 Phylactery

tateuch," and 4Q158, "Biblical Paraphrase," offer a different order of passages, omitting entire sections of the text and adding other "extra-biblical" texts. Tov defines this work as a "rewriting" of the biblical text, similar to that represented by the *Temple Scroll*.[24] Similar phenomena have also been observed in other non-biblical texts of anthological character, such as 4Q*Florilegium*, 4Q*Testimonia*, 4Q*Catena*ᵃ and texts recently published: *Psalms of Joshua* (4Q378–379), *Second Ezekiel* (4Q385–390) and *Pseudo-Moses* (4Q375–376). [25]

All these texts confront us with the task of clarifying the limits of the biblical text and, at the same time, of determining the authoritative function that these texts performed in the juridical, liturgical or exegetical fields among the Qumran covenanters, the Samaritans, or other Jewish groups.

The old tripartite scheme—Septuagint, MT and Samaritan Pentateuch—seems now to have been replaced with a scheme of shorter texts, intermediate texts, and longer texts. All these texts have their origin more in the process of edition and recension of the biblical texts than in the process of textual (mainly unconscious) transmission, towards which the attention of scholars has been primarily directed. The shorter texts (as the Hebrew original of the Septuagint) correspond to a first edition of some books, particularly in the prophetic literature. The intermediate texts, mainly those of the Masoretic textual tradition, correspond to a second or revised edition. The longer texts go also back to a pre-Maccabean date, as can be inferred particularly from the presumable antiquity of the Temple Scroll.[26] These longer texts could have reached a considerable diffusion and even become a kind of *koine* text acceptable to the Samaritans, the Qumran Essenes, and other Jewish groups.

---

Texts," *Madrid Qumran Congress*, 1.199–215; N. Jastram, "The Text of 4QNumᴮ," *Madrid Qumran Congress*, 1.177–198.

[24] E. Tov, "The Textual Status of 4Q364–367 (4QPP)," *Madrid Qumran Congress*, 1.43–82.

[25] C. Newsom, "The 'Psalms of Joshua' from Qumran Cave 4," *JJS* 39 (1988) 56–73; J. Strugnell and D. Dimant, "4QSecond Ezekiel," *Mémorial Jean Carmignac* (*RevQ* 13; [1988]) 45–58, pl. II; J. Strugnell, "Moses-Pseudepigrapha at Qumran: 4Q375, 4Q376 and Similar Works," *Archaeology and History in the Dead Sea Scrolls* (ed. L. H. Schiffman; JSPSup 8; Sheffield: Academic Press, 1990) 189–220.

[26] H. Stegemann, "The Origins of the Temple Scroll," *Congress Volume. Jerusalem 1986* (ed. J. A. Emerton; Leiden: Brill, 1988) 235–56.

The history of the Scriptures and the history of the Jerusalem Temple run parallel to one another, particularly in three critical moments: the restoration by Ezra, the Maccabean restoration, and the Rabbinic restoration. Recent excavations along the Western wall of the Jerusalem Temple have proved that the information provided by the Rabbinic sources about the extent of the Holy space corresponds to the Maccabean Temple, while the measures provided by Josephus correspond to the Herodian Temple. Even after the amplification by Herod, the truly Holy space where impure Jews and pagans were not allowed to enter continued to be the same as that in the Maccabean period.[27] In a similar way, we may say that the text fixed and authorized by the Rabbis, as well as the basic design of what was later to be known as the Hebrew canon, go back to the Maccabean restoration. However, some movements and groups knew and transmitted a wider corpus of Holy Scriptures, which probably included such books as *Jubilees*, *Enoch*, and the *Psalms of Joshua*. They also read the biblical books in longer and more paraphastic textual forms. Only in the context of such a textual plurality, which was even richer than so far assumed, can we appreciate that OT quotations present in the NT offer many textual variants which cannot be explained simply as Christian interpretative changes; and only thus can we understand why the Judeo-Christians could consider as inspired and canonical works like Tobit, Ben Sira, the Letter of Jeremiah, and others.[28]

The association of legal, narrative, and prophetic passages, constitutive of these new harmonistic or paraphrastic Qumran texts, was one of the first steps on the path of legitimating or conferring authority to certain *hălākôt*, midrashic interpretations, and apocalyptic conceptions. It is well known that a very expanded biblical text known to the Samaritans and also to other Jewish groups of Palestine combined the passages of Exod 20:17 and Deut 27:28; 11:29-30. The Samaritan Pentateuch took advantage of this textual combination to give Mosaic authority to the command of celebrating the cult at Garizin. The *Testimonia* literature also constituted the initial step for the development of the Christian theology. By associating different biblical passages a motif of the Christian kerygma was developed. The association of several of these motifs and of new

[27] D. Bahat, "Le Temple de Zorobabel à Hérode," *Le monde de la Bible* 60 (1989) 14.

[28] Contra R. T. Beckwith, *The Old Testament Canon of the New Testament Church and its Background in Early Judaism* (London: SPCK, 1985).

collections of biblical texts opened the path to creating new kerygmatic or theological developments.

## V. Scriptural and Text-Critical Value of the Marginal or Aberrant Biblical Text

The study of Qumran manuscripts containing Hebrew readings reflected by the Greek version contributed to the recognition of the critical value of the Septuagint. Now the discovery of new manuscripts containing "longer" and to a certain extent "aberrant" texts (in that their affiliation is not known) should call attention to a whole series of "marginal" readings, preserved in recensions of the Greek text, secondary versions and biblical quotations. Marginal readings of the Old Latin version (OL) preserved in some Spanish codices of the Vulgate recently published[29] present a rather high proportion of readings based on a Hebrew text different from the MT and also from the Hebrew reflected by the Septuagint and the Greek recensions. Researchers are eager to examine every piece of the Hebrew Qumran manuscripts. Yet I want to mention here that I heard someone say to Prof. John Strugnell that he would prefer to have a whole manuscript of the OL version than one more of the many Hebrew biblical manuscripts found at Qumran. I propose here two examples.

In 2 Kgs 13:17 (cf. OTG) the OL preserves a reference to a battle in *Aseroth quae est contra faciem Samariae*. The place name *Aseroth* is not mentioned anywhere in the Bible, but it appears in the Samaria ostraca of a period very near to that of the battle alluded to in the OL reading (Ḥaṣeroth, probably ʿAsīre es̆ Šemālīye to the North of Siquen). The Latin translator could not have fabricated this geographical reference. He was simply reproducing the Hebrew *Vorlage* at his disposal.

The second example is perhaps still more significant. In 2 Kgs 9:33 a Hexaplaric addition preserved in only three manuscripts (h i z, possibly representing the Hesychian recension) and in the Syro-Hexaplaric version, has Queen Jezebel thrown down from the balcony of the palace "to the ground" ($\dot{\epsilon}\nu\ \tau\hat{\omega}\ o\dot{\iota}\kappa o\pi\acute{\epsilon}\delta\omega$). Two OL

---

[29] A. Moreno Hernández, *Las glosas marginales de* Vetus Latina *en las biblias vulgatas españolas. 1–2 Reyes* (Textos y estudios "Cardenal Cisneros" 49; Madrid: C.S.I.C., 1992).

marginal glosses offer different versions: *in plano pede*, which is a quite literal translation of the Greek ("the site of a house"), and *in ruinoso loco* ("a place of ruins").[30] This second translation implies that the Greek term οἰκόπεδον corresponds to the Hebrew חרבה "ruins," "ruined dwellings" (cf. Ps 102:7 [LXX 101]; Ps 109:10 [LXX 108]; Sir 49:13). The Greek verb used, κυλίω/κυλίνδω (cf. the expression κυλίνδεσθαι κατὰ κόρπον = "roll, wallow in the dirt"), corresponds very well to the reading *in ruinoso loco*.

This reading provides a key for understanding the whole story. Jezebel's death is depicted with the same terms employed in the narratives about the death of the primordial monster, Yam or Leviathan, or about the profanation of an idol or a stele. Jezebel ("her eyes painted and her hair dressed" as an Ashtoreth) is declared "cursed" (הארורה הזאת), as Yam in Job 3:8, Leviathan in Job 41:1 and the snake of Paradise in Gen 3:14 (ארר) in the three cases. Jezebel is "trampled (רמס) by the horses" as Yam or ʿEreṣ (דרך על במות, Job 9:8. The members of her body are scattered as food for wild beasts and birds, as Leviathan in Ps 74:14, *tannîn* in Ezek 29:5 and Mot in UT 49 ii 35 (cf. Exod 32:20). Jezebel "thrown down" (שמם) recalls Ps 14:6, "slip on the rock . . . the earth cleft and broken up . . . the bones scattered at the mouth of Sheol."

Research still has ahead of it the great task of recovering fragments of marginal textual traditions, readings that were not "received" into the central tradition of the *receptus* and that cannot be accepted into a critical text since they are not traceable to any reconstructed original text. They are, however, vestiges of old texts that have reached us via recensions of marginal readings. At the present state of research, practitioners of textual criticism and defenders of an authorized text should probably operate with a broader concept of what constitutes an original text vs. an authorized text. Marginal readings can be as old as the original readings of a certain textual form or edition. At a given period or in a certain stream of Second Temple Judaism, marginal readings could have enjoyed an authority equal to that attained later by the corresponding massoretic readings. Scientific as well as canonical reasons converge today to recommend a polyglot, pluri-textual, and pluri-canonical study of the biblical texts.

---

[30] Ibid., 132.

# Biblical Texts as Reworked in Some Qumran Manuscripts with Special Attention to 4QRP and 4QParaGen-Exod

## Emanuel Tov

At Qumran many compositions have been found which in some way or other rework or rephrase the biblical text, or add exegetical comments to it. Several of these compositions were written by the Qumran community, while others were brought to Qumran from outside. The distinction between these two groups, though crucial, is usually not made for exegetical works and indeed is not an easy one to make. Yet it is significant to give some attention to this distinction, since too often scholars discuss what they call "biblical exegesis at Qumran," on the basis of exegetical compositions which may actually have been composed outside Qumran. In our view, only some of the compositions found at Qumran have been authored by that community,[1] while others were composed elsewhere. Hence, only some of the compositions from Qumran are relevant to the Qumran community. It is our impression, and we can speak only in terms of impressions, that most of the rewritten and rephrased biblical texts to be discussed below did not derive from the Qumran community. That is, these compositions do not reflect the characteristic features of the Qumran literature, although a few reflect the features of the Qumran scribal school. The Qumran community appropriated to itself the literary genre of the *pesharim* which may be considered an alternative to the rewritten and rephrased biblical texts. One of the texts to be discussed below,

---

[1] See E. Tov, "The Orthography and Language of the Hebrew Scrolls Found at Qumran and the Origin of These Scrolls," *Textus* 13 (1986) 31–57; idem, "Hebrew Biblical Manuscripts from the Judaean Desert: Their Contribution to Textual Criticism," *JJS* 39 (1988) 1–37. See further E. Tov, "*Tefillin* of Different Origin from Qumran?" *J. Licht Memorial Volume* (in press); idem, "Scribal Habits Reflected in the Documents from the Judean Desert and in the Rabbinic Literature: A Comparative Study," *Festschrift M. Haran* (ed. M. Fox et al., in press).

4QpGena, appears to reflect a middle course between the *pesher* and other rewritten Bible texts.

Another problem concerning the works discussed here concerns the definition of the various literary genres. The Qumran fragments representing the realm of the reworked, rephrased, expanded, and exegeted Hebrew Bible actually cover a wide range of literary genres. This has been recognized in the past, and scholars have tried to inventory the various categories of literary genres reflecting different forms of biblical exegesis. The most extensive analysis of the various levels of rewriting and/or exegesis reflected in the fragments found at Qumran is probably found in the writings of G. Vermes.[2] In our terminology, a distinction is made between reworking/rewriting which involved a limited intervention in the biblical text, and rephrasing involving a major intervention, often in such a way that the underlying biblical text is hardly recognizable. Adding exegetical comments to the biblical text is a form of rewriting.

## A. Reworked Bible Texts Found at Qumran

There are many aspects of the biblical exegesis reflected in the writings found at Qumran,[3] but in the present paper we are not involved with the whole spectrum of that topic. In its full scope, the discussion of the biblical exegesis in the Qumran writings involves a

---

[2] G. Vermes, "Bible Interpretation at Qumran," *Eretz Israel* 20 (1989) 184–91; E. Schürer, *The History of the Jewish People in the Age of Jesus Christ (175 B.C.–A.D. 135)* (3 vols.; rev. and ed. G. Vermes, F. Millar, and M. Goodman; Edinburgh: Clark 1986) 3.1.420–50.

[3] See the two works mentioned in the previous note and further: F. F. Bruce, *Biblical Exegesis in the Qumran Texts* (London: Tyndale, 1960); J. van der Ploeg, "Bijbelverklaring te Qumrân" (Mededelingen der Koninklijke Nederlandse Akademie van Wetenschappen, Afd. Letterkunde 23/8; Amsterdam 1960) 207–29; S. Lowy, "Some Aspects of Normative and Sectarian Interpretation of the Scriptures," *ALUOS* 6 (1969) 98–163; D. Patte, *Early Jewish Hermeneutic in Palestine* (SBLDS 22; Missoula, MT: Scholars Press, 1975); H. Gabrion, "L'Interprétation de l'Ecriture dans la littérature de Qumrân," *ANRW* II.19.1 (Berlin/New York: de Gruyter, 1979) 779–848; D. Dimant, "Qumran Sectarian Literature," *Jewish Writings of the Second Temple Period* (ed. M. E. Stone; CRINT 2/2; Assen: Van Gorcum; Philadelphia: Fortress, 1984) 483–549, esp. 503–32 ("Biblical Interpretation"); G. J. Brooke, *Exegesis at Qumran: 4QFlorilegium in its Jewish Context* (JSOTSup 29; Sheffield: JSOT Press, 1985). See further the extensive literature on the *pesharim*, esp. M. P. Horgan, *Pesharim: Qumran Interpretations of Biblical Books* (CBQMS 8; Washington, DC: Catholic Biblical Association of America, 1979) and earlier studies mentioned there.

discussion of several genres, including *pesharim*, quotations in the sectarian writings, and such literary genres as the Qumran hymns and sapiential writings. It could even involve some of the biblical scrolls. However, we limit ourselves to a specific group of Qumran writings, reflecting running biblical texts, that is, the Bible as reworked, expanded, and rephrased in some Hebrew compositions found at Qumran. By definition, this formulation excludes the Aramaic paraphrase of Genesis included in 1QapGen.

It is not easy to define the different gradations of reworking, rewriting, and rephrasing. In fact, as we shall see, several rewritten Bible texts found at Qumran are *sui generis*.

We first turn to some manuscripts of the Bible. When speaking of the reworked and rephrased biblical texts, by definition we exclude such manuscripts of the Bible. But some of the manuscripts could, by extension, be taken as borderline cases between biblical manuscripts and the reworked Bible. After all, editorial reworking is reflected in such Qumran texts as 4QpaleoExod$^m$ (published in *DJD* IX), 4QNum$^b$ (to be published in *DJD* XII), and 4QDeut$^n$ (*DJD* XIV), often named pre-Samaritan sources. But the process of editorial reworking in these texts belongs to the development of the biblical text itself.[4] These manuscripts are representatives of the biblical text and should not be considered as separate exegetical works.

The present analysis pertains to a category of compositions of a different type. We are concerned with compositions which stand outside the tradition of the biblical text, though continuing it in a special way. These compositions are based on an accepted form of the Bible. The compositions discussed here provide a running text of one or more biblical books, with additions, omissions, rearrangements, and changes. The exact wording of the biblical text is usually clearly recognizable in these compositions, but sometimes only vaguely. The organizing principle in our analysis is the degree of closeness of the exegetical compositions to the biblical text. Our survey moves from the compositions which are closest to the biblical text to compositions which are furthest removed from it. For this purpose we take the bib-

---

[4] In the pre-Samaritan sources and ɯ the reworking was to a great extent limited to the removal of assumed inconsistencies between the various books of the Pentateuch and within individual stories. Thus several verses from Deuteronomy 1–3 have been added to the parallel texts in the earlier books of the Pentateuch, in order to minimize the differences between Deuteronomy and these earlier books. In other instances sections were duplicated within stories, especially in the story of the plagues in Exodus, adding details concerning the execution of God's commands which were not explicitly reported in the biblical text.

lical text common to 𝔐, 𝔊, 𝔚, and non-aligned Qumran texts as representing what we may call "the biblical text," assuming that the compositions analyzed below were produced exegetically from the textual form common to those texts, or from one of them. These documents were not considered to reflect an authoritative text, although this assumption cannot really be proven. The rewritten biblical texts should be regarded, in a way, as literary exercises.

The two compositions which are closest to the biblical text are 4QRP (4QReworked Pentateuch) and the Temple Scroll (TS). Of these, 4QRP and 4QParaphrase of Gen and Exod are discussed at greater length than the other texts.

*a. 4QRP* presents a running text of the complete Pentateuch, but from time to time it changes the sequence of Pentateuchal pericopes or regroups them according to their content. The most salient characteristic, however, is the addition of exegetical elements, sometimes single words, but often one or two lines, and once as much as seven or eight lines. By the same exegetical principle, here and there words, verses, and even sections are omitted, that is, when according to the author of 4QRP a shorter text would present a more coherent picture. The special character of 4QRP is most clearly visible in quantitative differences, that is, in omissions and additions, since exegetical replacements of elements (that is, changes) are rare. On the surface it seems as if the number of deviations of 4QRP from the biblical text is larger than it is in reality. More specifically, if 𝔐 is taken as the base for the collation and analysis of 4QRP, the latter's deviations from 𝔐 are more numerous than its deviations from the biblical text were in reality. For 4QRP shares many elements with 𝔚 against 𝔐, especially in the so-called harmonizing pluses, and less frequently with 𝔊 against 𝔐. But these elements are not taken into consideration as deviations from the biblical text. They are exponents of the biblical text which happen to differ from 𝔐 while often agreeing with 𝔚. Such harmonizations involve the addition of sections from Deuteronomy in Exodus-Numbers and other additions within certain biblical stories.[5] Since in all these instances 4QRP faithfully reflects its underlying biblical *Vorlage*, these elements do not reflect 4QRP's exegetical character. We discuss the matter further below.

*b. The Temple Scroll* (TS) is in some of its sections closer to 𝔐 than 4QRP, while in others more removed from it.[6] The TS contains large

---

[5] The character of the reworking reflected in 4QRP is described below.

[6] The term Temple Scroll is used for a partially known composition which is represented by three or possibly four different texts, of which 11QT[a] is the main one. Other

sections which provide a running text of Deuteronomy with few differences from 𝔐, e.g., 11QT$^a$ LX 10–LXIV 6, as well as other stretches of text in which the main difference from the canonical text of the Pentateuch is the deviating internal sequence of 11QT$^a$, e.g., LIII 11–14a (Deut 23:22–24), LIII 14b–21 (Num 30:3–6), LIV 1–5a (Num 30:3–14 [different internal sequence]), LIV 5b–21 (Deut 13:1–7), LV 1–14 (Deut 13:13–19), LV 15–21 (Deut 17:2–5), LVI 1–21 (Deut 17:9–18).[7] On the whole, if the differences in sequence are disregarded, these sections are often closer to the biblical text than 4QRP, because of the latter's frequent exegetical additions and omissions. If indeed, as Wise believes, these sections of 11QT$^a$ derived from a separate source preceding TS, among the reworked biblical compositions that source would be the closest to the biblical texts.[8] However, the TS also contains sections which consist of a combination of two or more different Pentateuchal laws pertaining to a specific issue. For example, LII 1–5a combines elements from both Deut 16:22–17:1 and Lev 26:22 with reference to the prohibition of idols, with Deuteronomy serving as the leading text.[9] Furthermore, the TS rewrites the content of the biblical text from time to time, freely condensing the often verbose text of Deuteronomy, and altering some of its ideas, such as LIII 2–8 rephrasing Deut 12:20–28 and 15–19 and XXV 10–12 rephrasing Lev 23:27–29.[10] As a result of rewriting of this type, the TS is actually further removed from the biblical text than 4QRP. The TS provides evidence of all types of rewriting, from slight reworking to extensive paraphrasing, which removes the TS much from the biblical text. Many of the Pentateuchal laws are presented in a completely free fashion. Rather than presenting the corpus of the biblical laws as such, the TS presents an anthology, aiming at less completeness in certain

---

texts include 11QT$^b$ and 11QT$^c$ as well as 4Q365a, representing a nonbiblical text (see the forthcoming publication in *DJD* XIII), but none of these contains biblical segments.

[7] The various biblical texts are linked to each other by principles of associative connection, as if they reflected an exegetical chain of legal prescriptions. See G. Brin, "Concerning Some of the Uses of the Bible in the Temple Scroll," *RevQ* 12 (1987) 519–28.

[8] The view that the TS is composed of this and three additional sources was suggested by M. O. Wise, *A Critical Study of the Temple Scroll from Qumran Cave 11* (Studies in Ancient Oriental Civilization 49; Chicago: The Oriental Institute of the University of Chicago, 1990). The Deuteronomy source is named D by Wise.

[9] In the terminology of Wise, sections such as these also belong to the D source (*Critical Study*, 38).

[10] See E. Tov, "*Deut.* 12 and *11QTemple* LII–LIII: A Contrastive Analysis," *RevQ* 15 (1991) 169–73.

areas and more in others. Some chapters of Deuteronomy are covered rather well by the TS. Accordingly, when comparing the TS with the biblical text, one cannot speak in textual terms of omissions vis-à-vis the biblical text, since only a limited amount of the biblical laws was covered by the TS. At the same time, some areas or chapters were completely disregarded.

Other compositions further removed from the biblical text than the aforementioned 4QRP and the TS not only add and omit details but also change the wording of the biblical text. It is this type of reworking which is named paraphrasing, evidenced in the compositions in different gradations of intensity. In scholarship the term paraphrase is usually employed for extensive exegetical rewriting such as found in some of the Palestinian targumim, mainly Pseudo-Jonathan and the Fragmentary Targumim, and further the two Targumim of Esther. In these targumim it is often hard to recognize the wording of the biblical verse which is being paraphrased. In such cases, only the ideas are somehow recognizable in the Targum. Likewise, in the realm of the LXX, the Greek translations of Daniel and Esther paraphrase their source text to a great extent. In an again different area the rewritten biblical history by Josephus presents another instance of major rewriting. In the realm of the Qumran texts several such pervasive paraphrases are known, especially 1QapGen and the book of Jubilees as preserved in the Qumran fragments from Cave 4. In our analysis, however, we refer only to works which either follow the sequence of the biblical text or rearrange that text in some way. Compositions in which the underlying running Hebrew text is not easily recognizable are not included in this survey. The following survey is preliminary, since most of the compositions are still being prepared for publication. Besides, additional fragments probably ought to be included in this survey.

c. A running rewritten text is found in *4Q252* (*4QpGen*<sup>a</sup>), in spite of its being named a *pesher*.[11] This text probably reflects a middle course between a rewritten biblical text reflected in I–III and a *pesher* found in IV–VI. Those columns, containing segmented biblical texts accompanied by actualizing exegesis, reflect several of the characteristics of the *pesher* technique[12] including one explicit use of the term *pesher* (IV 5, explaining Gen 49:4).[13]

---

[11] Cf. T. Lim, "The Chronology of the Flood Story in a Qumran Text (4Q252)," *JJS* (1992) 288–98; G. J. Brooke, "4Q252: Structure and Themes" (in press).

[12] Actualizing sectarian-exegesis of the biblical text is preserved only once with reference to 49:10, but the lacunae may have contained more instances. On the other

BIBLICAL TEXTS AS REWORKED    117

Cols. I–III of 4Q252 contain a paraphrastic retelling of some of the biblical stories of Genesis between chapters 6 and 49. In this section the biblical text is quoted more or less verbatim, with verses omitted (e.g., the raven's flight in Gen 8:7), and with an added chronological framework for the period from Noah to Abraham. In the section about the flood, this chronology, often altered and expanded, seems to be the main focus of 4Q252.[14]

The paraphrastic rewriting involves many exegetical elements. For example, 4Q252 1 ii 7 contains an explanation of why Noah cursed his grandson Canaan and not his son Ham who, after all, was the one who had sinned (Gen 9:21–24): [ולוא] קלל את חם כי אם בנו כי ברך אל את בני נוח ("and he did not curse Ham but his [the latter's] son, since God had blessed the sons of Noah").

The paraphrased biblical text furthermore contains several minor exegetical changes, e.g.:

Gen 8:9     ותשב אליו ] חז [ ותבוא אליו     4Q252 1 i 15
Gen 8:9     ויסר נוח ] חז [ ויסר     4Q252 1 i 21
Gen 8:12    ומקץ שבעת ימים אחר[י]ם ] חז [ ויחל עוד שבעת ימים אחרים   4Q252 1 i 18
Gen 49:10   ולא יסור שליט משבט יהודה בהיות ] חז [ לא יסור שבט מיהודה לישראל ממשל   4Q252 1 v 1.

d. Similar paraphrastic retelling of the Pentateuchal narratives is found in 4Q225 and 4Q226,[15] named PsJub[a,b], because of the occurrence of the words יובל(ים) in 4Q226, frg. 1 6; 2 2 and שר המשטמה in 4Q225 2 i 9; 2 ii 13,14. The rewriting in these two texts is more pervasive than in the other compositions. While 4Q226 is too fragmentary for any analysis, the character of 4Q225 (PAM 43.251) can be determined better. In the exegetical sections only rarely can a word of the biblical text be recognized, but elsewhere in 4Q225 one finds quotations of sections from the biblical text freely rewritten, such as:

---

hand, it is not impossible that for the author of 4Q252, 49:10, traditionally conceived of as one of the most significant verses of Jacob's blessing, constituted a special case.

[13] At the same time, this word may have ocurred in the lacunae. In spite of the single occurrence of this word, 4Q252 is not a *pesher* such as known from other documents. The word *pesher* is used in 4Q252 as introducing an explanation of the biblical verse, and not as an introduction to its implication for the sect as in the other running *pesharim* on the Prophets and Psalms.

[14] Cf. Lim, "Chronology of the Flood Story," 295–98.

[15] Whether 4Q227 should be considered a text of Jubilees or a so-called Ps-Jubilees text is difficult to determine. See J. T. Milik, *The Books of Enoch: Aramaic Fragments of Qumrân Cave 4* (Oxford: Clarendon, 1976) 12.

ויאמר אברם אדני יהוה מה תתן לי ואנכי הולך ערירי ובן משק ביתי הוא Gen 15:2
דמשק אליעזר, paraphrased as follows in 4Q225 2 i 3:
א[ב̇ר̇הם אל אלוהים אדני הנני בא ע[רי]ר̇י ואלי[עזר.
הבט נא השמימה וספר הכוכבים אם תוכל לספר אתם Gen 15:5, paraphrased
in 2 i 5–6: שא צפא את הכוכבים וראה [ ] [הח̇כ̇ול אשר̇ על שפת
הים ואת עפר הארץ.
קח נא את בנך את יחידך אשר אהבת את יצחק Gen 22:2, paraphrased as follows in 2 i 11: קח את בנכה את ישחק את יחיד[כה.
Likewise, 2 i 12 = Gen 22:2 and 2 ii 9 = Gen 22:11.

e. 4Q464 (4QExposition on the Patriarchs), recently published by Stone and Eshel,[16] paraphrases various sections of Genesis, but because of its fragmentary nature little can be said about its character. Sometimes its underlying biblical text is clearly recognizable:
4Q464 3 ii 3–4 possibly reproduces Gen 15:13 without change:
כאשר אמר לאברה[ם ידוע תדע כי גר יהיה זרעכה בארץ לוא להמה]
ועבדום וענו̇ [אותם ארבע מאות שנה
Note the following slight change:
ויעלהו לעלה תחת בנו Gen 22:13 — [עשהו עולה]̇ 4 6 4Q464

f. Various documents are named "pseudo-", such as psEzek and psMoses, while the names of others consist of the word "apocryphon" and a second component, such as ApocrJer. To the best of my knowledge, most of these compositions do not actually present running biblical texts, although they reflect many words from their biblical counterparts. An exception should be made for some fragments of psEzek. However, an analysis of the type of paraphrase in the various fragments of 4QpsEzek can be embarked on only after the publication of these fragments by D. Dimant.[17]

The preliminary publication of 4Q385, frg. 24 presents a paraphrase of the first verses of Ezekiel 30. Note the following exegetical changes: יום אבדן גוים (line 2) for יהיה עת גוים (Ezek 30:3); יפולו בשער מצרים in line 5 for Ezek 30:4 בנפל חלל במצרים. For a different sequence, compare line 3 with Ezek 30:4.

---

[16] M. E. Stone and E. Eshel, "An Exposition on the Patriarchs (4Q464) and Two Other Documents (4Q464ᵃ and 4Q464ᵇ)," Le Muséon 105 (1992) 243–64.

[17] In the meantime, see D. Dimant, "New Light from Qumran on the Jewish Pseudepigrapha — 4Q390," The Madrid Qumran Congress: Proceedings of the International Congress on the Dead Sea Scrolls, Madrid 18–21 March, 1991 (2 vols.; ed. J. Trebolle Barrera and L. Vegas Montaner; STDJ 11; Leiden: Brill; Madrid: Editorial Complutense, 1992) 2.405–48; D. Dimant and J. Strugnell, "4QSecond Ezekiel," RevQ 13 (1985) 45–58; D. Dimant and J. Strugnell, "The Merkabah Vision in Second Ezekiel (4Q385 4)," RevQ 14 (1990) 331–48; D. Dimant, "From Prophecy to Pseudo-Prophecy: Ezekiel and Pseudo-Ezekiel at Qumran" (in press).

A condensed form of Ezek 37:4–9 is found in frg. 2 lines 5–9 of the same text, 4Q385.[18] That condensed text leaves out whole verses (vv. 5–7a as well as segments of verses, such as the omission of ובשר עלה in Ezek 37:8), adds details (compare lines 5–6 עצם אל [אל פרקו] עצמו ופרק with Ezek 37:7 עצם אל עצמו), and changes details (see ויעלו עליהם in line 6 compared with והנה עליהם in Ezek 37:8).

A similar paraphrase of the merkabah vision of Ezekiel 1 is reflected in a shortened version of that chapter in 4Q385, frg. 4. That fragment more or less follows the sequence of the biblical text, with omissions, some exegetical changes, and with a few changes in sequence, analyzed by Dimant and Strugnell.[19]

g. 2QExod[b] probably represents a rewritten Pentateuch text, although it is usually considered a biblical text. The remains of this text are fragmentary, but there are several indications of its not being a regular biblical manuscript. It contains several deviations from the biblical text (Exod 22:2, 15; 27:17, 18), all of them involving a longer text not preserved elsewhere. Especially interesting is frg. 8 of 2QExod[b], in which before Exod 34:10 two lines are found which are not known from the context in any of the textual witnesses. The first line reads ]ם ויגד מושה[, and the second line is not inscribed. In *DJD* III M. Baillet tentatively explained these two lines as representing Exod 19:9. It is, however, more likely that this fragment represents a nonbiblical addition before 34:10 similar to the additions in 4QRP to be discussed below. This solution comes close to Baillet's naming this text a possible *florilège*.[20] The fact that 2QExod[b] writes the tetragrammaton in the paleo-Hebrew and not the square script is a further argument in favor of the assumption that it does not represent a regular biblical text since this practice of writing the tetragrammaton is known only for nonbiblical texts with the exception of 2QExod[b] and 4QIsa[c].[21]

h. Some fragments of 4Q382 are, according to the unpublished manuscript of S. Olyan of his *DJD* edition "a part of a work recasting or quoting from the Elijah–Elisha stories in 1 and 2 Kings" (4Qpap paraKings et al., previously named papTehilot Ha'avot). The text of this composition is too fragmentary for comment.

---

[18] Dimant and Strugnell, "4QSecond Ezekiel."

[19] Dimant and Strugnell, "Merkabah Vision."

[20] M. Baillet, J. T. Milik, and R. de Vaux, *Les 'petites grottes' de Qumrân* (DJD 3; Oxford: Clarendon, 1962) 55.

[21] For a list of these texts, see E. Tov, *Textual Criticism of the Hebrew Bible* (Minneapolis: Fortress; Assen/Maastricht: Van Gorcum, 1992) 220.

*i*. A paraphrase of a special type is found in 4Q422 (4QParaGen–Exod, previously named 4QTraditions on Genesis), which is composed of fragments referring to both Genesis and Exodus and is to be published by the present author and T. Elgvin.[22] Both sections derived from one composition written by the same hand and deriving from the same scroll (cf. the similar shape of the fragments). Whether this composition covered much or most of the books of Genesis and Exodus is not known. One of the special features of this rewritten Bible text in the pericope of the ten plagues is its adherence both to the text of Exodus and to that of two historical psalms.

In the section of Exodus, frg. 9 first mentions briefly several events leading up to the description of the plagues: the two midwives, the secret arts of the sorcerers, the throwing of children into the Nile (?), the sending of Moses to the people, the appearance of God (in the burning bush?), the sending of Moses and Aaron to Pharaoh, and the hardening of Pharaoh's heart. Afterwards 4Q422 describes the plagues in detail, beginning with the plague of the blood.

The basic sequence of the plagues is that of Exodus as distinct from Psalms 78 and 105. Missing from the list is the plague of the boils, unless ל[ ]צ in line 9 refers to that plague. In that case the boils would pertain only to the cattle, while in Exod 9:10 they pertain to both humans and cattle. Note that this plague is the only one which is not mentioned in Psalm 105, and one of the four plagues not mentioned in Psalm 78. Also in the sequence of the last four plagues one notes the following divergence from the account in Exodus:

|           | Exodus | 4Q422 |
|-----------|--------|-------|
| blood     | 1      | 1     |
| frogs     | 2      | 2     |
| lice      | 3      | 3     |
| gnats (?) | 4      | 4     |
| pest      | 5      | 5     |
| boils     | 6      | 6?    |
| hail      | 7      | 8     |
| locusts   | 8      | 9     |
| darkness  | 9      | 7     |
| firstborn | 10     | 10    |

[22] "A Paraphrase of Exodus: 4Q422," *Biblical, Epigraphic, and Semitic Studies* (*Festschrift* Jonas Greenfeld, in press).

In the description of the last four plagues, that of the hail is mentioned before the plagues of the locusts and darkness. In this, the sequence of 4Q422 is identical with Psalm 105 where the last plagues are mentioned in the following sequence: hail (vv. 32, 33), locust (34, 35), death of firstborn (36).

The account of 4Q422 moves quickly from one event to the next, indicating each episode with a few words, pausing only at the description of the plagues, and describing each plague separately. It is not impossible that the episode of the plagues formed the main topic of the Exodus section of 4Q422.

The description of the plagues is structured in a poetical parallellistic form, similar to that of Psalms 78 and 105. Within that description 4Q422 elaborates on the biblical text with synonymously parallel phrases. Not all details are clear. After the plague of the blood, three distichs follow in which respectively two, one, and one or two plagues are mentioned. These three distichs are followed by three tristichs describing one plague each: darkness, hail, and locust. Within these tristichs the first two stichs describe the plague in synonymous words, and the third one describes an additonal feature.

ויופך לדמ[ מימ]יהֹמֹה
הצֿ[ ר]דעים בכול ארצֿ[ם ?]    וכנים בכול גבול[ם
[ער]וב [בב]תיהמה    ו[יפג]ע בכול פֿ[ן ]המה
ויגוף בדב[ר את/כול] מקניהמה   ובהמתם ל[ ]צ הסניר
יש[י]ח חו[שכ בארצֿם   ואפלה ב[בתי]המה   בלירא[ה] איש את אחיד[ו
ויך] בברד ארצם       ואדמת[ם ב]חנמל    לה[אביד את ]פרי אוֹצם
ויבא ארבֿה לכסות עין ה[אֹ]רץ]   חסל כבד בכול גבולם   לאכול כול ירוק בא[רצם

In this section the wording of 4Q422 depends in the first place on the historical Psalm 78, secondly on Psalm 105, and thirdly on the account in Exodus.

In the description of the plagues, as elsewhere in this composition, the actions of God are described in short sentences with God as the subject of the verb just like the historical psalms, but unlike the Exodus account. Third person verbal forms are rarely found in the Exodus narrative (see, however, ויהפך יהוה רוח ים חזק מאד in Exod 10:19). In that account situations rather than actions are depicted. On the other hand, in 4Q422 one finds: line 7 ויופך, line 8 ויגוף, line 9 הסניר, line 9 ישי[ח, line 10 ויבא, as well as a few reconstructed verbs.

The biblical text underlying 4Q422 is clearly recognizable, not only in its reliance on certain words, but also in its dependence on the structure of the historical psalms. See the following phrases:

Line 7 ויהפך לדם] מימ[יה

cf. Ps 105:29 ויהפך את מימיהם לדם and Ps 78:44 ויהפך לדם יאריהם, and secondarily also Exod 7:20 ויהפכו כל המים אשר ביאר לדם.

Line 8 הצ̇פ̇רדעים בכול ארצ̇[ם]

cf. Ps 105:30 שרץ ארצם צפרדעים and Exod 8:1 הצפרדעים בארץ מצרים (cf. also 8:2, 3).

Line 8 וכנים בכול גבול[ם

cf. Ps 105:31 אמר ויבא ערב כנים בכל גבולם.

Line 8 ערוב [בב]תיהםה

cf. Exod 8:17 ומלאו בתי מצרים את הערב and Ps 78:45 ישלח בהם ערב.

Line 9 ישי[ת חו]שך בארצם ואפלה ב[בתי]הםה

cf. Exod 10:22 ויהי חשך אפלה בכל ארץ מצרים שלשת ימים. The pair of juxtaposed and synonymous nouns is broken down in 4Q422 into two parallel stichs in accordance with the "break-up pattern."[23]

Line 9 בלירא[ה] איש את אחיד[ו

cf. Exod 10:23 לוא ראו איש את אחיו.

Lines 9–10 וי[ך] בברד ארצם ואדמת[ם ב]חנמל

cf. Ps 78:47 for a similar pattern of parallelism and for similar phrases: יהרג בברד גפנם ושקמותם בחנמל. Note that חנמל does not occur in the account of either Exodus or Psalm 105.

Line 10 ויבא ארבה̇ לכסות עין הא̇[רץ] חסל כבד בכו̇ל̇ גבולם

cf. Exod 10:5 וכסה את עין הארץ; cf. Ps 78:46 for a similar pattern of parallelism: ויתן לחסיל יבולם ויגיעם לארבה.

The text contains a few examples of added exegetical elements in small details, but the main exegetical dimension of the text is its swift moving from one episode to the next, which can be recognized in spite of the fragmentary nature of lines 1–6.

j. 4QpaleoParaJosh (4Q123), recently published in *DJD* IX,[24] possibly contains a paraphrase, about which little is known from the preserved fragments; at the same time, this text could also reflect a deviating biblical manuscript.

We now turn to a detailed analysis of one of the rewritten texts.

---

[23] Cf. E. Z. Melamed, "Break-up of Syereotype Phrases as an Artistic Devise in Biblical Poetry," *Scripta Hierosolymitana* 8 (1961) 115–53.

[24] P. W. Skehan, E. Ulrich, and J. E. Sanderson, *Qumran Cave 4 IV: Palaeo-Hebrew and Greek Biblical Manuscripts* (DJD 9; Oxford: Clarendon, 1992) 201–03.

## B. 4QRP

Within the framework of the hitherto published analyses of biblical exegesis at Qumran, little attention has been given to 4QReworked Pentateuch. In a way this is not surprising, since most of the fragments are still unpublished.[25] On the other hand, 4Q158, probably belonging to the same composition as 4Q364–367 (see below), and certainly belonging to the same literary genre, had been published long ago. But, published in 1968 by John Allegro as "Biblical Paraphrase,"[26] 4Q158 remained enigmatic especially because of the unusual sequence of its biblical text.[27] The enigma of the sequence of several fragments, however, was soon solved, when the similarities between 4Q158 and ωι were recognized.[28] It was therefore assumed that 4Q158 was based on an early text similar to and dating before the time of ωι. The sequence of the elements in that early text, like ωι, differed in details from 𝔐; hence the different sequence of some details in 4Q158. In other details, however, the internal sequence of texts in 4Q158 was arranged by the author of 4Q158 himself: frgs. 1–2: Gen 32:25–32, Exod 4:27–28; frg. 4: Exod 3:12 (?), 24:4–6. In addition to these unusual sequences, in both of these fragments exegetical elements were added in the text between the biblical texts, but because of their fragmentary status, their nature is not clear (see below). A large exegetical addition is found in frg. 14. The nature of that fragment is also not clear.

Little mention has been made of 4Q158 in research. The *editio princeps* by Allegro was improved by J. Strugnell,[29] but as far as I know, the text was mentioned as a special literary genre worth noting only in an article by Vermes.[30]

We now know, however, that 4Q158 does not stand alone. It forms part of a much larger group of fragments. Together with Sidnie

---

[25] The existence of 4Q364–367 was known from various lists, but segments of it as well as descriptions have been published only recently by E. Tov and S. White, "4Q364 & 365: A Preliminary Report," *The Madrid Qumran Congress*, 1.217–28.

[26] J. Allegro, *Qumrân Cave 4 I (4Q158–4Q186)* (DJD 5; Oxford: Clarendon, 1968) 1–6.

[27] According to the sequence of 𝔐: Exod 20:19–22; Deut 5:28–29, 18:18–22; Exod 20:12, 16, 17; Deut 5:30, 31; Exod 20:22–26.

[28] Cf. J. Strugnell, "Notes en marge du Volume V des *Discoveries in the Judaean Desert of Jordan*," *RevQ* 7 (1970) 172.

[29] Strugnell, "Notes en Marge," 168–75.

[30] Vermes, "Bible Interpretation at Qumran."

White, and on the basis of earlier identifications, transcriptions, and a draft of a commentary by John Strugnell, I am involved in the publication of four groups of fragments which are closely related to 4Q158, viz., 4Q364-367. In my view all these texts are part of the same composition. That work is now named 4QRP or 4QReworked Pentateuch, though formerly it was designated 4QPP or 4QPentateuchal Para-phrase.[31]

The reason for this change in terminology from 4QPP to 4QRP is the implication of the term "paraphrase." The work under consideration is not what we usually understand to be a paraphrase. That term should probably be reserved for large-scale exegetical deviations. In our view, the amount of rewriting extant in 4QRP is much smaller than in the compositions mentioned above, and therefore the name "paraphrase" is not appropriate for this composition. A general term like "Reworked Pentateuch" better describes the composition contained in 4Q158 (4QRP$^a$) and 4Q364-367 (4QRP$^{b,c,d,e}$).

## 1. Contents

The best preserved groups of fragments representing 4QRP are found in 4Q364 and 4Q365. The first fragment of 4Q364 starts with Genesis 2, and the next fragments cover the second part of that book (chapters 25-48). In Exodus 4Q364 covers chapters 19-26. Leviticus is not represented in this manuscript. In Numbers it contains isolated fragments of chapters 14 and 33, while in Deuteronomy it is represented by many fragments of chapters 1-14.

4Q365 contains a single fragment of Genesis 21 and many fragments of Exodus 8-39, Leviticus 11-26, Numbers 1-36, as well as two fragments of Deuteronomy (chapters 2 and 19). The coverage of 4Q365 is thus wider than that of 4Q364.

4Q366 contains merely one fragment of Exodus (chapters 21-22) as well as fragments of Numbers 29 and of Deuteronomy 14 and 16.

4Q367 contains only fragments of Leviticus (chapters 12-27).

4Q158 contains fragments of Genesis and Exodus, including fragments which in ₥ are included in Deuteronomy (for a list of contents, see above).

---

[31] Although Allegro named 4Q158, which probably reflects the same composition as 4Q364-367, "Biblical Paraphrase," it is now realized that that name is not appropriate.

Most of the fragments of 4QRP also contain exegetical pluses. **4Q365a**, though written by the scribe who wrote 4Q365, probably belongs to a different composition, parallel to 11QT$^a$.

## 2. *Internal Overlaps between the Fragments of 4Q364–367*

The fragments of 4Q364–367 belong to what once were four different scrolls, supposedly representing different copies of 4QRP. Since they cover a considerable amount of text, some overlaps would be expected. However, only two such overlaps have been noticed.[32]

The paucity of overlaps between 4Q364, 4Q365, 4Q366, and 4Q367 is probably mere coincidence. In any event, there are sufficient arguments against the assumption that some or all four manuscripts belonged to the same scroll.[33]

To the mentioned overlaps we should add the overlaps between 4Q364 and 4Q366 on the one hand and 4Q158 on the other.[34]

## 3. *The Relation between 4Q364–367 and 4Q158*

The main argument for ascribing 4Q158 to the same composition as 4Q364–367 is that they reflect the same features, which are described here from the angle of 4Q158:

a. 4Q158 contains running biblical texts interlaced with exegetical comments of 1–2 lines. In frg. 14, 4Q158 contains a large exegetical addition, but it is not certain that this fragment, written in the same handwriting as the remainder of 4Q158, belongs to that manuscript since it contains no running biblical text.

b. The biblical texts are presented in a sequence—not always understandable—which differs from the other witnesses. Note especially the sequences Gen 32:25–32, Exod 4:27–28; Exod 3:12, 24:4–6 in 4Q158.

c. 4Q158, like 4Q364, reflects the text of ɯ in its major harmonizing features visible in the deviating sequence of the biblical passages in 4Q158, frgs. 6–8 as well as in small details in other fragments. Thus

---

[32] See the discussion in E. Tov, "The Textual Status of 4Q364–367 (4QPP)," *The Madrid Qumran Congress*, 1.43–82.

[33] For details see Tov, "Textual Status of 4Q364–367."

[34] See Tov, "Textual Status of 4Q364–367."

4Q158, like m,[35] interweaves into the description of the Mount Sinai theophany in Exodus 20 sections from the parallel account in Deut 5:28–31. Likewise, it integrates into this pericope the divine command (Deut 18:18–22) to establish a prophet like Moses.

The evidence thus points to one composition, 4QRP, reflected by both 4Q158 and 4Q364–367. Only in a few fragments have actual overlaps been preserved, so that their common base cannot be proven beyond doubt. In one of the two fragments in which 4Q158 and 4Q364 overlap (4Q364 5 ii = 4Q158 1) they agree in three details against m, the third of which is a unique reading.[36]

## 4. Reconstruction of the Complete Composition of 4QRP

The reconstruction of the content and length of 4QRP remains a matter of speculation. The two large manuscripts, 4Q364 and 4Q365, contain both narrative and legal material. Sections from Genesis to Deuteronomy are included, not in one single scroll, but in the two texts together. One fragment of 4Q365 26 a–b actually preserves the transition from Leviticus to Numbers (Lev 27:34, Num 1:1–5). Of one single scroll, 4Q364, sections have been preserved of Genesis, Exodus, Numbers and Deuteronomy, and there is no reason to assume that Leviticus would have been excluded from that scroll. The other texts would probably also have included all of the Pentateuch. It thus stands to reason that 4QRP would have been a rather long text, longer than any preserved text from the Judean Desert.

It is questionable whether we can say anything more precise on the length of the complete scroll. On the basis of the extant material, H. Stegemann surmised in 1984 that 4Q365 comprised 25 meters.[37] He reached this conclusion by comparing the relation between known fragments of the scroll and the number of pages in *BHS*. This method allowed him to take into consideration the amount of deviation in length between the known sections of the scroll and the parallel sections of m as in *BHS*. If we assume that these differences between the two, mainly quantitative, are well represented by the preserved frag-

---

[35] The two are not identical, it should be noted. The differences have been described in E. Tov, "The Nature and Background of Harmonizations in Biblical Manuscripts," *JSOT* 31 (1985) 3–29 (see esp. n. 44).

[36] For details, see Tov, "Textual Status of 4Q364–367."

[37] See Stegemann's unpublished report on 4Q364–367 (August 1984).

ments we possess a solid basis for calculating the length of the whole scroll. On the other hand, if in certain sections of the Pentateuch, 4QRP would have been either much longer or much shorter than 𝔐, we must admit that any reconstruction of the length of the complete text is mere speculation. The preserved fragments make it likely that the margin of error would not have exceeded 10%. Taking Stegemann's calculation of 25 meters as point of departure, the length of the complete composition may thus be calculated as between 22 and 27 meters.

## 5. *Character of 4QRP*

The five manuscripts of 4QRP share important characteristics. These five groups of fragments should therefore be considered as reflecting the same composition, rather than, in general terms, the same literary genre. This composition contained a running text of the Pentateuch with exegetical additions and omissions. The greater part of the preserved fragments follows the biblical text closely, but many small exegetical elements have been added, while other elements have been omitted, and in other cases the sequence was altered. The exegetical character of this composition is especially evident from several exegetical pluses comprising half a line, a line, two lines, and even seven or eight lines. The most clear-cut example of this technique is found in the expanded "Song of Miriam" in 4Q365 6a ii and c and 4Q158 14. I have recently offered a detailed description of the exegetical character of 4QRP, with special attention to various types of exegetical elements in 4QRP in their relation to 𝔐.[38]

The *sequence* of the individual fragments of 4QRP cannot be reconstructed. In one instance a fragment juxtaposing a section from Numbers and Deuteronomy (4Q364 23a–b i: Num 20:17–18, Deut 2:8–14) probably derives from the rewritten text of Deuteronomy since a similar sequence is found in 𝔲. In the case of juxtaposed laws on a common topic (Sukkot) in 4Q366 4 i (Num 29:32–30:1; Deut 16:13–14) one does not know where in 4QRP this fragment would have been located. In our edition this fragment is placed as if occurring in Numbers.

We will now attempt to describe some of the principles behind the exegesis embedded in 4QRP. As a rule the biblical text which the author of 4QRP had in front of him was not changed by him, but from

---

[38] Tov, "Textual Status of 4Q364–367."

time to time he added or omitted minor or major details. In addition, 4QRP sometimes reflects a different textual base, often close to ⅏. Since some deviations of 4QRP from 𝔐 derive from the author's exegesis, and others from a different textual base, it is often difficult to decide to which factor a deviation should be assigned. The majority of the deviations should probably be ascribed to the author's exegesis, rather than to textual differences found in the author's source.

## i. *Topical Arrangement of the Constituting Elements of 4QRP*

4QRP rearranged some of the material, and when doing so it only seemingly omitted material intervening between the two or more pericopes which are now juxtaposed. Hence these are no real omissions.

1. The clearest proof of the technique of rearranging comes from the juxtaposition of two of the Sukkot laws in 4Q366 4 i (Num 29:32–30:1; Deut 16:13–14). This fragment juxtaposes the special sacrifices offered on the feast of Sukkot as described in Numbers 29 (only the last verses have been preserved: 29:32–39 and the summarizing verse 30:1) and in the brief laws of Deut 16:13–14 (probably including v. 15 as well). In the original text of 4QRP this fragment may have been followed by another text on Sukkot, now contained in the parallel manuscript 4Q365 23 (Lev 23:42–24:2, followed by a large nonbiblical addition). It is not known at which place in the original composition this fragment was located, in Numbers, Deuteronomy, or elsewhere.

2. A similar case of juxtaposing laws dealing with the same topic pertains to the narrative and laws about the daughters of Zelophehad. 4Q365 36 (Num 27:11; 36:1–2) combines these two texts referring to the daughters of Zelophehad. 4QRP probably started this pericope with Num 27:1, but presently only the last verse of this section has been preserved, viz., 27:11, followed by 36:1–2 (the complete text would have included the next verses as well). The modern researcher would probably consider chapter 36 a supplement to chapter 27, possibly by a later hand, dealing with the same issue. It is therefore understandable that 4QRP juxtaposed these texts. The two segments were considered so closely connected by the scribe of 4Q365 that no paragraph break was left between the two segments, as this scribe did so often elsewhere.[39]

---

[39] 4QNum$^b$ likewise fused the two chapters, though in a different way, with the contents of chapter 27. See 4QNum$^b$ frg. 36, as reconstructed by N. Jastram in *DJD* XII.

3. The first three lines of 4Q365 28 (Num 4:47–49) present the end of chapter 4 of Numbers (the last verses of the chapter, pertaining to the census of the Levites), followed by a blank line and the first verse of chapter 7 ("On the day when Moses had finished setting up the Tabernacle . . ."). The miscellaneous laws coming between these sections in m (about lepers, adultery, etc. in chap. 5 and Nazirites in chap. 6) have been left out, in this context, probably as irrelevant to the topic, which may be defined as the temple service.

No rearrangement is visible in the fragments covering the chapters dealing with the building of the tabernacle in the second part of Exodus (4Q365 8–13 covering chapters 28 until 39). Furthermore, two separate fragments have been preserved which present parallel segments that have not been combined into one account: 4Q365 15ab (Lev 11:17–[25]) 4Q366 5 (Deut 14:14–21), providing parallel sections of the list of unclean animals. As a consequence, it is not known whether this technique of rearrangement was used for all or most laws dealing with similar or identical topics.

Sometimes an *associative* thought may be discovered behind the linking together of different sections.

4. 4Q366 2 (Lev 24:20–22 [?]; 25:39–43) adduces immediately after the end of the *lex talionis* (preserved are Lev 24:20–22) the text of Lev 25:39–43 referring to the freeing of slaves. The juxtaposition of Lev 24:20–22 (?) and Lev 25:39–43 is probably instigated by the phrase "one law for the sojourner (גר) and native" in 24:22 and the sale of the Hebrews who are to be treated as a sojourner (תושב) in 25:40. Likewise, note that these two laws are juxtaposed in Exod 21:24–25, 26–27.

5. Several chapters of Leviticus are left out in 4Q367 2 between Lev 15:14–15 and 19:1–4, 9–15. The identification of the text adduced in these fragments is not without problems,[40] but beyond these problems the internal sequence of the components of the text remains difficult to understand. The sequence 19:1–4, 9–15 is understandable on the assumption that 19:5–8, dealing with the sacrifice of wellbeing was left out in this context, possibly since it was adduced elsewhere. The phrase "I am the Lord" occurring in both sections, in 19:4 (lines 6–7 in 4Q367) and 19:12 (line 11) may have formed the associative link between the two sections. More difficult is the sequence 15:14–15, 19:1–4 since much intervening material has been left out and the connection between the two sections is not easily understandable.

---

[40] The first two lines of the fragment could also be identified as 15:29–30, but that suggestion is less likely since these verses do not appear at the end of a section, while 15:14–15 do.

The material occurring between 15:14–15 and 19:1–4 has not been omitted, but was adduced elsewhere, since Lev 18:25–29 occurs in frg. 22 of 4Q365.

6. 4Q367 3 (? + Lev 20:13; 27:30–34). For the possible background of the juxtaposition of Lev 20:13 and Lev 27:30–34, cf. מות יומת in both 20:13 (lines 4–5) and in the verse preceding the verse to be quoted on the next line, that is Lev 27:29.

## ii. Exegetical Omissions

A topical arrangement is also visible in the next cases, but it would be better to describe them as exegetical omissions. Note that the first two instances occur in adjacent lines.

1. 4Q364 19a–b 7 (Num 33:38) מִצְרִים [ + החמישי בחדש לחדש באחד 𝔐 𝔰 𝔊 (τῷ μηνὶ τῷ πέμπτῳ μιᾷ τοῦ μηνός). Probably 4Q364 represents an exegetical shortening of the text omitting the date of Aaron's death.[41]

2. 4Q364 19 8 (Num 33:40) > 𝔊$^b$ ] habent 𝔐 𝔰 𝔊. Note the ס in 𝔐 after v. 39. 4Q364 omits v. 40: "And the Canaanite, the king of Arad, who dwelt in the Negeb in the land of Canaan, heard of the coming of the people of Israel" (RSV). This verse (almost identical with Num 21:1) contains a historical note found between two itineraries, and it has no apparent connection with the adjacent verses. This verse is likewise lacking in manuscript group b of 𝔊, usually identified with the Lucianic recension. The omission in this manuscript group of 𝔊 may have resulted from homoioteleuton. Such an assumption is less likely for the Hebrew text which was probably shortened exegetically.

3. 4Q365 12b iii 7 (Exod 39:5) $^{שה}$[מו{ת}] + השהם מסבת ויעשו את אבני$^6$ משבצת זהב מפתחת פתוחי חותם על שמות בני ישראל$^7$ וישם [וישמו 𝔰] אתם על כתפת האפד אבני זכרון לבני ישראל כאשר צוה ה' את משה 𝔐 𝔰 (with orthographic variants) 𝔊 (with minor differences). 4Q365 probably shortened the text, although homoioteleuton cannot be ruled out.

---

[41] The exact date of Aaron's death in 𝔐 𝔰 𝔊 is not parallelled by traditions about Moses and Miriam, so that it is remotely possible that 4Q364 reflects an ancient textual tradition in which Aaron's death was not mentioned.

## iii. Exegetical Additions

The following list mentions exegetical additions of 4QRP when its evidence differs from the other textual witnesses. Excluded from this list are instances of major exegetical expansions in which 4QRP agrees with ₥, since in those cases the common text of 4QRP ₥ presumably was based on a deviating biblical text. Because of the fragmentary preservation of 4QRP it is hard to know under which conditions such expansions are added (in some instances the expansion provides the actual text of a song or blessing mentioned in the context).

1. The largest addition preserved in 4QRP is a hitherto unknown poetical composition, preserved in part, following the Song at the Sea (Song of Moses) in Exodus 15 in 4Q365 6a ii and 6c.[42] The added poem in 4QRP repeats some of the elements found in the Song at the Sea, viz., the root גאה in lines 2 and 7 (cf. Exod 15:1,7) and במים אדירים, "in majestic waters" in line 5 (cf. 15:10). Most likely the unknown poem contained the "Song of Miriam," the nature of which is not clear in ₥. For in ₥ Miriam's song consists of one line only, viz., a repetition of the first line of the Song of Moses with one small alteration (Exod 15:1). The additional poem in 4Q365 was probably meant to provide the full text of that song since it immediately precedes 15:22, the verse after Miriam's song. It may have been the intention of the biblical text that Miriam repeated Moses's Song to the women. It is, however, understandable that an exegetical tradition developed which repeated Miriam's Song based on the contents of Moses' Song. The only such attempt known is 4QRP.

2. 4Q158 1-2 (Gen 32:25-32 + add., Exod 4:27-28). Gen 32:25-32 reports Jacob's encounter with the angel and the latter's blessing of Jacob. 4Q158 contains a direct quote from the biblical text, followed by three lines of exegetical expansion (lines 7-10)—the expansion probably contained the contents of the angel's blessing.

The connection between this pericope and the next section in 4Q158, Exod 4:27-28 (the story of the signs) is not clear, but it may be related to the meeting of Zippora and the angel in Exod 4:24-26, the section immediately preceding the lines quoted in 4Q158. On the basis of earlier statements by Rashbam *ad loc.*, and without referring to

---

[42] See S. White, "4Q364 & 365."

4Q158, M. Greenberg makes a connection between the two pericopes in question.[43]

3. Before the biblical text of 4Q364 3 ii 7–8 (Gen 28:6), 4QRP added at least 6 lines of text not known from other sources. This exegetical addition expanding the biblical story seems to contain material relating to Rebecca's address to the departing Jacob (line 3: מותכה) and Isaac's consolation of her. It can be partly supplemented in line 3 by the biblical phrase למה אשכל גם שניכם found in Gen 27:45 and especially by parallel matter in *Jub.* 27:14: "The spirit of Rebecca was grieved after Jacob her son" (cf. lines 5–6 in 4Q364); *Jub.* 27:17 "and we see him in peace" (cf. line 2 in 4Q364). The fragmentary addition may be translated as follows:

> [1] *him you* shall see [. . . . . . .] /[2] *you* shall see in peace [. . . . . . ] /[3] *your* death, and to *your* eyes [. . . . . . *lest I be deprived of even*] /[4] *the two of you. And Isaac* called [to Rebecca his wife . . . . and he told] /[5] her all these wor[ds. . .] /[6] after Jacob her son [and she cried. . .] /[7] And Esau saw that [. . . .]

4. 4Q364 14 1–2 places before Exod 24:12 not the text of v. 11 (𝔐 𝔖 𝔊) but at least two words from Exod 19:17, בתחתית ההר [ויתיצבו] (𝔐 𝔖 𝔊). It is not clear whether a larger segment of chapter 19 was included, because in line 1 the initial ש] (an ע is not possible) cannot be fitted into 19:16 or 17 at a convenient length before בתחתית ההר. The most likely explanation of the evidence is that the fragment does not present a sequence of Exod 19:17 and 24:12, but constitutes a freely rewritten text using elements of 19:17 before 24:12. In many ways Exodus 19 and 24 present parallel versions of the Mount Sinai episode, so that this fragment probably reflects a version in which elements from both chapters have been combined. The exact combination of the elements in this fragment is, in a way, more logical than the sequence of events in Exodus itself: the people took their places at the foot of the mountain (line 2 = Exod 19:17) and Moses is told to ascend the mountain (lines 3–6 = Exod 24:12ff). Exod 24:1–11 contains a parallel account which was excluded from the rewritten version.

---

[43] M. Greenberg, *Understanding Exodus* (New York, 1969) 111. In Greenberg's words:

> If a common denominator is to be sought for the two stories it is that the attack came at a moment fraught with susceptibility to harm—at night (the season of danger) on persons journeying toward danger—and that it was warded off, but at the cost to the survivors. . . .

5. The two lines of additional text after Exod 24:18 (4Q364 15 3–4) may have described what God showed Moses during the 40 days and 40 nights before His speech (chap. 25) at the end of that period. A similarly-dated revelation to Moses is recorded in *Jub.* 1:4ff. The relation between the two texts cannot be determined.

6. 4Q158 14 provides an unknown exegetical addition or commentary mentioning "Egypt," "I shall redeem them," and "the midst of the sea in the depths." This fragment, written in the same hand as the remainder of 4Q158, would reflect a rather long addition, relating to the story of Exodus.

## iv. Different Sequence

The internal sequence of the tribes in the list of the explorers in 4Q365 differs from that of the other sources. 4Q365 32 1–2 has the order Num 13:12,14,15,13,16 ] vv. 12–16 4QNum$^b$ 𝔐 𝔪 𝔊. In other words 4Q365 has the sequence: Dan (12), Naphtali (14), Gad (15), Asher (13), while other sources have the sequence: Dan (12), Asher (13), Naphtali (14), Gad (15).

The sequence of 4Q365 may well represent an early tradition, as it is also found in Exod 1:4. Note further that in Deut 33:20ff. Asher appears at the end of the list of tribes, as in 4Q365.[44]

## C. Concluding Remarks

The aforementioned texts have been discussed together as one coherent group, since all of them rework or rephrase the biblical text in some way or other. At the same time, different literary structures are involved. In our analysis a distinction was made between rewritten texts, involving mainly exegetical additions, omissions, and reordering of sections, and rephrased texts also changing the wording of the Bible itself. Furthermore, we find a large range of literary possibilities. The TS contains rewritten biblical texts as well as thematically arranged sections. 4QpGen$^a$ contains a mixture between a rewritten running text and a *pesher*. A text like 4QRP is actually very close to the biblical text itself. 4Q422 rewrites the story of Exodus in the style of a historical psalm (like Psalms 78 and 105). Because of

---

[44] For other sequences of the tribes, see Gen 49:16ff.; Num 1:12ff., 1:24ff., 2:14ff.; Deut 27:13; Josh 19:24ff.; Ezekiel 48.

these differences one wonders to what extent it is justifiable to discuss the texts mentioned above as one coherent literary genre. Indeed most of the texts are *sui generis*.

Because of its central place, the Bible gave much opportunity for rewriting and rephrasing in many more ways than described in this survey, not only in Hebrew, but also in the targumim, Greek translations, and in rabbinic literature. The rewritten biblical text should in a way be regarded as a literary exercise. The *Sitz im Leben* of these texts is not known, partly because of the fragmentary nature of the texts preserved. The TS was written in the first person, so that it was probably meant to create the impression of a more authentic form of the Torah than the traditional text. This rewritten Torah may have had an official status next to the other Torah. There is no indication that the other works had any such official status. All the compositions treated here probably were isolated literary documents, possibly created in different environments. Some of them may have been more popular than others. Thus 4QRP, preserved in five different manuscripts, probably encompassing all of the Pentateuch, was probably produced outside Qumran and also copied in Qumran.[45] It stands to reason that this composition was meant to make the reading in the Torah somewhat easier and "relevant," as it contained some exegetical elements and slightly rearranged the laws according to an organizing principle (see above). The background of the other compositions is less clear.

---

[45] An analysis of the orthography of the various manuscripts leads us to believe that two of its manuscripts (4Q366, 4Q367) were written outside Qumran, while the other three texts were written at Qumran (4Q158, 4Q364, 4Q365). See the analysis of these texts in Tov, "The Textual Status of 4Q364–367."

# Wisdom and Prayer

# Wisdom at Qumran

*Daniel J. Harrington, S.J.*

The wisdom books contained in the Jewish and Christian canons of Scripture were part of the Qumran library. There are fragments of Proverbs (4Q102–103), Job (4Q99–101) as well as 4Q and 11Q Targums of Job, Qohelet (4Q109–110), and Sirach (2Q18 and 11QPs<sup>a</sup> Sirach [= 51:13–20b, 30b]).[1]

Among the Qumran texts that have already appeared there are several Wisdom texts. 4Q184 (*DJD* 5.82–85), entitled by John Allegro *The Wiles of the Wicked Woman,* is in fact a Wisdom poem depicting the allurements of Dame Folly in the tradition of Proverbs 5, 7, and 9. It describes the evils associated with Dame Folly—her body, clothes, dwellings, and ways—and defines her mission as "leading men astray to the ways of the pit." 4Q185 (*DJD* 5.85–87) is an exhortation to wisdom: "Seek it and find it, grasp it and possess it." It appeals to the miracles that God did in Egypt at the exodus, envisions the possibilities of accepting or rejecting wisdom, and shows the effects of both choices. The Psalms Scroll from Cave 11 contains a Wisdom poem previously known as Psalm 154 or Syriac Psalm II (*DJD* 4.64–79). It defines the purpose of Wisdom as making known the glory of God and envisions a community enlivened by Wisdom:

> From the doors of the righteous her [Wisdom's] voice is heard, and from the congregation of the devout her song. When they eat their fill, she is mentioned, and when they drink in community together. Their meditation is on the Law of the Most High, and their words are for making known her strength (vv. 12–14).

This beautiful description of a Wisdom community raises the basic question regarding the Qumran origin of these Wisdom compositions.

---

[1] See E. Tov, "The Unpublished Qumran Texts from caves 4 and 11," *BA* 55 (1992) 94–104.

Though their content is appropriate to the Qumran sect, nothing in them is distinctively Qumranian. They may well have been composed elsewhere and simply brought to Qumran.

An even more basic question, of course, is this: What constitutes a Wisdom book? Many published Qumran texts of the clearly sectarian type have Wisdom elements. In the *Community Rule* (1QS) the Instructor or Master (for whom the book serves as a handbook) is called the *maśkîl*—a Wisdom term meaning "one who enlightens or instructs." The centerpiece of that work is the "Treatise on the Two Spirits" (cols. III–IV), which explains the structure of the cosmos as well as human nature and activity in terms of a schema of modified dualism.[2] Likewise, the "Songs of the Sage" in 4Q510–511 (*DJD* 7.215–262) contains psalms and poems of exorcism to be used by the *maśkîl*. The exhortations in the *Damascus Document*, while not Wisdom texts, often invoke themes of wisdom and knowledge: "God loves knowledge. Wisdom and understanding He has set before him, and prudence and knowledge serve him" (II 3).[3] And the *Thanksgiving Hymns* or *Hôdāyôt*(1QH) are full of Wisdom terminology and considerations from their opening proclamation in I 7 ("By [God's] wisdom all things exist from eternity") to their final description of "a creature of clay . . . illumined with perfect light forever" (XVIII 25–29).[4]

So on the one hand we have at Qumran Wisdom compositions with no sectarian features, and on the other hand sectarian compositions with Wisdom features. But was there a distinctively sectarian or Qumranian corpus of Wisdom writings?[5] The late Second Temple period saw several attempts at enlisting common-stock Wisdom tra-

---

[2] C. A. Newsom, "The Sage in the Literature of Qumran: The Functions of the Maśkîl," *The Sage in Israel and the Ancient Near East* (ed. J. G. Gammie and L. G. Perdue; Winona Lake, IN: Eisenbrauns, 1990) 373–82.

[3] A.-M. Denis, *Les thèmes de connaissance dans le Document de Damas* (Leuven: Publications Universitaires, 1967).

[4] S. J. Tanzer, "The Sages at Qumran: Wisdom in the Hodayot" (Dissertation, Harvard University, 1987).

[5] For general treatments of Qumran wisdom see J. E. Worrell, "Concepts of Wisdom in the Dead Sea Scrolls" (Dissertation, Claremont Graduate School, 1968); M. Hengel, *Judaism and Hellenism* (2 vols.; Philadelphia: Fortress, 1974) 1.218–24.

ditions in the service of particular theological viewpoints. Thus Ben Sira assigned Wisdom a home in the Jerusalem Temple (24:9–12) and identified Wisdom with the Law of Moses (24:23). The Enoch circle in *1 Enoch* (a literature very popular at Qumran) equated Wisdom with the heavenly mysteries. The book of Wisdom agrees with Ben Sira in linking Wisdom and the Torah but goes on to describe Wisdom as permeating all creation and functioning as kind of world-soul. The early Christians made Jesus the Wisdom teacher par excellence (see Matt 11:28–30) and developed their early christologies in Wisdom hymns (see John 1:1–18; Col 1:15–20).[6] In each case there is a fusion, or better an incorporation, of wisdom elements into a dominant theological perspective.

Can we find the same process in the Wisdom texts of the Qumran library? Perhaps the several Wisdom texts from Cave 4 will provide the evidence for this. A glance at the list of unpublished manuscripts at least inspires hope, for there appear to be several Wisdom books: "Words of a Sage to Sons of Dawn" (4Q298), "Book of Mysteries" (4Q299–301; see 1Q27 in *DJD* 1.102–105), "Meditation on Creation" (4Q303–305) and related works (4Q306–308), and several texts called "Sapiential Works" (4Q408, 410–413, 415–419, 420–421, 423–426).[7] These works are just beginning to be studied in a serious way, and anything said about them is necessarily preliminary. This paper will first report on one major text found mainly in 4Q416–418. Then as a way of getting perspective on that text it will make a few comparisons with a well-known Wisdom book from perhaps roughly the same period—the book of Sirach.

## A Sapiential Text from Qumran (4Q416–418)

The Qumran Sapiential text that John Strugnell and I have been working on is found chiefly in 4Q416–418 (also in 4Q415, 423, and 1Q26 and less likely in 4Q419). Reconstructed versions appear in

---

[6] D. J. Harrington, "The Wisdom of the Scribe according to Ben Sira," *Ideal Figures in Ancient Judaism: Profiles and Paradigms* (ed. J. J. Collins and G. W. E. Nickelsburg; SBLSCS 12; Chico, CA: Scholars Press, 1980) 181–88.

[7] See Tov, "Unpublished Texts."

the Wacholder–Abegg edition, fascicle 2, pp. 54–154.[8] Most of the work is a wisdom instruction cast in the second person singular. This report on our research is divided into five sections: our strategy for studying the text, a description of the content of some major sections, reflections on the nature of the work, observations about some distinctive words or ideas, and relations to other works.

## Strategy

There are three substantial versions of the work (4Q416, 417, and 418)—all written in the early Herodian formal hand (30–1 BCE). Parts of other versions may be found in 4Q415, 4Q423, and 1Q26.

From 4Q416 frg. 1 we can be sure about the start of the work, since there is a large margin before the writing begins. 4Q416 frg. 7 contains four columns, two of which are quite substantial, and so we can be sure about their order. The order of the smaller fragments in 4Q416 cannot be determined. There are two substantial fragments (1, 2) in 4Q417 along with several smaller pieces. 4Q418 consists of nearly 300 fragments, of which a few non-overlapping pieces (55, 69, 81, 103, 126–127) are the most substantial. For the most part, their order cannot be determined.

Imagine that you have three (or six) jigsaw puzzles of the same basic scene. But you do not know what the scene is, the pieces of each puzzle have been cut according to different patterns, and most of the pieces from each puzzle have been lost. Our task is to try to make sense out of this textual puzzle. We have been concentrating our research on the larger pieces. When we have fully edited them, we will try to see where the smaller pieces fit. Of course, in some cases it is possible to restore lacunae in the larger texts with the parallels in the smaller texts, since there are overlaps among 4Q415, 416, 417, 418, and 423 (and perhaps 1Q26).

## Content

To give you a sense of the nature of the work, I will provide brief summaries of ten of the major fragments.

---

[8] B. Z. Wacholder and M. G. Abegg, *A Preliminary Edition of the Unpublished Dead Sea Scrolls: The Hebrew and Aramaic Texts from Cave Four. Fascicle Two* (Washington, D.C.: Biblical Archaeology Society, 1992) 54–154.

(1) 4Q416, frg. 1 first speaks about God's orderly rule over creation—the heavenly hosts and luminaries (lines 1–10), and then about God's rewarding the righteous and punishing the wicked at the judgment (10–11), and about the reaction of all creation to God's judgment (12–14). The column ends (15–17) with reference to discerning between good and evil and to the "inclination (יצר) of the flesh." The language and style are reminiscent of the hortatory material in the *Manual of Discipline* and the *Hôdāyôt*, though there is nothing particularly sectarian (Qumranic).

(2) 4Q416, frg. 7 contains parts of four columns and is thus the most extensive piece of extant text. Only a few words can be read from the bottom left of column i. Column ii begins with comments about God's care for creation (7 ii 1–3) and about sensitivity to another's embarrassment (ii 3–4). The better preserved sections give instructions in the second person masculine singular imperative or imperfect about these topics: paying back loans or surety bonds quickly (ii 4–6), maintaining integrity in business and in serving others (ii 6–7), the rewards for serving God or one's master ("you will be for him a first-born son"; ii 7–13), avoiding what is hateful and oppressive and inappropriate (ii 13–16), selling yourself or your soul for wealth/possessions (ii 17–18), and balance in acquiring possessions and in boasting over poverty (ii 18–21). The second column ends (ii 21) with a warning against dishonoring "the vessel (כלי) of your bosom," i.e., your wife (see 1 Thess 4:4).

Columns iii and iv continue the second singular direct address. The speaker at several points reminds the one being instructed "you are poor." The units are short, consisting of a command plus some rationale. The language and structure are like Proverbs 22–23. The instructions concern caring for and restoring what has been deposited with you (iii 3–5), caution about accepting property or money from a stranger (iii 5–8), not desiring more than what God has allotted to you (iii 8–10), zeal for studying "the mystery of what is to come" (iii 12–15), honoring one's parents (iii 15–18), living in harmony with your wife and her children (iii 19–iv 1), dominion over your wife (iv 1–6), and the power to annul your wife's vows and votive offerings (iv 6–10).

To give you a feel for the style and content, let me quote a few lines from columns iii and iv: "Study the mystery that is to come and understand all the ways of truth and all the roots of iniquity you shall contemplate. Then you shall know what is bitter for a man and what is sweet for a human being" (iii 14–15). "You have taken a wife in your poverty; take her offspring in your lowly estate. But take care lest you be distracted from the mystery that is to come while you keep company together" (iii 20–21). "Over her spirit He has set you in authority so that she should walk in your good pleasure and so that she should not make numerous vows and votive offerings" (iv 6–7).

(3) 4Q417, frg. 1 is well preserved and substantial. The instructor urges the maven or "trainee" to forgive another ("the noble"?) unobtrusively and quickly because he himself has sinned ("do not overlook your sins") and God is the source of forgiveness (lines 2–6). Next he warns against associating with "a man of iniquity" (7–8) and against both coveteousness and overestimating the state of poverty (9–10). Then he urges the instructee: "Gaze upon the mystery that is to come, and understand the birth-time of salvation, and know who is to inherit glory" (11–12). Next there is a connection made between integrity in human judgment and God's willingness to forgive in the divine judgment (12–17). After short units on the moderate use of resources (17–18) and God as the ultimate provider (19–21), there is advice concerning borrowing and lending (21–28): Pay the loan back as soon as possible, be honest in dealing with others, and so on.

(4) 4Q417, frg. 2, col. i is a large text of twenty-seven lines. But most of the first five lines has been destroyed, a large part of lines 6–16 has lost its ink, and nearly two-thirds of the bottom part (from line 19 on) is absent. What can be read is an exhortation to the prospective sage to "meditate on the mystery of what is to come," which will bring truth and wisdom (lines 6–7). This "mystery" will enable you to discern between good and evil, and to understand their prospective outcomes. Line 15 refers to the "sons of Seth" (or "of perdition") and the "book of remembrance" (see Mal 3:16). In col. ii only the first few words in lines 3–16 are preserved. The vocabulary carries on from col. i ("the mystery of what is to come"), and the text warns in line 12: "Do not let the plan of the evil inclination deceive you."

(5) 4Q418, frg. 55 first describes the struggle and vigilance involved in the search for wisdom (lines 3–5) while tracing all truth and knowledge back to the "God of knowledge" (5–6; see 1 Sam 2:3) and promising "peace and quiet" as the reward for the quest (7). Then it offers the holy angels as models or as a goal for which the sage is to strive (8) and promises the inheritance of an eternal possession as a reward (9–12). Especially noteworthy here is the occurrence of the phrase (לפי) דעתם יכבדו איש מרעהו ("according to

their knowledge they shall be glorified each one more than his neighbor") in line 10, which is found also in 1QH X 27–28. Several explanations are possible: The Wisdom text could have copied from the *Hôdāyôt*; the *Hôdāyôt* could have copied from the Wisdom text; or both could have used a common source or simply repeated a cliché.

(6) In 4Q418, frg. 9 the "foolish of heart" (plural) are warned to expect death and eternal destruction, and at their judgment the "seekers of truth" and the "foundations of the firmament" will rise up against them (lines 4–10). Then (10–15) the "chosen ones of truth" are warned not to complain about toiling in understanding and pursuing knowledge, for their reward will be an eternal inheritance within the "council of the divine kings."

(7) Fragment 81 begins with a call to praise "the holy ones" (angels) and to separate yourself from all that God hates (lines 1–2). Next there is a reminder of the "good lot" that God has given you and a summons to respond with praise, fidelity, and love (3–8). Then there is another reminder of what God has done ("He opened up insight . . . he made you rule") and another summons to honor his "holy ones" (9–14). The column ends with an invitation to remember God's goodness in creating you and to increase instruction so as to enjoy God's goodness with even greater fullness (15–20).

(8) Fragment 103 begins (lines 1–5) with some agricultural images ("husbandmen . . . baskets . . . storehouses") and an application involving "times" and "living waters." Then (6–8) there is a section on "mixed things" (כלי״ם) such as mules, wool and linen, a bullock and ass yoked together, two kinds of seeds, along with an application. The point seems to be: Do not mix your property with that of your neighbor.

(9) The first part of frg. 126 (lines 1–10) describes God's work in creating the heavenly hosts and human beings, His separating the righteous from the "masters of iniquity," and His punishments for the wicked and rewards for the righteous. The second part (11–16) begins an exhortation to "walk with all the holy ones" and a promise of rewards from God.

(10) Fragment 127 contains six lines, much of them fairly well preserved. The first part reflects on human mortality, and the second part concerns God's gentleness and justice toward human beings. But beyond recognizing the familiar terms ("poverty . . . good pleasure . . . gentleness . . . scales of justice") it is hard to determine exactly what is being said.

## Nature of the Work

This Qumran sapiential work is a wisdom instruction expressed in small units and put together without much apparent concern for logical or thematic progression. In some places the sage's appeal is to pragmatism or to reward and punishment at judgment, while in other places there are deductions from Scripture and symbolic uses of Scripture. In form and content it is similar to Sirach, parts of Proverbs (especially chaps. 22–23), late Egyptian wisdom writings,[9] Jesus' instructions in the Synoptic Gospels, and the letter of James.

Much of the language in the more theological parts of the work can be found in the so-called sectarian writings from Qumran (*Manual of Discipline, Damascus Document, Hôdāyôt,* etc.). But the work presupposes a "non-sectarian" or at least non-Qumran and non-monastic setting in life. The one being instructed engages in business, has dealings with all kinds of people, and may marry a wife and have children. Moreover, the dualism of the work is not so metaphysical or psychological as it becomes in the sectarian documents (see 1QS III–IV). The work may have been pre-Qumranic in origin and thus a link in the early development of the later sectarian Qumran language and thought.

Wacholder and Abegg propose that our work is the *Raz Niheyeh* ("The Mystery of Being") and/or the "Vision of Haguy."[10] On the basis of 4Q417 frg. 2 i 14–18, they further suggest that the work was understood to have been etched on the heavenly tablets for Seth, son of Adam, who in turn handed it over to Enosh, and that it was studied by every member of the Qumran sect. The key text, however, admits of other translations and interpretations. At present, their suggestions seem to us to be a case of explaining the obscure by the more obscure.

Our preliminary translation of this text (admittedly obscure itself) runs as follows:

> Engraved is the ordinance, and ordained is all the punishment. For engraved is that which is ordained by God against all the

---

[9] M. Lichtheim, *Late Egyptian Wisdom Literature in the International Context: A Study of Demotic Instructions* (Fribourg: Univeritätsverlag; Göttingen: Vandenhoeck & Ruprecht, 1983).

[10] Wacholder and Abegg, *Preliminary Edition,* xii–xiv.

iniquities of the children of Seth (or, of perdition). And a Book of Memorial is written in His presence of those who keep His word. And that is the appearing (or, vision) of the meditating on a Book of Memorial. And He gave it as an inheritance to Man together with a spiritual people. For according to the structure of the Holy Ones is his fashioning. But no more was meditation given to fleshly spirit, for it knows not the difference between good and evil according to the judgment of its spirit (4Q417 frg. 2 i 14–18).

## Distinctive Words and Ideas

One of the most striking features of the document is its extensive vocabulary with regard to poverty: the nouns *maḥsor* and *rîš / rê(')š*, and the adjectives *rîš* and *'ebyôn*. Yet poverty is presented not so much as an ideal or a more perfect state as it is a symbol of human limitation and mortality. Though this vocabulary appears in other wisdom texts, it is particularly prominent in this work.

Another prominent term is *raz nihyāh* (or *nihyeh*). We have been translating it as "the mystery of what is to be (or, come)" since in some contexts it appears to refer to the eschatological plan of God. The term *raz* ("mystery") is frequent in Daniel (chap. 2 especially). The second element *nhyh* seems to be the niphal participle of the verb *hāyāh* ("be").

Another linguistic feature is the use of *'wṭ* as a noun. There may well be a relation to the adverb *'aṭ* or *'eṭ* ("gently"), and we are taking it as a noun "gentleness." It usually carries a masculine singular suffix *'ôṭô* ("his gentleness") and is sometimes a divine attribute and sometimes a human characteristic.

## Relations to Other Works

I have already mentioned in passing general relationships to Qumran sectarian documents, Jewish and Egyptian wisdom writings, and the New Testament. There seems to be some overlap in content and terminology with 4Q415, suggesting that it too was part of the sapiential work or somehow related to it. 4Q419, frg. 8, line 7 ("if he [= God] will shut his hand, and the spirit of all flesh be removed") overlaps with 4Q416, frg. 2, lines 2–3. But the content and style of the two works are quite different. There may also be a relationship with 4Q423 (see also 1Q26 in *DJD* I), as well as the so-called "Book of Mysteries" (4Q299–301) (see also *DJD* 1Q27).

For New Testament scholars this Qumran sapiential work is most important as an antecedent in form and content to the so-called ethical or paraenetic material. One minor but striking contribution, however, comes in 4Q416, frg. 7 ii 21, where the prospective sage is warned against dishonoring "the vessel" (כלי) of your bosom," i.e., your wife. This text provides an exact parallel to Paul's advice in 1 Thess 4:4: "that each one of you know to possess his own vessel (σκεῦος) in holiness and honor." Thus Paul's use of the term σκεῦος to refer to a wife echoes the Hebrew כלי found in our Qumran sapiential text.

## Some Comparisons with Sirach

The book of Sirach was known at Qumran (and Masada). It exists in many ancient versions and has been studied for many years. Its sheer bulk makes it a repository for Jewish wisdom in the third and second centuries BCE. There seems to be no direct relation of dependence between Sirach and the Qumran Wisdom text we have been studying. Thus my purpose is to bring out the distinctive character of the Qumran text by comparing it with the better known and better studied book of Sirach.

First I will look at the treatments of some issues of practical wisdom in both works: loans and surety, and parents and wives. Then I will try to get a glimpse at the theology of creation in each work and at the intellectual framework that creation provides for wisdom teachings. The works are similar in form (the use of the "wisdom essay" to instruct the prospective sage addressed as "my son"), content (common wisdom themes), concern for theology (wisdom placed in a theological framework and penetrated by it), and perhaps in date (early- to mid-second century BCE). But they have quite different interests and approaches.

### Loans and Surety

Ben Sira regards lending to a neighbor in need as a religious act (see 29:1), though he warns against lending to someone more powerful than oneself (8:12). He also envisions situations in which the scribe may need a loan. There his emphasis is on paying the loan back on time: "Pay back your neighbor when a loan falls due" (29:2). Our Qumran Wisdom text likewise stresses paying loans back as quickly as possible: "If men's money you borrow for your poverty, do not let there be [repose for you] day or night nor rest for your soul until you have restored to your creditor [your debt *in toto*]. Do not lie to him, lest you bear iniquity" (4Q417, frg. 1 i 21–23).

Ben Sira also considers standing surety for one's neighbor as the duty of a "good person" (29:14). But he goes on to warn about the dangers inherent in doing so: "Do not go surety beyond your means; think any pledge a debt you must pay" (8:13). In 29:16–20 Ben Sira describes how sinful people manipulate the surety system and bring about lawsuits and even exile. He begins his warning by addressing the prospective scribe: "Forget not the kindness of your backer, for he offers his very life for you (29:15). DiLella describes this as "an exaggeration to dramatize the point."[11]

There are passages in the Qumran wisdom text that indicate a special interest in the theme of surety. One who stands surety for another is described as having entrusted to a creditor "your hidden/treasure cup": "On account of your friends you have given away all your life for its price. Hasten and give what is his [the creditor's] and take back your cup" (4Q416, frg. 7 ii 5–6). What the precise meaning of the "cup" is remains unclear. But a text later in the same column suggests a connection with one's very life: "Do not sell yourself for money . . . do not sell your glory for any price nor give your heritage in exchange for surety for a sum of money, lest that money dispossess also your body" (4Q416, frg. 7 ii 17–18). Likewise in the context of how one should handle a deposit entrusted by a stranger, the maven is warned: "Do not let your spirit be taken as a pledge for it" (4Q416, frg. 7 iii 6–7). Perhaps this language is more "exaggeration to dramatize the point." But the Qumran wisdom text's repeated interest in it may indicate that some sad experience lay behind Ben Sira's comment that one who goes surety "offers his very life for you" (29:15).

*Parents and Wives*

There are some good parallels to what Ben Sira says about honoring one's parents (see 3:1–16) in the Qumran Wisdom text. Just as

---

[11] P. W. Skehan and A. A. DiLella, *The Wisdom of Ben Sira* (AB 39; Garden City, NY: Doubleday, 1987) 371.

Ben Sira says that "whoever honors his father will live a long life" (3:6), so the Qumran text urges the maven to honor the presence of his parents "for the sake of your life and the length of your days" (4Q416, frg. 2 iii 19). Ben Sira says that "His father's glory is a person's own glory" (3:11), and the Qumran text advises: "Honor them for the sake of your own honor" (line 18).

These standard biblical themes, however, serve to highlight the more unusual emphases of the Qumran Wisdom text on these matters. Attention is given to the economic/spiritual state of the one being instructed: "Honor your father in your poverty and your mother in your low estate" (lines 15–16). Then a daring comparison is offered: "For as God (reading אל rather than אב) is to a man, so is his father; and as a master is to a fellow, so is his mother" (line 16). The chief reason why one should honor and glorify one's parents is that "they uncovered your ear to the mystery that is to come" (line 18). This latter point presupposes a "family" rather than "monastic" setting for instruction and illustrates how the distinctive teachings of the movement have been interwoven with standard sapiential themes.

Ben Sira's views on women in general and wives in particular are notorious today: "Better a man's wickedness than a woman's goodness" (42:14). "With a dragon or a lion I would rather dwell than live with an evil woman" (25:16). "In a woman was sin's beginning; on her account we all die" (25:24).

The Qumran Wisdom text is much calmer. It (4Q416, frg. 2 iii 19–iv 11) assumes that the one being instructed will take a wife. But it warns against distraction: "Take care lest you be distracted from the mystery that is to come" (2 iii 20–21). The principal concern, however, is to reinforce the husband's authority over his wife. And most of the argument is based on allusions to biblical texts. Marriage is defined with reference to Gen 2:24: "Walk together with the helpmeet of your flesh according to the statute engraved by God that a man should leave his father and his mother . . . and that they should become one flesh" (2 iii 21–iv 1). Also included is a reference to Gen 3:16: "Toward you shall be her desire." These biblical texts are surrounded by comments to the effect that God has set the husband over the wife in authority, and that neither her father nor her mother retains authority over her. Any other man who claims authority over her "has displaced the frontier marker of his life" (2 iv 6). The discussion then focuses on the issue of the husband's authority over the vows and votive offerings made by the wife (as in Numbers 30): "Turn her spirit to your good pleasure; and every oath binding on her, to vow a vow, annul it according to a mere utterance of your mouth and at your good pleasure restrain her from performing her vow" (2 iv 8–9). The Qumran Wisdom text's section on the wife lacks the emotional and indeed obsessive tone found in Sirach. Its appeal is to the hierarchical relationship between husband and wife willed by God in the Scriptures that in turn provides the basis for the husband's absolute authority over his wife.

## Theology of Creation

Ben Sira treats creation in three long poems (16:24–18:14; 39:12–35; 42:15–43:33) that serve as theological underpinning for his many short wisdom essays. Much in these three creation poems simply echoes earlier biblical material. There is great emphasis on the order of creation and the divine wisdom made manifest in it, the central place of humankind within creation, the gift of the Law as the divinely revealed guide for human action, and the call for those who have strayed to repent and return to God.

Though quite biblical and traditional in his statements about creation, Ben Sira makes his own distinctive theological contribution (perhaps in response to Qohelet) with his treatment of theodicy in the context of creation. There he articulates what has come to be known as "the doctrine of the pairs."[12] This doctrine is summarized in Sir 42:24: "All of them come in twos, one corresponding to the other; yet none of them has He made in vain." It also appears in 33:15: "See now all the works of the Most High: they come in pairs, the one the opposite of the other." Both texts attribute absolute sovereignty to God the creator. But they account for the duality in human experience by appealing to the order of creation itself. This is a modified dualism (as at Qumran) but without an appeal to a subordinate evil power like the Angel of Darkness (as in 1QS III–IV).

For Ben Sira God's creations are objectively good but can result in punishment for the wicked: "For the good all these are good, but for the wicked they turn out evil" (39:27). This is, of course, a neat but simplistic solution to the question of theodicy. It leaves out the reality of innocent suffering and suggests that those who suffer natural calamities and the ravages of war must be among the wicked: "Fire and hail, famine, disease: these too were created for punish-

---

[12] G. L. Prato, *Il problema della teodicea in Ben Sira: Composizione dei contrari e richiamo alle origini* (Rome: Biblical Institute Press, 1975).

ment. Ravenous beasts, scorpions, vipers, and the avenging sword to exterminate the wicked: All these were created to meet a need and are kept in his storehouse for the proper time" (39:29–30).

Ben Sira's approach to creation is traditional. His innovative approach to theodicy is neat but somewhat timid. He acknowledges the existence of a certain duality in creation without developing it in much detail and declares that natural catastrophes are primarily intended to punish the wicked.

The appeal to creation as the theological basis for wisdom instruction is also prominent in the Qumran Wisdom text. But whereas Ben Sira seems intent on displaying and glorifying God's creation, the Qumran Wisdom text is less speculative and more interested in the moral consequences of creation and divine election. God has separated the wise from the "spirit of flesh." Therefore "you, separate yourself from everything that He (= God) hates and guard yourself from everything that His soul detests" (4Q418, frg. 81, line 2). The maven is urged repeatedly to recall his "inheritance" and his "portion" and his "glory" that God has granted him. As in Sirach, there are two kinds of people. But the Qumran Wisdom text puts much more emphasis on God's activity in choosing the righteous and on the responsibility that the righteous have in acting in a manner appropriate to their "lot" or "inheritance."

4Q418, frg. 126, lines 1–10 affirms God's sovereignty in the creation and preservation of the universe: "Nothing will cease from all their host. . . . He numbers all, and they did not come to be without his good pleasure" (lines 1, 5). It also stresses the discriminating judgment (election) of God that has already separated the good and the wicked, and looks forward to the future judgment that will bring vengeance on the "masters of iniquity" and vindication for the "poor ones."

God's plan for creation is called the *raz nihyeh* ("mystery of what is to be/come" or simply "mystery of being"). The many references to this phrase assume that both the speaker and the one being instructed know to what it refers, though we as outsiders are never informed. It could be a book (the Book of Hagu, according to Wacholder) or an epitome of basic teachings (as in 1QS III–IV). Or it could be the teaching itself concerning creation, election, and coming judgment. The title "mystery of being" seems too metaphysical and too truncated to capture the contexts in which the term appears. There seems to be an eschatological dimension, and the expression functions in an elusive and encompassing way—something like "kingdom of God" in the Synoptic Gospels. Here is a sample: "And thou, O understanding child, gaze on the mystery that is to come, and know that inheritance of everyone who lives and how he walks and the visitation of his deeds" (4Q417, frg. 2 i 18–19).

The attitude toward creation in the Qumran Wisdom text seems midway between Ben Sira's doctrine of the pairs and the fully fleshed out schema of 1QS III–IV with its Angel of Darkness. The Qumran Wisdom text assumes a God more active and involved in creation and human affairs than Sirach does. Its emphasis is on the election that God has imposed on creation and on the moral consequences of being the object of God's grace or good pleasure.

## Conclusion

All the manuscripts of our Qumran Wisdom text are Herodian in script, that is, they date from the first century BCE. The fact that there were several manuscripts of the work—three substantial ones (4Q416–418) and perhaps three additional ones (4Q415, 4Q423, 1Q26)—indicates the popularity of the work. If the community at Qumran constituted a sect—whether they be called Essenes or Sadducees—this Wisdom text clearly had great significance for them. Yet if the Qumran community lived anything like the monastic life according to the pattern laid down in the *Community Rule*, there was much in this Wisdom text that was irrelevant or did not pertain.

How can one put together these facts: multiple copies of a work from the late first century BCE, a popular and significant book, and a work whose life-setting is not monastic? And there is still another factor to be included: the linguistic and conceptual links to the so-called sectarian works found in Qumran (*Community Rule, Hôdāyôt, Damascus Document*).

One can imagine several explanations for these facts. The Qumran Wisdom text may simply have been popular at Qumran—as, for example, *1 Enoch* was—though not directly related to the sect at home at Qumran. Or the Qumran Wisdom text may be evidence for the wider non-monastic branch of the Essene or Qumran movement insofar as it provides guidance for members more thoroughly integrated into society. Thus it may have been composed in the first century BCE for such associate members.

Yet it is also possible—given the apparent popularity and significance of the work at Qumran—that this Wisdom text can be associated with the foundational, pre-Qumranic phase of the movement in the early second century BCE. Such a life-setting would explain both the clear links to the later and more sectarian works and the more secular setting presupposed by its teachings. Thus it would have been contemporary with the statutes in the second part of the *Damascus Document* and prior to the bill of particulars explaining the sect's separation in 4QMMT. It would also be contemporary with Sirach and thus would provide important evidence for a major turning point in Second Temple Jewish history. At any rate, a new area of Qumran research—Wisdom at Qumran—is opening up with the study of this and other Qumran Wisdom texts.

# Prayer, Hymnic, and Liturgical Texts from Qumran

*Eileen M. Schuller, O.S.U.*

In keeping with the focus of this conference on "the state of the Question," this paper will examine the corpus of hymns, prayers, and liturgical texts found in the manuscripts of the Dead Sea Scrolls from the dual perspective of a general survey and an articulation of selected questions. The survey is selective, not comprehensive. It reflects an attempt to call to mind and highlight the most significant texts that can now form the starting point for future discussions. The questions in particular are only exploratory, and I make no claim that this precise formulation will prove determinative as new issues emerge. At this stage of research, the issues are still very basic: Is there a common understanding of the terminology we use (psalm, song, hymn)? What, in terms of both form and usage, makes a specific text "liturgical"? Can we distinguish between sectarian and non-sectarian material in this corpus? Since this paper arises from my own attempts to grapple with these questions over the last several years, I have kept something of the more personal first-person approach that was part of the oral presentation at Notre Dame. I take this opportunity to thank the organizers of this conference for the opportunity to be part of these very stimulating and enjoyable days.

## Survey of Texts

When both general readers and even scholars who have worked more closely with the scrolls think of prayers/hymns in this corpus, it is usually the *Thanksgiving Scroll* (מגילת ההדיות) that first comes to mind. This large scroll, designated 1QH[a] (to distinguish it from a few fragments of a second manuscript of the same work also found in

Cave 1, 1QH<sup>b</sup>)[1], was among the first batch of manuscripts acquired by E. L. Sukenik in November 1947, and portions of it were among the first Dead Sea Scrolls texts to be published. Already in 1949–50 the Hebrew text of col. IV (one of the most complete columns) was made available in two different journals—complete with a translation into Latin![2] Both the plates and a complete transcription of the whole text were prepared by Sukenik, and after his death N. Avigad brought the work to publication in 1954 in Hebrew and 1955 in English.[3] Thus, we are dealing with a text available now for well over thirty-five years. Since this is a very well-known work, I need not go into much detail here. It is a collection of individual compositions of praise and thanksgiving, over thirty in number, each of which opens with a distinctive formula: "I praise you" אודכה אדוני, or "Blessed are you" ברוך אתה אדוני. In the 1960s, a variety of independent studies, working from quite diverse perspectives, arrived at a consensus—quite "unusual in Qumran literary criticism"[4]—namely, that there are two basic types of material: one group of texts closely modeled on the biblical "individual thanksgiving songs" with a more distinctive individual "I" figure and certain distinctive themes (persecution, revelation of knowledge); and another group of texts that are diffuse, more hymnic in character, again with distinctive vocabulary and themes about both divine salvific action and the human condition. These poems have frequently been scrutinized for the theological concepts they express (salvation, election, wisdom, predeterminism, angelology), and their

---

[1] For further discussion of the identification of 1QH<sup>b</sup>, see É. Puech, "Quelques aspects de la restauration du Rouleau des Hymnes (1QH)," *JJS* 39 (1988) 38–40. The identification of this manuscript as a copy of the Hodayot had been made much earlier and independently by both John Strugnell and H. Stegemann; for a very brief discussion see H.-W. Kuhn, *Enderwartung und gegenwärtiges Heil: Untersuchungen zu den Gemeindeliedern von Qumran* (SUNT 4; Gottingen: Vandenhoeck & Ruprecht, 1966) 17, n. 1.

[2] J.-M. P. Bauchet, "Une page d'un des manuscrits du désert de Judée," *RB* 56 (1949) 583–85; idem, "Transcription and translation of a Psalm from Sukenik's Dead Sea Scroll," *CBQ* 12 (1950) 331–35.

[3] In Hebrew under the title אוצר המגילות הגנוזות; in English with the title *The Dead Sea Scrolls of the Hebrew University* (Jerusalem: Magnes Press, 1955).

[4] As described by J. Murphy-O'Connor, "The Judaean Desert," *Early Judaism and Its Modern Interpreters* (ed. R. A. Kraft and G. W. E. Nickelsburg; Philadelphia: Fortress, 1986) 130. Major studies include G. Morawe, *Aufbau und Abgrenzung der Loblieder vom Qumran: Studien zur gattungsgeschichtlichen Einordnung der Hodajoth* (Berlin: Evangelische Verlagsanstalt, 1961); S. Holm-Nielsen, *Hodayot: Psalms from Qumran* (ATDan 2; Aarhus: Universitetsforlaget, 1960); G. Jeremias, *Der Lehrer der Gerechtigheit* (SUNT 2; Göttingen: Vandenhoeck & Ruprecht, 1963); and H.-W. Kuhn, *Enderwartung und gegenwärtiges Heil*.

poetic merit has been variously (sometimes harshly) evaluated. I have no doubt, however, that much of the ongoing appeal of these texts comes from the sense (rightly or wrongly) that here, among all the scrolls, we have access to something more personal and individual—as Sukenik expressed it, "songs expressing the views and feelings of one of the members of the sect."[5] Certainly the *Hôdāyôt* were our first evidence from the scrolls for a living, ongoing tradition of composing religious poetry. Now, with the hindsight of forty years, we need to remember how totally unexpected this discovery was in the 1950s, for in the scholarship of the period it was still often assumed that legalism had replaced piety in Second-Temple Judaism. The rich, extensive corpus of prayers and hymns preserved in apocryphal and pseudepigraphic literature, moreover, was largely ignored and unknown.[6]

In the early years of scrolls research, the *Hôdāyôt* stood in rather splendid isolation, much respected, but viewed as somewhat *sui generis*. There were other hymnic-type compositions in Cave 1, but these received much less attention, in part, at least, because they formed a sub-section of other genres, e.g., a lengthy poetic composition, very similar to the *Hôdāyôt*, that came at the end of the *Rule of the Community* (1QS X–XI) and the collection of victory hymns in the *War Scroll* (X–XIV). DJD 1, published in 1955, contained additional material: as an appendix to 1QS, 1QSb the *Words of Blessing* (דברי ברכה) for the *maśkil* to bless both specific individuals and the community; 1Q35 "Recueil de Cantiques d'Action de Graces," now properly identified as a second copy of the *Hôdāyôt*;[7] eight very fragmentary manuscripts (1Q30–31, 35–40) about which little could be said, except that they have some hymnic-type language and address someone/God in the second person; and some small fragments with the tantalizing title תפלה ליום כפורים (1Q34, 34[bis]). In the next year (1956), C.-H. Hunzinger published a preliminary description of the scroll material allotted to him for publication, and in so doing he alerted scholars to the existence of previously unknown liturgical

---

[5] Sukenik, *Dead Sea Scrolls*, 39.

[6] Even in the 1980s it was still necessary simply to survey and collect this material; for example, J. H. Charlesworth, "A Prolegomenon to a New Study of the Jewish Background of the Hymns and Prayers in the New Testament," *JJS* 33 (1982) 264–85; D. Flusser, "Psalms, Hymns and Prayers," *Jewish Writings of the Second Temple Period* (ed. M. E. Stone; CRINT 2/2; Assen: Van Gorcum; Philadelphia: Fortress, 1984) 551–77.

[7] See n. 1 above.

works, including collections of daily prayers.[8] A few years later, M. Baillet published the text plus extensive commentary for one of these, *The Words of the Luminaries*.[9]

While it is not my intent to go through a long list of publications and dates, I do want to point out that in the twenty-five years between 1955 and 1980, there was still little indication that prayer or liturgical-type material would be a significant component of the Qumran finds. Although there was some early interest in the *Hôdāyôt* on the part of Christian liturgical scholars (including an article by Jungmann[10]), these poems were usually viewed as the idiosyncratic works of an isolated desert community and thus of limited relevance or interest for the study of Jewish liturgy. Only S. Talmon, as early as 1959, working from the list of times of prayer at the end of 1QS, suspected that there must have been some sort of sectarian "Manual of Benedictions," parts of which he attempted to reconstruct as "the oldest Jewish prayerbook."[11] More bits and pieces of hymnic and prayer material surfaced slowly and haphazardly over the next years. In 1960 J. Strugnell published a small portion of a very different type of text, an "Angelic Liturgy" with an elaborate description of the heavenly temple, the angelic priesthood, and the merkavah.[12] Both in content and in the distinctive use of language (nominal syntax, lists, repetition) it was soon recognized that a text like this could only be understood, not by looking back to biblical psalmody but ahead to a style and vocabulary previously known only from much later Hekhalot lit-

---

[8] In the joint article "Le travail d'édition des fragments manuscrits de Qumrân," *RB* 63 (1956) 67.

[9] M. Baillet, "Un recueil liturgique de Qumrân, grotte 4: 'Les paroles des luminaires'," *RB* 68 (1961) 195–250.

[10] J. A. Jungmann, "Altchristliche Gebetsordnung im Lichte des Regelbuches von 'Ein Fescha'," *ZKT* 75 (1952) 215–19.

[11] S. Talmon, "The 'Manual of Benedictions' of the Sect of the Judaean Desert," *RevQ* 2 (1959–60) 475–500. The article was published a year earlier in Hebrew in *Tarbiz* 28 (1958) 1–20.

[12] J. Strugnell, "The Angelic Liturgy at Qumran—4Q Serek Širot ʿOlat Haššabbat," *Congress Volume: Oxford 1959* (VTSup 7; Leiden: Brill, 1960) 318–45. Although Strugnell already commented on links to later merkabah/hekhalot literature, the relationship was developed more fully only some years later by L. Schiffman, "Merkavah Speculation at Qumran: the 4QSerekh Shirot ʿOlat Hashabbat," *Mystics, Philosophers and Politicians: Essays in Jewish Intellectual History in Honor of Alexander Altmann* (ed. J. Reinharz and D. Swetschinski; Duke Monographs in Medieval and Renaissance Studies; Durham, NC: Duke University Press, 1982) 15–47.

erature. Another type of scroll was the beautifully written manusript, inscribed on deer skin, published by J. Sanders in 1965.[13] Though designated 11QPs$^a$, that is, as a copy of the biblical psalter, this scroll aroused far more interest than most biblical manuscripts because it contained—in addition to biblical psalms arranged in a quite different order than that of the Massoretic psalter—previously unknown texts (Hymn to the Creator, Plea for Deliverance, Apostrophe to Zion), works known only in translations (Psalms 151, 154, 155), and a massorah-type list of all the 4050 compositions of David. Although Sanders has steadfastly maintained that this is a "Qumran psalter," other scholars introduced once again the language of "prayer book/hymnbook."[14] I will to return to this problem shortly.

Although a few other small pieces were made available in these year, it was really only in 1982, when M. Baillet published all his allotted materials in *DJD* VII, that we began to get a better sense of the corpus as a whole: sets of prayers for morning and evening of each day of the month (4Q503); prayers for each day of the week (4Q504–506); prayers for feasts (4Q507–509); hymnic texts, similiar to the hodayot in vocabulary, yet quite distinctive in their purpose "to terrify and frighten all the spirits of the destroying angels" (4Q510–511); and blessings for purification (4Q512). And, in the last decade, the flow of material has continued: in 1985, the publication of the complete text of all the Sabbath Songs from Cave 4 and 11;[15] in 1986, two manuscripts (4Q380, 381) of non-biblical psalms attributed pseudepigraphically to various kings of Judah and prophets;[16] and more recently, preliminary presentations of smaller, independent texts, each presenting its own problems of interpretation. These include: 4Q372 1, a psalm of Joseph, part of a larger (still unpublished) narrative and psalmic collection;[17]

---

[13] J. Sanders, *The Psalms Scroll of Qumran Cave 11 (11QPs$^a$)* (DJD 4; Oxford: Clarendon, 1965).

[14] For a review of the debate and the bibliography, see J. Sanders, "The Qumran Psalms Scroll (11QPs$^a$) Reviewed," *On Language, Culture, and Religion: In Honor of E. A. Nida* (The Hague: Mouton, 1974) 79–99.

[15] C. Newsom, *Songs of the Sabbath Sacrifice: A Critical Edition* (HSS 27; Atlanta: Scholars Press, 1985).

[16] Schuller, *Non-Canonical Psalms from Qumran: A Pseudepigraphic Collection* (HSS 28; Atlanta: Scholars Press, 1986).

[17] E. Schuller, "4Q372 1: A Text about Joseph," *RevQ* 55 (1990) 349–76; eadem, "The Psalm of 4Q372 1 Within the Context of Second Temple Prayer,"*CBQ* 54 (1992) 67–79.

4Q373, an autobiographical psalm of David describing his victory over Goliath;[18] 4Q409, a short fragmentary hymnic call to praise in imperative form (הלל וברך והודו) linked to the feasts;[19] and the recently much-publicized but very difficult fragment of a scroll containing a portion of Psalm 154 and what seems to be a prayer that twice mentions King Jonathan.[20]

And we are awaiting more. Of the work still being prepared for publication, I would single out as especially significant, both in terms of length and content, the five manuscripts of blessings and curses (4Q286–290) now being prepared for *DJD* by B. Nitzan and the six copies of a collection of hymns, provisionally entitled *Barki Nafshi* (4Q434–439), that are being edited by M. Weinfeld. From among the six copies of the *Hôdāyôt* in Cave 4, we recover in 4QH$^a$ 7 a large fragment of some thirty-nine lines in two columns, which gives us a fascinating hymn virtually unpreserved in 1QH$^a$,[21] plus fragmentary bits of a few other hymns that are either not in 1QH$^a$ at all or in sections of that manuscript no longer preserved. And, although not a new text per se, our understanding of 1QH$^a$ is dramatically advanced by the rearrangement of the order of columns (28 in all) and the placement of many fragments on the basis of shapes and damage as this has been worked out—independently but with virtually the same results—by Stegemann and Puech.[22] Finally, according to the editor-

---

[18] E. Schuller, "A Preliminary Study of 4Q373 and Some Related (?) Fragments," *The Madrid Qumran Congress: Proceedings of the International Congress on the Dead Sea Scrolls, Madrid 18–21 March 1991* (2 vols.; ed. J. Trebolle Barrera and L. Vegas Montaner; STDJ 11; Leiden: Brill; Madrid: Universidad Complutense, 1992) 2.515–30. For the category of "autobiographical psalm," see S. Talmon, "Extra-Canonical Hebrew Psalms from Qumran—Psalm 151," *The World of Qumran from Within: Collected Studies* (Jerusalem: Magnes; Leiden: Brill, 1989) 258–64. In writing on the portion of this psalm found also in 2Q 22, Talmon interprets it as Moses describing his victory over Og.

[19] E. Qimron, "Times for Praising God: A Fragment of a Scroll from Qumran (4Q409)," *JQR* 80 (1990) 341–47.

[20] E. Eshel, H. Eshel, A. Yardeni, "A Qumran Composition Containing Part of Ps. 154 and a Prayer for the Welfare of King Jonathan and his Kingdom," *IEJ* 42 (1992) 199–229. A version of the article appeared also in Hebrew in *Tarbiz* 60 (1991) 295–324.

[21] A preliminary publication of this text, "A Hymn from a Cave Four Hodayot Manuscript: 4Q427 7 i + ii," is forthcoming in *JBL* in December, 1994.

[22] É. Puech, "Quelques aspects," 38–55; H. Stegemann, "Methods for the Reconstruction of Scrolls from Scattered Fragments," *Archaeology and History in the Dead Sea Scrolls: The New York University Conference in Memory of Yigael Yadin* (ed. L. H. Schiffman; JSPSup 8; ASOR Monographs 2; Sheffield: JSOT Press, 1990) 180–220, esp. pp. 200, 204.

in-chief's list of texts from Caves 4 and 11,[23] there remain to be published approximately twenty manuscripts described as prayer/hymnic/liturgical. To the best of my knowledge, most if not all of these are extremely fragmentary, and it remains to be seen how much we will eventually be able to recover from what is sometimes only a few words.[24]

## Articulating the Questions

With this quick and by no means comprehensive overview,[25] I have made the first and one of the most important of my points, namely, that the scrolls have given us a large corpus of previously unknown hymnic and prayer material. As I have also tried to indicate, a significant portion of this has only become available in the last ten years, and we are still awaiting first editions of a number of important texts. The boundaries of the corpus—what exactly belongs within this framework—are still fluid, and it has recently been proposed that some scrolls assumed to be biblical manuscripts or biblical paraphrases are in fact specific collections of texts gathered together for liturgical purposes.[26]

---

[23] E. Tov, "The Unpublished Qumran Texts from Caves 4 and 11," *JJS* 43 (1992) 101–36.

[24] Some of this material is known through papers presented at recent Conferences, e.g. E. Chazon on 4Q443 and 4Q457 at the Qumran Section of the Society of Biblical Literature meeting, 1992, and on 4Q444 at the World Congress of Jewish Studies, 1993; B. Nitzan on 11QBer and 4Q285 at the Society of Biblical Literature, 1992.

[25] For other types of surveys, see L. Schiffman "The Dead Sea Scrolls and the Early History of Jewish Liturgy," *The Synagogue in Late Antiquity* (ed. L. I. Levine; Philadelphia: ASOR, 1987) 33–48; the more comprehensive listing by J. Maier, "Zu Kult und Liturgie der Qumrangemeinde," *RevQ* 56 (1990) 543–86; M. Weinfeld, "Prayer and Liturgical Practice in the Qumran Sect," *The Dead Sea Scrolls: Forty Years of Research* (ed. D. Dimant and U. Rappaport; STDJ 10; Leiden: Brill; Jerusalem: Magnes, 1992) 241–58.

[26] At least two of the Deuteronomy manuscripts, Deut$^j$ and Deut$^n$, may fall into this category; see the discussion of S. A. White, "4QDeut$^n$: Biblical Manuscript or Excerpted Text?" *Of Scribes and Scrolls: Studies on the Hebrew Bible, Intertestamental Judaism and Christian Origins presented to John Strugnell on the Occasion of His Sixtieth Birthday* (ed. H. W. Attridge, J. J. Collins and T. H. Tobin; New York: University Press of America, 1990) 13–20; J. A. Duncan, "Considerations of 4QDt$^j$ in Light of the 'All Souls Deuteronomy' and Cave 4 Phylactery Texts," *Madrid Qumran Congress*, 1.99–216.

Thus, given the extent and diversity of the material and the relatively recent publication of a significant portion, the study of prayer and hymnic materials in the Dead Sea Scrolls is still in a very preliminary stage. In fact, in preparing the remainder of this paper, I cringed at the thought of presenting it here at Notre Dame in the presence of colleagues in the fields of both Bible and liturgy. I fear I am articulating very fundamental questions in a rather naive manner, but I do not think this reflects only personal ignorance and obtuseness. Rather, the process of thinking through the corpus as a whole, defining its boundaries and interrelating the various elements, is only beginning, and we have not really even tackled the task of correlating this material with non-Qumranic works, whether biblical texts (though certainly more has been done in this area), hymns and prayers of the apocrypha and pseudepigrapha, synagogue liturgy, or hekhalot hymns.

## Terminology and Genre

Let me give some examples. There is at present little agreement about terminology, even for such basic designations as psalm, hymn, song, prayer. Most often scholars use these terms without definition or introduce other, likewise undefined, terms. (For example, recently in trying to grasp how the editors understood the very puzzling document 4Q448,[27] I am not sure I was much the wiser after reading their single statement on genre "as for the literary genre of 4Q448, it may be called a 'paean'"!) But even common terms are less than clear. Are the compositions in 1QH$^a$ all hymns (as they are often designated in book titles such as *The Hymns of Qumran*[28]) or are they psalms (as in the title of the major commentary *Hodayot: Psalms from Qumran*[29])? What precisely does it mean to apply the term "psalm" to a non-biblical text? Should we call 4Q510 and 4Q511 "hymns" (as does B. Nitzan in a recent article[30]) or should we attempt to maintain the designation šir as it appears in the Hebrew text (4Q511 2 i 1, 8 4) and as Baillet did in the

---

[27] See n. 20 above.

[28] For instance, B. Kittel, *The Hymns of Qumran* (Chico, CA: Scholars Press, 1981); or M. Mansoor, *The Thanksgiving Hymns* (Grand Rapids, MI: Eerdmans, 1961).

[29] S. Holm-Nielsen, *Hodayot*.

[30] B. Nitzan, "Hymns from Qumran—4Q510–4Q511," *The Dead Sea Scrolls: Forty Years of Research*, 53–64.

*DJD* edition with the designation "Cantiques." In either case, is this meant to distinguish these compositions formally from others with a similiar purpose—"to frighten and terrify the evil spirits"—that scholars regularly designate as "psalms" (especially 11QPsAp<sup>a</sup>)?³¹ One possible solution is to decide to maintain Hebrew terminology (at least whereever this is in the text) rather than imposing modern form-critical terms which have been developed basicallly in light of the biblical psalter. But do specific terms—שיר, הודה, תפלה, תהלה, מזמר—have a technical and consistent usage in this period? The evidence is very unclear, as just two examples will illustrate. Psalm 145 is called תהלה in the MT, but תפלה in 11QPs<sup>a</sup>; the compositions in 1QH<sup>a</sup> are called in one rubrical heading הודות and תפלה (singular!) (1QH<sup>a</sup> XX 7 [= XII 4],³² also 4QH<sup>a</sup> 3 i 5 [למשכיל הודות) and in another section מזמור (1QH<sup>a</sup> XXV 34 [= frg. 8 10] למשכיל מזמ[ורים). A comprehensive study of these terms is clearly a desideratum, but this remains a work of the future.

A second issue that is only coming into focus as the full corpus becomes known is that of multiple texts which are very similiar, perhaps dependent upon one another, perhaps reworkings of yet another body of material. For example, Newsom recently has argued that the *Songs of the Maskil* can, in fact, be shown to be dependent upon the *Sabbath Songs*.³³ Somewhat more complicated is a segment of text of about ten lines that appears in three places: in a hymn in 4QH<sup>a</sup> 7; in the *War Scroll*, 4Q491 11 i, in that odd passage Baillet entitled (surely wrongly) "Cantique de Michel et cantique des justes"; and in a third, very fragmentary version in 4Q471b.³⁴ These three are clearly not identical, but more than fifteen phrases, often in the same order, are

---

³¹ This is the terminology of the editor, J. van der Ploeg, "Un petit rouleau de psaumes apocryphes (11QPsAp<sup>a</sup>)," *Tradition und Glaube: Das frühe Christentum in seiner Umwelt: Festgabe für Karl Georg Kuhn zum 65. Geburtstag* (ed. G. Jeremias et al.; Göttingen: Vandenhoeck & Ruprecht, 1971) 128–39, and has been maintained in subsequent discussion by, e.g., É. Puech, "Les deux derniers psaumes davidiques du rituel d'exorcisme 11QPsAp<sup>a</sup>," *The Dead Sea Scrolls: Forty Years of Research*, 64-89.

³² In references to 1QH<sup>a</sup>, the column and lines numbers listed first are according to the reconstruction of Stegemann and Puech (see note 22 above), and the second according to the *editio princeps* of Sukenik.

³³ C. Newsom, "'Sectually Explicit' Literature from Qumran," *The Hebrew Bible and Its Interpreters* (ed. W. Propp, B. Halpern, and D. N. Freedman; Winona Lake, IN: Eisenbrauns, 1990) 183–85.

³⁴ Although the original editors brought together under 4Q371 a group of fragments as a variant form of the War Scroll, the present editor, E. Eshel, has divided this into separate works; hence the designation 4Q471b. 4Q471b is not yet published.

shared by two or all three texts. Perhaps we are seeing a "floating text" that was incorporated in a number of different contexts, including into one of the hodayot. I suspect that more such interrelationships will come to light as the full corpus becomes known.

## The Designation "Liturgical"

One way that some texts or perhaps a majority of the texts that I have named to this point have typically been described is with the designation "liturgical," but again this is a term that is usually left undefined and simply treated as if its meaning were self-evident. I presume that the corresponding category is non-liturgical, though I find that term used much less frequently. I do not want to get sidetracked here into the quagmire of definitions, but when we use the term liturgy/liturgical, it is always with some working definition in mind, even if unexpressed. Indeed, I suspect that ultimately Qumran scholars will have to come to grips with the ways in which our confessional backgrounds are operative in how we even formulate questions like this. As has been much discussed in other contexts, it is by no means obvious that Christians and Jews in general, much less specific subgroups or individuals, mean the same thing when they use this language of liturgy/liturgical.[35]

I think it would be generally agreed now that different types of evidence converge to support the view that some public, fixed, non-sacrifical religious activity was part of the life of this group. Obviously, I am working toward a definition of liturgy as distinct from either spontaneous or private acts of devotion, on the one hand, and worship that is based on sacrifice, on the other.[36] Relevant data in support of a liturgy of prayer would include, first of all, descriptive statements in the documents themselves (e.g., 1QS VI 3 "together they

---

[35] See the brief comments of S. Reif, "Jewish Liturgical Research: Past, Present and Future," *JJS* 34 (1983) 168, and the essay of Arnold Goldberg, "Service of the Heart: Liturgical Aspects of Synagogal Worship," *Standing Before God: Studies on Prayer in Scriptures and in Tradition with Essays in Honor of John M. Oesterreicher* (ed. A. Finkel and L. Frizzell; New York: KTAV, 1981) 195–211.

[36] Here I am following the view that the authors of the Scrolls did not participate in the sacrifices of the Jerusalem temple but rather sought atonement and santification through prayer, study, and life as a community. For a summary of this complex topic and bibliography, see J. M. Baumgarten, "The Essenes and the Temple: A Reappraisal," *Studies in Qumran Law* (SJLA 24; Leiden: Brill, 1977) 57–74.

shall bless").³⁷ Secondly, as noted above, we do have a concrete body of actual texts with specific features of form and content (which we will examine more closely in a moment) that suggest a liturgical *Sitz im Leben*. Thirdly, as Talmon pointed out some years ago, there are specific sociological circumstances in the life and organization of the community conducive to "the emergence of institutionalized prayer."³⁸ The fourth type of evidence which could shed light on the liturgical life of this community, namely those practices that were shared in common by all Jews by the mid-second century BCE and that would have been simply inherited and continued, is, in fact, the most controversial, since there is so little scholarly agreement about the early (pre-70) development of non-temple worship.³⁹ However, when all this is brought together, we do have more bits and pieces of evidence than often realized about daily liturgical prayer (as distinct from special liturgies like the ceremony for entrance into the community described in 1QS I and II, or a liturgy for the end of days described in 1QM and 1QSb).

But can we be more specific about why we call a specific text "liturgical," but hesitate to apply that designation to others? Perhaps it is helpful to begin with some of the most obvious exemplars and then move to less certain material. In my survey of this material, I have noted that the manuscripts that are most consistently labelled liturgical are the collections of prayers for each day of the week (4QDibHam), prayers for each day of the month, and prayers for festivals. These share certain obvious features. Each is a series of self-contained, relatively short and simple compositions, in the first-person plural ("we"), to be used at a specific time ("on fourth day," "on Day of Atonement," "on day x in the evening"). Sometimes, we find the explicit formula יברכו וענו ואמרו.⁴⁰ There is a formal structure, consis-

---

³⁷ If identification is made with the Essenes, then we would want to include various statements in Josephus, such as the reference to "traditional prayers" before the rising of the sun *J. W.* 128). For a discussion of the very difficult passage in CD XI 21–XII 1 about the בית השתחות, see the forthcoming article of Annette Steudel in *RevQ*.

³⁸ S. Talmon, "The Emergence of Institutionalized Prayer in Israel in the Light of the Qumran Literature," *Qumrân: Sa piété, sa théologie et son milieu* (ed. M. Delcor; Paris: Gembloux, 1978) 265–84.

³⁹ For the view that there was little development of set prayer before the destruction of the Temple, see E. Fleischer, "On the Beginnings of Obligatory Jewish Prayer," *Tarbiz* 59 (1991) 397–441 (in Hebrew).

⁴⁰ This is most consistent in 4Q503. Note the same formula in 4Q266 in a liturgy for explusion of members from the community. See J. M. Baumgarten, "A New Qumran

tent within each collection, but with considerable variety when considered as a whole. For example, the prayers for the days of the week and the prayers for feasts conclude with a blessing (ברוך אדוני/האל) followed by a dual אמן אמן, while the daily prayers end with שלום עליכם ישראל. The daily prayers begin with a blessing (most often ברוך אל ישראל) and the prayers for the days of the week and the prayers for feasts with זכור אדוני.[41] Given that the *berakah* formula became normative for rabbinic statutory prayer, this formulation, though still far from the rabbinic standardization, points to a similar liturgical context. Furthermore, 4QDibHam distinguishes between petition on weekdays and praise on Sabbath, and this is a fundamental distinction in later statutory prayer.[42]

Recently E. G. Chazon has suggested that we should expect texts that were actually used liturgically in the life of the community to appear in a range of manuscripts over a period of time.[43] This suggestion is borne out with 4QDibHam (early Hasmonean, late Hasmonean, and Herodian manuscripts) and prayers for festivals (late Hasmonean to Herodian).[44]

However, if we are ready to agree that these prayers were used liturgically and then wish to move beyond these specific collections, things become much less clear. Were the biblical psalms used in the daily, public prayer in the community? Here I do not know how to evaluate the evidence. On the one hand, we do have 11QPs[a] with all its liturgical trappings (Psalm 145 with an antiphonal-type refrain; the liturgical catena in col. XVI, the doxological addition "there is none like the Lord" in Ps 135:6). As noted earlier, discussion has tended to focus on whether this is a variant psalter or a liturgical "hymnbook."

---

Substitute for the Divine Name and Mishnah Sukkah 4.5," *JQR* 83 (1992) 2. The formula also appears in liturgies of cursing (e.g., 4Q286 10 ii 2 וענו ואמרו). See J. T. Milik, "Milkî-sedeq et Milkî-reša; dans les anciens écrits juifs et chrétiens," *JJS* 23 (1972) 130.

[41] For more comprehensive study of the variations in the blessing formula, see E. Schuller, "Some Observations on Blessings of God in Texts from Qumran," *Of Scribes and Scrolls*, 139–42.

[42] E. Chazon, "4QDibHam: Liturgy or Literature?" *RevQ* 15 (1992) 447–55; eadem, "On the Special Character of Sabbath Prayer: New Data from Qumran," *Journal of Jewish Music and Liturgy* 15 (1992–93) 1–21.

[43] E. Chazon, "4QDibHam," 455.

[44] The fact that the daily prayers (4Q503) survive in only a single Hasmonean manuscript might support J. M. Baumgarten's suggestion that this collection, based on a lunar calendar, was not used liturgically in later stages of the community. See Baumgarten, "4Q503 (Daily Prayers) and the Lunar Calendar," *RevQ* 12 (1987) 399–407.

Yet, as Sanders himself and others have recognized,[45] this may not be the most helpful way to state the question since all psalters are, to some extent, liturgical collections. Schiffman has observed that many of the canonical psalms in 11QPs[a] are the same as those utilized in later rabbinic liturgy or are psalms that appear in talmudic discussions about prayer services. He concludes that "clearly, these same psalms, most notably Psalm 145, were used in a liturgical context by the Qumran sect."[46] Similarly, Weinfeld argues that the use of Psalms 145–150 in morning liturgy can be traced back already to Ben Sira and Qumran.[47] However, scholars of liturgy have been much less sanguine about the transference of psalmody from the realm of the Temple to the realm of the synagogue and insist that there is little documentation for a regular use of psalms in formal synagogue service until very much later.[48] This might at least give us pause when we think about whether the community of the Scrolls readily transferred psalmody to a non-Temple context. Certainly the large number of psalms manuscripts found at Qumran (thirty-nine, the largest number of manuscripts of any work at Qumran) attests to frequent use, but were these for study and private devotion or for liturgical purposes? It is to be noted that the recension with the most pronounced liturgical features exists in only two copies from Cave 11.[49]

If it is difficult to say how or if the biblical psalms might have been used in a non-Temple milieu, the question becomes more complicated when we move to non-biblical poetry. I first confronted this issue in working on the two manuscripts 4Q380 and 381, a collection of psalms not in the Masoretic psalter but clearly modelled on biblical psalms in topics, vocabulary, and headings, and incorporating extended quotations from biblical psalms. Though at least in the final

---

[45] J. A. Sanders, "Cave 11 Surprises and the Question of Canon," *McCormick Quarterly Review* 21 (1968) 292.

[46] L. H. Schiffman, "The Scrolls and Early Jewish Liturgy," 36.

[47] M. Weinfeld, "Traces of *Kedushat Yoṣer and Pesukey De-Zimra* in the Qumran Literature and in Ben-Sira," *Tarbiz* 45 (1976) 15–26 (in Hebrew).

[48] For example, P. Bradshaw, *The Search for the Origins of Christian Worship: Sources and Methods for the Study of Early Liturgy* (Oxford: Oxford University Press, 1992) 23; J. McKinnon, "On the Question of Psalmody in the Ancient Synagogue," *Early Music History* 6 (1986) 170–80; T. Zahavy, "From Temple to Synagogue: The Hallel in Early Rabbinic Judaism," *Studies in Jewish Prayer* (Lanham, MD: University Press of America, 1990) 103–09.

[49] For 11QPs[b], see J. P. M. van der Ploeg, "Fragments d'un manuscrit de Psaumes de Qumrân (11QPs[b])" *RB* 74 (1967) 408–13.

form of the manuscript these psalms are attributed not to David but to specific kings and prophets, I became interested in the methodological question of how one decides if these were used liturgically. Three of the compositions are called *tehillah* and one *tepillah*; the term *selah* occurs twice and can be reconstructed with a high degree of probability in five other places.[50] These terms most probably had precise liturgical significance at one stage in a Temple context, but by this time had they perhaps simply become stereotypical vocabulary without any liturgical significance?[51] There might be some hint of this in that *selah* is used somewhat differently than in biblical psalms, appearing here only at the conclusion of a psalm. Again, the fact that we have only one or perhaps two copies of the work may be significant.[52] Although I would hesitate to argue that 4Q380, 381 were used in the liturgy of the community, I am not sure there are clear grounds for making a decision (especially in contrast to the use of biblical psalms).

The issue becomes even more complicated when we move to the *Hôdāyôt*. There has, of course, been a long discussion about the possible *Sitz im Leben* for this collection and quite opposite conclusions have been proposed.[53] Some scholars highlight such features as the collapse of the standard psalmic forms, the extended length of some compositions, the presence of elaborate and complex expressions, and the irregular metric structure. For these reasons, they conclude that the *Hôdāyôt* were used primarily in an instructional or didactic context or for private meditation.[54] Others argue that these are truly "the Qumran community's liturgical prayers and songs of praise"—to quote Holm-Nielsen, who then becomes rather vague on specifics: "[the psalms] may be used anywhere in the service, without there being an established order and without their being linked to special holy

---

[50] For fuller documentation, see E. Schuller, *Non-Canonical Psalms from Qumran*, 25–27, 44–46.

[51] The same issue can be raised about the occurrence of *selah* in the *Psalms of Solomon* (17:31, 18:10) and in later synagogue inscriptions.

[52] Since there is no overlap of text, it is very difficult to decide if 4Q380 and 4Q381 are two copies of the same work or two different works; the similiarity of the material suggests the former.

[53] For a concise summary of past discussions and bibliography, see D. Dombrowski Hopkins, "The Qumran Community and 1QHodayot: A Reassessment," *RevQ* 10 (1981) 336.

[54] For example, H. Bardtke, "Considerations sur les cantiques de Qumrân," *RB* 63 (1956) 220–33; and most recently Schiffman, "The Dead Sea Scrolls and the Early History of Jewish Liturgy," 36.

occasions."⁵⁵ Weinfeld, however, finds clear links with morning prayers,⁵⁶ while Kuhn attempts to relate at least the Hymns of the Community to the ceremony for entrance into the covenant, although allowing that they could also have been used in daily prayer.⁵⁷

Here the Cave 4 *Hôdāyôt* manuscripts prove to be of particular significance. In the first place, it is now clear that there were multiple copies of the work in hands ranging from middle to late Hasmonean (4QH^(a,b)) to early Herodian (4QH^(d,e,f)). While I do not want to argue a simple equation that multiple copies imply liturgical usage, at least this is a consideration. Secondly, one of the standard criteria pointing to public, communal usage, as opposed to private meditation, is formulation of prayers in the first-person plural. While the presence in the *Hôdāyôt* of some "we" passages has always been recognized, these were so fragmentary in 1QH^a (e.g., a few lines from frg. 10 and the single word אוננו in frg. 18) as to have virtually no context. Thus these passages were overshadowed by the consistent "I" language. Now, however, we can draw into the discussion the large fragment 7 of 4QH^a. This fragment consists of about forty lines lines in two consecutive columns and overlaps with several small fragments (46 ii, 56 ii, 55 ii, 7 ii) that, in the reconstructed order of 1QH^a, form col. xxvi. This hymn contains typical "I" language in the first stanza (e.g., "as for me, my rank is with the heavenly beings") but moves to "we" language in the soteriological confession: דברנו, כיא ראינו, והכרנו, ידענוכה, והשכלנו. Similiarly, frg. 3 of 4QH^a overlaps with 1QH^a frg. 10 and enables us to read considerably more of this hymn in this first person plural (ונרננה, ואנחנו ביחד נועדנו, נוסרה). Furthermore, to return to the "new" hymn in 4QH^a 7, other sections are clearly liturgical. There is a long imperative summons to praise directed to the "beloved" ידידים (it is very difficult to know if this is a designation of the members of the community or the angels) with an extended series of imperative verbs (הביעו, ברכו, זמרו, שירו, שמחו, הרנינו, הללו, רוממו, הבו, הרימו). Three times we have the summons השמיעו ואמורו, followed by the actual text of an extended

---

⁵⁵ Holm-Nielsen, *Hodayot*, 348. See also the chapter "For What Purpose were the Hodayot Written?" (332–48).

⁵⁶ This view was first expressed by J. P. Hyatt, "The View of Man in the Qumran 'Hodayoth,'" *NTS* 2 (1955–56) 276. Weinfeld has promised a full article on this view, but so far has mentioned it only in passing in a review article in *BO* 41 (1984) 712–13 and in "The Morning Prayers (Birkhoth Hashachar) in Qumran and in the Conventional Jewish Liturgy," *RevQ* 13 (1988) 483, 491.

⁵⁷ H.-W. Kuhn, *Enderwartung und gegenwärtiges Heil*, 29–33.

blessing of God ברוך אל המפלי פלאות גדול אל עושה פלא, and (if the restoration is correct) a third blessing of God as creator. Although the evidence cannot be presented here, there are some indications that certain of the 4Q manuscripts do not contain the large compilation of hymns found in 1QH<sup>a</sup> but only smaller units of material, perhaps sources that circulated independently.[58] 4QH<sup>a</sup> seems to be a specific collection of material, much of which is suited to liturgical usage. Whether these hymns functioned in the same way when they were joined with others of quite different style in the manuscript that we know as 1QH<sup>a</sup> is difficult to say, but the presence of these hymns with strong liturgical features is one factor that calls us to think again about where we place the Hodayot on the liturgical/non-liturgical spectrum.

Some of the same questions can be raised about the *Songs of the Sabbath Sacrifice*. Newsom has called these thirteen related compositions "a coherent liturgical cycle,"[59] noting in particular certain formal elements—especially the repeated imperative call to praise (הללו אלהי המרים) and the use of first-person plural language in at least one hymn (4Q400 2 6–8 ): "what can we reckon like them . . . let us praise the God of knowledge." There are multiple manuscripts in late Hasmonean to full Herodian hands. While Newsom entertains the possibility that we could be dealing with a text that, while liturgical in origin, was not adopted for actual liturgical use by the community but "consulted only as a study text for the speculations on the heavenly world that it contained,"[60] she and most other commentators work with the assumption that the text was somehow used liturgically over the course of the first thirteen (or all?) of the sabbaths of the year.

My point in this last section has been simply to point out some of the problems and implications surrounding the use of the concept "liturgical." If we cast our net very broadly and envision the biblical psalms, various apocryphal psalms, the *Hôdāyôt*, and the *Songs of the Sabbath Sacrifice* as part of the daily or weekly liturgical practice of the

---

[58] The evidence will be presented more fully in an article I am preparing for *JQR Supplement*, 1994. The most convincing argument can be made for 4QH<sup>c</sup>, where the physical arrangement of the manuscript with very narrow columns of only twelve lines suggests that this contained only the Hymns of the Teacher.

[59] C. Newsom, "Merkabah Exegesis in the Qumran Shabbath Shirot," *JJS* 38 (1987) 12. Also "'Sectually Explicit' Literature from Qumran," n. 13: "The liturgical form of the document assumes a rather well-organized community."

[60] C. Newsom, "'Sectually Explicit' Literature from Qumran," 181. Newsom attributes the suggestion to H. Stegemann.

community, we come to a very different point than if we eliminate some or all of these as "non-liturgical" and relegate them to the realm of private devotion or study. If we understand liturgy as both forming and sustaining self- and religious-identity, the issue of what texts are to be included has far ranging implications. Much more work remains to be done.

## Sectarian vs. Non-Sectarian

Finally, as in many other areas of Qumran studies, the attempt to distinguish between sectarian and non-sectarian authorship of specific prayer and hymnic texts has come more and more to the fore in recent years. In contrast to the working hypothesis of earlier scholars that any non-biblical work found in one of the Qumran caves is sectarian unless proven otherwise, the pendulum has swung almost to the point where it is now the sectarian authorship that must be proved, not assumed. Various attempts have been made to list criteria for separating sectarian and non-sectarian,[61] and recently Newsom nuanced the question still further by distinguishing carefully between sectarian authorship per se; sectarian reading of an "adopted text" that originated in non-sectarian circles; and non-sectarian, that is, non-polemical, non-self-defining texts authored by a member of the community.[62]

The attempt to develop criteria and distinguish between sectarian and non-sectarian prayers is not a theoretical exercise for some abstract purpose of classification but a practical consideration with major implications. If certain prayers like 4QDibHam are pre-Qumran in origin and reflect more broadly based Second-Temple practice rather than specific sectarian developments, this helps to account for what Schiffman has noted as "certain almost shocking corespondences in prayer language"[63] between these texts and later Tannaitic usage. These prayers now become important not so much for the study of

---

[61] Arguments which have been brought forth in support of sectarian composition of a particular text include paleographic dating; characteristic vocabulary, terminology, and ideas; organizational or temporal features (e.g., language of yaḥad and presence of the figure of the Teacher of Righteousness); use of the tetragrammaton; the calendrical system reflected; evidence of a distinct scribal school. See E. G. Chazon, "Is *Divrei ha-meʾorot* a Sectarian Prayer?" *The Dead Sea Scrolls: Forty Years of Research*, 3–17.

[62] C. Newsom, "'Sectually Explicit' Literature from Qumran," 172–80.

[63] L. H. Schiffman, "From Temple to Torah: Rabbinic Judaism in Light of the Dead Sea Scrolls," *Shofar* 10 (1992) 10.

sectarian liturgy per se, but because we have here a window onto a previously inaccessible stage of Jewish liturgical development, and perhaps even insight into specific aspects such as the nature (literary or oral) of the development of prayer texts.

However, although I applaud the attempt to distinguish sectarian and non-sectarian and am confident that we can and will refine our methodology in the coming years, I suspect that this body of texts will remain the most resistant to such a distinction. The very essence of prayer/hymnic discourse, whether sectarian or non-sectarian, is its dependence on a common stock of stereotypical and formulaic, biblically-based phraseology. Those precise features that scholars have singled out as hallmarks in recognizing "sectarian"—whether institutional clues (Teacher of Righteousness, calendar) or theological concepts (predeterminism, dualism)—are least likely to come to expression in a prayer text. Although this is readily recognized on one level, I am afraid that at times we work with very outdated understandings of the function of liturgical language, still conceiving it as predominately cognitive and fundamentally a vehicle for polemical and theological discourse.[64] Qumran scholarship has much to learn by turning to historians, liturgists and sociologists who have studied the liturgical life of other dissident groups. Do the generating impulses that lead to division and a new self-identity necessarily find expression in "new" prayers? What are retained of "old" prayers, and how are they undestood?[65]

## Conclusion

This brings me to my final point. The fundamental work of producing first-editions of the major texts is not yet over, but we can almost see the end with regard to prayer and hymnic texts. As we seek to move the questions forward in the three areas that I have been discussing (genre, liturgical vs. non-liturgical, sectarian vs. non-

---

[64] For discussion of the same issue in terms of rabbinic liturgy, see L. Hoffman, "Censoring In and Censoring Out: A Function of Liturgical Language," *Ancient Synagogues: The State of Research* (ed. J. Gutman; BJS 22; Chico, CA: Scholars Press, 1981) 19–38.

[65] I am still haunted by the question put a few years ago during a discussion at the Haifa Conference when Daniel Schwartz asked, "Well, is the Our Father a Protestant prayer?"

sectarian), I am increasingly convinced that real progress will be made in the next years only if Qumran scholarship now becomes less isolated and more cognizant of and involved in other related disciplines. A few years ago, P. Bradshaw lamented the fragmentation that has characterized much of scholarship:

> Such work as has been done has on the whole been pursued in separate, seemingly watertight, departments: Jewish scholars have worked largely in isolation from NT scholars, NT scholars largely in isolation from liturgical scholars, and so on, with the result that hardly at all have the findings in one area been related to those in another.[66]

And Qumran scholars have been off working in still another separate corner! As I hope I have indicated here, the prayer and hymnic texts found in the caves at Qumran have much to offer to us all, not only Qumran specialists but students of both Jewish and Christian liturgy, but it will require our cooperative efforts to uncover and explore their richness in the years ahead.

---

[66] P. Bradshaw, *Daily Prayer in the Early Church* (New York: Oxford University Press, 1982) ix.

# Apocalypticism, Messianism, and Eschatology

# Apocalyptic Texts at Qumran

*Devorah Dimant*

Ever since Jewish apocalypses became an object of scientific inquiry, their origins and significance were a subject of diverse interpretations. Nonetheless, their antiquity and Jewish character were early recognized and completely vindicated by the discoveries of the Qumran manuscripts. Works such as *1 Enoch, Jubilees*,[1] and the *Testament of Levi* were discovered there in their original Aramaic and Hebrew versions and the study of these and other Jewish apocalypses was thus established on a sound footing: they are products of the Second Temple period, authored mostly in the Land of Israel.

Yet, inspite of the progress made during the last two decades in the study of Jewish apocalypses, their origins and background have remained obscure. Even their relation to the biblical literature is not sufficiently understood. A decade ago it was still debated whether the apocalypses are rooted in biblical prophecy or in biblical wisdom.[2] Scholars today tend to see biblical prophecy as the matrix of Jewish apocalypses and apocalypticism, but the question of origins is by no means settled.

Although presented as heavenly revelations divulged and explained to *biblical* sages, Jewish apocalypses contain much that is not biblical. Among the prominent themes are the periodization of history, an angelic world developed far beyond that of the biblical one, an emphasis on the last judgment, and a belief in afterlife or resurrection. Since the early days of critical inquiry, the presence of such non-biblical elements has been attributed to external influences

---

[1] *Jubilees* as a whole is considered here as an apocalypse, for it contains ingredients constitutive of the genre: it is a pseudepigraphon attributed to the Angel of Presence, who reveals to Moses on Sinai the sequence of past and future history.

[2] Cf. the reviews in M. A. Knibb, "Prophecy and the Emergence of the Jewish Apocalypses," in *Israel's Prophetic Tradition: Essays in Honour of Peter Ackroyd* (ed. R. Coggins, A. Phillips, M. Knibb; Cambridge: Cambridge University Press, 1982) 155–80; M. E. Stone, "Apocalyptic Literature," *Jewish Writings of the Second Temple Period* (ed. M. E. Stone; CRINT 2.2; Assen: Van Gorcum; Philadelphia: Fortress, 1984) 384–89.

on Second Temple Judaism: Canaanite,[3] Babylonian,[4] Persian,[5] and Hellenistic.[6] Especially emphasized were Mesopotamian elements in the Book of Daniel: mythological and astrological themes, as well as components of historical realia.[7] Long considered the earliest Jewish apocalypse, the Book of Daniel was viewed as evidence for the Mesopotamian origins of Jewish apocalyptic literature.[8]

Such a view is corroborated by the presence of Babylonian elements in *1 Enoch*, and the list has been augmented in recent studies. Babylonian influence can be detected, for instance, in the figure of Enoch as the seventh prediluvian patriarch,[9] in the mythical geography of *1 Enoch* 17–36,[10] and in the astronomy of the *Astronomical Book* (*1 Enoch* 72–82).[11] Other Babylonian elements have been identified in a newly discovered Aramaic work, unearthed at Qumran and related to the Enochic cycle, the *Book of Giants*.[12]

---

[3] Cf. P. Hanson, "Jewish Apocalyptic against its Near Eastern Environment," *RB* 78 (1971) 31–58.

[4] Cf. J. J. Collins, "Jewish Apocalyptic against its Hellenistic Near Eastern Environment," *BASOR* 220 (1975) 27–36; H. G. Kvanvig, *Roots of Apocalyptic* (WMANT 61; Neukirchen-Vluyn: Neukirchener Verlag, 1988) 2–11.

[5] Cf D. S. Russell, *The Method and Message of Jewish Apocalyptic* (Philadelphia: Westminster, 1964) 257–62; J. J. Collins, *The Apocalyptic Imagination* (New York: Crossroad, 1984) 22–26.

[6] Cf. T. F. Glasson, *Greek Influence on Jewish Eschatology* (London: SPCK, 1961); M. Hengel, *Judaism and Hellenism* (2 vols.; Philadelphia: Fortress, 1974) 1.181–218.

[7] See the summary in J. J. Collins, "Genre, Ideology and Social Movements in Jewish Apocalypticism," *Mysteries and Revelations: Apocalyptic Studies since the Uppsala Colloquium* (ed. J. J. Collins and J. H. Charlesworth; JSPSup 9; Sheffield: JSOT Press, 1991) 25–32.

[8] Cf. the review in Collins, *Apocalyptic Imagination*, 20–22.

[9] Cf. J. C. VanderKam, *Enoch and the Growth of an Apocalyptic Tradition* (CBQMS 16; Washington: Catholic Biblical Association, 1984) 33–51; Kvanvig, *Roots of Apocalyptic*, 231–36.

[10] Cf. P. Grelot, "La géographie mythique d'Hénoch et ses sources orientales," *RB* 65 (1958) 33–69.

[11] Cf. O. Neugebauer, "The 'Astronomical' chapters of the Ethiopic Book of Enoch (72 to 82)," in M. Black, *The Book of Enoch or I Enoch* (SVTP 7; Leiden: Brill, 1985) 387–88.

[12] They appear in the names of two giants: one is called *[g]lgmyš* (4Q531 = 4QBook of Giants$^c$) or *glgmys* (4Q530 = 4QBook of Giants$^b$), apparently the Sumerian and Old Babylonian hero Gilgamesh; the other is *ḥwbbš* (4Q203 = 4QEnGiants$^a$), which was plausibly related by Milik to the monster *Humbaba*, another character from the *Gilgamesh Epic*. Cf. J. T. Milik, *The Books of Enoch* (Oxford: Clarendon Press, 1976) 312–13.

The presence of Babylonian traditions in the Book of Daniel as well as in *1 Enoch* is of particular importance for the dating and origin of the apocalyptic literature, since the two works are considered the oldest Jewish apocalypses. The Qumran fragments have shed new light on this question by showing that at least two Enochic works may be older than the final edition of the Book of Daniel:[13] the *Book of the Watchers*,[14] and the *Astronomical Book*.[15]

Nevertheless, while the greater part of the cave 4 texts was unpublished, Qumran's contribution to the clarification of the nature and origin of the apocalyptic literature remained problematic. Connected with this issue was the attempt to define the character of the Qumran community and its literature. Whereas earlier scholars saw the Qumran community as an "apocalyptic community,"[16] and therefore closely related to the apocalyptic literature, more recently an

---

For details, cf. J. C. Reeves, *Jewish Lore in Manichaean Cosmogony* (HUCM 14; Cincinnati: Hebrew Union College, 1992) 125.

[13] The final version of the Book of Daniel known from the Massoretic Text is usually dated to 164 BCE at the latest.

[14] This work consists of at least four independent units (*1 Enoch* 1–5, 6–11, 12–16 and 17–36), which in themselves must be older. Cf. G. Beer, "Das Buch Henoch," *Die Apokryphen und Pseudepigraphen des Alten Testaments* (2 vols.; ed. E. Kautzsch; Tübingen: Mohr, 1900) 2.224–26. Already at Qumran these units were incorporated into one work, as is evident from the Aramaic copies. At least some form of the narrative source of *1 Enoch* 6–11 was known to the Maccabean-era *Book of Dreams* (*1 Enoch* 86–89:1), for it attempts to harmonize elements from two originally different legends about the Fallen Angels, the one about Shemihaza, the other about Azael, the combination of which is already present in the aggadic source of *1 Enoch* 6–11. For an analysis of this relationship, see my "The Fallen Angels in the Dead Sea Scrolls and in the Apocryphal and Pseudepigraphic Books Related to Them" (Dissertation, Hebrew University of Jerusalem, 1974) 85–87 (in Hebrew). Given the early date of the *Book of the Watchers*' sources, it has been argued that the affinity detected between the throne-scene of Daniel 7 and *1 Enoch* 14 may reflect dependence of Daniel 7 on *1 Enoch* 14 rather than the other way around. Cf. Kvanvig, *Roots of Apocalyptic*, 561–64.

[15] The evidence for this work rests especially on the manuscript 4Q208 (= 4QEnastr$^a$), which Milik dates to the turn of the second century BCE. Cf. Milik, *Books of Enoch*, 273.

[16] Cf. F. M. Cross, *The Ancient Library of Qumran & Modern Biblical Studies* (rev. ed.; Grand Rapids: Baker, 1980) 78. J. J. Collins has recently reformulated the same position by concluding that the affinities between the apocalypses and some of the community's writings suggest "the same general milieu as the apocalyptic movements." Cf. his comments in "Was the Dead Sea Sect an Apocalyptic Movement?" *Archaeology and History in the Dead Sea Scrolls: The New York Conference in Memory of Yigael Yadin* (ed. L. H. Schiffman; JSPSup 8; Sheffield: JSOT Press, 1990) 46.

apocalyptic character has been denied to the Qumran community.[17] However, the terms of the debate were defined on the basis of the partial Qumran evidence available at the time. The situation has now radically changed. With the cave 4 texts either preliminarily published or available for study in photographs, a more accurate and refined evaluation of the relevance of Qumran to the apocalyptic literature may be attempted. Moreover, the cave 4 materials can now be studied against the backdrop of the entire Qumran library. New perspectives have been brought to bear on the Qumranic materials, and they suggest new ways of understanding the sources and background of the apocalyptic literature.

In the following, I attempt to describe all the Qumran cave 4 fragments which, in my opinion, are closely related to the apocalyptic literature in theme, literary form, and central preoccupation. This is made possible by the use of a list I have recently compiled, which reclassifies the entire Qumran collection according to subject matter and literary genre.[18] Aiming at reconstructing the intact library, the list takes each manuscript as a single unit, disregarding the amount of text preserved. The 800 manuscripts of the library are thus divided into three categories: biblical manuscripts, works related to the Qumran community, and works unrelated to it.[19] Significantly, the shares of each category are more or less equal: one third of the manuscripts are biblical texts (excluding the apocrypha, which are assigned to non-biblical works).[20] Somewhat less than a

---

[17] By H. Stegemann, "Die Bedeutung der Qumranfunde für die Erforschung der Apokalyptik," *Apocalypticism in the Mediterranean World and the Near East: Proceedings of the International Colloquium on Apocalypticism, Uppsala, August 12–17 1979* (2d ed.; ed. D. Hellholm; Tübingen: Mohr-Siebeck, 1989) 513–14. The uncertainty surrounding Qumranic apocalyptic texts was well described by K. Koch more than twenty years ago, and the numerous new texts published since have not changed that. Cf. K. Koch, *The Rediscovery of Apocalyptic* (SBT 22; London: SCM Press, 1972) 32–33.

[18] The list with introductory comments is being published in "The Qumran Manuscripts: Contents and Significance," *Time to Prepare the Way in the Wilderness: Papers on the Qumran Scrolls by Fellows of the Institute for Advanced Studies of the Hebrew University, Jerusalem, 1989–1990* (ed. D. Dimant and L. H. Schiffman; Leiden: Brill, forthcoming).

[19] Such a definition involves some subjective criteria, for no generally accepted definition of community versus non-community literature has yet been worked out. In compiling the list, an effort was made to use a more precise terminology.

[20] These include the following writings: the *Wisdom of Ben Sira*, the Qumran fragments of which are re-edited in *The Book of Ben Sira* (Jerusalem: Academy of Hebrew Language, 1973) (in Hebrew); *Tobit* (unpublished); the *Letter of Jeremiah*, published by M. Baillet, *Les 'Petites Grottes' de Qumrân* (DJD 3; Oxford; Clarendon, 1962) 143;

third are works related to the community. These works are distinctive in that they employ specific terminology and ideas connected with a particular community. The third category comprises works with no such terminology, but which nevertheless display a particular character.

Reviewing the Qumran library as a whole, one is immediately struck by the peculiar place held by texts related to the apocalyptic literature. First, they do not contain terminology distinctive to the Qumran community.[21] Second, most of the texts which can be termed apocalypses or which involve related themes and styles are written in Aramaic rather than in Hebrew. The comparison between these Aramaic and Hebrew texts is in itself instructive.

In the preliminary observations offered below on this segment of the Qumran library, the following terms are employed: An *apocalypse* is a discourse in the first person relating divine revelation granted to a wise seer and interpreted through divine wisdom.[22] Such a revelation often concerns history and is usually set in a third-person narrative framework that identifies the speaker, normally a biblical sage, and determines the circumstances of the speech. The narrative is, therefore, the main vehicle for establishing a pseudepigraphic framework. As a rule, the bulk of an apocalypse consists of the protagonist's autobiographical account. A *testament* is a discourse in the first person containing instructions and sometimes forecasts addressed by an authoritative figure (father/king/wise man) to his subordinates (sons/subjects/disciples) on his deathbed. This type of discourse also has a narrative framework that functions in a way similar to that of an apocalypse. An *aggadic narrative* is a legendary, third-person narrative sequence, occasionally interspersed with smaller units of other forms, such as discourses and dialogues.

---

Psalm 151 and *Apocryphal Psalms*, published by J. A. Sanders, *The Psalms Scroll of Qumrân Cave 11 (11QPs$^a$)* (DJD 4; Oxford: Clarendon, 1965).

[21] These manuscripts were therefore assigned in my classification to the category of non-community texts. The absence of apocalypses from the literature of the community was noted by J. J. Collins, "The Jewish Apocalypses," *Semeia* 14 (1979) 48–49 and Stegemann, "Bedeutung der Qumranfunde," 511 n. 52.

[22] For definitions emphasizing the literary nature of the apocalypses, cf. M. E. Stone, "Apocalyptic Literature," 394, 433–34; Stegemann, "Bedeutung der Qumranfunde," 498. Compare Koch, *Rediscovery of Apocalyptic*, 28–33 and Collins, "The Jewish Apocalypses," 28, with his qualifying comments in "Genre," 12–13.

## Qumran Apocalyptic Texts in Aramaic

Some twenty-five Aramaic literary works have turned up at Qumran, beside a few magical, astronomical, and astrological texts. Almost all the literary works were unearthed in cave 4. Copies of three works were also found in other caves: the *Book of Giants*, the *New Jerusalem*, and the *Testament of Levi*. The only exception is the aggadic narrative *Genesis Apocryphon*, which was found only in cave 1, with no copies in cave 4. But this may be accidental.

Inspite of the fragmentary state of the texts, which does not always permit a precise understanding of their literary form, it is quite clear that the Aramaic texts from Qumran used only a limited number of forms: of the twenty-five Aramaic works, ten can be defined as apocalypses or visionary narratives; another nine as aggadic narratives; and the other six as testaments. Compared with the plethora of genres and forms displayed by the Hebrew non-community literature at Qumran, the limited range of forms used in Qumranic Aramaic texts is notable. As it happens, all these literary forms—visions, testaments, and aggadic narratives—constitute the building blocks from which many Jewish apocalypses are built. So, even if not every Aramaic text constitutes a real apocalypse, all are relevant to the understanding of the apocalyptic literature. For the purpose of this discussion, however, I will limit myself to texts which may be defined as apocalypses or texts closely related to them.

### Apocalypses

The work which goes under the name of *1 Enoch* was preserved in its entirety only in Ethiopic. It is, in fact, a collection of several compositions related to Enoch. Qumran cave 4 yielded fragments of four out of the five literary units which constitute *1 Enoch*, all of them in Aramaic.[23] Only two of them are clearly visionary in form:

---

[23] The second section, the so-called *Book of Parables* (1 Enoch 37–71), was not found at Qumran. Milik believed this fact indicated that the work is late and of Christian authorship (*Books of Enoch*, 89–100, 183). Others have noted that the composition shows no trace of distinctive Christian beliefs. It has been suggested that some allusions in the work may point to the beginning of the first century CE as the date of composition. Cf. J. C. Greenfield and M. E. Stone, "The Enochic Pentateuch and the Date of the Similitudes," *HTR* 70 (1977) 51–65. Cf. also C. L. Mearns, "Dating the Similitudes of

the *Book of Dreams* (*1 Enoch* 83–90) and the *Apocalypse of Weeks* (*1 Enoch* 93:1–10; 91:12–17). Both concern the historical sequence revealed to the biblical patriarch Enoch.

In *1 Enoch* dream visions serve as a medium not only for revelation about history, but also for ascents to the heavenly temple. An early specimen of such an ascent is found in *1 Enoch* 14–16. Another one is described in the *Testament of Levi* 2–5.[24] But although ascents have a distinct setting and genre, it is significant that these two early examples culminate in disclosures about history and the imminent future. The throne vision in Daniel 7, which shares features with *1 Enoch* 14, also involves a revelation about history, and it too takes place in a dream vision.

The act of incorporating revelations of this type in throne scenes signifies that the mysteries of history belong to the domain of divine knowledge and are safeguarded above. Consequently they can be divulged to mortals either through an angelic intermediary descending to earth, or by having a human being ascend to the heavenly temple.[25] Both procedures are employed by the apocalypses, and in the early examples the revelation is granted only in dream visions, since dream visions are the proper medium of communication with the heavenly world.

In *1 Enoch* heavenly ascent is carefully distinguished from a different type of activity, which takes place when Enoch embarks with angels on journeys to remote, mythical places in the universe. As described in the *Book of the Watchers* (*1 Enoch* 17–36) and the *Astronomical Book*, these journeys purport to take place in real time

---

Enoch," *NTS* 25 (1979) 360–69; M. A. Knibb, "The Date of the Parables of Enoch: A Critical Review," *NTS* 25 (1979) 345–59.

[24] Among the Qumran Aramaic fragments of *1 Enoch*, there are some which correspond to chap. 14 (4Q204 = 4QEn$^c$ 1 vi–vii); cf. Milik, *Books of Enoch*, 192–200, 348–49. Also fragments of an Aramaic Levi text were found at Qumran (1Q21; 4Q213, 4Q214). Cf. J. T. Milik, "Le Testament de Lévi en araméen: Fragment de la grotte 4 de Qumran," *RB* 62 (1955) 398–406. All the Qumranic texts published to date, together with some Geniza leafs, are assembled by K. Beyer, *Die aramäischen Texte vom Toten Meer* (Göttingen: Vandenhoeck & Ruprecht, 1984) 193–209. The Aramaic and Greek fragments of the primitive Aramaic Levi are assembled and translated by J. C. Greenfield and M. E. Stone in H. W. Hollander and M. de Jonge, *The Testaments of the Twelve Patriarchs: A Commentary* (SVTP 8; Leiden: Brill, 1985) 457–69. For the Cairo Geniza fragments, cf. J. C. Greenfield and M. E. Stone, "Remarks on the Aramaic Testament of Levi from the Geniza," *RB* 86 (1979) 214–30.

[25] Cf. M. Himmelfarb, "Apocalyptic Ascent and the Heavenly Temple," *SBLSP* 26 (1987) 210–17.

and space.[26] Again, the different medium of transmission indicates that a different type of knowledge is involved: this time the mysteries revealed to Enoch concern earthly localities within the domains of various angels.[27] Such knowledge is transmitted directly by the angels in the earthly sphere and therefore does not require a dream vision.

The distinction between dream visions and cosmic journeys becomes somewhat blurred in later Jewish apocalypses. Mysteries that in the *Book of the Watchers* (*1 Enoch* 17–36) are revealed during cosmic journeys—such as the course of the luminaries—are now granted to seers during their heavenly ascents. This may be due in part to the change in the cosmological picture: later apocalypses, such as 3 (Greek) *Baruch*, 2 (Slavonic) *Enoch* and the *Apocalypse of Abraham*, describe heavenly ascents in terms of multiple heavens, reflecting contemporary Hellenistic cosmology. In this complex system, the borderline between the heavens and the earthly world is perceived in a way different from the more rudimentary Mesopotamian picture of the world underlying the cosmic journeys of Enoch.

## New Jerusalem

Another type of vision is described in a different Qumran Aramaic work, the so-called *New Jerusalem*.[28] Preserved in numerous fragments, this work is presented as an autobiographical account of a seer, a pseudepigraphic device popular among the apocalyptic authors. The seer is shown a huge city and its temple.[29] Neither his

---

[26] Note *Jub* 4:21, which states that Enoch spent three hundred years with the angels (based on Gen 5:22). The course of his journeys is traced by *1 Enoch* 17–36 in an earthly and precise geographical context. The *Book of Parables* does, in fact, describe similar journeys, but its geography is less realistic.

[27] Note especially *1 Enoch* 17–18, where the list of the angelic responsibilities is presented.

[28] For most of the fragments published to date, cf. Beyer, *Die aramäische Texte*, 214–22. The fragments of an 11Q copy (11Q18) were recently edited by F. García Martínez, "The Last Surviving Columns of 11QJN," *The Scriptures and the Scrolls* (ed. F. García Martínez, A. Hilhorst, and C. J. Labuschange; Leiden: Brill, 1992) 178–92. For discussions see J. T. Milik, "Description de la Jérusalem nouvelle," *Les 'Petites Grottes' de Qumrân* (DJD 3; Oxford; Clarendon, 1962) 184–93 (on 5Q15); F. García Martínez, *Qumran and Apocalyptic: Studies on the Aramaic Texts from Qumran* (STDJ 9; Leiden: Brill, 1992) 180–213.

[29] The vision of the temple is preserved especially in the 11Q copy.

name nor that of his guide was preserved. However, the style and subject matter draw heavily on the vision of the eschatological Jerusalem and temple revealed to the prophet Ezekiel (Ezekiel 40–48). The seer in the Qumranic work may, therefore, be Ezekiel himself or someone going through a similar experience. That Jerusalem and the temple of the eschatological future are intended is evident from the gigantic dimensions of the city,[30] from its ideal plan, and from its being made of precious stones.[31] Thus, although the tour is conducted at an actual concrete site and not a symbolic one, it is nevertheless not a place thought to exist in an ordinary sense. The author may have envisaged a kind of visionary time machine which projected the seer into the eschatological future city. If so, this "tour" also has a "historical" dimension and therefore belongs with the dream visions concerned with eschatological realities. Another possible interpretation visualizes the future city and temple as already existing in historical time in some supernatural way.[32] Be that as it may, the tour must have taken place in a vision.

The foregoing review shows that the majority of the Aramaic apocalypses from Qumran concern history. It is noteworthy that the new texts have not yielded any specimen of heavenly ascents or cosmic journeys besides the ones already known from *1 Enoch*. This silence shows that these forms had only limited use at the early stage of the apocalyptic literature. Moreover, it suggests that ascents, journeys, and tours had a distinctive history and may have originated in different genres and settings.[33] In broad terms, then, the

---

[30] This motif is based on Isa 54:2–3. For later elaboration, cf. the Qumranic *Apostrophe to Zion* (= 11QPs$^a$ XXII 14–15); *1 Enoch* 90:36; 4 Ezra 10:26.

[31] Based on Isa 5:11–12. This is taken up in the description of the eschatological Jerusalem in Tob 13:18–19. In a pesher on the same verse of Isaiah 54 (4Q164 = 4QpIs$^d$) the Qumran community applied the simile to itself. Cf. M. P. Horgan, *Pesharim: Qumran Interpretations of Biblical Books* (CBQMS 8; Washington: Catholic Biblical Association, 1979) 125–31. The theme of the magnificence of the future Jerusalem is developed in contemporary literature on the basis of Isa 52:1; 54:1–2,11–12; cf. Bar 5:1–2; Tob 13:16–19; *Ps. Sol.* 11:7. Compare *1 Enoch* 90:29; 4 Ezra 10:25–26.

[32] Perhaps involving the notion of the heavenly Jerusalem. Cf. Revelation 21; 4 Ezra 10:26. Cf. the comments of M. E. Stone, *Fourth Ezra* (Hermeneia; Minneapolis: Fortress Press, 1990) 327–28. On the early Jewish sources of this idea, see my analysis "Jerusalem and the Temple in the Animal Apocalypse (*1 Enoch* 85–90) in the Light of the Thought of the Dead Sea Sect," *Shenaton* 6–7 (1983) 177–93 (in Hebrew).

[33] No "tours of hell" were discovered at Qumran. This confirms the impression that such tours form a distinct, later genre, which is attested mainly in later Jewish and Christian examples. Cf. M. Himmelfarb, *Tours of Hell: An Apocalyptic Form in Jewish and Christian Literature* (Philadelphia: Fortress, 1983) 60–61.

Qumran evidence justifies the basic distinction between "historical apocalypses" and "otherworldly journeys,"[34] although more refined secondary distinctions may yet need to be made.

## Visions and Forecasts in a Court Setting

Visions about history form the center of another type of literary setting, that of the court tale. The more general type of court tale is that of a plot against the successful and wise courtier, his downfall, and his eventual restoration. This was a motif widely disseminated in the ancient Mediterranean world.[35]

Drawing upon the biblical precedent of the Joseph story (Genesis 39–41), Jewish adaptation of the court-tale motifs turned the courtier into a Jew serving at the Babylonian or Assyrian court. In this form the court-tale pattern appears in Esther, Tobit, and Daniel 3, 6. The main concern of these works is the situation of Jews living in the diaspora; they therefore tell about rivalries with gentile courtiers, faith in divine providence in face of dangers menacing Jews, their eventual delivery, and the final vindication of the God of Israel.

However, in Daniel 2, 4, and 5 the court-tale framework has been adapted for a different purpose: it accommodates enigmatic visions of history and forecasts, which are interpreted by the divinely inspired Jewish courtier, Daniel. It is this last type of court tale which displays the closest affinity to apocalypses and apocalypticism. Using such Aramaic stories (Daniel 2–6) to build up the narrative framework for the Hebrew apocalypse (Daniel 7–12), the final editor of the Book of Daniel must have been well aware of this affinity.

As it happens, a surprising number of the Aramaic texts from Qumran belongs precisely to this type of court tale. A number of

---

[34] Cf. Collins, "Jewish Apocalypses"; idem, "Genre," 13–14.

[35] As is evident from the numerous versions of the *Story of Ahikar*, the oldest of which is a fifth-century BCE Aramaic copy from Elephantine. Cf. G. R. Driver, *Aramaic Documents of the Fifth Century B.C.* (Oxford: Clarendon, 1965). The presence of this copy in the Jewish military settlement, and the references to Ahikar in the Jewish book of Tobit (1:21–22; 2:10; 11:19; 14:10) attest to the knowledge of this work in Jewish circles as early as the fifth century BCE. Cf. J. M. Lindenberger, "Ahiqar," *The Old Testament Pseudepigrapha* (2 vols.; ed. J. H. Charlesworth; Garden City: Doubleday, 1983–85) 2.479–507. For a review of this work and other court-tales, cf. Cf. L. M. Wills, *The Jew in the Court of the Foreign King* (HDR 26; Philadelphia: Fortress Press, 1990) 39–74.

fragments have preserved a narrative about a royal court, referring to a king and his courtiers. In all these texts, the protagonist is a wise courtier and/or dream interpreter who converses with the king. Essentially this is the scene in both the so-called *Aramaic Apocalypse* (4Q246)[36] and the *Four Kingdoms* apocalypse (4Q552–553).[37] In these two texts the court-tale scene is the occasion for unfolding history, interpreted by or to the protagonist. In the *Aramaic Apocalypse* a seer foretells the succession of kingdoms and the final reign of a supernatural person, a son of God. The *Four Kingdoms* apocalypse introduces a symbolic vision, in which the protagonist sees four trees, apparently representing four kingdoms, a scheme perhaps similar to the one used in Daniel 2 and 7. The vision is apparently being explained to the seer by someone, since a few fragments have preserved the seer's questions about what he sees.

Also set against the background of a royal court are the so-called *Proto-Esther* text (4Q550)[38] and the *Prayer of Nabonidus* (4Q242).[39] Only narrative material from the two texts has survived, but originally they may also have contained visions or dreams. The *Proto-Esther* text tells about a Jewish dream interpreter at the court of the Persian king, whereas the *Prayer of Nabonidus* concerns a Jewish sage who informs the king that his mysterious illness was caused by his sinful idolatry.

Three other texts, an *Aramaic Vision* (4Q556, 557, 558),[40] the text that has been known as the *Elect of God* (4Q534),[41] and the so-called *Aaronic Text* (4Q541),[42] may also have constituted visions, but

---

[36] Cf É. Puech, "Fragment d'une apocalypse en araméen (4Q246 = pseudo-Dan^d) et le "royaume de Dieu," *RB* 99 (1992) 98–131. Cf. also the comments of G. Vermes, "Qumran Forum Miscellanea I," *JJS* 43 (1992) 301–03.

[37] Published by R. H. Eisenman and M. Wise, *The Dead Sea Scrolls Uncovered* (Rockport: Element, 1992) 72–73; K. Beyer, *Die aramäischen Texte vom Toten Meer – Ergänzungsband* (Göttingen: Vandenhoeck & Ruprecht, 1994) 108–09.

[38] Cf. J. T. Milik, "Les modèles araméens du livre d'Esther dans la grotte 4 de Qumrân," *RevQ* 15 (1992) 321–406.

[39] Cf. J. T. Milik, "'Prière de Nabonide' et autres écrits d'un cycle de Daniel," *RB* 63 (1956) 411–15.

[40] For 4Q588, cf. Beyer, *Ergänzungsband*, 93–94.

[41] Cf. the edition of Beyer, *Die aramäischen Texte*, 269–71, and his additions in the *Ergänzungsband*, 125–26.

[42] Cf. É. Puech, "Fragments d'un apocryphe de Lévi et le personnage eschatologique. 4QTestLévi^{c-d} (?) et 4QAJa," *The Madrid Qumran Congress: Proceedings of the International Congress on the Dead Sea Scrolls, Madrid 18–21 March, 1991* (2 vols.; ed. J. Trebolle Barrera and L. Vegas Montaner; STDJ 9; Leiden: Brill, 1992) 2.449–502.

they are too fragmentary to be reconstructed with certainty. From the *Aramaic Vision* only extremely fragmentary references to angels, the wicked, and the end of the kingdom have survived. The *Aaronic Text* has somewhat more, but not enough to understand fully the intriguing allusions to an extraordinary person, endowed with divine wisdom and authority, who is to suffer greatly. It has been plausibly conjectured that an eschatological setting is indicated here. The *Elect of God* text details the physical characteristics of yet another outstanding figure, whom scholars tend to identify as Noah.[43]

It is interesting to note that most of the Qumranic court tales do not explicitly mention Israel or her fortunes. At most, we hear about a wise Jewish exile, such as the protagonist in the *Prayer of Nabonidus* and the *Proto-Esther* text. Moreover, most of the pieces set in a royal court are permeated with a general pietistic atmosphere, of the type found in Daniel 2, 4–5 and in the *Story of Ahikar*. This strongly suggests a common Aramaic milieu, though perhaps not a distinctly Jewish one.

In the light of this observation, it should be noted that, inspite of the general similarity between the Qumran texts and the Danielic court tales, very few of the Qumranic court tales actually mention Daniel. Even the *Prayer of Nabonidus*, which is believed to belong with the Daniel cycle because of its affinity with Daniel 4, does not mention the biblical sage, at least not in the surviving fragments. In fact, the only Aramaic work from Qumran to do so is the so-called *Pseudo-Daniel* text (4Q243–244).[44] Set against the same type of royal court, it nevertheless differs from other Aramaic texts in that it contains a long and detailed review of biblical history. Allusions to the flood, the tower of Babel, and Egypt survive. This is at variance with both the Danielic stories and the court tales from Qumran, neither of which makes any reference to prediluvian or patriarchal events. It shows that two types of Aramaic texts figured among the

---

[43] The identification was first proposed by J. A. Fitzmyer, "The Aramaic 'Elect of God' text from Qumran Cave 4," *Essays on the Semitic Background of the New Testament* (Atlanta: Scholars Press, 1974) 127–60 (originally published in *CBQ* 27 [1965] 348–72). For a recent discussion, cf. García Martínez, *Qumran and Apocalyptic*, 1–24. See also the additions in Beyer, *Ergänzungsband*, 125–26.

[44] Partly published by Milik, "Prière de Nabonide," 411–15. Milik considered 4Q245, too, as a copy of the same work, but an examination of the photo (PAM 43.259) does not confirm this claim. The text does indeed contain the name of Daniel, but it also has the names Qahat, Ben Simeon, and Solomon. In any case, the fragmentary surviving text does not suggest a visionary or a royal-court context. I therefore consider it as a separate text.

sources of the apocalyptic literature: texts of a general pietistic character, which may even have been cultivated outside Judaism, and texts with a biblical orientation.[45]

## Visions as Subordinate Units

The limited scope of this presentation does not permit me to deal in detail with other Aramaic texts, such as the *Visions of Amram* (4Q543–548).[46] Although defined by the first editor, J. T. Milik, as "visions," the basic literary framework is that of a testament. Part of the testament is a dream vision seen by Amram and told to his children, just as Levi relates his visionary ascent in the *Testament of Levi*. Amram's vision is, nevertheless, not about history but about a demonic individual. It is therefore not included in the discussion here.

As for the *Book of Giants*, although it draws upon Enochic traditions, it does not share the visionary form of some Enochic works. Nor does Enoch relate his experiences in a pseudepigraphic form. Rather, its basic framework is a third-person narrative. The work should, then, be classified as a legendary narrative.[47]

In summarizing the discussion on the Aramaic texts from Qumran related to the Jewish apocalypses, one may discern two types of compositions: (1) works related to biblical figures and themes, which include the Enochic works, the *New Jerusalem*, and *Pseudo-Daniel*; and (2) works, mostly court tales, concerning dream visions about history and eschatological events, with only slight or no relationship to the Bible.

---

[45] Wacholder sees the Aramaic texts as Judeo-Aramaic, pre-Qumranic literature and explains their presence at Qumran as works "considered to be the ancestral patrimony of the sect itself." Cf. B. Z. Wacholder, "The Ancient Judeo-Aramaic Literature (500–165 BCE): A Classification of Pre-Qumranic Texts," in Schiffman, ed., *Archaeology and History in the Dead Sea Scrolls*, 273.

[46] Cf. J. T. Milik, "4Q Visions de ʿAmram et une citation d'Origène," *RB* 79 (1972) 77–97.

[47] This is one of my reasons for rejecting Milik's conjecture, advanced in *Books of Enoch*, 58, that the *Book of Giants* formed part of the original Enochic collection at Qumran. Cf. my remarks in "The Biography of Enoch and the Books of Enoch," *VT* 33 (1983) 16 n. 8. Similar observations were made by Reeves, *Jewish Lore*, 55.

## Qumran Apocalyptic Texts in Hebrew

Turning now to Hebrew apocalyptic texts at Qumran, one is immediately struck by two facts: first, their paucity; second, the difference in setting and style as compared with the Aramaic texts. Altogether absent from the Hebrew texts are works of the court-tale type. Also, aggadic narratives are poorly represented in Hebrew, with the possible exception of some fragments about the miraculous birth of Noah (= 1Q19; 1Q19bis).[48] Most intriguing, however, is the situation regarding apocalyptic and pseudepigraphic Hebrew texts. As for pseudepigrapha, we find hardly any pseudepigraphic patriarchal testaments in Hebrew, except for the meager and problematic fragments attributed to the *Testament of Naphtali* (4Q215).[49] Even more significant is the marked difference between the Aramaic and Hebrew works: whereas the Aramaic pseudepigraphic visions are attributed to a prediluvian figure, Enoch, the Hebrew pseudepigrapha are attributed to Moses (in the case of *Jubilees*) and to Ezekiel (in the case of *Pseudo-Ezekiel*).[50] There is also a narrative work related to Jeremiah.[51] The difference between Hebrew and Aramaic pseudepigrapha is apparent not only in the choice of pseudepigraphic protagonists but also in literary approach: whereas the Aramaic works treat their biblical models with considerable freedom, the Hebrew pseudepigrapha slavishly reproduce their model source.

Generally speaking, very few Hebrew "historical" apocalypses have turned up at Qumran. Only *Jubilees, Pseudo-Ezekiel,* and

---

[48] The text was edited by J. T. Milik, *Qumran Cave I* (DJD 1; Oxford: Clarendon, 1955) 84–86, 152.

[49] Cf. J. T. Milik, "Ecrits prééssénions de Qumran: d'Hénoch à Amram," *Qumrân: Sa piété, sa théologie et son milieu* (ed. M. Delcor; BETL 46; Gembloux: Duculot, 1978) 91–106.

[50] Extant in at least five copies: 4Q385, 4Q386; 4Q387; 4Q388; 4Q391. Cf. my list in "New Light from Qumran on the Jewish Pseudepigrapha – 4Q390," *The Madrid Qumran Congress*, 2.409–13. This article should be used to qualify previous discussions of *Pseudo-Ezekiel*: J. Strugnell and D. Dimant, "4Q Second Ezekiel," *RevQ* 13 (1988) 45–58; D. Dimant and J. Strugnell, "The Merkabah Vision in *Second Ezekiel* (4Q385 4)," *RevQ* 14 (1990) 331–48.

[51] The so-called *Apocryphon of Jeremiah*, extant in at least four copies: 4Q383; 4Q385; 4Q387; 4Q389. Cf. the list and my comments in "New Light." I have edited 4Q385 16 in the *Proceedings of the Paris Congress of Qumran Studies* (forthcoming). Since I have discussed them extensively elsewhere, I have not elaborated here on *Pseudo-Ezekiel, Pseudo-Moses*, and the *Apocryphon of Jeremiah*.

*Pseudo-Moses* may be so termed, but certain qualifications are necessary. Hebrew "otherworldly" apocalypses are altogether absent from the library. This should be connected with the absence of apocalypses from the distinctive literature of the community, already noted above.[52] Obviously, the Qumranites were not engaged in writing apocalypses. Whoever did write apocalypses in Hebrew attributed them only to figures belonging to the proper history of Israel, while authors writing in Aramaic attributed their apocalypses to prediluvian or patriarchal figures.[53]

The central place at Qumran held by Aramaic court tales points to the importance of this type of material for the understanding of the nature and origins of the Jewish apocalyptic literature. Perhaps not only a Babylonian phase is to be looked for, but also an Aramaic one.

The complex relationship between Hebrew and Aramaic texts at Qumran has a bearing on a number of issues related to the biblical canon. With the presence of both Hebrew apocalyptic texts and Aramaic court tales at Qumran, the combination of these two types of material in the Book of Daniel may not appear so unusual. In any case, both types of literature were circulating side by side during the Second Temple period, and, in the case of Qumran, were read by the same people. One may, then, well ask: How and why were the tales attributed to Daniel selected and invested with authority? And what was the attitude of contemporary readers, or of the Qumranites themselves, to many other similar tales? Similar questions may be asked about the status of the Hebrew pseudepigrapha. What, for instance, would have been the attitude toward a work such as *Pseudo-Ezekiel*, which purports to come directly from Ezekiel but which obviously produces passages not found in the authoritative version of Ezekiel's prophecies? That the Qumranites may have been aware of the difference is suggested by the fact that they possessed copies of the biblical Ezekiel which are identical to the Massoretic Text.[54]

---

[52] The case of *Pseudo-Moses* is more complex, for it contains terminology closely related to the *Damascus Covenant*. However, I do not think that it can be simply equated with the terminology of the community. Cf. my discussion in "New Light."

[53] Perhaps the use of Hebrew as the linguistic vehicle for divine revelations after Moses was based on the theological belief, expressed in *Jubilees*, that Hebrew—the divine, angelic language of creation—had been the revelatory language since the days of Moses. Cf. *Jub* 2:15; 12:25–27.

[54] Cf. J. Lust, "Ezekiel Manuscripts in Qumran: Preliminary Edition of 4QEz$^a$ and $^b$," *Ezekiel and His Book* (ed. J. Lust; BETL 74; Leuven: Peeters, 1986) 90–100.

No less intriguing is the status of the Enochic compositions. Many of the traditions found in these compositions concern subject matter treated in the first chapters of Genesis. What is the historical relationship between the two,[55] and how did the Qumranites evaluate these ancient traditions?

The inquiry into these texts is in its initial stage. Nevertheless, we may already realize that the study of the earliest Jewish apocalyptic texts, and the question of their origins, cannot be studied in isolation from the overall picture emerging from Qumran.

---

[55] Although one may not agree with Milik (*Books of Enoch*, 31) that Genesis 6–9 refers to the *Book of the Watchers*, the relationship between the two requires further investigation, given the early dating of the Enochic work.

# Appendix:
## Qumranic Texts Related to the Apocalyptic Literature

| Hebrew Pseudepigrapha | | Aramaic Texts | |
|---|---|---|---|
| Jubilees | 4Q176 19–20; 4Q216; 4Q218–224;1Q17–18; 2Q19–20; 3Q5; 11Q12 | Book of Giants | 4Q203; 4Q530–532; 4Q533(?); 1Q23; 1Q24(?); 2Q26(?); 6Q8 |
| Text Close to Jubilees | 4Q482–483 | New Jerusalem | 4Q554–555; 1Q32; 2Q24; 5Q15; 11Q18 |
| Pseudo-Jubilees | 4Q217; 4Q225–227 | Visions of Amram | 4Q543–548 |
| Testament of Naphtali | 4Q215 | Aramaic Levi | 4Q213–4Q214; 1Q21 |
| Words of Moses | 1Q22 | Apocryphon of Levi | 4Q537; 4Q540–541 |
| Moses Apocryphon | 2Q21 | Testament of Qahat | 4Q542 |
| Pseudo-Ezekiel | 4Q385–388; 4Q391 | Patriarchal Pseudep. | 4Q538–539 |
| Pseudo-Moses | 4Q385a; 4Q387a; 4Q388a ; 4Q389; 4Q390 | Aramaic Apocalypse | 4Q246 |
| Pseudepigraphic Work | 4Q459–460 | Prayer of Nabonidus | 4Q242 |
| Prophetic fragments | 4Q522; 1Q25; 2Q23; 6Q10 | Proto-Esther (?) | 4Q550 |
| | | Daniel-Susanna | 4Q551 |
| | | (?)Elect of God | 4Q534 |
| | | Four Kingdoms Apoc. | 4Q552; 4Q553 |
| | | Vision (?) | 4Q556–558 |
| | | Words of Michael | 4Q529 |
| | | Miscellaneous | 4Q535–536; 4Q549 |
| | | Tobit | 4Q196–199 |
| | | Genesis Apocryphon | 1Q20 |
| | | 1 Enoch | Enoch: 4Q201–202; 4Q204–207; 4Q212; Astronomical Book: 4Q208–211 |

# Teacher and Messiah? The One Who Will Teach Righteousness at the End of Days

*John J. Collins*

In the sixth column of the *Damascus Document*, there is a notoriously controversial reference to "one who will teach righteousness at the end of days." The controversy, of course, centers on the relation between this figure, who is clearly future, and the Teacher of Righteousness, who appears elsewhere in the document as a figure from the past, and also the "Interpreter of the Law" who is mentioned in the same passage, a few lines earlier. The passage is an exposition of a verse from Num 21:18: "the well which princes dug, which the nobles of the people delved with the staff." According to the exposition:

> The well is the Law, and those who dug it were the converts of Israel who went out of the land of Judah to sojourn in the land of Damascus . . . The Staff is the Interpreter of the Law of whom Isaiah said, He makes a tool for His work; and the nobles of the people are those who come to dig the well with the staffs with which the staff ordained that they should walk in all the age of wickedness—and without them they shall find nothing—until he comes who shall teach righteousness at the end of days.

In the early days of Scroll research, this passage gave rise to some rather wild speculation that the historical Teacher was expected to return at the end of days.[1] A consensus developed, however, that the figure expected at the end of days cannot be identified with the Teacher who played a role in the beginning of the community. Rather, that Teacher is referred to in this passage as the Interpreter of the Law, and the eschatological figure remains in the future. This

---

[1] For a summary of the early debate see G. Jeremias, *Der Lehrer der Gerechtigkeit* (Göttingen: Vandenhoeck & Ruprecht, 1963) 275–81; J. Carmignac, "Le Retour du Docteur de Justice à la fin des jours?" *RevQ* 1 (1958–59) 235–48.

consensus was challenged by Philip Davies, who argued that this passage comes from an earlier stratum of the document than the other references to the Teacher of Righteousness. On his view, the historical Teacher claimed to be the fulfilment of the expectation articulated in VI 11, and so might be described loosely as a messianic figure.[2] The Interpreter of the Law would then be another, less significant figure from the early days of the movement before the true Teacher came along. Davies then supposes that the dispute between the Teacher and the Man of the Lie, or the Scoffer, who rejected his teaching, was in effect a disagreement as to whether the Teacher was the fulfilment of eschatological expectations.

There are obvious problems with Davies' proposal, many of which have been pointed out by Michael Knibb.[3] "Interpreter of the Law" appears as an eschatological title, for a figure who is to appear with the Branch of David at the end of days, in the *Florilegium*, a document that is closely related to CD.[4] It also appears in CD VII 18 with reference to the star of Balaam's oracle, which usually has eschatological connotations. This suggests that such titles as Interpreter of the Law and Teacher of Righteousness could be variously used to refer to figures past or future, and that they are interchangable. Indeed, the *Community Rule* requires that every group of ten should include a man who interprets the law (איש דרש בתורה) so the title Interpreter of the Law could obviously have more than one referent. The expectation of "one who will teach righteousness at the end of days" is retained in the final redaction of CD, even though the career of the historical Teacher is clearly past. The document clearly envisages two Teachers, one of whom was dead at the time of the final redaction and one who was still to come. It is gratuitous to multiply teachers without cause, by identifying the Interpreter of the Law as yet a third figure who preceded the historical Teacher.

---

[2] P. R. Davies, *The Damascus Covenant* (JSOTSup 25; Sheffield: JSOT, 1983) 124; "The Teacher of Righteousness at the End of Days," *RevQ* 13 (1988) 313–17.

[3] M. Knibb, "The Teacher of Righteousness—A Messianic Title?" *A Tribute to Geza Vermes: Essays on Jewish and Christian Literature and History* (ed. P. R. Davies and R. T. White; JSOTSup 100; Sheffield: JSOT, 1990) 51–65.

[4] On the relationship between the *Florilegium* and CD see George J. Brooke, *Exegesis at Qumran: 4QFlorilegium in its Jewish Context* (JSOTSup 29; Sheffield: JSOT, 1985) 206–09. The Interpreter of the Law is also mentioned in the *Catena* (4QCatena[a] II 5; F. García Martínez, *Textos de Qumrán* [Madrid: Trotta, 1992] 261) but the passage is too fragmentary to show whether the reference is past or future.

Davies has been supported, however, by Michael Wise, who argues in his dissertation not only that the Teacher was the one who had been expected, but that the *Temple Scroll* is the new law that he wrote for the end of days.[5] Since many scholars have argued for various reasons that the *Temple Scroll* was authored by the Teacher of Righteousness[6] or that it is a law for the eschatological period,[7] this argument deserves some consideration.

## The Understanding of the "End of Days"

The expression אחרית הימים occurs one other time in CD, in IV 4, which interprets the "sons of Zadok" of Ezek 44:15 as "the elect of Israel, the men called by name who (shall) stand at the end of days." The verb "stand" is a participle (עמדים) and so it is uncertain whether the reference is present or future.[8] It should be noted, however, that the same verb (עמד) is used of the figure who will teach righteousness in CD VI 11, of the "prince of the congregation" who is the sceptre of Balaam's oracle in CD VII 20 and of the "Branch of David" who will arise with the Interpreter of the Law in *Florilegium* I 11. In each of these cases the reference is to the eschatological future. The most significant parallel to CD VI 11 is found in the *Florilegium*, which refers to the "Branch of David" who will arise with the Interpreter of the Law at the end of days. Since there is no

---

[5] Michael O. Wise, *A Critical Study of the Temple Scroll from Qumran Cave 11* (Studies in Ancient Oriental Civilization 49; Chicago: The Oriental Institute of the University of Chicago, 1990) 184; idem, "The Temple Scroll and the Teacher of Righteousness," *Mogilany 1989: Papers on the Dead Sea Scrolls, Vol. 2* (ed. Z. J. Kapera; Kraków: Enigma, 1991) 121–47.

[6] So Y. Yadin, *The Temple Scroll: The Hidden Law of the Dead Sea Sect* (London: Weidenfeld and Nicolson, 1985) 226–28; B. Z. Wacholder, *The Dawn of Qumran: The Sectarian Torah and the Teacher of Righteousness* (Cincinnati: Hebrew Union College, 1983) passim; F. García Martínez, "Qumran Origins and Early History: A Groningen Hypothesis," *Folia Orientalia* 25 (1989) 121.

[7] M. Fishbane, "Use, Authority and Interpretation of Mikra at Qumran," *Mikra. Text, Translation, Reading and Interpretation of the Hebrew Bible in Ancient Judaism and Early Christianity* (ed. M. J. Mulder; CRINT 2.1; Assen: Van Gorcum; Philadelphia: Fortress, 1988) 365. Fishbane takes the *Temple Scroll* as a Torah for the New Age, after the final war, and so for a later point in the eschatological timetable than the "end of days" as understood by Wise.

[8] See Davies, *The Damascus Covenant*, 91 for a discussion of the various scholarly positions.

evidence that the Branch of David was thought to have come already, the "end of days" is surely future from the perspective of the *Florilegium*. Nonetheless, George Brooke has argued that "This future time, this time before the end, is already being experienced. The latter days herald and anticipate, even inaugurate the end, but they are not the end, except proleptically . . . ."[9] One may grant, however, that the "latter days" are not the end, or the final culmination of history, without granting that they are being already experienced.

Wise also takes the אחרית הימים as referring to a time before the end, but he sees this as the first stage of a two-stage eschatology. Against Brooke, he argues that there is no unambiguous use of אחרית הימים which refers to the present, but many that refer to the future.[10] 4QMMT is an exception here, in so far as it claims that some of the blessings and curses foretold in the book of Moses have come about, and that "this is the end of days."[11] It is very doubtful, however, whether the *Damascus Document*, the *Pesharim*, *Florilegium* or *Catena* regard the אחרית הימים as already inaugurated. The difference between 4QMMT and these documents might be explained in various ways. They may reflect different periods in the history of the sect, or different contemporaneous viewpoints, but in any case 4QMMT appears to be exceptional on this point.

The eschatological expectations of the *Florilegium* have been much debated, and no consensus has been reached. Much of the debate has centered on the various temples mentioned in the *Florilegium*.[12] The extant fragments of this composition begin with an exposition of 2 Sam 7:10. The beginning of the verse is not preserved, but it is the basis of the following interpretation. The verse reads "And I will appoint a place for my people Israel and will plant them, so that they may live in their own place and be disturbed no more." The interpretation follows:

> That is the house which [he will build] for him in the latter days, as it is written in the book of [Moses], "The sanctuary of the Lord which thy hands have established . . . And foreigners shall not make it desolate again, as they desolated formerly the sanctuary of Israel because of their sin. And he said to build

---

[9] Brooke, *Exegesis at Qumran*, 176.

[10] M. Wise, "4QFlorilegium and the Temple of Adam," *RevQ* 15 (1991) 115 n. 45.

[11] 4QMMT C 22 (numbering of *The Qumran Chronicle* 2 [1990] Appendix A).

[12] For a summary of research, see Wise, "4QFlorilegium," 107–10.

for him a מקדש אדם, for there to be in it for him smoking offerings...."[13]

The מקדש אדם has been variously interpreted as the Qumran community or as a physical temple, and has often been identified with the sanctuary of the Lord, mentioned in the citation from Exodus 15 at the beginning of the passage. Wise, who envisages a physical temple, points out that the sentence "and he said to build for him a מקדש אדם" is not preceded by a new citation, and so he argues that it continues the explanation of 2 Sam 7:10–11. There is no formal parallel, however, for the sentence introduced by "and he said," and so the form-critical observations do not really support any interpretation. Daniel Schwartz has plausibly suggested that this sentence is a paraphrase of 2 Sam 7:13a ("he will build me a temple"), which in its original context promises that Solomon will build the temple.[14] If this is correct, then the מקדש אדם is not necessarily identified with the "sanctuary of the Lord" which is promised for the "end of days," since it is related to a different lemma. Even if we do not accept Schwartz's suggestion, however, and suppose that the מקדש אדם is an "additional explication" of 2 Sam 7:10, as Wise suggests,[15] it does not necessarily follow that the two temples should be identified. A scriptural verse may have more than one referent, as can be seen clearly from 1QpHab II 1–10, à propos of Hab 1:5, which we will cite later. It seems to me, moreover, that the מקדש אדם, however understood, by its very terminology implies a contrast with the "sanctuary of the Lord," which will be built in the "latter days."[16] It should also probably be distinguished from the "temple of Israel" which was defiled. I suggest, then, that the מקדש אדם, whether understood as a real temple or as "a sanctuary consisting of men," is not an eschatological temple that belongs to the "end of days." Rather it is an in-

---

[13] Trans. Brooke, *Exegesis at Qumran*, 92, except that he translates מקדש אדם as "a sanctuary of men."

[14] D. R. Schwartz, "The Three Temples of 4QFlorilegium," *RevQ* 19 (1979–81) 88. Schwartz infers that the reference in the *Florilegium* is to Solomon's temple, but this does not necessarily follow. By omitting the actual citation, the author avoids the question of who will build this temple.

[15] "4QFlorilegium," 120.

[16] Other scholars who have argued that the מקדש אדם is made by humans include Michael Knibb, *The Qumran Community* (Cambridge: Cambridge University Press, 1987) 258–62, and Devorah Dimant, "4QFlorilegium and the Idea of the Community as Temple," *Hellenica et Judaica: Hommage à Valentin Nikiprowetzky* (ed. A. Caquot, M. Hadas-Lebel and J. Riaud; Paris/Leuven: Peeters, 1986) 165–89.

terim arrangement, pending the construction of the "sanctuary of the Lord" in the end of days. It may possibly refer to the sectarian community, as Brooke and others have argued, but it does not imply that the "end of days" has been inaugurated in the history of the community.

Yigael Yadin already drew attention to a possible parallel between the temples of the *Florilegium* and those of 11QTemple col. XXIX,[17] and the parallel has been pursued by Wise. 11QTemple col. XXIX speaks of "the house upon which I will cause my name to d[well] . . ." on which God will cause his glory to dwell "until the Day of Creation, when I myself shall create my temple, to establish it for me forever, according to the covenant which I made with Jacob at Bethel." The *Temple Scroll* does not use the expression אחרית הימים, but Wise argues that the period of the temple where God causes his glory to dwell, or the period immediately prior to the "Day of Creation," is in fact the period called the "end of days" in the *Florilegium*.[18] This argument depends on his identification of the penultimate temple of the *Temple Scroll* with the מקדש אדם in the *Florilegium*, on the one hand, and the "sanctuary of the Lord" which is to be made in the "end of days" on the other. This argument, however, forces him to reject the plain meaning of the quotation from Exod 15:17, which implies that the "sanctuary of the Lord" will be made directly by God ("the sanctuary of the Lord which thy hands have established")[19] and so is more naturally correlated with the new temple on the day of creation (if indeed the two passages should be so correlated at all). It seems to me, then, that only one temple in the *Temple Scroll*, the final one on the day of creation, can properly be called eschatological: the new temple which God will make on the day of creation is the same as the one promised in the *Florilegium* for the אחרית הימים. This has implications both for the supposed eschatological character of the *Temple Scroll* and for its possible authorship by the one who would teach righteousness at the end of days.

---

[17] Y. Yadin, "Le Rouleau du Temple," *Qumrân: sa piété, sa théologie et son milieu* (ed. M. Delcor; BETL 46; Paris: Duculot; Leuven: Leuven University Press, 1978) 115-19; idem, *The Temple Scroll, Volume One: Introduction* (Jerusalem: Israel Exploration Society, 1977) 140-44.

[18] Wise, "4QFlorilegium," 115. Wise translates the מקדש אדם as "the temple of Adam," implying a return to a paradisiac state.

[19] Contrast the MT, which reads "thy sanctuary, O Lord." Wise admits this problem ("4QFlorilegium," 115) but dismisses it in light of his other arguments.

Up to this point, we have argued that the אחרית הימים is still in the future from the perspective of the *Damascus Document* (at all stages of its redaction) and of the *Florilegium*. We are told only a few important characteristics of this period. It will be a time of refining (עת מצרף, 4QFlor II 1). It will be marked by the coming of the Branch of David and the eschatological Interpreter of the Law, and by the sanctuary made by God. This picture can be elaborated only to a slight extent from other texts. The time of testing is reflected in 4QCatena[a] II 9–10, which also speaks of the purification of the hearts of the men of the community and of the conflict between the lots of light and darkness.[20] It is also reflected in the *Pesher on Habakkuk*, which refers to traitors and ruthless ones at the end of days (1QpHab II 5–6; cf. 4QpNah 3–4 ii 2). The Branch of David is also associated with the "end of days" in the pesher on Isaiah (4QpIsa[a]) and the messiah of Israel, who is presumably to be identified with the Branch of David, appears in the "Rule for all the congregation of Israel in the end of days" (1QSa).[21] This latter document, also known as the *Messianic Rule*, shows that the אחרית הימים is not the end of history, and does not imply a perfect world. There is still provision for marriage and for the education of children, and there are still laws to limit the roles of simpletons and of people smitten with various forms of uncleanness. The pesharim also allude to the activity of the Kittim in this period (1QpHab IX 6–7) and to war and turmoil (4QpIsa[a] 7–10; 22–25; 4QpIsa[b] II 1; 4QCatena[b] III 7–8). The end of days, then, is not a period of perfection and peace, but includes the final turmoil and at least the dawn of the messianic age.

---

[20] F. García Martínez, *Textos de Qumrán*, 261; cf. J. Strugnell, "Notes en marge du volume V des 'Discoveries in the Judaean Desert of Jordan'," *RevQ* 7 (1970) 244. Annette Steudel, "4QMidrEschat: 'A Midrash on Eschatology' (4Q174 + 4Q177)," *The Madrid Qumran Congress: Proceedings of the International Congress on the Dead Sea Scrolls, Madrid 18–21 March 1991* (2 vols.; ed. Julio Trebolle Barrera and Luis Vegas Montaner; STDJ 11; Leiden: Brill; Madrid: Editorial Complutense, 1992) 2.531–41, argues that the *Catena* and the *Florilegium* are two parts of the same composition.

[21] On this text see L. H. Schiffman, *The Eschatological Community of the Dead Sea Scrolls* (SBLMS 38; Atlanta: Scholars Press, 1989).

## The Temple Scroll and the End of Days

Is this characterization of the אחרית הימים reflected in the *Temple Scroll*? A crucial part of Wise's argument rests on his redactional study of the use of Deuteronomy in 11QTemple.[22] He argues that the Scroll did not draw directly from Deuteronomy, but from a source D that had already excerpted portions of the biblical book.[23] The redactor of the *Temple Scroll* left out portions of D which would cease to function at the end of days. So it omits laws relating to the גר, in accordance with their exclusion from the eschatological temple in the *Florilegium*. Passages on lending to Israelites are omitted, as are laws relating to slaves. Yet, as Wise recognizes, the *Temple Scroll* does not omit everything we would expect to be irrelevant to the "end of days." It retains laws on adultery and rape, expiation for an unknown murderer and the stoning of a rebellious youth.[24] Wise's explanation, that inconsistency is human, and that the author's concept of righteousness allows for some individual lapses, is weak. If Wise is right that the author of *Temple Scroll* was working with a D source rather than with the book of Deuteronomy itself, then we do not know whether these laws were already omitted from the source. It would also seem that many of the omissions could be explained by the author's relative lack of concern for social issues. While it is true that the אחרית הימים does not necessarily imply a perfect world, the argument that relevance to the end of days is a redactional principle in the *Temple Scroll* is not compelling.

One of the most consistent trade-marks of the אחרית הימים is the coming of the messiah. We should expect then that the portrayal of the king in the *Temple Scroll*, in the so-called "Law of the King" (11QT LVII 1–LIX 11),[25] would show some messianic traits. But this is not the case. We should not be surprised that the king is subordinated to the authority of the High Priest ("at his word he shall go and at his word he shall come," LVIII 19). The Branch of David is also subjected to priestly authority in the pesher on Isaiah, and this arrangement is compatible with the expectation of two messiahs

---

[22] Wise, *A Critical Study of the Temple Scroll*, 167–79; idem, "The Eschatological Vision of the Temple Scroll," *JNES* 49 (1990) 155–72.

[23] *A Critical Study of the Temple Scroll*, 35–38.

[24] Ibid., 175.

[25] Wise attributes the Law of the King to a "Midrash to Deuteronomy" source (ibid., 101).

elsewhere in the scrolls.²⁶ It is surprising, however, to find that the reign of this king is conditional and that the law envisages the possibility that his posterity would be cut off for ever (LIX 14–15). Where else is such a possibility raised with reference to a messianic king? There is no hint here that this king is engaged in an eschatological war, no mention of the Kittim or of a time of testing. Most striking of all is the lack of any allusion to messianic prophecy that might link the kingship as envisaged here with the אחרית הימים.

It is instructive to contrast the portrayal of the king with such messianic passages as *Psalms of Solomon* 17 and the *Scroll of Blessings*, 1QSb. Wise has argued that the three-fold emphasis on the king as warrior, judge and man of purity in the *Temple Scroll* is reminiscent of the Psalm.²⁷ The two texts share a peculiarity in so far as they add the words "for war" in their adaptations of Deuteronomy 17.²⁸ The Psalm, however, is resonant with messianic imagery: the king will "smash the sinners' arrogance like a potter's vessel" and "with a rod of iron break in pieces all their substance" (*Pss. Sol.* 17:23–24, cf. Ps 2:9). God has created him strong in the holy spirit, and wise in prudent counsel, together with strength and righteousness, like the shoot of David foretold in Isaiah 11 (*Pss. Sol.* 17:37). The blessing of the Prince of the Congregation in 1QSb 5 also draws heavily on Isaiah 11. There are no such allusions in the Temple Scroll. Neither the Psalm nor the Blessing contains any hint that the line of the messianic king could be discontinued. Instead the Psalm declares confidently that "there will be no unrighteousness among them in his days, for all shall be holy, and their king shall be the Lord Messiah" (*Pss. Sol.* 17:32). The functions of the king remain substantially the same whether a passage is eschatological or not. There is a huge qualitative difference, however, between the fallible king of the *Temple Scroll* and the messianic king of the Psalm, who is declared "pure from sin" (17:36).

---

²⁶ See my essay, "Method in the Study of Messianism," *Methods of Investigation of the Dead Sea Scrolls and the Khirbet Qumran Site: Present Realities and Future Prospects* (ed. J. J. Collins, N. Golb, D. Pardee, and M. Wise; New York: New York Academy of Sciences, forthcoming).

²⁷ "The Eschatological Vision of the Temple Scroll," 167–68.

²⁸ *Pss. Sol.* 17:33: "Nor shall he increase his store of gold and silver for war." 11QT LVI 16: "nor lead the people back to Egypt to war." See D. Rosen and A. Salvesen, "A Note on the Qumran Temple Scroll 56:15-18 and Psalm of Solomon 17:33," *JJS* 38 (1987) 99–101.

Perhaps the aspect of the *Temple Scroll* that most strongly suggests that it is an eschatological law is the gargantuan size of the temple.[29] As is well known, the temple envisaged is too large for the site of Jerusalem, being about three times the size of the Herodian enclosure. Nonetheless, Wise has argued that there are some indications of compromise between the ideal dimensions of the temple, which were probably derived from an earlier source, and the necessities of real life—e.g., the distance of the latrine from the city is disproportionately short in relation to the width of the city. He infers that the "redactor of TS was probably willing to make such compromises because he really intended to build his temple."[30] Johann Maier has also argued that the design is not entirely outside the range of possibility, noting that "the Qumran community, in its opposition to the cultic reality of Jerusalem, naturally favored ideal norms (as does every opposition group) and therefore concentrated ... on traditions that stressed the differences from the existing situation."[31] In any case, the temple described in the *Temple Scroll* is not the final temple which will God will create on the "day of creation" according to 11QT XXIX 9, but rather an ideal temple for the interim period. This temple is obviously utopian. Whether it is eschatological is perhaps a matter of definition, but I have argued that it should not be identified with the temple which the *Florilegium* assigns to the אחרית הימים. That temple is more likely to correspond to the one that God will create on the "day of creation." It seems to me then that the *Temple Scroll* is not a law for the אחרית הימים, and is reformist rather than eschatological. However unrealistic it may seem to us, it would seem to be intended as an ideal for this age, prior to the final tribulation and the coming of the messiah.

---

[29] M. Broshi, "The Gigantic Dimensions of the Visionary Temple in the Temple Scroll," *BAR* 13 (1987) 36–37.

[30] *A Critical Study of the Temple Scroll*, 84.

[31] J. Maier, "The Temple Scroll and Tendencies in the Cultic Architecture of the Second Commonwealth," *Archaeology and History in the Dead Sea Scrolls* (ed. L. H. Schiffman; JSPSup 8; Sheffield: JSOT, 1990) 68. Compare also H. Stegemann, "The Institutions of Israel in the Temple Scroll," *The Dead Sea Scrolls: Forty Years of Research* (ed. D. Dimant and U. Rappaport; Leiden: Brill, 1992) 162: "the author of the *Temple Scroll* did indeed have in mind the actual temple in Jerusalem, not some utopian or heavenly model of it."

## The Teacher and the End of Days

Both CD VI 11 and the *Florilegium* locate the eschatological Teacher/Interpreter of the Law firmly in the אחרית הימים. If this figure were to come, the "end of days" would presumably be underway. If Wise is right, as I think he is, that the "end of days" refers to a future time in these scrolls,[32] it follows that the eschatological Teacher/Interpreter had not yet come, from their perspective. This applies not only to CD and the *Florilegium*, but also to the *Pesharim*, which make frequent reference to the Teacher of Righteousness as a historical figure[33] and to the אחרית הימים.[34] In the *Pesher on Habakkuk* we read, à propos of Hab 1:5,

> [The interpretation of the passage concerns] the traitors together with the Man of the Lie, for [they did] not [believe the words of] the Teacher of Righteousness (which were) from the mouth of God. And it concerns the trai[tors to] the new [covenant,] f[o]r they were not faithful to the covenant of God [but they profaned] his holy name. Likewise, the interpretation of the passage [concerns the trai]tors at the end of days. They are the ruthless [ones of the coven]ant who will not believe when they hear all that is going to co[me up]on the last generation from the mouth of the priest into [whose heart] God put [understandi]ng to interpret all the words of his servants the prophets . . . .

This passage clearly looks back to the Teacher of Righteousness, and forward to the end of days. The author of the pesher, then, cannot have viewed the historical teacher as the fulfillment of the expectation of CD VI 11. There is in fact no evidence anywhere in the scrolls that the historical Teacher was so regarded. The Teacher may or may not have been the author or redactor of the *Temple Scroll*, but he was not an eschatological figure, the scroll was not an

---

[32] Wise, "4QFlorilegium," 115.

[33] 1QpHab I 13; II 2; V 10; VII 4; VIII 3; IX 9–10; XI 5; 4QpPss[a] 1–10 iii 15, 19; iv 8, 27; 4QpPss[b] I 4; II 2.

[34] 1QpHab II 5–6; IX 6; 4QpIsa[a] 2–6 ii 26; 7–10 iii 22; 4QpIsa[b] II 1; 4QpIsa[c] 6–7 ii 14; 13 4; 23 ii 10; 4QpNah 3–4 ii 2; 3–4 iii 3; 4QpMic 6 2.

eschatological law. In fact, the notion of a new law for the eschatological period remains very poorly attested in ancient Judaism.[35]

The use of such titles as Interpreter of the Law and Teacher of Righteousness for figures of the historical past and the eschatological future underlines a feature of the eschatology of the scrolls that has often been noted. This eschatology has a restorative aspect, and involves the fulfillment and perfection of the institutions of past and present.[36] This is true of the offices of king and High Priest. It is also true of the office of Teacher. The homologies between past, present and future sometimes engender confusion on the part of modern interpreters. The situation is rendered all the more confusing by the fact that the relationships of Teacher/Interpreter to other offices, present or future, are not clearly defined.

## Teacher and Prophet

The historical Teacher was a priest. This is explicit in the pesher on Ps 37:23-24 (4QpPs$^a$ 1-10 iii 15). There is no evidence that he was ever High Priest in Jerusalem, despite frequent claims to the contrary.[37] It is more difficult to say whether he was also regarded as a prophet. He is a priest to whom God has given the power "to interpret all the words of his servants the prophets" (1QpHab II 8-9), "to whom God made known all the mysteries of the words of his servants the prophets" (1QpHab VII 4-5). Despite some lacunae, it ap-

---

[35] W. D. Davies, *Torah in the Messianic Age and/or the Age to Come* (SBLMS 7; Philadelphia: SBL, 1952) adduces very little evidence for it. The clearest passage is the medieval Yalqut Shimoni on Isaiah 26 (Davies, *The Damascus Covenant*, 74; cf. Wise, "The Temple Scroll and the Teacher of Righteousness," 146).

[36] See the remarks of S. Talmon, "Waiting for the Messiah: the Spiritual Universe of the Qumran Covenanters," *Judaisms and their Messiahs at the Turn of the Christian Era* (ed. J. Neusner, W. S. Green, and E. S. Frerichs; Cambridge: Cambridge University Press, 1987) 125.

[37] The view that the Teacher was High Priest was proposed by H. Stegemann, *Die Entstehung der Qumrangemeinde* (Bonn: published privately, 1971) 102 nn. 328-29 and supported by J. Murphy-O'Connor, "The Damascus Document Revisited," *RB* 92 (1985) 239. See the critique of this position in my article "The Origin of the Qumran Community: A Review of the Evidence," *To Touch the Text: Biblical and Related Studies in Honor of Joseph A. Fitzmyer, S. J.* (ed. M. P. Horgan and P. J. Kobelski; New York: Crossroad, 1989) 166 and the fuller treatment of the issue by M. Wise, "The Teacher of Righteousness and the High Priest of the Intersacerdotium: Two Approaches," *RevQ* 14 (1990) 587-613.

pears that the same pesher also claims that the words of the Teacher were from the mouth of God (1QpHab II 2–3), which is reminiscent of Num 12:6–8, where Moses is distinguished from the prophets by the fact that God speaks to him "mouth to mouth."[38] Yet he is never called a prophet, as he is called a priest.

Ever since the early years of scroll research, scholars have repeatedly canvassed the view that the Teacher was the prophet like Moses, envisaged in the passage from Deuteronomy 18 cited in the *Testimonia*, and in the famous reference to "the prophet and the messiahs of Aaron and Israel" in 1QS IX.[39] This view encounters some difficulties, however. It implies that the passages in question were written before the historical Teacher came on the scene. The context in 1QS IX bears considerable similarity to the passage in CD VI which we considered at the beginning of this paper. It refers to "the primitive precepts in which the men of the Community were first instructed" which will remain in effect "until there shall come the Prophet and the Messiahs of Aaron and Israel." Similarly CD VI refers to the ordinances of the "Interpreter of the Law" which will remain in effect "until he comes who shall teach righteousness at the end of days." If, as is generally assumed, these passages refer to the same sect or movement, then the historical Teacher/Interpreter should be associated with the "primitive precepts" rather than with the coming of the messiahs. If he was the "Interpreter of the Law" who laid down the precepts in which people "should walk in all the age of wickedness" (CD VI 10), then he was indeed, in a sense, a "new Moses" but he was not necessarily the prophet like Moses, expected at the end of days.[40] We should also expect that if the Teacher were regarded as the eschatological prophet, this would have been made explicit at some point.

A much stronger case can be made for identifying the eschatological prophet with the one who will teach righteousness at the

---

[38] Wise, "The Temple Scroll and the Teacher of Righteousness," 144, regards this as "a transparent claim that the T of R was a typological Moses."

[39] N. Wieder, "The 'Law Interpreter' of the Sect of the Dead Sea Scrolls: The Second Moses," *JJS* 4 (1953) 158–75; A. S. van der Woude, *Die Messianischen Vorstellungen der Gemeinde von Qumrân* (Assen: van Gorcum, 1957) 186; H. M. Teeple, *The Mosaic Eschatological Prophet* (SBLMS 10; Philadelphia: SBL, 1957) 54; G. Vermes, *The Dead Sea Scrolls: Qumran in Perspective* (Philadelphia: Fortress, 1977) 185–86; Wise, "The Temple Scroll and the Teacher of Righteousness," 142.

[40] See the comments of Jeremias, *Der Lehrer der Gerechtigkeit*, 274–75.

end of days, of CD VI 11. The biblical source of the prophet like Moses is Deut 18:18, which is quoted in the *Testimonia*:

> A prophet like you I shall raise up for them from the midst of their brothers, and I shall put my words in his mouth, and he will tell them all that I command him. Whoever does not listen to my words which the prophet will speak in my name, I shall seek a reckoning from him.[41]

It is certainly possible to view this prophetic figure as a teacher. Moreover, Hos 10:12, "until he comes and teaches righteousness for you," the passage from which the language of CD VI 11 is drawn, is applied to Elijah in later Jewish tradition.[42] Van der Woude argued over a quarter of a century ago that the eschatological Interpreter of the Law should be identified with Elijah.[43] CD VII 18 identifies the star of Balaam's oracle as "the Interpreter of the Law who will come (הבא) to Damascus."[44] Van der Woude argued that this was an allusion to 1 Kgs 19:15, where Elijah is told "Go, return on your way to the wilderness of Damascus; when you arrive you shall anoint Hazael as king over Aram."[45] The wilderness of Damascus could be taken to suggest Qumran, and the fact that Elijah is charged to anoint someone recalls a later tradition, according to which Elijah would anoint the messiah.[46] Whether van der Woude is justified in inferring that the Interpreter of the Law here is identified with Elijah seems less than certain. The allusion hangs only on the men-

---

[41] Brooke, *Exegesis at Qumran*, 317, notes that the *Testimonia* follows the Samaritan text of Exod 20:21 in combining Deut 5:28b–29 and Deut 18:18–19.

[42] So e.g. Rashi, interpreting *b. Bek.* 24a. See L. Ginzberg, *An Unknown Jewish Sect* (New York: Jewish Theological Seminary, 1976) 211–22, who notes that "in no fewer than eighteen passages in the Talmud, Elijah appears as one who, in capacity of precursor of the Messiah, will settle all doubts on matters ritual and juridical"; G. Molin, "Elijahu de Prophet und sein Weiterleben in den Hoffnungen des Judentums und der Christenheit," *Judaica* 8 (1951) 81; J. Jeremias, "Elias," *TDNT* 2.932; H. M. Teeple, *The Mosaic Eschatological Prophet*, 54–55; G. Jeremias, *Der Lehrer der Gerechtigkeit*, 286.

[43] Van der Woude, *Die Messianischen Vorstellungen*, 55.

[44] Debate has raged as to whether this figure should be regarded as past or future. See the recent treatment by M. Knibb, "The Interpretation of Damascus Document VII,9b–VIII,2a and XIX,5b–14," *RevQ* 15 (1991) 248–50.

[45] Van der Woude, *Die Messianischen Vorstellungen*, 55. C. Rabin, *The Zadokite Fragments* (Oxford: Oxford University Press, 1954) 30, suggested a reference to 2 Kgs 8:7 and Elisha.

[46] Justin, *Dialogue with Trypho* 49.

tion of Damascus. The Interpreter is not said to anoint anyone in CD. Nonetheless the suggestion is an attractive one, and strengthens the case for viewing the eschatological Teacher as the prophet who was to come.

## Teacher and Priest

A case can also be made, however, for viewing the eschatological Teacher/Interpreter as a priest, who should be identified with the messiah of Aaron. George Brooke has argued that "The essential link between the functions of this eschatological figure as Interpreter of the Law and as priest is provided by the fortunate preservation among the fragments of 4QFlor (6–11) of a section of Deuteronomy 33."[47] Deut 33:10 says of the descendants of Levi: "They teach Jacob your ordinances and Israel your law." This passage is also cited in the *Testimonia*, which is usually taken as a string of eschatological proof texts, so that the blessing of Levi would refer to the eschatological priest.[48] The teaching function of Levi is noted, in language reminiscent of Deuteronomy 33, in Isaac's blessing of Levi in *Jubilees* 31.[49]

The eschatological High Priest, then, could aptly be described as "Interpreter of the Law" or "Teacher of Righteousness." In light of this, the Interpreter of the Law and Branch of David in the *Florilegium* may be plausibly equated with the figures known elsewhere as the messiahs of Aaron and Israel.[50] This understanding of the eschatological Interpreter also fits the disputed passage at the end of CD VII:

> The star is the Interpreter of the Law who shall come (הבא) to Damascus; as it is written, A star shall come forth out of Jacob and a sceptre shall rise out of Israel. The sceptre is the Prince of

---

[47] Brooke, *Exegesis at Qumran*, 204.

[48] J. A. Fitzmyer, "'4QTestimonia' and the New Testament," *Essays in the Semitic Background of the New Testament* (Missoula, MT: Scholars Press, 1974) 82–84.

[49] J. C. VanderKam, "Jubilees and the Priestly Messiah of Qumran," *RevQ* 13 (1988) 363.

[50] On the messiahs of Aaron and Israel see Talmon, "Waiting for the Messiah," 111–37.

the whole congregation, and when he comes he shall smite all the children of Sheth.

Since the sceptre here is clearly eschatological, the star is most naturally interpreted in this sense too. In the *Testaments of the Twelve Patriarchs*, the star is associated with the "new priest" of *T. Levi* 18, while the sceptre is associated with kingship and the descendant of Judah in *T. Judah* 24. In CD VII, then, we have the familiar messianic duality.[51] The Prince of the Congregation is the figure elsewhere called the Branch of David or the messiah of Israel. The Interpreter of the Law is the eschatological High Priest or messiah of Aaron.

Corroboration for the notion that the eschatological High Priest would also function as Teacher comes now from the fragmentary text 4QAaronA, recently published by Émile Puech.[52] In frg. 9 i we read of a figure who

> will atone for all the sons of his generation and will be sent to all the sons of his [peopl]e; his word is like a word of heaven and his teaching is in accordance with the will of God. His eternal sun will shine, and his fire will burn in all the corners of the earth and it will shine on the darkness. Then the darkness will pass away from the earth and deep darkness from the dry land ....

The role of atoning for sin is expressly assigned to the משיח אהרון וישראל in CD XIV 19 (whether the reference be to one figure or two). The passage in 4QAaronA goes on to say that he will encounter lies and adversity, which suggests a parallel between his career and that of the historical Priest/Teacher in his struggle with the Man of the Lie.

Puech notes the parallel between 4QAaronA and *T. Levi* 18, which says that:

---

[51] Brooke argues that this passage is an interpolation, intended to introduce the notion of two messiahs into CD (*Exegesis at Qumran*, 302–04).

[52] É. Puech, "Fragments d'un apocryphe de Lévi et le personnage eschatologique. 4QTestLévi$^{c-d}$(?) et 4QAJa," *The Madrid Qumran Congress*, 2.449–501. The text is printed with an English translation in R. Eisenman and M. Wise, *The Dead Sea Scrolls Uncovered* (Rockport, MA: Element, 1992) 142–45.

> Then will the Lord raise up a new priest,
> To whom all the words of the Lord will be revealed;
> And he will execute true judgement on earth for many days.
> And his star will arise in heaven, as a king,
> Lighting up the light of knowledge as the sun the day;
> And he will rank as great in the world until he is taken up.
> He will shine forth like the sun on the earth,
> And dispel all darkness from under heaven....

T. *Levi* 18 is Christian in its present form, and refers to Christ as both priest and king,[53] but it is widely held to incorporate an earlier Jewish document which looked for two messiahs, the priestly star of T. *Levi* 18 and the royal sceptre of T. *Judah* 24.[54]

While it is not certain that 4QAaron A or T. *Judah* refer to the same figure as CD or the *Florilegium*, they are certainly closer in time and setting to the Dead Sea Scrolls than the medieval Jewish traditions about Elijah. There seems then to be more reason to identify the "one who will teach righteousness at the end of days" with the messiah of Aaron, or eschatological High Priest, than with the "prophet like Moses," although admittedly the priestly interpretation does not clarify the association with Damascus in CD VII. I do not, however, claim that the expectations of the Dead Sea sect were necessarily consistent in this matter. We know little as yet of the historical development of eschatological ideas in the corpus of scrolls.[55] The prophet and eschatological Priest may not have been always clearly distinguished. In fact, Elijah, the prototypical eschatological prophet, was also identified as eschatological High

---

[53] M. de Jonge, "Two Messiahs in the Testaments of the Twelve Patriarchs," *Tradition and Re-Interpretation in Jewish and Early Christian Literature: Essays in Honour of Jürgen C. H. Lebram* (Leiden: Brill, 1986) 150–62.

[54] Van der Woude, *Die Messianischen Vorstellungen*, 190–216; J. Liver, "The Doctrine of the two Messiahs in Sectarian Literature in the Time of the Second Commonwealth," *HTR* 52 (1969) 149–85 (rept. in *Messianism in the Talmudic Era* [ed. L. Landman; New York: KTAV, 1979] 354–90); A. Hultgard, *L'eschatologie des Testaments des Douze Patriarches I. Interprétation des Textes* (2 vols.; Uppsala: Almqvist & Wiksell, 1977) 1.15–81, 268–381.

[55] Several developmental theories have been proposed. The best known is that of J. Starcky, "Les quatres étapes du messianisme à Qumrân," *RB* 70 (1963) 481–505, which has been widely criticized. The sketchy views of P. R. Davies, "Eschatology at Qumran," *JBL* 104 (1985) 39–55 do not withstand scrutiny. The entire question of chronological development will have to be re-opened now that the scrolls are fully available.

Priest in later Jewish tradition, through an association with Phineas and their shared motif of zeal.[56] The association with Elijah, then, could imply a priestly motif as well as a prophetic one, and an eschatological High Priest could also have a prophetic persona.

## Conclusion

The historical Teacher evidently anticipated to some degree the roles of his eschatological counterpart. He is explicitly said to have been a priest, and he also had some prophetic characteristics. He was, in a sense, a new Moses. If our analysis is correct, however, he was not himself regarded as the fulfillment of eschatological expectation, either as the "prophet like Moses" or as the "messiah of Aaron," and he did not write a law for the end of days. There was yet a more definitive Teacher to come, and this, perhaps, is a reason why the historical Teacher remains such a shadowy figure in the Dead Sea Scrolls.

---

[56] Molin, "Elijahu," 84–85, notes that Elijah is frequently called *kahana rabba* in the Targumim. See also Ginzberg, *An Unknown Jewish Sect*, 245–47; N. Wieder, "The Doctrine of the Two Messiahs among the Karaites," *JJS* 6 (1955) 14–23; van der Woude, *Die Messianischen Vorstellungen*, 55–57; Jeremias, "Elias," 932–33.

# Messianism in the Scrolls

## James VanderKam

From very early days in Qumran studies scholars have been writing that the group which copied and composed the scrolls expected the arrival of two messiahs. This was hardly surprising because the *Manual of Discipline*, one of the seven scrolls found in Cave 1, contained the now-famous statement: "They shall depart from none of the counsels of the Law to walk in the stubbornness of their hearts, but shall be ruled by the primitive precepts in which the men of the Community were first instructed until there shall come the Prophet and the Messiahs of Aaron and Israel" (1QS IX 9–11).[1] The text does not, of course, specify how many messiahs there would be, but use of two names, Aaron and Israel, at least suggests there would be two. This statement was thought to clarify the more ambiguous data in the *Damascus Document*, made available some 40 years before the scrolls were found, in which there are four instances of the phrase "the messiah of/from Aaron and Israel" (CD XII 23–XIII 1; XIV 18–19; XIX 10–11; XIX 33–XX 1). On the basis of information from the *Rule of the Congregation*, an appendix to or continuation of the *Manual of Discipline*, it was also concluded that the Messiah of Aaron, who is mentioned first in 1QS IX 11, took a certain sort of precedence over the Messiah of Israel, since the former is the one who presides over the meal which is described in the second column. In the last few years, some new texts with references to messianic characters have been made available. Naturally, they have elicited new discussion and some new proposals regarding the chararcter of messianic expectation as evidenced in the Qumran documents.

---

[1] Translation of G. Vermes, *The Dead Sea Scrolls in English* (3rd ed.; Sheffield: Sheffield Academic Press, 1987). All renderings of the scrolls given between quotation marks, unless otherwise indicated, are from this volume.

In this paper I offer a brief overview of Qumran messianism. To do that, I first collect the evidence from different scrolls about the titles used for the davidic or non-priestly messiah and the functions he performs. In the second part I do the same for the priestly messiah.

## I. The Davidic Messiah

The various scrolls that speak of a political leader in the latter days use three main titles for him. Certain equivalences indicate that the three titles refer to the same individual.

### A. משיח (Messiah)

1. The *Manual of Discipline* uses the title in IX 11: עד בוא נביא ומשיחי אהרון וישראל ("until there shall come the Prophet and the Messiahs of Aaron and Israel"). The copy from cave 1 has been dated on paleographical grounds to ca. 100 BCE, but the work which it contains is now attested not only in this one almost complete copy but also in ten additional fragmentary ones from cave 4.[2] In the cave 1 copy, the messianic reference concludes a section that deals with the original or pioneer community (VIII 1–IX 11) and precedes one on guidance for the instructor of that early congregation (IX 12–26). Little is said about the messianic and prophetic trio other than that they will come (עד בוא) and that their advent will mark the end of a period in history in which the group being addressed is to walk according to the precepts in which they were initially instructed (ונשפטו במשפטים הרשונים אשר החלו אנשי היחד לתיסר בם [line 10]).

One problem that scholars have had with this rather straightforward statement in 1QS IX 9–11 has to do with the now-familiar fact that the messianic sentence is not present in the oldest copy of the *Manual of Discipline*—a fact which Milik announced years ago. His words are worth quoting:

---

[2] See Vermes, "Preliminary Remarks on the Unpublished Fragments of the Community Rule from Qumran Cave 4," *JJS* 42 (1991) 250–55; and "Qumran Forum Miscellanea I," *JJS* 43 (1992) 300–01.

The evolution of their belief in the Messiah or Messiahs is hard to trace; especially its character at the beginning is unknown to us, since the relevant section in the *Rule* (1Q S IX.10 f.) does not occur in the oldest manuscript (4Q S$^e$) of the work. This copies 1Q S IX.12 directly after VIII.16. It is accordingly probable that a later addition was made, although the shorter redaction leaves the impression of abruptness and may represent an intermediate stage between the original text and that found in 1Q S.[3]

The manuscript in question—4Q259—may indeed contain an earlier version of the *Manual*, but it is also possible that it, not 1QS, is defective at this point. It may be significant that virtually the same words occur just before the missing section and one line after it. In VIII 15 1QS has: היאה מדרש התורה [אשר] צוה ביד מושה לעשות ככול הנגלה עת בעת. Nearly the same words recur in IX 13 (note also עת ועת in IX 12): לעשות את רצון אל ככול הנגלה לעת בעת. 4QS$^e$ has: [צוה ביד משה אלה הח]וקים. The oldest copy has the text of 1QS as far as the words that are repeated in VIII 15 and IX 13. This would not be a classic case of haplography because IX 12 intervenes between the repeated expressions. The repetition may betray signs of editorial adjustment after an addition was made, or it could be that in the tradition represented in copy *e* an omission was made and a scribe felt the need to add the heading of the new section (in IX 12) to make sense of what follows.[4] But, whatever may be the relation between the two copies, it is a fact that in a document from cave 1, copied in ca. 100 BCE, one finds the expression "the Messiahs of Aaron and Israel." When one recalls what a central document the *Manual* seems to have been (the number of copies is impressive) and how clearly it presents Essene traits as known from other sources, this is a fact of some importance.

2. *The Rule of the Congregation* (1QSa):[5] The title משיח occurs three times in the second column of this text which belongs to the same manuscript as 1QS. Beginning in II 11 the column deals with the procedures to be followed in the מושב (session) of the men of renown.

---

[3] *Ten Years of Discovery in the Wilderness of Judaea* (SBT 26; London: SCM, 1959) 123–24.

[4] When this paper was presented, Geza Vermes agreed that one could explain the evidence of ms. e in this way but not that of another of the cave 4 copies.

[5] For the text and notes, see *DJD* 1.107–18; and L. H. Schiffman, *The Eschatological Community of the Dead Sea Scrolls* (SBLMS 38; Atlanta: Scholars Press, 1989) 53–67.

a. In II 12 the form המשיח (the messiah) occurs in a context that has caused much debate, and from which little can be inferred with certainty. Whatever may have been the wording at the end of line 11 and the beginning of line 12, the text does say that the messiah is present with others and apparently accompanied by a priest.

b. In II 14 מש[י]ח ישראל (the mess[i]ah of Israel) presides over the heads of various groups, arranged in military order before him, and over their contingents.

c. In II 20 משיח ישראל (the messiah of Israel) stretches out his hand to the food after the priest has blessed both it and the drink.

3. *The Damascus Document*: The title appears at least four times in this text which is known in medieval copies and now in one from cave 5 and eight from cave 4 (cf. also II 12 where משיחו [his messiah] seems a mistake for the construct plural [the anointed ones of]).[6]

a. According to XII 23–XIII 1, in a rule of the מושב ה[מ]חנות] (the session of the camps) for those who walk in certain precepts in the period of wickedness, they are told to obey them before a set time is reached: עד עמוד משוח אהרן וישראל (until the anointed one of Aaron and Israel stands). Their appearance,[7] then, as in the *Manual of Discipline*, serves to mark the end of a period during which certain laws prevail. That is, their arising marks a key eschatological turning point.

b. XIV 18–19 gives some of the same information. The context specifies certain precepts in which they are to walk עד עמוד משי[ח אהרן וישראל ויכפר עונם (until the messi[a]h of Aaron and Israel stands and makes atonement for their sin). Here the intriguing new element is the added clause ויכפר עונם.

c. XIX 10–11 is another passage in which the arrival of the messianic fugures defines an eschatological moment: אלה ימלטו הפקדה והנשארים ימסרו לחרב בבוא משיח אהרן וישראל (these will escape the visitation and those who are left will be handed over to the sword when the messiah of Aaron and Israel comes).

---

[6] The most recent edition of the Cairo Geniza texts is by E. Qimron in M. Broshi, ed., *The Damascus Document Reconsidered* (Jerusalem: IES/The Shrine of the Book, Israel Museum, 1992). The cave 4 texts have been transcribed in B. Z. Wacholder and M. G. Abegg, *A Preliminary Edition of the Unpublished Dead Sea Scrolls: The Hebrew and Aramaic Texts from Cave 4*, fascicle 1 (Washington: Biblical Archaeology Society, 1991) 1–59.

[7] For evidence that the referent is plural, see below in the section on the eschatological priest.

d. XIX 33–XX 1 teaches that the ones who renege on the new covenant will not be considered part of the council מיום האסף מורה היחיד עד עמוד משיח מאהרון ומישראל (from the day when the teacher of the community is gathered up until a messiah from Aaron and from Israel stands). In this way again the arrival of the messiahs serves to define a period.

4. 4Q252: While explicating Gen 49:10, especially the Shiloh reference, the author writes in col. V 3–4: עד בוא משיח הצדק צמח דויד כי לו ולזרעו נתנה ברית מלכות עמו עד דורות עולם (until the messiah of righteousness, the branch of David, comes, for to him and to his descendants the covenant of the kingship of his people has been given for the generations of eternity).[8] The royal, davidic associations are strong in these lines, and the kingship in question is eternal. Note that here, too, his arrival is used to identify an eschatological moment.

5. 4Q521: In the first line the term appears in an interesting context. It is unfortunate that the text is too broken to tell whether anything else is associated with this anointed one. 4Q521 1 ii 1 reads: הש[מ]ים והארץ ישמעו למשיחו (the heav]ens and the earth obey his messiah). The restoration הש[מ]ים is obvious, but the unknown factor is what came before the heavens and the earth—the angels? As is well known, the activities noted at the end of the column (heal the sick, raise the dead, etc.) have been compared to what Jesus does in Luke 7:18–23. There certainly are similarities, but it remains unclear whether the messiah of the first line or the Lord who is mentioned several times thereafter is the one who does these miracles. The context favors the latter option.[9]

---

[8] The text may be found in Wacholder–Abegg, *A Preliminary Edition of the Unpublished Dead Sea Scrolls: The Hebrew and Aramaic Texts from Cave Four*, fascicle 2 (Washington: Dead Sea Scroll Research Council/Biblical Archaeology Society, 1992) 215.

[9] For 4Q287 frg. 4 13 the Preliminary Concordance records the reading ונח]ה על משיחו רוח קוד[ש (p. 1353), and R. M. Eisenman and M. Wise have reproduced the text in the same way, translating: "... The [*sic*] Holy Spirit [sett]led upon His Messiah ...". (*The Dead Sea Scrolls Uncovered: The First Complete Translation and Interpretation of 50 Key Documents Withheld for Over 35 Years* [Shaftesbury/Rockport/Brisbane: Element, 1992] 228, 230; cf. the comments on p. 226). However, J. T. Milik ("*Milkî-ṣedeq et Milkî-rešaʿ; dans les anciens écrits juifs et chrétiens,*" *JJS* 23 [1972] 134), to whose article Eisenman and Wise refer (p. 255), had published a different transcription already in 1972: [. ].. ולדבר ס]ר[ה על משיחי רוח קוד[שו (= 4Q287 frg. 4 13). Milik was able to compare similar readings in 4QD^e 2 ii 13–14, CD V 21–VI 1 (= 4QD^b 2 i 5–6). On PAM 43.314 the disputed letter (ו or י) is fairly clearly a י, as its thicker hook at the top indicates (compare the other י in משיחי and contrast them with the ו's in רוח and קוד[שו ). The

Summary: These 10 occurrences of *messiah* come from three different kinds of texts: legal (1QS, 1QSa, CD—8 instances), a text which comments on the blessing of Judah in Gen 49:10 (4Q252); and a different sort of text (4Q521). The messiah or messiahs are mentioned frequently in contexts in which the writers are referring to an eschatological time when current conditions will end (1QS, CD—all 4; 4Q252). CD XIV 19 says that they will atone for the sins of some group; and 4Q521 notes that heaven and earth or perhaps those in heaven and on earth will obey his (God's) messiah—thus indicating that he is still subject to God.

## B. צמח דויד *(The Branch of David)*

The title occurs in four texts.

1. 4Q161 (4QpIsa<sup>a</sup>) 7–10 iii 22:[10] צמח] דויד העומד באח[רית הימים (the branch of] David who stands in the latt[er days). Though the first term must be restored, it is highly likely in view of the plant imagery in Isa 11:1, the passage under consideration here. In Isa 11:1–5, all of which is quoted in the *pesher*, the words *shoot* and *branch* are used of the davidic descendant who also receives the spirit of various virtues, judges justly, kills the wicked, and embodies righteousness and faithfulness. In addition to his standing in the latter days, he does something to his foes, God will sustain him with a spirit of strength, he will have a glorious throne, a holy crown, splendid clothes, and he will rule over the nations, whom his sword will judge. As will be noted in the second part of the paper, some group teaches him at a later point in the text (lines 28–29).

2. 4Q174 *(Florilegium)* I 1–13:[11] The title occurs in a section which deals with 2 Sam 7:11–14 where the Lord promises to build David a house, raise his seed after him, and establish the throne of his kingdom forever. He will also become father to him and David's offspring will be a son to God. The author of the *pesher* identifies who this promised one is: הואה צמח דויד העומד עם דורש התורה אשר

---

same fragment can be viewed on PAM 41.588 and 42.418. Since the plural construct is the more likely reading here, 4Q287 frg. 4 13 can be left out of consideration because it, like the other plurals in the *Damascus Document* mentioned by Milik, may well refer to the prophets.

[10] The text was published by J. Allegro in "Further Messianic References in Qumran Literature," *JBL* 75 (1956) 177–82, and by him also in *DJD* 5.11–15

[11] Allegro, "Further Messianic References," 176–77, and *DJD* 5.53–57.

בצי[ון בא]חרית הימים ... (he is the branch of David who stands with the interpreter of the law ... in Zi[on in the la]tter days). He then cites Amos 9:11 (the Lord will "raise up the booth of David that is fallen")[12] and interprets that fallen booth to be the one who "will stand to save Israel" (אשר יעמוד להושיע את ישראל). So this branch of David will have company when he stands in the latter days to save Israel.

3. 4Q252 V 3–4: The passage has been cited in connection with the title משיח above. Here it is of special interest, not only because of the obvious davidic content, but also because it identifies the messiah of righteousness with the branch of David. It is possible that this text, which has long been available,[13] also mentions the דורש התורה (the interpreter of the law; see below). The branch is here associated with righteousness and unending kingship over God's people.

4. 4Q285 frg. 5 3–4:[14] The fragmentary text builds upon the end of Isaiah 10 and the beginning of chap. 11 (it names the prophet in line 1). It quotes the plant language from Isa 11:1 and, after a break in the fragment, mentions on the next line ] צמח דויד ונשפטו את [ (the branch of David, and they will enter judgment with [or: be judged with]). The next line is the one that recently stirred a storm of controversy: והמיתו נשיא העדה צמ]ח דויד (and the prince of the congregation, the bran[ch of David] will kill him). The reference to judging in line 3 may relate to Isa 11:3–4; but, whereas Isaiah says the future scion of David will do the judging, this text has a plural verb. The killing in line 4 probably develops Isa 11:4 where the prophet predicts: והכה ארץ בשבט פיו וברוח שפתיו ימית רשע ("he shall strike the earth with the rod of his mouth, and with the breath of his lips he shall kill the wicked"). Naturally, the biblical base makes it very likely indeed that the individual named in line 4 does the killing. There has been some dispute about the last visible letter on line 4. If one follows the reading given here, the text identifies two messianic titles: the prince of the congregation is the branch of David who kills someone. Another possibility is to read, not צמ]ח,

---

[12] Biblical quotations are from the *NRSV*.

[13] It was first published by J. Allegro, "Further Messianic References," 174–76.

[14] The text is given in Wacholder–Abegg, *A Preliminary Edition*, fascicle 2.223–27. For a study of the passage cited above, see Vermes, "The Oxford Forum for Qumran Research Seminar on the Rule of War from Cave 4 (4Q285)," *JJS* 43 (1992) 85–90.

but צב]א, as in the Preliminary Concordance to the cave 4 texts and hence in the Wacholder–Abegg edition.

Summary: These four instances exhaust the uses of the title "the branch of David" for the messiah. It is employed in connection with eternal davidic kingship which is strengthened by God, with victory over foes, rule over the nations, the latter days, salvation for Israel, and righteousness. One text identifies the branch of David and the messiah of righteousness (4Q252) and one less certainly identifies him with the prince of the congregation (4Q285). In each case the title is closely tied to a biblical source: Isa 11:1-5; 2 Sam 7:11-14 (with Amos 9:11); and Gen 49:10. The branch of David is also associated with the interpreter of the Torah.

## C. נשיא העדה *(The Prince of the Congregation)*

At least five documents resort to this title for the royal leader of the latter days.

1. 1QSb V 20–29:[15] The text, which includes blessings of various leaders, identifies these lines as a blessing for the prince of the congregation (למשכיל לברך את נשיא העדה [for the instructor, to bless the prince of the congregation]). In the course of the blessing itself one reads of the hope that his kingdom will be established forever, that he will reprove properly, walk perfectly in the Lord's ways, that God will exalt him, his staff will place the earth under the ban, he will kill the wicked, have the kinds of spirits mentioned by Isaiah, trample the foe, be a sceptre, and subdue the rulers. In other words, the blessing calls for him to rule all rightly and forever with divine backing. The text is clearly drawing upon Isaiah 11.

2. CD VII 18–21: In the preceding context the writer explains Amos 5:26-27; 9:11. After offering his understanding of who the *star* in Amos 5:26 is, he adduces Num 24:17 and its famous star prophecy. "The *star* [of Amos 5:26] is the Interpreter of the Law who shall come to Damascus; as it is written, *A star shall come forth out of Jacob and a sceptre shall rise out of Israel* (Num. xxiv, 17). The *sceptre* is the Prince of the whole congregation [נשיא כל העדה], and when he comes [ובעמדו] *he shall smite all the children of Seth* (Num. xxiv, 17)." This royal (note his "scepter") individual will be victorious over his enemies. He seems, given the collocation of texts here and the refer-

---

[15] See *DJD* 1.118–30.

ence to both a star and a scepter in Num 24:17, to be associated with the interpreter of the law (cf. 1QM XI 6–7).

3. 4Q161 (4QpIsa$^a$) 2–6 ii 19: As the commentator deals with Isa 10:24, in which Assyria strikes Judah with a rod (בשבט) and staff (מטה), he explains the staff as the prince of the congregation. The text is badly broken, but the prince seems to be involved in turning aside the enemy.

4. *The War Scroll* V 1: The line indicates what is written on his shield: "And on the sh[ield of] the Prince of all the congregation they shall write his name, together with the names of Israel, Levi and Aaron, and the names of the twelve tribes of Israel according to the order of their precedence, with the names of their twelve chiefs." He is clearly the leader of all Israel in the eschatological war.

5. 4Q285

a. Frg. 6 2 refers to נשי[א העדה וכול ישר]אל (the prin]ce of the congregation and all Isra[el) in a broken context where there are words about evil being smitten and apparently regarding war with the nations (frg. 6 1, 5, 8).

b. Frg. 6 6 mentions him in the same general setting: נש[יא העדה עד הים ה]גדול (the pri]nce of the congregation as far as the [great] sea).

c. Frg. 6 10, after what may be some lines about war, says that someone is brought before the prince of the congregation (יביאוהו לפני [נשיא ]העדה).

d. Frg. 5 4, as noted above in connection with the branch of David, may identify the prince of the congregation with him and probably says that he kills someone. Isaiah 11 is the biblical text reflected.

Summary: The prince of the (whole) congregation is named eight times, four in two small fragments which belong to 4Q285. This title, too, is attached to Isaiah's prophecies in chaps. 10 and 11 (1QSb, 4Q161, 4Q285 frg. 5 4) and with Num 24:17. The prince has military duties, apparently in all of the texts that mention him, but the title is also associated with the qualities that Isaiah predicts for the descendant of David. These are the three principal messianic titles for the davidic messiah, and as noted earlier, the three are equated with one another.[16]

---

[16] 4Q246 has been left out of the survey because it is not certain that it is referring to a messiah. It contains the words "He shall be called son of God, and they shall designate him son of the Most High" (II 1); but since in II 4 the people of God arise (or someone raises them) and an eternal kingdom is inaugurated, it appears that the sequence from Daniel 7 underlies the fragmentary text and that, as a result, the king who

## II. The Eschatological Priest

### A. 1QS IX

The passage which speaks of the coming of the messiahs of Aaron and Israel has been quoted above. Some of the imagery in the context in which the reference occurs is worth noting. In dealing with the establishment of the community in Israel the writer speaks of them as a sanctuary (VIII 5–6): ". . . the Council of the Community shall be established in truth. It shall be an Everlasting Plantation, a House of Holiness for Israel, an Assembly of Supreme Holiness for Aaron." Here the use of the two terms "Israel" and "Aaron" is of some interest; the latter is, as one might expect, a section (holy of holies) separate from the former (holy place). There is later a reference to its being a "Most Holy Dwelling (מעון קודש קודשים) for Aaron" and a "House of Perfection and Truth in Israel" (VIII 8–9). The text mentions separation (VIII 10, 12), and this separation leads to a series of rules. There is also talk of the community's atoning for the land and offering non-animal sacrifices of prayer. Note, too, the statement:

> At that time, the men of the Community shall set apart a House of Holiness [for Aaron—omitted in Vermes' translation] in order that it may be united to the most holy things and a House of Community for Israel, for those who walk in perfection. The sons of Aaron alone shall command [ימשלו; literally, rule] in matters of justice and property, and every rule concerning the men of the Community shall be determined according to their word (IX 5–7).

---

is called by these divine titles would be someone like Antiochus IV Epiphanes. In other words, the author of 4Q246 would be reporting what others called him but would not himself be adopting those designations for him. On this text, see now the thorough study in É. Puech, "Fragment d'une apocalypse en Araméen (4Q246 = pseudo-Dan[d]) et le 'royaume de Dieu'," *RB* 99 (1992) 98–131, especially 115–16. In this case, no messiah is mentioned, and the people of God are the (singular) subject of the verbs in the remainder of the column. For a messianic reading of the title, see J. J. Collins, "A Pre-Christian 'Son of God' Among the Dead Sea Scrolls," *BR* 9 (1993) 34–38, 57.

Thus, the context shows that there is a difference in meaning for the two designations "Aaron" and "Israel" and that they do not express the notion of "all Israel," as some have suggested for the messianic designation in IX 11.

## B. 1QSa

This text, of which only the one copy has been found, has played a prominent role in the scholarly understanding of the dual messianism in the scrolls. It was edited by D. Barthélemy,[17] who incorporated a number of Milik's proposals in his presentation. The key passage for the present purposes stands after a section in which sundry types of blemished individuals are denied access to the community which defines itself as "... the men of renown, the members of the assembly summoned to the Council of the Community in Israel before the sons of Zadok the Priests" (II 1–3). Once he has tended to these matters, the writer turns his attention in II 11 to the prescriptions for the מו[ש]ב (session) of the men of renown (further defined almost exactly as in II 1–3). The remainder of the column, which also seems to conclude the document, centers about the procedures for this מושב (lines 11–22).

The passage is messianic in the literal sense because the word משיח occurs three times, two of which are certain and the other nearly so. The context for המשיח in line 12 (the only case in which it is not in the construct state and thus not defined by another noun) is less clear than one would have wished. The word that ends line 11 and the first word or two of line 12 are uncertain—at the end of 11 because of the damage to the manuscript, and at the beginning of 12 because the leather is lost. For the last word of line 11 neither of the photographs supplied in *DJD* 1 is especially helpful; and for the beginning of 12 only a single dot survives from the ink of the 6–7 letters that probably once appeared here. Barthélemy read the verb of line 11 as יוליד (he will beget) and wrote: "Après une étude par transparence aussi attentive que possible la lecture de ce mot apparaît pratiquement certaine."[18] He did add, however, that with this reading אתם (with them) in line 12 would be difficult and that the problem would be alleviated by Milik's hunch that יוליד was a blun-

---

[17] *DJD* 1.108–18 (with plates xxii–xxiv). It is numbered as 1Q28a.
[18] *DJD* 1.117.

der for יוליך (he will bring).¹⁹ Consequently, he read the disputed section as ואם יוליך [אל] א[ת] המשיח אתם: "au cas où *Dieu* mènerait le Messie avec eux." In the gap which follows the words המשיח אתם יבוא he read הכוהן (the priest). This, too, was Milik's idea, and he compared the priest with the כוהן הרואש (chief priest) who plays a role in the *War Scroll*.

The verb at the end of line 11 has been the subject of a lengthy debate. A number of skilled paleographers who have actually seen the manuscript insist that יוליד is the correct reading, while others restore another verb such as יתועד or יועד (J. Licht, followed by L. Schiffman).²⁰ The beginning of line 12 is no less controversial and can be restored only on the basis of how one interprets the entire passage. What can be stated securely is that the one letter which has left the only trace (it occupies about the fourth space) has a high left corner and could well be from an א, as Barthélemy read it. It is less likely to be any of the letters that Schiffman proposes (בעת [קץ]). For the second gap in line 12, placing הכוהן is highly likely in the present context, though one should read the preposition ב after it.²¹ The sequel establishes this point clearly.

In the section devoted to the מושב there is a pattern for introducing the different individuals and groups who participate. Recurring phrases mark off three sections, the first of which probably involves a priestly leader (the case in question) and certain priests, the second a military figure and his subjects, and the third the heads of the congregation.

Section A (lines 12–14)
1. X will come as head of all the congregation of Israel (12).
2. The group over which he is head is defined as "all [his brethren, the sons of] Aaron the Priests" (they are then further defined) (12–13).

---

¹⁹ *DJD* 1.117.

²⁰ Note Cross's comments in *The Ancient Library of Qumran & Modern Biblical Studies* (rev. ed.; Grand Rapids: Zondervan, 1980) 87–88 n. 67 (he also accepts Milik's proposal about the scribal blunder). É. Puech ("Fragment d'une apocalypse en Araméen," 100 and n. 6) refers to the reading יוליד as certain. For the view of J. Licht, see his מגילת הסרכים (Jerusalem: Bialik Institute, 1965) 267–69; and for Schiffman's reading, see his *The Eschatological Community*, 53–54.

²¹ Cross, *The Ancient Library of Qumran*, 88 nn. 70–71; Puech, "Fragment d'une apocalypse en Araméen," 100 n. 6.

3. "they shall sit [before him, each man] in the order of his dignity" (13–14).

Section B (lines 14–15) is separated from the actions of A by the word אחר (afterwards)
1. "[the Mess]iah of Israel shall [come]" (14).
2. The group over which he presides is "the chiefs of the [clans of Israel]" (14–15).
3. they "shall sit before him [this element precedes the identification of the group], [each] in the order of his dignity" (14–15).

Section C (lines 15–17)
1. (No one enters because the two leaders are already present.)
2. The group is "all the heads of [family of the congreg]ation" (it is further described [15–16]).
3. They will sit "before *them*," "each in the order of his dignity" (16–17).

This pattern establishes a certain likelihood that a priest was mentioned in line 14. All the other priests sit before him, as Joshua's priestly colleagues sat before him according to Zech 3:8 (יהושע הכהן הגדול אתה ורעיך הישבים לפניך). Moreover, the priest is mentioned in the subsequent description of the meal—a description which follows the same order of characters as in lines 12–17. Again, the text is somewhat broken, but the priest (line 19) does bless the meal and is the first to do so (lines 18–22). As in line 14, the word אחר separates his activity from that of the messiah of Israel who next extends his hand to bless. The entire group finally joins in the benediction.

The text is saying, then, that when God (?) gives birth to (or brings) the messiah or when the messiah assembles with them, the priest will enter, leading the entire congregation of Israel. He presides over the priests, and the messiah of Israel presides over others. There is no textual support for understanding המשיח in line 12 as referring to the priest. It is more likely that the priest does something when the messiah appears.[22] That is, in this text, the only individual who is termed messiah is the messiah of Israel. The broken text in lines 11–12 leaves open the possibility that the messiah here was identified as a priest, but the extant portions of text do not entail this. It is important to stress, however, that whatever title the

---

[22] See, for example, Cross, *The Ancient Library of Qumran*, 88 n. 68; Schiffman, *The Eschatological Community*, 54 n. 5. One should certainly reject Vermes' rendering as thoroughly unlikely: ". . . when [the Priest-]Messiah shall summon them He shall come . . ." (102).

priest may have had, when the messiah of Israel is present a priest is with him and is mentioned first in the description of the מושב and has at least a ceremonial precedence in the account of the meal.

## C. 1QSb (= 1Q28b)

Milik, who published the first edition of the *Rule of Benedictions*,[23] considers it, with 1QSa, another continuation of the scroll that contains the *Manual of Discipline*—a point that can be demonstrated materially. He suggests that the Blessings originally covered six columns, from which remnants of just five have survived. He admits that his proposed arrangement has only a hypothetical value but thinks that the sequence of the four large fragments from the bottoms of cols. III–IV is certain. Moreover, several pieces of evidence showed to his satisfaction that the succession of fragments at the tops of these columns was assured. Nevertheless, the arrangement of scraps for cols. I and II remains a suggestion. He analyzes the full text into four divisions: I 1–20: A general blessing for all members of the community; I 21–III 20: Blessings of the High Priest; III 21–V19: Blessings of the Priests; and 5:20– : Blessings of the Prince of the Congregation. All of these divisions are explicit in the text except the Blessings of the High Priest: 1QSb I 1–3 preserve enough letters to show that those who fear God, keep the commandments, adhere to the covenant, walk perfectly, and are chosen are the ones to be blessed (note that the plural is abandoned already in I 3; the singular is still used in I 7, and one also appears in I 26); in III 22 the sons of Zadok the priests are mentioned after the same formula of introduction as in I 1; and in V 20 the same is the case for the נשיא העדה.[24]

Milik proposed that the section of blessings for the high priest began in I 21, although the text of the line is totally lost. He based his claim on a paragraph marker in the left margin under 1QSa II 22.[25] If one may infer that the arrow marks the beginning of a section or the end of the previous one and that it pointed to that spot in the next column (Milik thinks 1QSb followed 1QSa on the manuscript), then there is a material indicator of a new section. He also main-

---

[23] *DJD* 1.118–30 (with plates xxv–xxix).
[24] *DJD* 1.119.
[25] See *DJD* 1.119, 122.

tains that certain phrases in col. III (he notes lines 1, 2, and 6) entail that in this section blessings are pronounced on a priest of higher rank than an ordinary one. Presumably he had in mind the unmistakable cultic language of III 1 (including יושבי לכה[ונתכ]ה, though the phrase is curious). But the item he mentions specifically is the word עדתכה (your congregation) in III 3, which suggests that the priest in question has his own עדה. There are, of course, a number of verbal echoes here (and elsewhere in the text) of the priestly benediction of Numbers 6 (which is pronounced by priests, not on priests).

It has to be admitted, however, that too little of the text remains either to demonstrate or refute Milik's thesis. There are, moreover, some features that at least in the first instance do not look very priestly—יתן לכה ומלכות in III 5; אלפיכה in III 7; and the partially restored להכנ]יע לכה לא[ומי]ם ר[ב]ים in III 17. The problems with his view have elicited other proposals for understanding the arrangement of the text. It has been argued that the high priestly section would be disproportionately long. Licht held that the text moves from the lowest group to the most important eschatological figures (using the groups of 1QSa for comparison). If such is the pattern, then one would expect the high priest to appear more toward the end of the text. He proposed that the high priestly blessing could be seen in IV 22–28 (it must have started before this because the normal introductory words of a new section are not present in line 22), an unidentified blessing in V 18–19 (the intervening text is badly broken), and the one for the prince of the congregation in V 20–29.[26] IV 22–28 do in fact contain some intriguing expressions, e.g., ואתה כמלאך הפנים במעון קודש (but you are like the angel of the presence in an abode of holiness) in IV 24–25.

It would not be at all surprising if a high priestly figure received blessings in this text, but none is ever mentioned by a recognizable title in the extant parts. If 1QSb is to be included in the case for a messianic or eschatological priest at Qumran, the argument would have to be a more general one: the other blessings are addressed to familiar groups (the community, the priests) and to the prince of the congregation (a messianic title); surely a high priest would be included. There is a certain plausibility to this approach, but the fact is that there is no surviving and recognizable evidence for a priestly messiah in 1QSb.

---

[26] מגילת הסרכים, 274–75.

## D. 4Q175 = *Testimonia*[27]

*Testimonia* often figures in analyses of Qumran messianism, not because the word messiah appears in it, but because a familiar cast of eschatological characters and texts dominates it. The surviving manuscript may have been copied in the early first century BCE. It contains quotations from several biblical passages arranged as follows:

1. Deut 5:28–29 and 18:18–19 (Exod 20:21 in the Samaritan Pentateuch), with the latter pair of verses promising a prophet like Moses who will tell the people all that the Lord commands—a theme that relates to the contents of the former pair.

2. Num 24:15–17, an oracle of Balaam about a star from Jacob and a scepter from Israel. The quotation includes the passage about crushing the borderlands of Moab and destroying the children of Sheth. That is, the distant figure of the text exercises military functions. This pericope is interpreted in messianic senses elsewhere in the scrolls (see above) and in non-Qumran texts.

3. Deut 33:8–11, the blessing of Levi includes statements about his functions (urim, tummim, teaching the Law, sacrificing).

4. Josh 6:26 which is explained by reference to the *Psalms of Joshua*. It deals with the rebuilding of a city by three (a father and two sons), and the city seems to be Jerusalem.

The argument is that *Testimonia* is a collection of messianic texts, the last perhaps fitting less well than the first three. Citations 1–3 deal with the same characters as the trio of 1QS IX 11: a prophet, a secular messiah, and a priestly messiah (a different order than in 1QS; the word *messiah* does not occur). The manuscript itself supplies no context for the citation groups, but the Deuteronomy passage and Balaam's oracle are known messianic sections, and a book such as *Jubilees* uses words from the blessing on Levi in Deut 33:8–11 to exalt Levi and his priesthood (a move that seems to lie behind the priestly messianism of Qumran).

---

[27] The text, edited by Allegro, is in *DJD* 5.57–60.

## E. 4Q174 = Florilegium[28]

A late first-century BCE manuscript, the *Florilegium* uses parts of 2 Samuel 7 as a base text to which it adds interpretations. It also employs an assortment of other biblical texts (e.g., Ps 1:1; Isa 8:11; and Ezek 44:10, to deal with wayward Zadokites; Ps 2:1, with an actualizing commentary that relates it, through Dan 12:10, to the coming time of trial). The document refers explicitly to the latter days (I 2, regarding the house the Lord will build; and in I 12).

The lines of special interest in this connection are I 10–13. The writer first quotes words from 2 Sam 7:11–14 which speak of the Lord's constructing a house for David and establishing his seed forever as the divine son. The explanation is:

> He is the Branch of David who shall arise [העומד] with the Interpreter of the Law [דורש התורה] [to rule] in Zion [at the end] of time [בא]חרית הימים]. As it is written, *I will raise up the tent of David that is fallen* (Amos ix, 11). That is to say, the fallen *tent of David* is he who shall arise to save Israel.

The branch of David is a familiar messianic title (see above) and is mentioned in close proximity with the prince of the congregation in 4Q285. Here he stands with an individual who is titled the interpreter of the law. Someone in this duo will stand to save Israel—presumably the davidic figure.

Who is the interpreter of the law? Some other fragments of the *Florilegium* provide a clue that he may have been a priestly leader. There are tantalizing hints among the pieces that they may have dealt with messianic topics: י[שראל ואהרון] (I]srael and Aaron) in frg. 5 2—note the order; and החוזים (the seers) in frg. 5 4 could point to Num 24:16 according to G. Brooke;[29] דורש (interpreter) in frg. 23 1. But frgs. 6–7 3–6 offer a more connected text which shows that Deut 33:8–11—the blessing of Levi—was cited here as well. That is, in an explicitly eschatological setting one meets the priestly blessing (the context is not given in *Testimonia*). Line 7 preserves a bit of what appears to be a *pesher* on the passage (it takes up the terms *urim* and

---

[28] See *DJD* 5.53–57.

[29] *Exegesis at Qumran: 4QFlorilegium in its Jewish Context* (JSOTSup 29; Sheffield: JSOT Press, 1985) 160–61. Brooke numbers the lines in frg. 5 differently, so that this one is frg. 5 5 for him and the reference to Israel and Aaron is in frg. 5 3.

*tummim*). With regard to the identification of the interpreter of the law, it may be significant that one of the levitical functions in Deut 33:10 is to teach the Torah (יורו משפטיכה ליעקוב ותורתכה לישראל—all of this must be restored in the present text). A number of other biblical passages also attest the intimate connection of priest and Torah (e.g., Jer 18:18). It is perhaps worth adding that *T. Levi* 18:3 uses the star imagery of Num 24:17 with respect to the future priest.[30] It is possible, then, that *Florilegium* also points to the time when the davidic messiah stands with a priestly colleague.[31]

## F. The Damascus Document

Though this literary composition, which also goes under the name "The Zadokite Fragments" or the "Damascus Covenant," is probably older than *Testimonia* or *Florilegium* (the oldest copy of CD dates from the first half of the first century BCE), it is appropriate to treat it here because it contains more occurrences of the title "interpreter of the law" and "prince of the congregation" along with other messianic expressions. CD uses the word *messiah* in the plural in two cases, probably as a designation for prophets (see II 12–13; V 21–VI 1). In CD 7, however, one meets eschatological leaders whose role is reminiscent of the one assigned to a prophet and the messiahs of Aaron and Israel in 1QS IX 11. In CD VII 14–21 the author begins by quoting Amos 5:26–27 ("You shall take up Sakkuth your king, and Kaiwan your star-god, your images, which you make for yourselves; therefore I will take you into exile beyond Damascus, says the Lord, whose name is the God of hosts"; this is abbreviated in CD). The passage serves to explain the escape to the north by those who hold fast. The interpretation is:

> The Books of the Law are the *tabernacle* [= the Sakkuth] of the king; as God said, *I will raise up the tabernacle of David which is fallen* (Amos ix, 11). The *king* is the congregation; and *the bases* [the Kaiwan] *of the statues* are the Books of the Prophets whose sayings Israel despised. The *star* [= Amos 5:27] is the Interpreter of the Law who shall come to Damascus [הבא דמשק;

---

[30] Brooke, *Exegesis at Qumran*, 197–205, esp. 203–05.

[31] In 4QCatena A (4Q177), frgs. 10–11 2–3, what seems to be Zech 3:9 is quoted. In line 5 there is reference to דורש התורה.

see Amos 5:27]; as it is written *A star shall come forth out of Jacob and a sceptre shall rise out of Israel* (Num. xxiv, 17). The *sceptre* is the Prince of the whole congregation, and when he comes *he shall smite all the children of Seth* (Num. xxiv, 17).

Here the interpreter of the law and the prince of the congregation appear together (with the interpreter/star first as in the biblical lemma) in an eschatological context and in connection with statements from Amos 5:26–27; 9:11; and Num 24:17. It is worth noting that the words "the star is the interpreter of the law" in VII 18 are now attested in 4QD$^b$ 3 iv 7; and bits of it are in copies d (frg. 2 15) and f (frg. 5 2) as well.[32]

A second type of messianic reference in CD is, of course, the four passages in which one meets the word משיח/משוח in association with אהרון/ישראל. Some of these show strong parallels in wording and theme with 1QS IX. In CD XII 23–XIII 1 there is the "rule for the assembly [מושב] of the camps." "Those who follow these statutes in the age of wickedness until the coming [עמוד] of the Messiah [משוח] of Aaron and Israel shall form groups of at least ten men . . . ." (Note that XII 20–22 have verbal echoes of the context in 1QS IX.) That is, as in 1QS IX, certain rules are to prevail until the anointed one stands. The second reference, also in manuscript A, appears at XIV 18–19: "*This is the exact statement of the statutes in which [they shall walk until the coming of the Messia]h* (= מש[יח) *of Aaron and Israel who will pardon* (= ויכפר) *their iniquity.*" The messianic function is once more to define a unit of time. This passage has been important in the old debate about whether the title משׁו/יח אהרון וישראל refers to one or two individuals. The reason is

---

[32] The Well Midrash in CD 6 (introduced with: "But God remembered the Covenant with the forefathers, and He raised from Aaron men of discernment and from Israel men of wisdom, and He caused them to hear" [6:2–3]) explains Num 21:18 ("*the well which the princes dug, which the nobles of the people delved with the stave*") in these words: "The *Well* is the Law, and those who dug it were the converts of Israel who went out of the land of Judah to sojourn in the land of Damascus. God called them all *princes* because they sought Him, and their renown was disputed by no man. The *Stave* [מחוקק] is the Interpreter of the Law of whom Isaiah said, *He makes a tool for His work* (Isa. liv, 16); and the *nobles of the people* are those who come to dig the *Well* with the staves with which the *Stave* ordained that they should walk in all the ages of wickedness—and without them they shall find nothing—until he comes who shall teach righteousness at the end of days [עד עמד יורה הצדק באחרית הימים]" (VI 4–11). Here the interpreter seems to be a historical character, a figure of the present age. Thus, at least one end-time title was held by someone in the present.

that the following verb is also in the singular; from this some have concluded that the messiah is one individual who carries out the atoning work. L. Ginzberg already raised the possibility that the verb be read as a pual, but this does not seem to be the most obvious reading of the form.³³ Actually, the number of the verb is not decisive because it simply agrees with the singular subject משיח. The meaning of the messianic designation must be gleaned from the words which form the construct phrase. It is difficult to imagine why a single messiah would be said to be of Aaron and Israel. If only one were intended, why not say "messiah of Israel," since Aaron would be included in the more comprehensive designation? It seems preferable to take the phrase as intending two messiahs, and to argue that it is another instance of a singular construct noun which is to be understood with each of two (or more) absolutes. Other examples are מלך סדום ועמרה (Gen 14:10); ראש ערב וזאב (Judg 7:25); and from the scrolls שם ישראל ואהרון (1QM III 13); and שם ישראל ולוי ואהרון (1QM V 1). Milik had originally suggested that the singular of the *Damascus Document* was a correction by a medieval copyist, but he soon retracted that view when he learned that the singular is supported by 4QD^b 18 iii 12.³⁴ The function here attributed to the משיח (atoning) is, of course, a preeminently priestly one (cf. Leviticus 16; Exod 28:38; Zech 3:9).

The remaining references are in manuscript B. In XIX 10–11, after citing Zech 13:7, the author explains: "The humble of the flock [a term that occurs in Zechariah] are those who watch for Him. They shall be saved at the time of the Visitation whereas the others shall be delivered up to the sword when the Anointed of Aaron and Israel shall come [בבוא], as it came to pass at the time of the former Visitation . . ." (XIX 9–11). The arrival of the messianic age is associated with punishment. The last passage is XIX 33–XX 1—an interesting one for several reasons.

> None of the men who enter the New Covenant in the land of Damascus, and who again betray it and depart from the fountain of living waters, shall be reckoned with the Council of the people or inscribed in its Book from the day of the gathering in

---

³³ L. Ginzberg, *An Unknown Jewish Sect* (Moreshet Series 1; New York: The Jewish Theological Seminary of America, 1976) 252–53. (He first published his views in 1914 and 1922.)

³⁴ See *Ten Years of Discovery*, 125–26.

of the Teacher of the Community until the coming [עמוד] of the Messiah out of Aaron and Israel.

The repeated preposition מ- (from, out of) in the formulation here adds weight to the claim that two messiahs are meant. As elsewhere, the appearance of the messiahs marks the end of an era—a time separated by an interval from the death (?) of the Teacher.

## G. *The War Scroll*

The passages adduced from the *War Scroll* are those which refer to כוהן הרואש (the chief priest) and his activities during the eschatological warfare. In X 2 the priest (no other title) stands and addresses those about to enter battle (cf. Deut 20:2–4); in XIII 1ff. the high priest (the title is restored on the basis of parallels) and his brothers the priests and levites bless and curse (cf. 4Q491, frgs. 1–3); in XV 4: ועמד כוהן הראש with his colleagues (he recites the prayer for the time of war); in XVI 13 the head priest strengthens their hands in battle and speaks to the troops; in XVIII 5 he and others bless all Israel; and in XIX 1 he approaches (context broken). At least one can say that in this text the chief priest has eschatological roles, while the prince of the congregation has a more directly military part to play.

## H. *Other References*

The pattern of a priest, regardless whether he is termed a messiah, appearing with a secular leader of the end time is repeated in other texts.

1. 4Q161 = 4QpIsa$^a$ 8–10[35]: The lines of these fragments cite Isa 10:33, 34; 11:1–5 and offer a *pesher* on them. After a long scriptural quotation from Isaiah 11, the expositor writes:

> 17 [*Its interpretation concerns the Shoot of*] David who will arise [העומד] at the e[nd of days . . . 18 . . . ] his [*ene*]mies, and God will sustain him with [. . . *the* ] Law [. . . 19 . . . th]rone of glory, a ho[ly] crown, and garments of variegat[ed stuff . . . 20 . . . ] in his hand, and over all the G[*entile*]s he will rule, and Ma-

---

[35] *DJD* 5.13–15.

gog [21 . . . al]l the peoples shall his sword judge. And as it says, 'Not [22 . . . ] or decide by what his ears shall hear': its interpretation is that [23 . . . ] and according to what they [!] teach him so shall he judge, and according to their [!] command [24 . . . ] *with him*, one of the priests of repute shall go out with garments of [. . . ] in his hand [. . . ³⁶

2. 4Q285 3–5: "3] the Branch of David and they will enter into judgement with [4 ] and the Prince of the Congregation, the Bran[ch of David] will kill him [ 5 by stroke]s and by wounds. And a priest [of renown (?)] will command [."³⁷

## I. Unclear Texts

1. 4Q167 = 4pHos B, frg. 2: In interpreting Hos 5:13–15, which it cites, the pesherist includes these words: "*Its interpretation con]cerns the Last Priest* [כוהן האחרון] *who will send forth his hand against* [the text says "to strike"] *Ephraim.*"³⁸

2. 4Q173 = 4QpPs B (Ps 127:2–3): In frg. 1 4 the text refers to the teacher of righteousness, and in line 5 to "a/the pri]est at the end of ti[me."³⁹

3. 1Q30: It mentions מ[שיח הקודש in line 2 and perhaps the books of the pentateuch in line 4.

4. 4Q252: Allegro restored "[. . . the Interpreter of (?) the Law, with the men of the community" in col. V 5.⁴⁰ If he is correct, the interpreter of the law would again be mentioned with the messiah, the branch of David in this text.

5. 4Q375 and 376⁴¹

---

³⁶ The translation is Allegro's (*DJD* 5.14).

³⁷ Translation of Vermes, "The Oxford Forum for Qumran Research Seminar on the Rule of War from Cave 4," 88. Vermes also notes the possibility of reading כוהן [הראש] in line 5.

³⁸ Allegro, *DJD* 5.33. The commentator may be interpreting the words "For I will be like a young lion to Ephraim."

³⁹ *DJD* 5.51–52.

⁴⁰ "Further Messianic References," 175.

⁴¹ The readings from these texts may be found in J. Strugnell, "Moses-Pseudepigrapha at Qumran: 4Q375, 4Q376, and Similar Works," *Archaeology and History in the Dead Sea Scrolls: The New York University Conference in Memory of Yigael Yadin* (ed. L.

375 1 i 9: ה[כוהן המשיח] (see Lev 21:10)
376 frg. 1 1: הכ<ו>הן המשיח

There is insufficient context to allow further identification of this anointed priest. A prophet is also under consideration in 4Q375.

6. 4Q521: a fragment speaks of its anointed ones: וכל משיחיה. M. Wise and J. Tabor take this as a reference to the prophets in line with the usage in CD and in the Psalms.[42]

## Summary

1. The texts surveyed range over at least the first century BCE, with some such as 1QS and CD probably being earlier and the *War Scroll* possibly later.

2. In them a priestly eschatological figure puts in appearances and bears different titles. In some cases he is termed משיח (1QS IX 11; CD XII 23–XIII 1; XIV 18–19; XIX 10–11; XIX 33–XX 1) and possibly elsewhere. A second title, found in more than one document, is דורש התורה (4QFlor I 11; CD VII 18–19 [cf. VI 7]; see also Catena A [4Q177] frgs. 10–11 5). A third title is כוהן הראש (variously spelled) that is frequent in the *War Scroll*. In some cases this character is styled simply הכוהן (1QSa II 12?) or a priest with some other noun attached (השם in 4QpIsa[a] and perhaps in 4Q285; האחרון in 4QpHos frg. 2 3).

3. Several functions are carried out by the priestly figure alone or with the davidic heir. In 1QS and CD the time when they stand or come is used to define the end of a period of wickedness during which certain laws are in force. In CD the task of atoning is also mentioned. 1QSa has the priest lead the whole congregation, preside over his priestly colleagues, and offer the first blessing at the meal. The title דורש התורה underscores his work of clarifying and teaching Torah with which he also seems to advise the davidic figure. One text speaks of the last priest as extending his hand to defeat Ephraim.

4. Several of the references studied here attach mention of a priestly messiah to biblical texts. Prominent among the explicit ones

Schiffman; JSPSup 8, JSOT/ASOR Monographs 2; Sheffield: Sheffield Academic Press, 1990) 221–56 (see 226, 236).

[42] "The Messiah at Qumran," *BAR* 18 (1992) 65, n. 11. The fragment and line are 4:9 in Eisenman and Wise, *The Dead Sea Scrolls Uncovered*, 22.

are Deut 33:8–11 and Num 24:17. The star imagery of Num 24:17 is related to the star named in Amos 5:26. CD also talks of the historical interpreter of the law in connection with Numbers 21, and the *pesher* on Hosea finds a reference to the last priest in the young lion who opposes Ephraim.

The evidence does allow one to conclude, then, that at Qumran there was a dual messianism, with one messiah being priestly and the other davidic.[43]

---

[43] The Melchizedek text (11QMelch) has been left out of consideration because the figure described there is not a messiah. He appears to be an angel—perhaps the equivalent of the archangel Michael. See P. J. Kobelski, *Melchizedek and* Melchirešaʿ; (CBQMS 10; Washington, DC: Catholic Biblical Association of America, 1981).

# Messianism, Resurrection, and Eschatology at Qumran and in the New Testament[*]

*Émile Puech*

Since the first publication of manuscripts, a number of studies have focused on messianism in the Dead Sea Scrolls.[1] This subject is an important part of, or at least related to, a main theme, that of eschatology.[2] Eschatology concerns mainly "the last days" (אחרית הימים/אחרון קץ) and what follows "at the end of days"—the general judgment, the destruction of the wicked, and the salvation of the just. Against this background, is it possible to situate and understand better the theological concepts of messianism and resurrection, particularly at Qumran, themes which occupy such an important place in New Testament theology?[3] My purpose here is not to deal with all the aspects of each of these themes in the Qumran texts and in the New Testament, but to underline some main points in order to sketch an outline of these subjects. Then, perhaps, parallels and differences will emerge.

---

[*] I warmly thank Prof. J. Taylor for the revision of my English draft.

[1] For a general bibliography on Qumran messianism, see J. A. Fitzmyer, *The Dead Sea Scrolls: Major Publications and Tools for Study* (rev. ed.; SBLRBS 20; Atlanta: Scholars Press, 1990) 164–67, to which must be added J. T. Milik, *Ten Years of Discovery in the Wilderness of Judaea* (SBT 26; Naperville, IL: Allenson, 1959) 123–28.

[2] See for example H.-W. Kuhn, *Enderwartung und gegenwärtiges Heil: Untersuchungen zu den Gemeindeliedern von Qumran, mit einem Anhang über Eschatologie und Gegenwart in der Verkündigung Jesu* (SUNT 4; Göttingen: Vandenhoeck & Ruprecht, 1966).

[3] For instance, G. W. E. Nickelsburg, *Resurrection, Immortality and Eternal Life in Intertestamental Judaism* (HTS 26; Cambridge: Harvard University Press, 1972); H. C. C. Cavallin, *Life after Death: Paul's Argument for the Resurrection of the Dead in 1 Cor 15. Part I: An Inquiry into the Jewish Background* (ConB 7/1; Lund: Gleerup, 1974); idem, "Leben nach dem Tode im Spätjudentum und im frühen Christentum. I: Spätjudentum," *ANRW* II.19.1 (1979) 240–345.

## The Available Sources

It is clear that not all the texts found in the Qumran caves are Essene compositions. Besides the biblical manuscripts, the Aramaic compositions are at present being increasingly identified as pre-Essene works by a majority of scholars.[4] Among the copies found at Qumran, some predate the Essenes' occupation of the site in the middle of the second century BCE, while the others were possibly copied there more than once during the two centuries of occupation. Even if these Aramaic compositions are not Essene works, they can still be used in this study because they were surely read by Essenes, as is proved by numerous copies found at Qumran. Moreover, they have (or could have) influenced the theological concepts of this religious group. For our purposes, it is also possible to utilize some books of Karaite authors who knew and copied Essene books after a discovery of manuscripts at Qumran in the Byzantine era (ca. 790 CE).[5] Especially notable are Daniel al-Qumisi (end of ninth century) and Yefeth ben ʿAli.[6] All this must be taken into account in order to understand the origin and evolution of these important theological concepts of the Essene movement.

## Messianism

One of the oldest and clearest witnesses to messianic expectation in the Scrolls is certainly the testimony of 1QS IX 10–11, which states that the members of the community shall depart from none of the counsels of the Law according to the primitive precepts "until the coming of a Prophet and of the Messiahs of Aaron and of Israel." It is true that 4QSᵉ, the oldest copy, has the material in 1QS IX 12

---

[4] See J. T. Milik, "Écrits prééesséniens de Qumrân: d'Hénoch à Amram," *Qumrân: Sa piété, sa théologie et son milieu* (ed. M. Delcor; BETL 46; Paris/Gembloux: Duculot, 1978) 91–106. But this qualification is not yet accepted by all scholars; see, for instance, on the New Jerusalem, F. García Martínez, *Qumran and Apocalyptic: Studies on the Aramaic Texts from Qumran* (STDJ 9; Leiden: Brill, 1992) 207–13.

[5] This phenomenon recalls that of Aramaic (pre-Essene) manuscripts copied at Qumran. Compare, for instance, the discovery of CD or *Testament of Levi* in the Geniza of a Karaite synagogue in Cairo.

[6] See A. Paul, *Écrits de Qumrân et sectes juives aux premiers siècles de l'Islam: Recherches sur l'origine du Qaraïsme* (Paris: Letouzey et Ané, 1969) 115–30.

directly after VIII 16, and so lacks this important evidence. Yet, it is not at all clear that this shorter redaction is the primitive one, because it leaves an impression of abruptness and disharmony.[7] Thus, the 4QS[e] text cannot be used to establish an earlier concept of messianic expectation different from that known from 1QS IX 11.

Consequently, a date at the beginning of the first century BCE is to be assigned to three passages that belong to the same scroll and hand: 1QS IX, 1QSa II 11–12 (the full reading of which, of course, must be reconstructed: אם יוליד [אל ה]מ[ל]ך[ ] המשיח אתם, "When God will bring forth the king Messiah with them");[8] 1QSb (benediction of the high priest, the priests, and the king, נשיא העדה); and, also belonging to the same hand, 4Q175 (Testimonia). All four of these texts describe the expectation of two Messiahs: the priest and the king. Even 1QSa and b show a hierarchic precedence of the priestly Messiah over the royal one. This hierarchy is not disproved by the different order reflected in 4Q175, which, as has been correctly noted, relies on the order of the biblical quotations of the Pentateuch.[9]

The same messianic conception, which must prevail during the age of wickedness, is found in CD XIV 19 "until the coming of the Messi]ah of Aaron and (of) Israel and he will atone for their iniquity";[10] in CD XII 23–XIII 1; and again in CD XIX 33–XX 1:

> Thus, none of the men who entered the New Covenant in the Land of Damascus and who left, and who betrayed, and who

---

[7] But see Milik, *Ten Years*, 124–25, who would after all consider this passage a later addition, and J. Pouilly, *La Règle de la Communauté de Qumrân: Son évolution littéraire* (CahRB 17; Paris: Gabalda, 1976) 26–28, following J. Murphy O'Connor, who assigns IX 3–11 to stratum 1 but VIII 16b–IX 2 to stratum 2! Thus it appears that the anteriority of the text of 4QS[e] is a subject of debate. Can this missing section be better explained by the omission of a full column in the copy by a scribe?

[8] It does not seem that in this text the banquet is the eschatological one; rather, the reference seems to be to any (cultic) banquet during the messianic period where the king would be present.

[9] First Exod 20:21b (in the Samaritan recension with the same introductory formula); next Num 24:15–17; then Deut 33:8–11; and finally Psalms of Joshua for the figure of Antichrist.

[10] CD XIV 19 has a singular substantive, משיח, present even in the oldest manuscript, 4QD[d] (first half of the first century BCE), but the translation given here is grammatically the only possible interpretation. See, for instance, מלך אתור ומצרין in 4Q246 i 6. Cf. É. Puech, "Fragment d'une apocalypse en araméen (4Q246 = Pseudo-Dan[d]) et le Royaume de Dieu," *RB* 99 (1992) 98–131, esp. n. 17 (pp. 102–03).

departed from the fountain of living waters, shall be reckoned with the council of the people or inscribed in their book from the day of the gathering in of the Teacher of the Community until the coming of the Messiah out of Aaron and out of Israel.

This same dyarchy is found in yet another passage of CD (VII 18–20) that identifies "the star" as "the interpreter of the Law" and "the scepter" as "the Prince of the whole Congregation." This passage thus lends support to the interpretation of the previously quoted passages of CD.

The title נשיא, "Prince"—an Ezekielian designation of the davidic Messiah to whom Isa 11:1–5 is applied—refers to the king Messiah (Ezek 34:23–24; 37:25; 45:7–25). 4Q252 1 v 3–4 also refers to the king Messiah in its comment on Genesis 49. There he is qualified as "shoot of David" (עד בוא משיח הצדק צמח דויד). The Pesher on Isaiah, 4Q161 7–10 iii 15–29, presents the davidic Messiah as judge in association with a priest, as does 4Q252 1 v 4–5, where the interpreter of the Law (= the priestly Messiah) also accompanies the davidic Messiah. The same idea is found again in 4Q174 1–2 i 11–12.

We always find these two main figures—the priestly and the davidic Messiahs—in the Rules and in texts that are roughly contemporaneous with them (CD, 4Q175), in the slightly later Eschatological Midrash (4Q174 + 177), in 4Q252, and in the *Pesharîm*.[11] The role of the royal shoot is confined to political leadership, and that of the high priest is focused on cultic leadership as well as on an emerging interpretative function. The priestly Messiah has to perform the cult—in particular, the atonement rites (CD XIV 19; see also 11QMelch ii 7–11; 4QTestLevi^d[?])[12]—and to act as the last Interpreter of the Law.

Such a clear dyarchy remains consistent throughout the Qumranic period and even has some roots in pre-Qumranic texts. It does not represent a totally new concept (see *T. Levi* 18; *T. Judah* 21:2–5;

---

[11] Thus it is not possible to accept the hypothesis of four stages to explain the evolution of messianism as proposed by J. Starcky, "Les quatre étapes du messianisme à Qumrân," *RB* 70 (1963) 481–505. See Puech, "Fragment d'une apocalypse en araméen."

[12] É. Puech, "Fragments d'un apocryphe de Lévi et le personnage eschatologique. 4QTestLévi^c-d(?) et 4QAJa," *The Madrid Qumran Congress: Proceedings of the International Congress on the Dead Sea Scrolls Madrid 18–21 March, 1991* (2 vols.; ed. J. Trebolle Barrera and L. Vegas Montaner; STDJ 11; Leiden: Brill; Madrid: Editorial Complutense, 1992) 2.449–501.

24¹³; *Jub* 31:12–20).¹⁴ It goes back to biblical texts, principally Gen 49:10–12; Psalms 2, 89, 110; Isaiah 9, 11; Jer 23:5–6; and especially Zech 3:8;6:12–13, where the prophet establishes, through Zerubbabel, a connection with the davidic messianism of 2 Samuel 7 (see also Hag 2:23). Zech 6:12–13 speaks about two figures: the davidic shoot who will wear the royal insignia and rebuild the sanctuary of Yahweh and a priest who is "at his side" (LXX) or "on his throne" (MT).

Only by chance do we know that some Karaite commentators on the Twelve Prophets—Daniel al-Qumisi and Yefeth ben ʿAli, whose theological affinities with Essenism are well known—described the two-pronged messianism¹⁵ that is already expressed in the Dead Sea Scrolls. As we have noted, the expectation of two Messiahs appears to be well rooted in the pre-Qumranic period, in biblical as well as in pseudepigraphical texts, both of which were well known in the Essene movement. But the situation of conflict at the origin of the split of the Hasidean movement—which gave birth to the Pharisees on the one hand and to the Essenes on the other—must have raised in the mind of those who were excluded the desirability, or even the necessity, of a separation of the central power for the present time. This must have had a direct consequence on the future, principally on the concept of eschatology, with the rise of a strong counterpoise in the form of the High Priesthood, which had already gained considerable influence since the fall of Jerusalem in 587 and the end of the kingship. The image of pairs—Joshua and Zerubbabel, etc.—during the peaceful period of Persian domination in Palestine that was at the origin of Zechariah's oracles must have left a powerful imprint on the religious consciousness of pious people and especially on the priesthood. The

---

¹³ These texts were not found in the Qumran caves; however, remains of the *Testament of Levi* and the *Testament of Judah* are attested there, yet in a longer recension. The messianic concepts should have been the same in both recensions.

¹⁴ The book of *Jubilees* is well known in the Qumran Caves. See J. T. Milik, *Ten Years*, 32; J. C. VanderKam and J. T. Milik, "The First *Jubilees* Manuscript from Qumran Cave 4: A Preliminary Publication," *JBL* 110 (1991) 243–70; idem, "A Preliminary Publication of a Jubilees Manuscript from Qumran Cave 4: 4QJub$^d$ (4Q219)," *Bib* 73 (1992) 62–83.

¹⁵ See Paul, *Écrits de Qumrân*, 128–29. Commentary on Zech 4:14 and 6:12–13, I. Markon, *Commentarius in librum Duodecim Prophetarum quem composuit Daniel al*-Kūmissi, *saec. IX* (Jerusalem, 1957) 66, 68) and on Mal 3:24 (ibid., 125ff.). These commentaries are important because they assure us that Zechariah and Malachi are the direct biblical sources of the messianic conception of the Essenes.

result was that the excluded high priest and his colleagues tried to support the same dyarchy, even granting a hierarchic precedence to the priestly messianic figure over the all-encompassing authority of the davidic Messiah. Moreover, the two-pronged messianic expectation that emerges from the published texts of Qumran had a similar continuation in the later period with the pair Eleazar–Bar Kosiba (the latter of whom bore the title נשיא ישראל) and in rabbinic texts (for instance, in ʾAbôt de Rabbi Nathan A 34).[16]

But as we have seen, 1QS IX 11 expected another figure "until the coming of a Prophet and the Messiahs of Aaron and of Israel" (עד בוא נביא ומשיחי אהרון וישראל). The Teacher of Righteousness was surely considered a prophet by the members of his community, and he was the (exiled) high priest, the true interpreter of the Law whom God had sent in those difficult times. After his death, the members were asked to follow his teaching and his interpretation of the Law until the coming of a Prophet and of the priestly Messiah. A prophet like Moses whom God would raise up was to tell to their brethren all that God commanded him (4Q175 1–8). But this function of teaching the eschatological Law is also that of the Priestly Messiah (CD VI 10–11, VII 18–19; 4Q174 1–2 i 11). What, then, was the precise function of the Prophet like Moses to be, except that of a precursor of the Messiahs? This view perhaps finds support in 4Q375,[17] since the mosaic eschatological Prophet might have been at Qumran, as in Mal 3:23, identical with Elijah *redivivus* and therefore could hardly have been identified with the eschatological high priest and expected to arrive on the scene before himself. Yet the Karaite Daniel al-Qumisi identified Elijah with the teacher, and later in the tenth century David ben Abraham al-

---

[16] ʾAbôt de Rabbi Nathan A 34:

Similarly, with the verse, *These are the two anointed ones, that stand by the Lord of the whole earth* (Zech 4:14). This is a reference to Aaron and the Messiah, but I cannot tell which is the more beloved. However, from the verse, *The Lord hath sworn, and will not repent : Thou art a priest for ever after the manner of Melkisedek* (Ps 110:4), one can tell that the Messianic King is more beloved than the righteous priest (trans. J. Goldin, *The Fathers according to Rabbi Nathan* [Yale Judaica Series 10; New Haven: Yale University Press, 1955] 137–38).

[17] Published by J. Strugnell, "Moses-Pseudepigrapha at Qumran: 4Q375, 4Q376, and Similar Works," *Archaeology and History in the Dead Sea Scrolls: The New York University Conference in Memory of Yigael Yadin* (ed. L. H. Schiffman; JSOT/ASOR Monographs 2; JSPSup 8; Sheffield: JSOT Press, 1990) 221–56.

Fasi identified the priestly Messiah with Elijah.[18] Thus this figure who has been identified with the teacher (= the true Prophet) and/or the priestly Messiah, was not so clearly understood already in ancient times.

A small fragment of an Aramaic composition of Cave 4 contains a free translation of Mal 3:23: "³the eighth as elect. And behold I shall puri[fy(?) . . .] ⁴I shall send you Elijah befo[re . . ." (4QarP).[19] Here the coming of Elijah *redivivus* is linked to the day of the Lord. The Prophet has to prepare hearts, to convert people before the coming of the day of judgment (Mal 3:1, 22–24). This same passage (Mal 3:24) is partly quoted in a Hebrew manuscript which I have called "a messianic apocalypse," precisely in a messianic context and just before an allusion to the king Messiah. The text reads: "I shall deliver them by [your mouth /the word of your mouth, because] ²it is certain: the fathers go back to the sons" (4Q521 2 iii 1–2).[20] If Sir 48:10–11 from the first half of the second century BCE is taken into account (see also 1 Macc 14:41 and 4:46, where the prophetic precursor is called a true Prophet), it is clear on the one hand that the coming of a New Elijah was expected among pious circles of that period and, on the other hand, that the Essenes in particular kept alive this biblical prophetic teaching.

For Essene history, this means that during the lifetime of the Teacher there was no need to expect a Prophet like Moses or a priestly Messiah, because he was himself the true Prophet and the authentic high priest, the anointed one. The Essenes were awaiting only the coming of a messianic ruler, other than the Hasmoneans, who could be both rulers and high priests.[21] But shortly after the

---

[18] Paul, *Écrits de Qumrân*, 128–29, quoting N. Wieder, "The Doctrine of the Two Messiahs Among the Karaites," *JJS* 6 (1955) 14–23.

[19] See J. Starcky, "Les quatre étapes," 497–98, and É. Puech, *La croyance des Esséniens en la vie future: Immortalité, résurrection, vie éternelle? Histoire d'une croyance dans le Judaïsme ancien* (2 vols.; Ebib 21–22; Paris: Gabalda, 1993) 2.669–92.

[20] See É. Puech, "Une apocalypse messianique (4Q521)," *RevQ* 15 (1992) 475–522; idem, *La croyance des Esséniens*, 2.627–92. I use "apocalypse" in its broad sense, as a revelation to the *maskil(im)* about the eschatological times with a transcendent dimension involving afterlife and cosmic judgment. The composition describes themes and a theology of history developed in the apocalypses.

[21] The point is apparently different from that of 1 Macc 14:41 about the fusion of both powers in the same person (except in the case of Alexandra). This is still reflected in 1QSa II 11–12 ("When God will bring forth the king Messiah with them"), but this remark is valid also for the period after.

death of the Teacher, the community was in need of these figures, the priestly and royal Messiahs and the Prophet. This situation is also reflected in 4Q521 and in the later redactional stages of 1QS, 1QSa and b, CD, and 4Q175 around 100 BCE. The same conception obtained until the end of the community, as we can see in the later compositions, 4QMidrEschat, 4Q252 and the *Pesharim*.[22]

At the next stage of development, the prophecy of Malachi known to Ben Sira (48)—the one concerning individual conversion through the observance of the Law in view of the restoration of the tribes by the servant of the Lord (Isa 49:6)—was kept alive but the role of Elijah underwent an evolution. First linked to the parousia of Yahweh for the judgment, the coming of Elijah is now related to the coming of the Messiahs who will prepare the final judgment. The restoration of a new eschatological kingdom by the king Messiah becomes an important element of the messianic times. This is clearly present already in 4Q521 2 (see also *Psalms of Solomon* 17, 18; *Testaments of the Twelve Patriarchs*; etc.).

So the expectation of the coming of Elijah and of the Messiah(s) at the end of days is well attested both in the Qumran literature and outside Qumran (at Ben Sira 48 etc.). This recognition sheds a great deal of light on passages in the NT that envision Elijah as a forerunner of the Messiah, an identification which can in no way be a *novum* as some scholars have recently written.[23] On the best understanding of Mark 9:2–13//Matt 17:1–13 the idea is that, according to the scribes, Elijah must come first, before the Messiah or Son of Man (which is a messianic title) or beloved Son of God (which is a declaration of the messianic sonship of Jesus) suffers, dies, and rises again (see John 1:27; Matt 3:11; Luke 1:17).[24] This popular belief lies in the background of the question of certain Jews to John regarding Elijah the prophet (John 1:19–21, quoting precisely Isa

---

[22] See Puech, "Fragment d'une apocalypse en araméen."

[23] With D. C. Allison, "Elijah Must Come First," *JBL* 103 (1984) 256–58; *contra* M. M. Faierstein, "Why Do the Scribes Say that Elijah Must Come First?" *JBL* 100 (1981) 75–86; J. A. Fitzmyer, "The Aramaic 'Elect of God' Text from Qumran Cave 4," *Essays on the Semitic Background of the New Testament* (London: Chapman, 1971) 137; idem, "More About Elijah Coming First," *JBL* 104 (1985) 295–96.

[24] Against Fitzmyer, "More About Elijah Coming First," 295, who understands the sense of the passage to be "before the rising of the dead, or before the son of man rises from the dead." The question regarding the coming of Elijah emerges from his presence in the story of the transfiguration. Then, since Elijah does come first and restores all things, how can the son of man suffer, die, and rise?

40:3). It is implicit in Jesus' recognition of John as a prophet (Matt 11:7–14; Luke 7:26–35, quoting Mal 3:1). It underlies the general presentation of the Baptist in Mark 1:1–8 (quoting Mal 3:1) and Luke 1:16–17 (quoting Mal 3:23–24; Sir 48:10–11). And it even informs speculation about Jesus as Elijah, a prophet, and the Messiah (Mark 6:15, 8:28; Matt 16:14; Luke 9:19).

These passages of the NT can no longer be taken as something novel. Indeed, the very presence of Moses and Elijah (the representatives of the Law and the Prophets) with Jesus in the transfiguration scene (Matthew 17 and parallels) signifies that Jesus is neither the expected Prophet like Moses nor Elijah *redivivus*, but the Messiah coming to inaugurate his messianic kingdom (cf. Acts 3:20–28; 1:6; 2:30).

In many passages in the Gospels, from the narratives of the annunciation until the passion narratives and the answer to Caiaphas, we find such formulas as the Son of God, the Son of the most High, the Messiah, the Son of Man, the king of Jews. These titles show without a doubt that Jesus was regarded as the king Messiah, on the one hand. On the other, his priestly character appears in the Gospels in the institution of the Lord's Supper, where Jesus gives himself as a perfect victim for many, for the forgiveness of sins, to seal the New Covenant. Jesus takes on himself the task of universal redemption that Isaiah had assigned to the servant of the Lord (Isa 42:6; 49:6; 53:12; cf. Heb 8:8; 9:15; 12:24 and 4QTestLevi$^d$[?] 9 i 2–7, 24 ii [?][25]). This is also apparent in Luke 4:16–21, which quotes Isa 61:1–2, a text that was applied to the high priest during his consecration (61:1, 10).[26] It is to be noted that a liberation of captives accompanied this investiture, as in a sabbatical year.

To be sure, as an answer to the priests and Levites from Jerusalem, John declared himself openly to be neither the Christ (= Messiah), nor Elijah, nor the Prophet (John 1:19–24). But in response to the next question, he confessed the one who is coming after him, the lamb of God that takes away the sin of the world, the Chosen One of God (John 1:25–34)—designations that underline once more the priestly character of the expected figure.

However, from prison John sent his disciples to ask Jesus: "Are you the One who is to come, or have we to wait for someone else?"

---

[25] See Puech, "Fragments d'un apocryphe de Lévi."

[26] See P. Grelot, "Sur Isaïe LXI: La première consécration d'un grand-prêtre," *RB* 97 (1990) 414–31.

(Matt 11:2–3//Luke 7:18–20). The question concerns the messiahship of Jesus, in connection with his prophetic announcement (Matt 3:11–12//Luke 3:16–17).

Jesus does not directly answer the question by telling John that he is the powerful one, the judge separating the wicked and the just, baptizing the good with the Holy Spirit and sending the wicked into fire, as one might expect. Instead, he answers with a sentence containing a series of signs that he is doing—the works of Christ, which effectively are the signs of the coming of the messianic kingdom. Even Luke adds that "just then he cured many people of diseases and afflictions and of evil spirits, and gave the gift of sight to many who were blind" (Luke 7:21). As a matter of fact, the enumeration of the signs is not a pure sequence of biblical quotations mostly from Isaiah, but an announcement that the kingdom of God is present there now among people. There exists a close link between the kingdom and the person preaching it by his acts. Jesus is "the one who is to come" because "he has been sent" (Matt 10:40), but he is coming in a somewhat different way than John expected.[27] This is why Jesus tells John about his works. Since these works fulfill the scriptures that spoke about Jesus and his mission, it is up to John and his disciples to arrive at an answer about him.

The messianic works that show the fulfilment of the scriptures do not refer precisely to the king Messiah, and the climax of the six works of Jesus is the proclamation of the good news to the poor, which is not "a work of power." Two of them feature in Isa 61:1–2, a text on which Jesus comments in the synagogue of Nazareth on a sabbath: "The spirit of the Lord . . . has anointed me. He has sent me *to bring the good news to the poor*, to proclaim liberty to captives and *to the blind new sight*, to set the downtrodden free, to proclaim the Lord's year of favor." To these words Jesus adds, "This is being fulfilled today even as you listen" (Luke 4:16–30 and parallels). The other works point to Isa 29:18 ("that day the deaf will hear the words of the book and *the eyes of the blind will see*"); Isa 35:5–6 ("then *the eyes of the blind shall be opened*, the ears of the deaf unsealed, then the lame shall leap like a deer and the tongues of the dumb sing for joy"); and Isa 26:19 ("*your dead will come to life, their corpses will rise; awake*, exult all you who lie in the dust"). Of the actions enumerated in Jesus' answer—"Go back and tell John what

---

[27] Jesus did not try to deliver John from prison, in spite of the messianic text of Isa 61:1–2, which mentions such a deliverance.

you hear and see: *the blind see again* and the lame walk, *lepers are cleansed* and the deaf hear, *the dead are raised to life,* and *the good news is proclaimed to the poor*, and happy is the man who does not lose faith in me" (Matt 11:4–5//Luke 7:22–23)[28] —only one, the cleansing of lepers, is not part of an eschatological oracle of the prophets. But the healing of lepers (Mark 1:40–44; Matt 8:2–4; Luke 5:12–14; 17:11–18; cf. 4:27), which has its biblical basis in Lev 13:45–46; 14:1–32; 2 Kgs 5:13–15, is a work that demonstrates the power of God as healer and signifies the coming of the kingdom.

Although less miraculous, the last work to which Jesus points—"the good news is proclaimed to the poor"—is the central act in the preaching of the kingdom (Matt 5:3; Luke 6:20) and refers to the theme of the defense of the poor in Torah, Prophets and Wisdom literature.

All this is to say that the answer of Jesus is intended to point up the full significance of all the miracle narratives that show the power of God which accompanies the inbreaking of the eschatological kingdom on earth.

A similar list of messianic benefits is to be read in 4Q521 2 ii 8, 12–14: "⁸(the Lord) *gives liberty to prisoners, restores sight to the blind*, straightens the bent" (Ps 146:7b–8b) and "¹²*He will cure the mortally wounded and raise the dead, He will proclaim the good news to the poor* ¹³and satisfy the weak, He will lead the uprooted and enrich the hungry and [. . .]", because the Lord will do marvelous deeds which have never been done when He will [judge ?] and reward a good deed (lines 10–11). As it is, the list is without parallel, but it evidently draws on Ps 146:7b, 9a; Isa 26:19, 61:1; Deut 32:39b; Hos 6:1; and Ps 22:27. Only three themes are explicitly shared by the Qumran text and the NT: the blind, the dead, and the good news. One can add the liberty to prisoners of Isa 61:1 quoted in Luke 4:18 and the promise that "those who hunger will be satisfied" in the beatitude of Matt 5:6. But the purpose of both lists is similar insofar as the description of the signs tells of the inbreaking of the divine power on earth to usher in the kingdom of God. In 4Q521, God himself accomplishes these signs (probably in the days of the Messiah and through his messenger) by the pouring out of the spirit

---

[28] After the present tense in Matthew 11 (as opposed to the past tense of Luke), the sequence is grouped two by two with a καί in Matthew (a+b, c+d, e+f) but juxtaposed in two stichs of three in Luke (a,b,c + d,e,f); compare the sequence of 4Q521 2 ii 12–13, which is very close to that in Matthew.

of holiness—a theme present in the next column after that of the new Elijah. In the gospels, by contrast, Jesus as the Messiah and shoot of David (Luke 1:27, 32, 69) acts by himself as the Elect, the Son of God.

In conclusion, we find in both the Qumran literature and the NT very similar messianic ideas, including the coming of the new Elijah as a forerunner of the king Messiah. If in the Qumran texts the high priesthood belongs to the priestly Messiah, in the NT Jesus himself fulfills in his person both messianic expectations, as anointed high priest and king and as a very special messenger of God, the Son of God. Moreover, John the Baptist was also the son of a priest, Zechariah (Luke 1:5, 8–22).[29] But contrary to Qumran, where atonement is expected for the members of the group, the just Essenes, Jesus makes expiation for all the world. His kingdom is not political and national, but universal and spiritual.

## Resurrection

The resurrection of the dead, we have noted, is one of the benefits of the messianic times when God will manifest his power and his victory over sin and death. Did the Essenes believe in the resurrection of the dead, eternal life after death, or in immortality of the soul? This question has received different answers. Some scholars assert that the Essenes shared the Jewish belief in the resurrection of the body.[30] Others deny that any form of such a belief existed among the Essenes.[31] And some recognize in the scrolls the Essene doctrines noted by Josephus,[32] who ascribes to the Essenes a neo-pythagorean belief: the fall of immortal and preexistent souls who are enmeshed with bodies which serve them as prisons until, freed from the bonds of the flesh, they rise up to the heavenly world. The evil souls are relegated to a dark pit full of unending

---

[29] See above for the identifications proposed by the Karaites Daniel al-Qumisi and David ben Abraham al-Fasi, and recall that according to Sir 48:10–11 the new Elijah will have the power to raise the dead.

[30] For instance K. Schubert, "Das Problem der Auferstehungshoffnung in den Qumrantexten und in der frührabbinischen Literatur," *WZKM* 56 (1960) 154–67.

[31] R. B. Laurin, "The Question of Immortality in the Qumran «Hodayot»," *JSS* 3 (1958) 344–55; J. Le Moyne, *Les Sadducéens* (Ebib; Paris: Gabalda, 1972) 167–68.

[32] J. Carmignac, "Le retour du Docteur de Justice à la fin des jours?" *RevQ* 1 (1958) 235–48, Nickelsburg, *Resurrection*.

chastisements (*J. W.* 2 §§ 151–158). But according to Hippolytus of Rome, the Essenes believed in the resurrection of the flesh, the final judgment, a conflagration of the universe, and an eternal punishment of the wicked.

Accordingly, some scholars have tried to find a basis for these contradictory views in the same passages of the scrolls. Is it possible to propose a solution? Since most of the very badly preserved passages are subject to diverse interpretations, do we even have enough internal testimony for a solution?

Pertinent to the issue are three groups of texts: (1) the pseudepigrapha known and copied at Qumran, such as *1 Enoch, Jubilees,* and some Testaments; (2) the Aramaic texts found at Qumran, such as 4QTestament of Qahat, 4QVisions of Amram, 4QPseudo-Daniel, New Jerusalem; and (3) Qumran text such as 1QS, 1QH, 1QM, CD, 11QMelchizedek, 4Q180–181, 4Q280, 286–287, Eschatological Midrash, and the *Pesharim*. One might also include the Hebrew manuscript 4Q*Dibrê ha-me'ôrôt*, to which the Hebrew manuscripts 4QDeutero-Ezekiel and 4Q521 must now be added.

The earliest texts from group two (4QTestQah 1 ii 3–8 and 4QVis Amr$^f$ 1–2 ii),[33] which date from the end of the third to the beginning of the second century BCE, testify to hope in the resurrection of the just for the great judgment. As representatives of the two-way theology, these texts are to be situated in the tradition of Isa 26:14, 19, but they antedate the brief formulation of Dan 12:1–3. According to both linear and personal eschatology, they envision the just going to peace, eternal joy and light at the time of the great judgment, when they will be enlightened and will live again forever and see the wicked going to death and cast into Abaddon, fire, abyss and a darkened cave forever.

If the context of the eschatological war is not present or at least preserved in these manuscripts, it is present in 4QPseudo-Daniel$^{c-d}$ and New Jerusalem, which mention a war that the judgment will bring to an end. The contrast between the wicked who will stray in blindness and the just who will share in the resurrection is very explicit in the last column of 4QPseudo-Dan$^c$, lines 2–6. The opposition of "these and those" clearly alludes to Dan 12:2; the opposition also implies a resurrection and probably a return to the New Jerusalem on a renewed earth. Similarly 4QPseudo-Dan$^d$ insists peculiarly on the

---

[33] The attribution of this manuscript to Visions of Amram is not certain, only probable.

victory of the people of God over the impious kings and on establishing the kingdom of the saints on an earth free from enemies. Even the abyss will obey him (the Messiah or the people of God?) for eternity. Both texts know Daniel 12 and 7.

The same dependence on the book of Daniel is to be found in the Hebrew composition 4QDibrê ha-me'orôt (which may be Qumranic).[34] 4Q504 1-2 vi 11-16 reads, ". . . and deliver your people, Israel, from all the countries, near or far away, [where you have banished them]. All those who are written in the book of life [will stand before you or stand up/revive and stay] to serve you and give thanks to your holy Name." The inscription in the book of life must allude precisely to a concept of resurrection as in Daniel 12, or to survival at the divine judgment in the final time of distress. At any rate, this precision shows a change from a national eschatology such as that reflected in Isa 26:19 to an individual and personal eschatology as in Daniel 12. The people of Israel are identified exclusively with the pious, the *verus Israel* of the renewed covenant, the Ḥasîdîm waiting for the divine benedictions. This identification constitutes one of the reasons for tentatively attributing this Hebrew manuscript to the Essenes, as a composition written after the Book of Daniel.

To the same period must be dated 4QDeutero-Ezekiel. Its attribution to the Essenes is debated. It has a probable allusion to splits among the Hasideans, and it tries to console members of the community after the breaches caused by fratricidal fighting over the Law and Covenant. In view of the final events, God will shorten the time of distress because of his pious ones, "those who have walked in the ways of justice and have loved your name." "They will be compensated for their piety" because God is the redeemer (גואל) of his people. The parable of the dry bones (taken from Ezekiel 37) is used here to comfort the pious with the hope of resurrection according to an individual eschatology, as in Daniel 12 and 4QDibrê ha-me'orôt. The retribution implies a belief in the resurrection of the pious, whose bones ensure the personal identity of the revived who then will bless God, as in 4QVis Amr[f], 4Q521 7, and 4QDeutero-Ezekiel.

---

[34] E. Chazon, "4QDibHam: Liturgy or Literature?" *Mémorial Jean Starcky: Textes et études qumrâniennes II* (ed. É. Puech and F. García Martínez; *RevQ* 15 [1992]) 447-55, concludes that this weekly liturgy "was probably not composed at Qumran but rather in a pre-qumranic milieu." But there is not yet a clear-cut answer.

Concerning the Pseudepigrapha (group one, above), there is in the *Book of Watchers* of *1 Enoch* a clear affirmation of individual existence after death, meaning the *post-mortem* retribution of the righteous and wicked. The immortality of the souls or spirits of the just and the impious, who wait in separate compartments during the intermediate state between death and eternal judgment, does not exclude a resurrection of the righteous. But the separation of souls in compartments also implies some kind of individual judgment after death. Again, in the Enochic *Book of Dreams* (90:33) there is a possible allusion to the resurrection that is closely associated with the restoration of the people of Israel. Further references are to be found in the *Epistle of Enoch* (91:10//92:3–4; 100:5; 102:4–5; 103:3–7;[35] and 104:2–5), which are to be compared with Dan 12:3. After a period of wickedness, the Lord will come to judge and punish the impious; then the resurrection of the pious will occur: "the righteous shall arise from his sleep." The new life involves transformation into eternal light and glorification. But the resurrection of a glorified body must be implied—and not the existence of the spirit or soul, as some have supposed.[36] Moreover, the association of the blessed with the angels in glory is related to the day of the great judgment (and not to the death of the just). This belief is more clearly presented in the Enochic *Book of Parables* (which was not found at Qumran), especially chaps. 51 and 61. Here we read of the resurrection of the just on the new earth in the company of the Elect One, who presides over the judgment, while the impious perish in eternal fire. Consequently, the *Book of Enoch*, whose composition extended over almost two centuries, presents a non-unified eschatology. Yet eternal life is consistently described as a glorified life in light, radically different from the earthly life, and is normally associated with the resurrection of the just at the time of the last judgment. Clearly the end of history and the status of the dead seem more important to the authors than the anthropological aspects.

It is clear from the discovery of all these compositions in the Qumran library—often in many exemplars—that they, along with

---

[35] See 7Q4 1 and 7Q8; G. W. Nebe, "7Q4 — Möglichkeit und Grenze einer Identifikation," *Mémorial Jean Carmignac: Études qumrâniennes* (ed. F. García Martínez and É. Puech; *RevQ* 13 [1988]) 629–33.

[36] For instance, P. Grelot, "L'eschatologie des Esséniens et le Livre d'Hénoch," *RevQ* 1 (1958) 121; Nickelsburg, *Resurrection*, 136.

the biblical books of Isaiah, Ezekiel, and Daniel, must have influenced the beliefs of the members of the Community.

Do we find similar or different concepts of eschatology in the typical compositions of the Essenes? To the Essene compositions of the first generations, if not to the teacher himself, must belong the essential part of 1QS, 1QSa–b, 1QH, and the oldest part of 1QM.

1QS (III–IV, XI) hints at the reasons for the Community's existence as one destined to become the legacy of the saints in association with the sons of heaven, even while the group is still living among a sinful people and a wicked humanity. But the divine visitation or judgment is central in the Instruction on the Two Spirits, which tries to explain the origin of evil by the opposing presence of two spirits in the heart of mankind and to motivate the ethical behavior of human beings. God has put an end to the rule of evil and to the impious who will perish forever, while he will purify and reward the just at the time of the renewal of creation. The description of rewards and chastisements takes up and develops the terms of Daniel 12, and these lists are found again in a number of hymns. Clearly they concern the present life under divine judgment, as well as the end of time expected in the near future. The term "resurrection" is absent, but can the concept be ignored when reference is made to Daniel 12? The rewards presuppose a return to paradise in a purified world, made free of sin, of its cause, evil, and of its consequence, death. Thus, all the glory of Adam is promised again to the just; the living will be healed and transformed, while the dead will revive according to Daniel 12, which is the basis of this instruction.

A similar eschatology is to be found in the hymns of 1QH, whose didactic purposes are also evident. Instructed in the divine mysteries, the instructor (משכיל) and the wise know the present and future, the struggle of the two spirits in the heart of mankind, and the final result, the everlasting punishments and rewards at the time of the visitation, the universal conflagration, and the renewal of creation. To enter the community and to persevere in the trials are necessary for participating in the promised inheritance and future rewards at the end of time. The present Community is not the final realization of salvation,[37] but only the first step, because the authors know a linear eschatology that ends with the universal conflagration and a total renewal; they also know an intermediary

---

[37] We cannot speak of a purely realized eschatology in the Hymn Scroll, as understood by Kuhn, *Enderwartung*.

state in different spheres of the heavens, earth, and sheol. 1QH thus testifies to both an individual and a collective eschatology. In the Hymns, judgment, visitation, reward and punishment are sometimes linked to the eschatological war (XI 30ff., XIV 32ff., VII 30 ff.)[38] with the final fall of Belial and the enemies who will burn in Abaddon. There is also a linkage with the resurrection of the just and the transformation of the living, as in Daniel 12 and Isa 26:19 (mainly in XIV 37, V 28–29, XIX 15–16). The faithful know that they will receive the benefit of salvation by the grace of God and put on the glory of Adam in length of days (= immortality), after being purified of the great sin, which is an allusion to the primitive sin (XI 12). The curse which had fallen on humankind will be changed into blessing for the faithful so that Eden and life with God will be given back to them. This is compared to an exaltation into the eternal height, a communion with the assembly of the sons of God, and an elevation of mankind above the angels (XXIV 3) in the eternal light. All creation will be concerned in the last judgment. Thus the eschatology of the Hymns is the same as that of 1QS in its dependence on Daniel.

The *War Scroll* knows and develops the theme of the war of extermination in Daniel 11–12: the sons of light will win and no enemy will escape; they will all be killed and handed over to fire in Abaddon, while the just will shine for ever. This final war, which is described in liturgical fashion, will extirpate evil forever and usher in a new era in a transformed world, like a return to the origins. The theme of Daniel 12 is indeed present in cols. XIII–XIV; yet despite some attempts, it is not possible to find any direct allusion to resurrection in col. XII.[39] Still, the names of the chosen are written in books in heaven (cf. Daniel 12). It is true that in the scroll in its present state, there is no mention of resurrection, but there are also no dead among the just during these battles. However, inasmuch as the author has worked to a great extent on the basis of Daniel 11–12, it would be fair to conclude that he has also accepted Daniel's belief in the eternal chastisement of the wicked and in the resurrection–

---

[38] I quote according to my rearrangement of columns and fragment in É. Puech, "Quelques aspects de la restauration du rouleau des Hymnes (1QH)," *JJS* 39 (1988) 38–55.

[39] For instance, by A. Dupont-Sommer, "Règlement de la Guerre des Fils de lumière. Traduction et Notes," *RHR* 148 (1955) 25–43, 141–80, esp. p. 132.

transformation–exaltation of the righteous, according to a schema of both individual and collective eschatology.

A similar view is expressed in CD: at the end of time the total destruction of the wicked and the reward of the just will take place. The just will themselves have to be converted and enter the Community, until the king Messiah comes and leads the war of extermination before the visitation. "Those who adhere to the Law will live for ever and all the glory of Adam will belong to them" (III 20). This is a kind of terrestrial eschatology, no doubt, but is this complete change of condition at the end so different from that of Daniel 12?

An eschatology similar to that expressed in Daniel 12 is found again in 4Q180–181 (*Pesher of Periods*). 4Q181 knows Dan 12:1–3 and the resurrection[40] to eternal life in a celestial exaltation in the company of angels for the service of God. "The wicked will be for everlasting shame and for the destruction in Abaddon and the just] for everlasting life[". The same conception is found in 4QTohorôt and Berakôt. The *Eschatological Midrash* (4Q174 + 177) formally quotes the prophet Daniel (Dan 11:35; 12:10) and must also have accepted Daniel's collective and individual eschatology. The *Pesher* on Ps 37:10–22 (4Q171 1–10 ii–iii) mentions the end of the rule of the impious and the life of the just for a thousand generations, with the delights of Paradise and the inheritance of Adam, which means: on a new earth without sin and death, as at the beginning.

The last judgment, over which Melchizedek will preside, will seal his own victory and the destruction of Belial's rule (11QMelch). The change of era involves the renewal of the world and the coming of eternal bliss at the end of the tenth jubilee.

From this short presentation of the content of some scrolls, it is clear that an essentially identical conception of eschatology is present in the Essenes' own compositions and in the pre-Qumranic or pseudepigraphical texts found at Qumran. This understanding of the texts is confirmed by the recently published 4Q521, where belief in the resurrection of dead is certain: "the cursed one will be for death [when] the One who is giving life [will resurre]ct the dead of His people."[41] We find here the same conception as that in 4QVis Amr$^f$, 4QTestQahat, 4QPseudo-Daniel$^{c-d}$ and Daniel 12 and in the contemporary or somewhat later Essene compositions, such as 1QS (see

---

[40] This is not based on the translation of מעמד (4Q181 1 ii 4), as proposed by Cavallin, *Life after Death*, 65, but on lines 5–6.

[41] See É. Puech, "Une apocalypse messianique (4Q521)," *RevQ* 15 (1992) 475–523.

above). There the resurrection of the dead is understood as a new creation, in such a way that God the creator can create anew when he renders justice to the righteous by opening the tombs. As we have noted, the same idea is already present in 4QDeutero-Ezekiel. But there is more, because this manuscript[42] says something about the place and condition of the cursed and blessed. After crossing the bridge over the abysses, the cursed ones will go rigid, probably falling down into Abaddon or freezing hell, while the blessed ones will be welcomed by the heavens to live in the company of the angels (5 ii). This new and unique notion recalls, on the one hand, the Bridge of the Sorter in Zoroastrianism[43] and, on the other hand, the conviction in the Essene compositions that at the time of the visitation the just will stand before God in the company of angels and be similar to them. This means also that the state of resurrection is not a pure return to life on earth but a spiritual transformation in glory for the living as well as for those who have come to life again on a new earth for a perfect service of God.

The Essenes' eschatology connects with the protological concept of awaiting entry to the lost paradise. They expected the restoration of mankind to the state he was in before the original fall. Thus, it is easier to understand the state of the resurrected body or flesh, already present in the books of Enoch, a concept of resurrection that some scholars have understood as a purely spiritual one. The holy spirit will cover the blessed ones who will sit on a royal throne forever (4Q521 2 ii 6–7).

Consequently, the Essenes did not adopt a purely realized eschatology, as many scholars have stated. Rather, they expected the coming of a messianic kingdom and the day of visitation–judgment in the eschaton, with the glorification–resurrection–transformation of the righteous on a new earth and the eternal destruction of the wicked in the fire of hell.

---

[42] As I have shown ("Une apocalypse messianique," 515–19), the cancelling of the tetragrammaton in biblical quotations (for instance in Psalm 146) and the use of אדוני as a substitute in free composition argue in favor of a date for 4Q521 (whose paleographic date is ca. 80 BCE) that is post-Danielic and contemporary with 1QH, 1QS, and 1QM. Even some well-known vocabulary in these latter three texts features in 4Q521. Thus an Essene attribution for this work seems to be justified or at least quite possible.

[43] Others aspects of the belief depend on contacts with this Persian religion (e.g., universal conflagration).

The consistency of the Essenes' eschatology throughout all the scrolls, which is identical with that of the Hasideans Ḥasîdîm ) of the pre-Qumranic pseudepigrapha, is confirmed by the archeological data from the cemeteries of Qumran and of ʿAin el-Ghuweir, where the dead lie facing toward the north ready to enter the paradise of justice. But it is also confirmed by the external data of the notice of Hippolytus, who ascribed to the Essenes belief in the resurrection of the flesh, the universal conflagration, and the renewal of the earth with an intermediary state of rewards and chastisements according to a linear eschatology.[44] This belief, which is very similar to that of the Pharisees in the second and first centuries BCE, could not evolve too far because of the attachment of the disciples to the instructions and revelations of the teacher.[45] Alas, the state of preservation of 4Q521 does not give us a clear relationship between the days of the Messiah and the day of judgment–resurrection (a millennium?), but it clearly opposes belief in a general resurrection of all, wicked and righteous. Only the blessed among the true people of God will revive and recover all the glory of Adam.[46]

The eschatology of the NT writings, which are about one century later than the latest Essene compositions presented here, is in many aspects very close to that of the Essenes.[47] Both insist on a linear eschatology of history that nevertheless includes an individual eschatology. Almighty God, the creator and judge, must do justice, if not on this earth then surely in the world to come, when he will reward the just and punish the ungodly. The plan of salvation at the basis of God's covenant with his people must succeed, and the rule of Belial–Satan will surely end. Therefore, the coming of the messianic kingdom in both eschatologies is of the greatest importance.

But while still awaited by the Essenes, this coming is, in the outlook of the NT writings, realized by the birth, teaching, and mes-

---

[44] The presentation of Flavius Josephus does not give us a correct picture of the Essenes' belief, and at least on this point he cannot be trusted.

[45] As in the Pharisaic texts of this period and earlier in the Bible, we do not yet find the Semitic formula תחית המתים in the Essenes' manuscripts. But in itself, this point cannot contradict our conclusion regarding the Essenes' belief in the resurrection of the dead; other formulas are unequivocal. The same would be true for the Pharisees!

[46] For a more detailed presentation and discussion, see Puech, *La croyance des Esséniens*, chapter XI (2.627–702).

[47] It is not possible in this short presentation to quote all the relevant passages from the NT or to discuss all aspects of NT eschatology.

sianic acts of Jesus the Messiah, the Son of God. Jesus' death and resurrection have atoned for the sins of all forever and have ushered in the new creation, the new human or new Adam in the divine glory. Jesus is the first-fruits of all who have fallen asleep and the first born of the new creation (1 Corinthians 15; 2 Pet 3:13; etc.) that was eagerly awaited by the Essenes. God has realized for Jesus the Just what he had promised, victory over death, the last enemy, after victory over Belial–Satan and his rule. And he will do this for all the just at the eschaton. Meanwhile, the kingdom of God is growing in secret in the hearts of those who believe in Jesus, the Messiah of God, until the parousia of Christ at the end of time (1, 2 Thessalonians etc.). As in the scrolls, so too in the NT there is a clear distinction between the days of the Messiah and the end of time or parousia of God for the last judgment. This is the time of the church, or of the millennium in some writings. But as in the *Parables* of Enoch and perhaps in 11QMelchizedek, it is the Messiah who will judge in the name of Yahweh, sitting on the throne of his glory, to reward the just and punish the ungodly. This is the Day of Yahweh, regarded in Christian writings as the fulfilment of Malachi's prophecies.

An emphasis on the revival of bones or the opening of tombs (an emphasis proper to the Shammai school as well) reflects adherence to a notion of resurrection that insists on the continued personal identity of the resurrected just. The narratives of the empty tomb and of the appearances of the risen Jesus fulfill this purpose in the NT, by showing that he was recognized as the same person before and after the crucifixion. As this identity of the person is underlined in the scrolls by the inscription of names in the celestial books, so it is in the NT as well (Luke 10:20; cf. Rev 20:12; and note the comparisons of the seed and of the clothing in 1 Cor 15:35–50 and 2 Cor 5:1–5, respectively).

Continuity but also discontinuity and novelty were part of the Essenes' eschatology. Resurrection was considered a new creation by the Essenes (as also by Hillel's school, which viewed resurrection as a kind of new birth). This idea also comes to expression in the NT writings, with diverse imagery including that of the new Adam, new Jerusalem, and divine sonship in the Son of God and the Holy Spirit, which ensures one's inheritance in the heavenly kingdom. But contrary to the Essenes, who constituted a closed entity, Christians maintained that all just believers in Jesus the Messiah—Jews and non- Jews—will take part in his kingdom at the time of the renewal

(Matt 19:28). Both the scrolls and the NT point out the glory and spiritual form of the resurrected body.

The scrolls testify to a resurrection of the just, and the NT also knows of the last day (John 11:24)—a universal resurrection of the just and wicked (Matt 25:31–46; John 5:29; Acts 24:15)—which is a belief expressed from time to time among the Pharisaic sources of the period by means of a new and literal interpretation of Daniel 12 (LXX).

Rewards and entry into eternal life through resurrection or through transformation of the living for the just, everlasting chastisements in Hell (Abaddon–Gehenna) for the wicked destined for death—these are the eschatological expectations we find in both the scrolls and the NT, except that the terms *just* and *wicked* do not receive exactly the same meaning in both of them. But like the scrolls, the NT seems to have accepted the representation of a differentiated intermediary state for the dead awaiting the last judgment.

Using the language and the images of their cultural milieu, the authors of both the scrolls and the NT also proceeded to demythologize the awaited future: The religious experience of life with God in this world must go on after death in an eternal life with the one who rewards the pious and changes their being into a resurrected–transformed one, in the light of the divine glory at the day of judgment. Thus an existentialist interpretation of human existence stood alongside a linear, eschatological interpretation.

# Indexes

# Biblical Passages

## Hebrew Bible

*Genesis*
| | |
|---|---|
| 2 | 124 |
| 2:24 | 148 |
| 3:14 | 110 |
| 3:16 | 148 |
| 6–9 | 190 n.55 |
| 8:3-4 | 35 |
| 8:7 | 117 |
| 8:9 | 117 |
| 8:12 | 117 |
| 9:21-24 | 117 |
| 14:10 | 230 |
| 15:2 | 118 |
| 15:5 | 118 |
| 15:13 | 118 |
| 19–26 | 124 |
| 21 | 124 |
| 22:2 | 118 |
| 22:11 | 118 |
| 22:13 | 118 |
| 25–48 | 124 |
| 27:45 | 132 |
| 28:6 | 132 |
| 32:25-32 | 123, 125, 131 |
| 34 | 14 n.38 |
| 39–41 | 184 |
| 49:4 | 116 |
| 49:10-12 | 239 |
| 49:10 | 116–17 n.12, 117, 215, 216, 218 |
| 49:16ff. | 133 n.44 |

*Exodus*
| | |
|---|---|
| 1:4 | 133 |
| 3:12 | 123, 125 |
| 4:24-26 | 131 |
| 4:27-28 | 123, 125, 131 |
| 7:20 | 122 |
| 8–39 | 124 |
| 8:1 | 122 |
| 8:2 | 122 |
| 8:3 | 122 |
| 8:17 | 122 |
| 10:5 | 122 |
| 10:19 | 121 |
| 10:22 | 122 |
| 10:23 | 122 |
| 15 | 131, 197 |
| 15:1 | 131 |
| 15:7 | 131 |
| 15:10 | 131 |
| 15:17 | 198 |
| 15:22 | 131 |
| 19 | 132 |
| 19:9 | 119 |
| 19:16 | 132 |
| 19:17 | 132 |
| 20 | 126 |
| 20:12 | 123 n.27 |
| 20:16 | 123 n.27 |
| 20:17 | 86 n.22, 108, 123 n.27 |
| 20:19-22 | 123 n.27 |

260  INDEX OF BIBLICAL PASSAGES

| | | | |
|---|---|---|---|
| 20:21 | 226 | 23:11 | 34 |
| 20:21b | 237 n.9 | 23:15 | 34 |
| 20:22-26 | 123 n.27 | 23:27-29 | 115 |
| 21–22 | 124 | 23:42–24:2 | 128 |
| 21:24-25 | 129 | 24:20-22 | 129 |
| 21:26-27 | 129 | 24:22 | 129 |
| 22:2 | 119 | 25:39-43 | 129 |
| 22:15 | 119 | 25:40 | 129 |
| 24 | 132 | 26:22 | 115 |
| 24:1-11 | 132 | 27:29 | 130 |
| 24:4-6 | 123, 125 | 27:30-34 | 130 |
| 24:12 | 132 | 27:34 | 126 |
| 24:12ff. | 132 | | |
| 24:18 | 133 | *Numbers* | |
| 25 | 133 | 1–36 | 124 |
| 27:17 | 119 | 1:1-5 | 126 |
| 27:18 | 119 | 1:12ff. | 133 n.44 |
| 28:38 | 230 | 1:24ff. | 133 n.44 |
| 32:20 | 110 | 2:14ff. | 133 n.44 |
| 34 | 42 | 4 | 129 |
| 34:10 | 119 | 4:47-49 | 129 |
| 35 | 42 | 5 | 129 |
| 39:5 | 130 | 6 | 129, 225 |
| | | 7 | 129 |
| *Leviticus* | | 12:6-8 | 205 |
| 11–26 | 124 | 13:12-16 | 133 |
| 11:17-25 | 129 | 14 | 124 |
| 12–27 | 124 | 20:17-18 | 127 |
| 13:45-46 | 245 | 21 | 234 |
| 14:1-32 | 245 | 21:1 | 130 |
| 15:14-15 | 129, 129 n.40, 130 | 21:18 | 193, 229 n.32 |
| 15:29-30 | 129 n.40 | 24:15-17 | 226, 237 n.9 |
| 16 | 230 | 24:16 | 227 |
| 18:25-29 | 130 | 24:17 | 218, 219, 228, 229, 234 |
| 19:1-4 | 129, 130 | | |
| 19:4 | 129 | 27 | 128 |
| 19:5-8 | 129 | 27:1 | 128 |
| 19:9-15 | 129 | 27:11 | 128 |
| 19:12 | 129 | 29 | 124, 128 |
| 20:13 | 130 | 29:32-30:1 | 127, 128 |
| 21:10 | 233 | 29:32-39 | 128 |

# INDEX OF BIBLICAL PASSAGES

| | | | |
|---|---|---|---|
| 30 | 148 | 18–22 | 43 |
| 30:1 | 128 | 18 | 205 |
| 30:3-14 | 115 | 18:18-22 | 123 n.27, 126 |
| 30:3-6 | 115 | 18:18-19 | 226 |
| 33 | 124 | 18:18 | 206 |
| 33:38 | 130 | 19 | 124 |
| 33:39 | 130 | 20 | 47 |
| 33:40 | 130 | 20:2-4 | 231 |
| 36 | 128 | 23:22-24 | 115 |
| 36:1-2 | 128 | 27–28 | 14 |
| | | 27:13 | 133 n.44 |
| ***Deuteronomy*** | | 27:28 | 108 |
| 1–14 | 124 | 28:69–32:47 | 14 n.35 |
| 1–3 | 113 n.4 | 32 | 87 n.25 |
| 1:1 | 62 | 32:1-43 | 86 n.25 |
| 2 | 124 | 32:39b | 245 |
| 2:8-14 | 127 | 33 | 207 |
| 5:28-31 | 126 | 33:8-11 | 226, 227, 234, 237 n.9 |
| 5:28-29 | 123 n.27, 226 | | |
| 5:30 | 123 n.27 | 33:10 | 207, 227 |
| 5:31 | 123 n.27 | 33:20ff. | 133 |
| 11:29-30 | 108 | | |
| 12 | 115 n.10 | ***Joshua*** | |
| 12:1 | 104 n.19 | 6:26 | 226 |
| 12:5 | 86 n.22 | 7:11 | 98 |
| 12:11 | 86 n.22 | 7:13 | 100 |
| 12:14 | 86 n.22 | 7:16 | 98 |
| 12:18 | 86 n.22 | 7:24 | 98 |
| 12:20-28 | 115 | 8:10 | 100 |
| 13:1-7 | 115 | 8: 30-35 | 14 |
| 13:13-19 | 115 | 8:33 | 99 |
| 14 | 124 | 8:34 | 100 |
| 14:14-21 | 129 | 19:24ff. | 133 n.44 |
| 16 | 124 | 24:28 | 100, 101 |
| 16:13-14 | 127, 128 | 24:31 | 101 |
| 16:15 | 128 | | |
| 16:22–17:1 | 115 | ***Judges*** | |
| 17 | 201 | 2:6 | 100, 101 |
| 17:2-5 | 115 | 2:7 | 98, 101 |
| 17:9-18 | 115 | 7:25 | 230 |
| 17:18 | 45 | 10:10 | 101 |

## 262  INDEX OF BIBLICAL PASSAGES

| | | | |
|---|---|---|---|
| 20:2 | 99 | 17–18 | 89 |
| 20:25 | 98 | 27:11 | 102 n.14 |
| | | 27:12 | 100 |
| *1 Samuel* | | 30:25 | 102 n.14 |
| 1 | 89, 89 n.40 | | |
| 2:3 | 142 | *2 Samuel* | |
| 2:11-26 | 99 | 3:18b | 100 |
| 2:13 | 99, 102 n.14 | 3:21 | 99 |
| 2:14 | 99 | 3:37 | 100 |
| 2:22 | 99 | 5:2 | 100, 101 |
| 2:23 | 99 | 6:21 | 100 |
| 2:24 | 99 | 7 | 227, 239 |
| 8:3 | 102 n.14 | 7:7 | 100 |
| 8:9 | 102 n.14 | 7:8 | 100 |
| 8:11 | 102 n.14 | 7:10-11 | 197 |
| 9:9 | 105 n.20 | 7:10 | 100, 196, 197 |
| 9:16 | 99 | 7:11-14 | 216, 218, 227 |
| 10:1b | 99 | 7:13a | 197 |
| 10:25 | 45, 102 n.14 | 7:19 | 103 n.17 |
| 10:27b–11:15 | 99 | 8:15 | 102 n.14 |
| 11 | 88 n.39 | 14–15 | 89 n.39 |
| 11:4 | 99 | 15:2 | 102 n.14 |
| 11:5 | 99 | 15:4 | 102 n.14 |
| 11:7 | 99 | 15:6 | 102 n.14 |
| 11:11 | 99 | 22:23 | 102 n.14 |
| 11:12 | 99 | | |
| 11:14 | 99 | *1 Kings* | |
| 11:15 | 99 | 1:1–2:11 | 103 |
| 12:10 | 101 | 1:20 | 99 |
| 13:16 | 99 | 2:3 | 102 n.14, 103, 104 n.19 |
| 13:22 | 99 | | |
| 14:2 | 99 | 2:12–21:43 | 103 |
| 14:3 | 99 | 2:12 | 104 |
| 14:17 | 99 | 3:3 | 102 n.14, 103 – 04 n.18 |
| 14:18-23 | 99 | | |
| 14:20 | 99 | 3:11 | 102 n.14 |
| 14:24 | 98 | 3:14 | 102 n.14, 103 – 04 n.18, 104 n.19 |
| 14:27 | 98 | | |
| 14:38 | 98 | | |
| 15:1 | 100 | 3:28 | 102 n.14 |
| 15:30 | 99 | | |

| | | | |
|---|---|---|---|
| 6:12 | 102 n.14, 103 – 04 n.18, 104 n.19 | 12:15-16 | 99 |
| | | 14:1-20 | 102– 03 n.15, 105 n.20 |
| 8:5 | 99 | 14:5 | 105 n.20 |
| 8:45 | 102 n.14 | 14:8 | 103 – 04 n.18 |
| 8:58 | 102 n.14, 103 – 04 n.18, 104 n.19 | 16:16b-17 | 99 |
| | | 16:21a | 99 |
| | | 18:18 | 103 – 04 n.18 |
| 8:59 | 102 n.14 | 19:15 | 206 |
| 8:61 | 102 n.14, 103 – 04 n.18, 104 n.19 | 20:15b | 101 |
| | | 22:5 | 105 n.20 |
| | | 22:7 | 105 n.20 |
| 8:62 | 99, 101 | 22:8 | 105 n.20 |
| 9:4 | 102 n.14, 103 – 04 n.18, 104 n.19 | **2 Kings** | |
| | | 1:2 | 105 n.20 |
| | | 1:3 | 105 n.20 |
| 9:6 | 102 n.14, 103 – 04 n.18, 104 n.19 | 1:6 | 105 n.20 |
| | | 1:16 | 105 n.20 |
| 10:9 | 102 n.14 | 3:11 | 105 n.20 |
| 11:11 | 102 n.14, 103 – 04 n.18, 104 n.19 | 5:13-15 | 245 |
| | | 8:7 | 206 n.45 |
| | | 8:8 | 105 n.20 |
| 11:33 | 102 n.14, 103 – 04 n.18, 104 n.19 | 9:33 | 109 |
| | | 10:31 | 103 |
| | | 13:17 | 109 |
| 11:34 | 102 n.14, 103 – 04 n.18, 104 n.19 | 14:6 | 103 |
| | | 17:13 | 102 n.14, 103, 104 n.19, 105 n.20 |
| 11:38 | 102 n.14, 103 – 04 n.18, 104 n.19 | 17:15 | 104 n.19 |
| | | 17:16 | 104 n.19 |
| | | 17:19 | 102 n.14, 104 n.19 |
| 12:1 | 99 | 17:34 | 102 n.14, 103, 104 n.19 |
| 12:3 | 99 | | |
| 12:5 | 99 | 17:37 | 102 n.14, 103, 104 n.19 |
| 12:6 | 99 | | |
| 12:7 | 99 | 18:6 | 104 n.19 |
| 12:9 | 99 | 21:8 | 103 |
| 12:10 | 99 | 22:8 | 103 |
| 12:12 | 99 | 22:11 | 103 |
| 12:13 | 99 | 22:13 | 105 n.20 |

| | | | |
|---|---|---|---|
| 22:18 | 105 n.20 | 25:11-12 | 13 |
| 23:3 | 102 n.14, 104 n.19 | 29:10 | 13 |
| 23:24 | 103 | 31:1-14 | 13 |
| 23:25 | 103 | 31:15-22 | 13 |
| | | 31:23-30 | 13 |
| *Isaiah* | | 31:31-34 | 13 |
| 5:11-12 | 183 n.31 | 31:35-40 | 13 |
| 8:11 | 227 | | |
| 9 | 239 | | |
| 10 | 217, 219 | *Ezekiel* | |
| 10:24 | 219 | 1 | 119 |
| 10:33 | 231 | 3:1-3 | 83 |
| 10:34 | 231 | 4:4-6 | 13 |
| 11 | 201, 217, 219, 231, 239 | 29:5 | 110 |
| | | 30 | 118 |
| 11:1-5 | 216, 218, 231, 238 | 30:3 | 118 |
| 11:1 | 216, 217 | 30:4 | 118 |
| 11:3-4 | 217 | 34:23-24 | 238 |
| 11:4 | 217 | 37 | 248 |
| 23:1-14 | 90 n.43 | 37:4-9 | 119 |
| 26:14 | 247 | 37:5-7a | 119 |
| 26:19 | 244, 245, 248, 251 | 37:7 | 119 |
| 29:18 | 244 | 37:8 | 119 |
| 30:15 | 36 | 37:25 | 238 |
| 35:5-6 | 244 | 40 – 48 | 183 |
| 40:3 | 242– 43 | 44:10 | 227 |
| 42:6 | 243 | 44:15 | 195 |
| 49:6 | 242, 243 | 45:7-25 | 238 |
| 52:1 | 183 n.31 | 48 | 133 n.44 |
| 53:12 | 243 | | |
| 54:1-2 | 183 n.31 | *Hosea* | |
| 54:2-3 | 183 n.30 | 5:13-15 | 232 |
| 54:11-12 | 183 n.31 | 6:1 | 245 |
| 54:16 | 229 n.32 | 10:12 | 206 |
| 61:1-2 | 243, 244, 244 n.27 | | |
| 61:1 | 243, 245 | *Amos* | |
| 61:10 | 243 | 5:26-27 | 218, 228, 229 |
| | | 5:26 | 218, 234 |
| *Jeremiah* | | 5:27 | 228, 229 |
| 18:18 | 228 | 9:11 | 217, 218, 227–29 |
| 23:5-6 | 239 | | |

## INDEX OF BIBLICAL PASSAGES 265

*Micah*
| | |
|---|---|
| 7:11 | 22 |

*Habakkuk*
| | |
|---|---|
| 1:5 | 197, 203 |

*Haggai*
| | |
|---|---|
| 2:23 | 239 |

*Zechariah*
| | |
|---|---|
| 1:12-17 | 13 |
| 3:8 | 239 |
| 3:8 | 223 |
| 3:9 | 228 n.31, 230 |
| 4:14 | 239 n.15 |
| 6:12-13 | 239, 239 n.15 |
| 7:5 | 13 |
| 13:7 | 230 |

*Malachi*
| | |
|---|---|
| 3:1 | 241, 243 |
| 3:16 | 142 |
| 3:22-24 | 241 |
| 3:23-24 | 243 |
| 3:23 | 240, 241 |
| 3:24 | 239 n.15, 241 |

*Psalms*
| | |
|---|---|
| 1:1 | 227 |
| 2 | 239 |
| 2:1 | 227 |
| 2:9 | 201 |
| 14:6 | 110 |
| 22:7 | 245 |
| 37:10-12 | 252 |
| 37:23-24 | 204 |
| 74:14 | 110 |
| 78 | 120, 121, 133 |
| 78:44 | 122 |
| 78:45 | 122 |
| 78:46 | 122 |
| 78:47 | 122 |
| 89 | 239 |
| 102:7 | 110 |
| 105 | 120, 121, 122, 133 |
| 105:30 | 122 |
| 105:31 | 122 |
| 105:32 | 121 |
| 105:33 | 121 |
| 105:34 | 121 |
| 104:35 | 121 |
| 105:36 | 121 |
| 105:29 | 122 |
| 109:10 | 110 |
| 110 | 239 |
| 110:4 | 240 n.16 |
| 135:6 | 164 |
| 127:2-3 | 232 |
| 145–150 | 165 |
| 145 | 161, 164, 165 |
| 146 | 253 n.42 |
| 146:7b-8b | 245 |
| 146:7b | 245 |
| 146:9a | 245 |
| 150 | 91 |

*Proverbs*
| | |
|---|---|
| 22–23 | 141, 144 |

*Job*
| | |
|---|---|
| 3:8 | 110 |
| 9:8 | 110 |
| 41:1 | 110 |

*Daniel*
| | |
|---|---|
| 1–6 | 91 n.50 |
| 2–6 | 184 |
| 2 | 184, 185, 186 |
| 3 | 184 |
| 4–5 | 186 |
| 4 | 184 |
| 5 | 184 |

| | | | |
|---|---|---|---|
| 6 | 184 | *Ezra* | |
| 7–12 | 184 | 2:3 | 13 |
| 7 | 181, 185, 219 n.16, 248 | *1 Chronicles* | |
| 2 | 145 | 11:2 | 101 |
| 9:24 | 13 | 17:6 | 100, 101 |
| 11–12 | 251 | 17:9 | 100 |
| 11:35 | 252 | 28:11-19 | 45 |
| 12 | 248, 250–52, 256 | *2 Chronicles* | |
| | | 2:6 | 99 |
| 12:1-3 | 247, 252 | 10:1 | 99 |
| 12:2 | 247 | 10:16 | 99, 101 |
| 12:10 | 227, 252 | 36:20-22 | 13 |

# Apocrypha

| | | | |
|---|---|---|---|
| *Tobit* | | 33:15 | 149 |
| 1:21-22 | 184 n.35 | 39:12-35 | 149 |
| 2:10 | 184 n.35 | 39:27 | 149 |
| 11:1 | 184 n.35 | 39:29-30 | 150 |
| 13:16-19 | 183 n.31 | 42:14 | 148 |
| 13:18-19 | 183 n.31 | 42:24 | 149 |
| 14:10 | 184 n.35 | 42:15–43:33 | 148 |
| | | 48 | 242 |
| *Sirach* | | 48:10-11 | 241, 243, 246 n.29 |
| 3:1-16 | 147 | | |
| 3:6 | 148 | 49:13 | 110 |
| 3:11 | 148 | 51:13-20b | 137 |
| 8:12 | 146 | 51:30b | 137 |
| 8:13 | 147 | | |
| 16:24 –18:14 | 149 | *Baruch* | |
| 24:9-12 | 139 | 5:1-2 | 183 n.31 |
| 24:23 | 139 | | |
| 25:16 | 148 | *1 Maccabees* | |
| 25:24 | 148 | 4:46 | 241 |
| 29:1 | 146 | 13:24 | 49 |
| 29:2 | 147 | 14:41 | 241, 241 n.21 |
| 29:14 | 147 | | |
| 29:15 | 147 | *Psalms* | |
| 29:16-20 | 147 | 151 | 91 |

# New Testament

## Matthew
| | |
|---|---|
| 3:11-12 | 244 |
| 3:11 | 242 |
| 5:3 | 245 |
| 5:6 | 245 |
| 8:2-4 | 245 |
| 10:40 | 244 |
| 11 | 245 n.28 |
| 11:2-3 | 244 |
| 11:4-5 | 245 |
| 11:7-14 | 243 |
| 11:28-30 | 139 |
| 16:14 | 243 |
| 17 | 243 |
| 17:1-13 | 242 |
| 19:28 | 256 |
| 24:15 | 82 n.14 |
| 25:31-46 | 256 |

## Mark
| | |
|---|---|
| 1:1-8 | 243 |
| 1:40-44 | 245 |
| 6:15 | 243 |
| 8:28 | 243 |
| 9:2-13 | 242 |
| 13:14 | 82 n.14 |

## Luke
| | |
|---|---|
| 1:5 | 246 |
| 1:8-22 | 246 |
| 1:16-17 | 243 |
| 1:17 | 242 |
| 1:27 | 246 |
| 1:32 | 246 |
| 1:69 | 246 |
| 3:16-17 | 243 |
| 4:16-30 | 244 |
| 4:16-21 | 243 |
| 4:16-20 | 80 |
| 4:18 | 245 |
| 4:27 | 245 |
| 5:12-14 | 245 |
| 6:20 | 245 |
| 7:18-23 | 215 |
| 7:18-20 | 244 |
| 7:21 | 244 |
| 7:22-23 | 245 |
| 7:26-35 | 243 |
| 9:19 | 243 |
| 10:20 | 255 |
| 16:16 | 81 n.11 |
| 16:29 | 81 n.11 |
| 16:31 | 81 n.11 |
| 17:11-18 | 245 |
| 24:27 | 81 n.11 |
| 24:44 | 82 |

## John
| | |
|---|---|
| 1:1-18 | 139 |
| 1:19-24 | 243 |
| 1:19-21 | 242 |
| 1:25-34 | 243 |
| 1:27 | 242 |
| 5:29 | 256 |
| 11:24 | 256 |

## Acts
| | |
|---|---|
| 1:6 | 243 |
| 2:30 | 243 |
| 3:20-28 | 243 |
| 24:15 | 256 |
| 26:22 | 81 n.11 |
| 28:23 | 81 n.11 |

## 1 Corinthians
| | |
|---|---|
| 7 | 9 n.22 |

15                235 n.3, 255
15:35-50          255

*2 Corinthians*
5:1-5             255

*Colossians*
1:15-20           139

*1 Thessalonians*
4:4               146

*Hebrews*
8:8               243
9:15              243
12:24             243

*2 Peter*
3:13              255

*Revelation*
20:12             255

# Ancient Literature

## Qumran

**CD = (Damascus Document):**

| | |
|---|---|
| I 1-8 | 13 |
| II 3 | 138 |
| II 11-12 | 13 |
| II 12-13 | 228 |
| II 14-III 20 | 13 |
| IV 4 | 195 |
| IV 11-12 | 22 |
| V 2-3 | 33 |
| V 8-9 | 9n.20 |
| V 21-VI 1 | 228 |
| VI | 205, 229n.32 |
| VI 10-11 | 240 |
| VI 11 | 195, 203, 206 |
| VI 19 | 12 |
| VII | 207-209 |
| VII 11 | 203 |
| VII 14-21 | 228 |
| VII 18-21 | 195, 218, 233, 237 |
| VIII 1-IX 11 | 212 |
| VIII 29 | 12 |
| IX 11 | 212 |
| X 6 | 18 |
| X 8-10 | 82n.17 |
| XI 21-XII 1 | 163n.37 |
| XII 23-XIII 1 | 211, 214, 229, 233, 237 |
| XIII 2 | 18 |
| XIV | 208 |
| XIV 7-8 | 18 |
| XIV 18-19 | 208, 211, 214, 216, 233, 237, 238 |
| XVI 1-4 | 18 |
| XVI 3 | 28 |
| XVI 3-4 | 82n.17 |
| XIX 10-11 | 211, 214, 230, 233 |
| XIX 33-XX 1 | 211, 214, 230, 233, 237 |

**1Q28 = (1QS; Community Rule):**

| | |
|---|---|
| I | 163 |
| I 1-3 | 81n.12 |
| I 6-7 | 18 |
| I 16-II 25 | 10 |
| II | 163 |
| III-IV | 138, 144, 149-151, 250 |
| VI 3 | 162 |
| VIII 1-IX 11 | 212 |
| VIII 5-6 | 220 |
| VIII 8-9 | 220 |
| VIII 10, 12 | 220 |
| VIII 15 | 212 |
| VIII 16 | 237 |
| IX | 205, 213, 220, 229, 237 |
| IX 5-7 | 220 |

| | | | |
|---|---|---|---|
| IX 9-11 | 211, 212, 226, 228, 236, 237, 240 | XIX 15-16 | 251 |
| | | XX 7 | 161 |
| | | XXIV 3 | 251 |
| IX 10-12 | 236 | XXV 34 | 161 |
| IX 12-26 | 212 | 10 | 167 |
| IX 13 | 213 | | |
| X-XI | 155 | | |

**1QM = (War Scroll):**
| | |
|---|---|
| III 13 | 230 |
| V 1 | 219, 230 |
| X-XIV | 155 |
| X 2 | 231 |
| XI 6-7 | 219 |
| XII | 251 |
| XIII 1 | 231, 251 |
| XV 4 | 231 |
| XVIII 5 | 231 |
| XIX 1 | 231 |

**1Q28a = (1QSa; Rule of the Congregation):**
| | |
|---|---|
| I 9-10 | 9n.20 |
| II 1-3 | 221 |
| II 11-12 | 237, 241n.21 |

**1Q28b = (1QSb):**
| | |
|---|---|
| I-V | 224 |
| III-V | 225 |
| V 20-29 | 218 |

**1QpHab:**
| | |
|---|---|
| I 13 | 203n.33 |
| II 1-10 | 197 |
| II 2 | 203n.33 |
| II 2-3 | 205 |
| II 5-6 | 199, 203n.34 |
| II 8-9 | 204 |
| V 10 | 203n.33 |
| VII 4 | 203n.33 |
| VII 4-5 | 204 |
| VIII 3 | 203n.33 |
| IX 6-7 | 199, 203n.34 |
| IX 9-10 | 203n.33 |
| XI 5 | 203n.33 |

**4Q27 = (4QNum$^b$):**
| | |
|---|---|
| 36 | 128n.39 |

**4Q84 = (4QPs$^b$):**
| | |
|---|---|
| I 4 | 203 |
| II 2 | 203 |

**4Q158 = (4QRP$^a$):**
| | |
|---|---|
| 1-2 | 131 |
| 6-8 | 125 |
| 14 | 125, 127, 133 |

**1QH = (Hôdāyôt Scroll):**
| | |
|---|---|
| V 28-29 | 251 |
| VII 30 | 251 |
| X 27-28 | 143 |
| XI 30 | 251 |
| XIV 32 | 251 |
| XIV 37 | 251 |

**4Q161 = (4QpIsa$^a$):**
| | |
|---|---|
| 2-6 ii 19 | 219 |
| 2-6 ii 26 | 203n.34 |
| 7-10 | 199, 203n.34, 216 |
| 7-10iii 15-29 | 238 |
| 8-10 | 231 |
| 22-25 | 199 |

**4Q162 = (4QpIsa$^b$):**
| | |
|---|---|
| II 1 | 199, 203n.34 |

## INDEX OF ANCIENT LITERATURE

**4Q163 = (4QpIsa$^c$):**
| | |
|---|---|
| 6-7 ii 14 | 203n.34 |
| 13 | 203n.34 |
| 23 ii 10 | 203n.34 |

**4Q167 = (4QpHos$^b$):**
| | |
|---|---|
| 2 | 232 |
| 2 3 | 232 |

**4Q168 = (4QpMic):**
| | |
|---|---|
| 6 2 | 203n.34 |

**4Q169 = (4QpNah):**
| | |
|---|---|
| 3-4 ii 2 | 203n.34 |

**4Q171 = (4QpPs$^a$):**
| | |
|---|---|
| 1-10 ii-iii | 252 |
| 1-10 iii 15 | 203n.33, 204 |

**4Q173 = (4QpPs$^b$):**
| | |
|---|---|
| I 4 | 232 |

**4Q174 = (4QFlor):**
| | |
|---|---|
| I 1-13 | 216, 227 |
| I 11 | 233 |
| II 1 | 199 |
| II 3 | 81n.13 |
| 1-2 i 11 | 240 |
| 1-2 i 11-12 | 238 |
| 5 2 | 227 |
| 5 4 | 227 |
| 6 | 227 |
| 6-11 | 207 |
| 23 1 | 227 |

**4Q177 = (4QCatena$^a$):**
| | |
|---|---|
| II 9-10 | 199 |
| 10-11 5 | 233 |
| 10-11 6 | 22n.56 |

**4Q182 = (4QCatena$^b$):**
| | |
|---|---|
| III 7-8 | 199 |

**4Q252 = (4QpGen$^a$):**
| | |
|---|---|
| V 3-4 | 215, 217 |
| V 4-5 | 238 |

**4Q267 = (4QD$^b$):**
| | |
|---|---|
| 2 15 | 229 |
| 3 iv 7 | 229 |
| 5 2 | 229 |
| 18 iii 12 | 230 |

**4Q285 = (Serekh ha-milḥamah):**
| | |
|---|---|
| 3-5 | 232 |
| 5 3-4 | 217, 219 |
| 6 1, 2, 5, 6, 8 | 219 |

**4Q286 = (4QBer$^a$):**
| | |
|---|---|
| 10 ii 2 | 164n.40 |

**4Q287 = (4QBer$^b$):**
| | |
|---|---|
| 4 13 | 215n.9 |

**4Q364 = (4QRP$^b$):**
| | |
|---|---|
| 3 ii 7-8 | 132 |
| 14 | 132 |
| 15 | 133 |
| 19 | 130 |
| 23a-b | 127 |

**4Q365 = (4QRP$^c$):**
| | |
|---|---|
| 6a ii | 127 |
| 8-13 | 129 |
| 12b iii 7 | 130 |
| 15 a-b | 129 |
| 22 | 130 |
| 23 | 128 |
| 26 a-b | 126 |
| 28 | 129 |

| | | | |
|---|---|---|---|
| 32 | 133 | 11 i | 161 |
| 36 | 128 | | |

**4Q504 = (4QDibHam$^a$):**
1-2 vi 11-16     248

**4Q366 = (4QRP$^d$):**
2        129
4 i      127, 128
5        129

**4Q511 = (4QShir$^b$):**
2 i 1    160
8 4      160

**4Q367 = (4QRP$^e$):**
2        129
3        130

**4Q521 = (Messianic Apocalypse):**
1 ii 1      215
2           242
2 ii 6-7    253
2 ii 8      245
2 iii 1-2   241

**4Q400 = (ShirShabb$^a$):**
2 6-8    168

**4Q416 = (Sap. Work A$^b$):**
1        141
2        145, 148
7        141, 146, 147

**4Q542 = (4QTestQah):**
1 ii 3-8    247

**4Q548 = (4QVisAmr$^f$):**
1-2 ii      247

**4Q417 = (Sap. Work A$^c$):**
1        142, 147
2        142, 144, 145, 151

**11Q5 = (11QPs$^a$):**
XVI         164
XXII 14-15  183n.30
XXVII 11    82n.16

**4Q418 = (Sap. Work A$^a$):**
9        143
55       142
81       143, 150
103      143
126      143, 150
127      143

**11Q19 = (11QT; Temple Scroll):**
II 1-XLVII 18    46
XIII 9-XXIX 1    46
XXIX             198
XXIX 2-10        43, 50
XXIX 9           202
XLVIII 1-LI 10   46
XLVIII 3-21      47
LI 11-LVI 21     46
LII-LIII         115n.10
LIII-LVI         115
LVI-LIX          45, 49

**4Q419 = (Sap. Work B):**
8        145

**4Q427 = (4QH$^a$):**
3 i 5    161, 167
7        161, 167

**4Q491 = (M$^a$):**

| | | | |
|---|---|---|---|
| LVI 12-LIX 21 | 46, 49 | LIX 14-15 | 201 |
| LVI 16 | 201n.28 | LX 1-LXVI 17 | 46 |
| LVII 1-LIX 11 | 200 | LX 10-LXIV 6 | 115 |
| LVIII 19 | 200 | LXI 12-LXII 16 | 47 |

## Josephus

*Ant.:*

| | | | |
|---|---|---|---|
| 5.20 | 88n.38 | | |
| 13.293-298 | 30 | | |
| 13.297 | 33 | | |
| 18.16 | 34 | | |

*J.W.:*

| | |
|---|---|
| 2.151-158 | 247 |
| 2.164-165 | 31 |

*Life:*

| | |
|---|---|
| 1.12 | 27n.1 |

## Rabbinic Literature

| | | | |
|---|---|---|---|
| m.ʿErub.3:4; 4:10 | 41n.20 | b.Sanh.11a | 17n.42 |
| m.Para.3:7 | 29 | b.Sanh.90b | 32n.16 |
| m.Yad.4:6 | 16 | b.Shab.30b-31a | 15 |
| m.Yad.4:7 | 29 | b.Soṭa.48b | 17n.42 |
| t.Soṭa.6:2 | 17n.42 | b.Yoma.9b | 17n.42 |
| b.B.Bat. 14b | 81n.10 | ʾAbot R. Nat. | 32n.16 |
| b.Kidd. 66a | 32 | S. ʿOlam Rab.6 | 20n.51 |
| b.Menaḥ.66a | 34n.23 | Zohar3.134a | 38 |

# Subjects

*Aaronic Text* (4Q541) 185, 186
Aramaic compositions: as pre-Essene works 236
Abul-Fath 28
aggadic narrative: defined 179
ʾaḥarît hay-yamîm 195–96, 198–203
Alexander Jannaeus 30, 49 Qumran prayer text mentioning 158
angelology 154
*Angelic Liturgy* 156; see also *Songs of Sabbath Sacrifice*
apocalypse: defined 179
apocalyptic texts at Qumran: Aramaic texts 180–88; apocalypses 180–82; *New Jerusalem* 182–84; visions and forecasts in court setting 184–87; visions as subordinate units 187; Hebrew texts 188–90
*Apostrophe to Zion*: text in 11QPsª 157
*Aramaic Apocalypse* (4Q246) 185
*Aramaic Vision* (4Q556–558) 185, 186
Ashtoreth 110

*Astronomical Book* (1 Enoch 72–82) 176, 177, 181
Azariah de Rossi 36
*Barki Nafshi* (4Q434–439): collection of hymns 158
Ben Sira 146–50, 242
Boethusians: 7; and halakhic controversies in tannaitic sources 34; proposed identification with Essenes 36
*Book of Giants* 176, 180, 187
Branch of David: 194, 195, 196, 199, 200, 208, 215, 216–18, 227
*Book of Dreams* (1 Enoch 83–90) 181, 249
*Book of Parables* (1 Enoch 37–71) 249, 255
*Book of the Watchers* (1 Enoch 17–36) 176, 177, 181, 182, 249

Christianity: as early Jewish faction 7; pluriform character of before 70 CE 92
Christians: collections of books of Scriptures among 93; wisdom christologies of 139
community of the Renewed Covenant: and other varieties of Judaism 3, 5–7,

18; method in study of 5–7; as unique socio-religious phenomenon 5–7; socio-religious characterizations of 8; Qumran covenanters as subgroup of 8, 23; abstinence from sexual relations in 9–10; immersion in not identical to baptism 10; foundation documents of 11–12; self-identification with ancient Israel 12–17; community understanding of covenant in 13–15; categories and genres of sacred literature in 15–20; prophetic inspiration in 20–21; aspects of theology of 24

*Community Rule/Manual of Discipline* (1QS): as foundation document of Qumran covenanters 11, 28, 144; wisdom elements in 138; monastic life reflected in 151; poetic portion at end of 155; messiah(s) in 212–13, 236–37; eschatological priest in 220–21; eschatology in 250, 252

*Damascus Document* (CD): as foundation document of Qumran covenanters 11, 144; juxtaposition of *Jubilees* to Torah in 18; view of oral law in 33; legal section of 65, 66; in relation to 4QMMT 68; wisdom themes in 138; reference to "one who will teach righteousness at end of days" in 193; Messiah in 214–15, 228. 229; Prince of the Congregation in 218–19, 229; eschatological priest in 228–31; Interpreter of the Law in 229; eschatology in 252

Daniel al-Qumisi 236, 239, 240
David ben Abraham al-Fasi 240–41
Dositheans: Schechter's identification of Zadokite sect with 28
Durkheim (Emile) school of sociology 95

*Elect of God* text (4Q534) 185, 186
Elijah: as eschatological figure 206, 209–10, 240–43
end of days: see *'aḥarît hay-yamîm*
*Epistle of Enoch* 249
eschatological priest: in 1QS IX 220–21; in 1 QSa 221–24; in 1QSb (=1Q28b) 224–25; in 4Q175 (= *Testimonia*) 226; in 4Q174 (= *Florilegium*) 227–28; in *Damascus Document* 228–31; in *War Scroll* 231; other references to 231; unclear texts relating to 232–33; summary of texts relating to 233
eschatological High Priest 207, 208
eschatological teacher/interpreter: 203, 207–210
eschatology at Qumran: 196, 235, 252–56; see also apocalytic texts at Qumran;

end of days; eschatological priest; eschatological teacher/interpreter; messianism; resurrection
Essenes: alleged identification with Qumranians 7– 8, 30, 65, 151; alleged identification with Boethusians 36; text traditions acceptable to 107; Aramaic compositions read by 236; messianic expectations of 241; eschatological beliefs of 246 – 56; early compositions of 250

*Four Kingdoms* Apocalypse (4Q552–553) 185
*Florilegium* 194 –96, 198 –99, 200, 202, 203, 207, 209; eschatological priest in 227–28

*Genesis Apocryphon* 180

Ḥasidim 7, 254
Hasmoneans 30, 49, 55, 241
Hesychian recension 109
Hexaplaric recension/version 109
Hippolytus of Rome: on the Essenes 247, 254
historical apocalypses 184
*Hôdāyôt* (1QH): as foundation of Qumran covenanters 11, 144; wisdom themes in 138; among corpus of hymns, prayers, and liturgical texts from Qumran 153 –56, 158, 160, 161, 166 – 68; eschatology in 250 –51
Hymn to the Creator: text in 11QPs$^a$ 157
Hymns (1Q36–40): 155
Interpreter of the Law: 193, 194, 195, 199, 204, 206, 207, 208, 217, 227, 228, 229

Jerusalem Temple 108, 138, 202
Jesus 21, 80, 139; messianic expectations centered on 242– 46
Jews: collections of books of Scriptures among 93
Jezebel 109, 110
Judaism: pluriform character of before 70 CE 92
Judeo-Christians 101, 108
John the Baptist: and popular messianic expectations 242–26
John Hyrcanus 30, 48, 49, 50
Jonathan the Hasmonean 49;
Josephus: on the Essenes 7, 10, 35, 246; on the Sadducees 31, 33 –35; description of Second Temple in 45; rewriting of biblical text in 116

*kaige*: recension of Greek Bible 102; sections of 1 and 2 Kings 103 – 05
Karaites 236, 239

Leviathan 110

Man of the Lie/Scoffer 194, 208

Masada: Mas1$^f$ (Ps$^b$): 91
Massoretic Text (MT): 19, 106; as collection of disparate texts 93
*Messianic Rule/Rule of the Congregation* (1QSa): as foundation document of Qumran covenanters 11; Messiah in 213 –14; eschatological priest in 221–24
messianism: Davidic messiah 212–19; Messiah 212–16; Branch of David 216 –18; Prince of the Congregation 218 –19; eschatological priest 220 –33; in reference to Teacher of Righteousness and eschatological teacher/interpreter 193 –210; at Qumran and in New Testament 236 – 46; in 1QS 236 –37; in CD 237–38; in 4Q252 238; in 4Q161 238; in 4Q174 + 177 238; biblical basis for 239; in Karaite commentators 239; dyarchic character of at Qumran 234, 236 – 40
*miqdaš ʾadam* 197–98

*New Jerusalem* 180, 182– 84, 187
New Jewish Publication Society Translation 101
NT writings: eschatology of 254 –56

Old Greek text 90, 91, 106
Old Hebrew text 106
Old Latin text 106
otherworldly journeys 184

*Pesher on Habakkuk* (1QpHab): as foundation document of Qumran covenanters 11
Pharisees: controversies with Sadducees 28, 29–32; authority of traditional ordinances among 33, 35; extra-biblical traditions of 52; as opponents of Qumranite authors 65; texts of 106
Philo: on the Essenes 7; 35; 53
Phineas 210
plagues: of the Exodus 120 –21
Plea for Deliverance: text in 11QPs$^a$ 157
Pliny the Elder: on the Essenes 7
prayer, hymnic, and liturgical texts at Qumran: survey of texts and history of research on 153 –59; genre labels applied to 160 – 62; liturgical vs. non-liturgical character of 162– 69; sectarian vs. non-sectarian provenance of 169–70
*Prayer of Nabonidus* (4Q242) 185, 186
predeterminism 154
Prince of the Congregation 195, 201, 208, 218 –19, 225, 227, 228, 229
Prophet like Moses 209, 210, 226, 239, 241

INDEX OF SUBJECTS 279

*Proto-Esther* text (4Q550) 185, 186
*Pseudo-Daniel* text (4Q243–244) 186, 187
*Pseudo-Ezekiel* text 188, 189
*Pseudo-Moses* text 189

Qumran Literature:
CD: 9, 11, 28, 194, 195, 209, 216, 228, 229, 233, 234, 237, 238, 242, 247, 252
1QIsa$^a$: 39
1QpHab: 203 nn. 33-34
1Q16 (pPs$^a$): 82 n. 15
1Q19 (Noah): 188
1Q19$^{bis}$ (Noah): 188
1Q20 (apGen): 113, 116
1Q26 (SapWorkA): 139, 140, 151
1Q27 (Myst): 139
1Q28 (S): 9, 11, 138, 156, 213, 216, 226, 229, 233, 240, 242, 247, 250, 251, 252, 253n. 42
1Q28$^a$ (S$^a$): 199, 213, 216, 221, 224, 225, 233, 237, 241n. 21, 242, 250
1Q28$^b$ (1QS$^b$): 155, 163, 201, 219; Prince of the Congregation in 218, 224, 225; eschatological priest in 224–25, 237, 242, 250
1Q30–31 (Liturgical Texts?): 155, 232
1Q33 (M): 11, 163, 247, 250, 253n. 42
1Q34 (LitPr$^a$): 155
1QH: 11, 138, 153, 158, 161n. 32, 167, 168, 247, 250, 251, 253n. 42
1Q35 (H$^b$):154, 155
1Q36 (Hymns): 155

1Q37–40 (Hymnic Compositions?): 155
1Q71–72 (Dan $^{a,b}$): 91n. 49
2Q3 (Exod$^b$): 119
2Q18 (Sir): 137
4QDeutero-Ezekiel: eschatology in 247, 248, 252, 107n. 25, 118n. 17, 119n. 18, 188n. 50, 247, 248, 253
4Q1 (Gen-Exod$^a$): 81n. 7, 85n. 20
4Q2–8 (Gen$^{b-h}$): 85n. 20
4Q9–10 (Gen$^{j-k}$): 85n. 20
4Q11 (paleoGen-Exod): 81n. 7
4Q17 (Exod-Lev$^f$): 81n. 7
4Q22 (paleoExod$^m$): 85, 106, 113
4Q23 (Lev-Num$^a$): 81n. 7
4Q25–26 (Lev$^{c,d}$): 86n. 23
4Q27 (Num$^b$): 86, 106, 107n. 23, 113, 128n. 39
4Q28–39 (Deut$^{a-l}$): 86n. 25
4Q37 (Deut$^j$): 106, 159n. 26
4Q37, 41 (Deut$^{j,n}$): 87n. 26
4Q41 (Deut$^n$): 106, 113, 159n. 26
4Q47–48 (Josh$^{a,b}$): 88
4Q49 (Judg$^a$): 87n. 27
4Q51 (Sam$^a$): 88n. 39
4Q52–53 (Sam$^{b,c}$): 89n. 39
4Q54 (Kings): 87n. 28
4Q57 (Isa$^c$): 119
4Q71 (Jer$^b$): 90
4Q73 (Ezek$^a$): 189n. 54
4Q74 (Ezek$^b$): 189n. 54
4Q84 (Ps$^b$): 90n. 47, 165n. 49
4Q87 (Ps$^e$): 91
4Q99–101 (Job$^{a-b}$, paleoJob$^c$): 137
4Q102–103 (Prov$^{a-b}$): 137
4Q109–10 (Qoh$^{a-b}$): 87n. 29,

# INDEX OF SUBJECTS

137
4Q112–14 (Dan$^{a-c}$): 91n. 49
4Q123 (paleoparaJosh): 88
4Q158 (RP$^a$): 107, 123, 124, 125, 126, 127, 131, 132, 133, 134
4Q159 (Ord$^a$): 52
4Q161 (pIsa$^a$): 199, 203n. 34, 216, 219, 231, 233, 238
4Q162 (pIsa$^b$): 199, 203n. 34
4Q163 (pIsa$^c$): 203n. 34
4Q164 (pIsa$^d$): 183n. 31
4Q167 (pHos$^b$): 232, 233
4Q168 (pMic?): 203n. 34
4Q169 (pNah): 199, 203n. 34
4Q171 (pPs$^a$): 82n. 15, 203n. 33, 252
4Q172 (pUnid): 82n. 15
4Q173 (pPs$^b$): 82n. 15, 232
4Q174 (Flor): 107, 112n. 3, 194n. 4, 195, 196n. 10, 197nn. 14-15, 198n. 18, 199n. 20, 203, 207, 209, 216, 227, 228, 238, 240, 242, 252
4Q175 (Test): 107, 207n. 43, 226, 228, 237, 238, 240, 242
4Q177 (Catena$^a$): 107, 194n. 4, 199n. 20, 228n. 31, 238, 242, 252
4Q180 (AgesCreat): 247, 252
4Q181 (AgesCreat): 247, 252
4Q182 (Catena$^b$): 199
4Q184 (Wiles of the Wicked Woman): 137
4Q185 (sapiential work): 137
4Q203 (EnGiants$^a$): 176n. 12
4Q208 (Enastr$^a$): 177n. 15
4Q215 (TNaph): 188
4Q225 (PsJub$^a$): 117, 118
4Q226 (PsJub$^b$): 117
4Q227 (PsJub$^c$): 117n. 15

4Q242 (PrNab): 185
PseudoDan: 247
4Q243 (PsDan$^a$): 186
4Q244 (PsDan$^b$): 186
4Q245 (psDan$^c$): 186n. 44, 252
4Q246 (Apocalypse): 185, 219n. 16, 237n. 10, 252
4Q252 (pGen$^a$): 35, 112, 116, 117, 133, 215, 216, 217, 218, 232, 238, 242
4Q259 (S$^e$): 213, 236, 237
4Q266 (D$^a$): 163n. 40
4Q267 (D$^b$): 215n. 9, 229, 230
4Q269 (D$^d$): 237n. 10
4Q270 (D$^e$): 9, 215n. 9
4Q280 (Ber$^f$): 247
4Q285 (Serekh ha-milḥamah): 159n. 24, 217, 218, 219, 232, 233
4Q286 (Ber$^a$): 158, 164n. 40, 247
4Q287 (Ber$^b$): 158, 215n. 9, 216, 247
4Q288 (Ber$^c$): 158
4Q289 (Ber$^d$): 158
4Q290 (Ber$^e$): 158
4Q298 (CrA Words of Sage): 139
4Q299 (Myst$^a$): 139, 146
4Q300 (Myst$^b$): 139, 146
4Q301 (Myst$^c$): 139, 146
4Q306 (Men of People who Err): 139
4Q307 (sapiential frags.?): 139
4Q308 (sapiential frags.?): 139
4QReworked Pentateuch (4QRP; 4Q158, 364–367): 41– 42, 92n. 51, 107, 119, reworking of biblical texts

in 114–16, 123–33; contents
of 124–25; internal overlaps
between fragments of 125;
relation between fragments
of 125; reconstruction of complete
composition of 126–27;
exegetical character of
127–28; topical arrangement
of elements in 128–30;
exegetical omissions in 130;
exegetical additions in 131–
33; different sequence in
4Q365 133; *see also*
reworked biblical texts at
Qumran
RP: 41n. 16, 114, 115, 116, 119,
123, 124, 125, 126, 127, 128,
131, 133, 134,
4Q364 (RP$^b$): 41n. 19, 92n. 51,
107n. 24, 123, 124, 125, 126,
127, 130, 132, 133, 134
4Q365 (RP$^c$): 41, 92n. 51,
107n. 24, 123, 124, 125, 126,
127, 128, 129, 130, 131, 133,
134
4Q365a (T?): 42, 48, 115n. 6,
125
4Q366 (RP$^d$): 92n. 51, 107n. 24,
123, 124, 125, 126, 127, 128,
129, 134
4Q367 (RP$^e$): 41n. 19, 92n. 51,
107n. 24, 123, 124, 125, 126,
127, 129, 130, 134
4Q371 (apocrJoseph$^a$): 161n. 34
4Q372 (apocrJoseph$^b$): 157
4Q373 (apocrJoseph$^c$): 158
4Q375 (apocrMosesB): 107,
232, 240
4Q376 (3 Tongues of Fire): 107,
232, 240n. 17
4Q378–9 (Psalms of

Joshua$^{a,b}$): 107
4Q380 (Non-Canonical Psalms
A): 157, 165, 166
4Q381 (Non-Canonical Psalms
B): 157, 165, 166
4Q382 (pap paraKings et al.):
119
4Q383 (apocrJer A?): 188n. 51
4Q385 (psEzek$^a$): 107, 118, 119,
188nn. 50-51
4Q386 (psEzek$^b$): 107, 188n. 50
4Q387 (psEzek$^c$): 107,
188nn. 50-51
4Q388 (psEzek$^d$): 107, 188n. 50
4Q389 (psMos$^d$): 107, 188n. 51
4Q390 (psMos$^e$): 33n. 21, 107,
118n. 17, 188n. 50
4Q391 (pap psEzek?$^g$):
188n. 50
4QMMT: 11, 22, 54, 57, 61, 62,
63, 65, 68, 70, 71, 72, 82, 196,
214; history of the *editio
major* 57–60; calendaric
section of 61–62; legal
section of 62–67; hortatory
epilogue of 67–70; historical
significance of 70–73; date
of 70–71; group language in
70–71; literary genre of
70–72; not as letter but legal
proclamation 72
4Q394 (MMT$^a$): 61, 62
4Q395 (MMT$^b$): 61
4Q400 (ShirShabb$^a$): 168
4Q408 (sapiential work): 139
4Q409 (liturgy): 158
4Q410–13 (sapiential works):
139
4Q415–19 (Sap. Work A,B):
139, 140, 141, 142, 143, 144,
145, 146, 147, 148, 150, 151
4Q420–21 (Ways of

Righteousness$^{a,b}$): 139
4Q423 –26 (Sapiential Works): 139, 140, 146, 151
4Q422 (Treatise on Gen and Exod): 120, 121, 122, 123, 133
4Q427 (Hod$^a$): 158, 161, 167, 168
4Q428 (Hod$^b$): 167
4Q429 (Hod$^c$): 168
4Q430 (Hod$^d$): 167
4Q431 (Hod$^e$): 167
4Q432 (papHod$^f$): 167
4Q434 (Barki Nafshi$^a$): 158
4Q435 (Barki Nafshi$^b$): 158
4Q436 (Barki Nafshi$^c$): 158
4Q437 (Barki Nafshi$^d$): 158
4Q438 (Barki Nafshi$^e$): 158
4Q439 (work similar to Barki Nafshi): 158
4Q443 (prayer): 159n. 24
4Q448 (Apocr. Psalm and Prayer): 160
4Q457 (Prayer): 159n. 24
4Q464 (Exposition on the Patriarchs): 118
4Q464$^a$ (unclassified frag.): 118n. 16
4Q464$^b$ (unclassified frag.): 118n. 16
4Q471 (Prayer of Michael): 161
4Q491 (M$^a$): 161, 231
4Q503 (papPrQuot): 157, 163n. 40, 164n. 44
4QDibrê ha-měorôt : 163, 164, 169, 248n. 34
4Q504 (4QDibHam$^a$): 157, 248
4Q505 (4QDibHam$^b$): 157
4Q506 (4QDibHam$^c$): 157
4Q507 (PrFetes$^a$): 157
4Q508 (PrFetes$^b$): 157
4Q509 (PrFetes$^a$): 157
4Q510 (Shir$^a$): 138, 157, 160
4Q511 (Shir$^b$): 138, 157, 160
4Q512 (papRitPur): 157
4Q513 (Ord$^b$): 52
4Q514 (Ord$^c$): 52
4Q521 (Messianic Apocalypse): 31, 215, 216, 233, 241, 242, 245, 247, 248, 252, 253, 254
4Q530 (Book of Giants$^b$): 176n. 12
4Q531 (Book of Giants$^c$): 176n. 12
4Q534 (Elect of God): 185
4Q537 (AJ$^a$): 185n. 42, 208n. 52
4Q540 (AhA$^{bis}$) = TLevi$^c$ ?: 185n. 42, 208n. 52, 238n. 12
4Q541 (AhA) = TLevi$^d$ ?: 185, 208, 209, 238, 243
4Q542 (TQahat): 247, 252
Visions of Amram: 247, 248
4Q543 (Visions of Amram$^a$): 187
4Q548 (Visions of Amram$^f$ ?): 187, 252
4Q550 (PrEsther$^{a-e+f}$): 185
4Q552 (Four Kingdoms$^a$): 185
4Q553 (Four Kingdoms$^b$): 185
4Q556 (Vision$^a$): 185
4Q557 (Vision$^c$): 185
4Q558 (papVision$^b$): 185
6Q7 (papDan): 91n. 49
7Q4 (pap biblical text ?): 249
7Q8 (pap unclassified): 249
11Q5 (Ps$^a$): 82, 90, 91, 137, 157, 161, 164, 165, 179n. 20
11Q6 (Ps$^b$): 91, 165n. 49
11Q11 (ApPs$^a$): 161
11Q13 (Melch): 234n. 43, 238, 247, 252, 255

11Q14 (Ber): 159n. 24
11Q18 (JN): 182n. 28
11QT (Temple Scroll): 40, 41n. 16, 50, 106, 195, 198, 200, 201, 202
11Q19 (T$^a$): 38, 39, 40, 41, 42, 48, 114n. 6, 115
11Q20 (T$^b$): 40, 41nn. 16 –17, 42, 115n. 6
11QT$^c$: 41n. 16, 115n. 6

*Raz Niheyeh* 144
reworked biblical texts at Qumran: 111–34; 4QRP 114, 123 –33; *Temple Scroll* 114 –16; 4Q252 (4QpGen$^a$) 116 –17; 4Q225 –226 (4QPsJub$^{a,b}$) 117–18; 4Q385, frg. 24 (4QSecondEzekiel) 118 –19; 2QExod$^b$ 119; 4Q382 (4QpapparaKings) 119; 4Q422 (4QParaGen-Exod): 120 –22; 4Q123 (4QpaleoParaJosh) 122; *see also* 4Q Reworked Pentateuch (4QRP); scriptures at Qumran
resurrection: denial of by Sadducees 27, 32; at Qumran and in the New Testament 246 –56;

Sadducees: paucity of sources relating to 27; association with Karaites 27; association with Zadokites 28; in controversy with Pharisees over purity 29; and 4QMMT 30, 35, 65; as earliest members of Qumran sect 30; as described by Josephus 31; theological beliefs of distinct from those of Qumran sect 31; denial of resurrection by 32; rejection of traditional Pharisaic ordinances by 33; lack of esteem for tradition among 34; areas of congruity and incongruity with Qumran halakhah 34 –36; and founding of Qumran sect 47– 48, 65; association with community at Qumran 151
Samaritan Pentateuch 19, 85 – 86, 92, 107, 226
Samaritans 7; and collection of books of Scripture 86, 93; as dissident group 101; text traditions acceptable to 107
sapiental text from Qumran (4Q408, 410 – 413, 415, 423 426, 416 – 419): 137–152; versions of 139– 40; content of 140 – 44; genre of 144 – 45; distinctive words and ideas in 145; relation to other works 145 – 46; compared to Sirach 146 –51; on loans and surety 146 – 47; on parents and wives 147– 49; theology of creation 149 –51; place in history of Qumran community 151–52
scriptures at Qumran: external shape of collection(s) of 78 – 82; number and distribution of manuscripts of 78 –79; multiple literary editions of books and passages of 83 – 85; review of individual books of 85 –91;

and history of biblical text 92, 97; pluriform character of 92; determining original text of 92; and Bible translation 93; authoritative functions of 95–110; sociological analysis of 95–96, 98; conscious and unconscious changes in text of 97–102; "Israelitization" of text of 98–101; systematic revisions and recensions of 102–06; harmonistic or paraphrastic text of 106–09; and parallel history of Jerusalem Temple 108; marginal or aberrant biblical text of 109–10; *see also* reworked biblical texts at Qumran

*Scroll of Blessings* (1QSb) 201

Septuagint 19, 107; as collection of disparate texts 93; critical value of 109

Shimʿon ben Shetach 33

Sukkot: laws pertaining to in 4QRP (4Q366) 127–28

song of Miriam: expanded form of in 4QRP (4Q365 and 4Q158) 127

*Songs of the Sabbath Sacrifice* 157, 161, 168; *see also* Angelic Liturgy

*Story of Ahikar* 186

Syro-Hexaplaric version 109

Targumim 116

Teacher of Righteousness: and 4QMMT 70–72; as forerunner of eschatological counterpart 193, 194, 210; as messianic figure 194; as author of *Temple Scroll* 195; and end of days 203–04; as priest 204–05; as prophet 205–07

*Temple Scroll* (11QT): 9, 11; acquisition of 38–39; text and manuscripts of 38–42; contents of 42–46; sources of 46–48; dating of 48–51; law of the king in 49–50, 200; theology of law in 51–53; relation to Qumran corpus 53–55; significance of 55; in relation to 4QMMT 66; lack of sectarian features in 68, 106; reworking of biblical text in 114–16; as eschatological law 195; and Teacher of Righteousness 195; on end of days 200–03

testament: defined 179

*Testament of Levi* 180, 181, 187

*Testament of Naphtali* (4Q215) 188

*Testimonia* (4Q175) 107, 205, 206, 207; eschatological priest in 226

Theodotion 19

Vision of Haguy 144

*Visions of Amram* (4Q543–548) 187

Vulgate 106

*War Scroll* (1QM): victory hymns in 155; Prince of the Congregation in 219; eschatological priest in 231; eschatology in 251–52

Weber (Max) school of socioloy 96

Wicked Priest: and 4QMMT
    70–72
*Words of Blessing* (1QSb) 155
*Words of the Luminaries* 156

Yam 110
Yefeth ben ʿAli 236, 239
Yehoshua ben Parachyah 33
Yose ben Yoʿezer 33

Zadokites: alledged identification with Sadducees 28, 65
Zealots 7
Zelophehad: narratives and laws about daughters of in 4QRP (4Q365) 128

# Modern Authors

Abegg, M. 41n.16, 140, 140n.8, 144, 144n.10, 214n.6, 215n.8, 217n.14, 218
Albrektson, B. 96, 96n.5, 106
Allegro, J. 123, 123n.26, 124n.31, 137, 216nn.10,11, 217n.13, 226n.27, 232, 232nn.36,38,40
Allison, D. C. 242n.23
Avigad, N. 154
Bahat, D. 108n.27
Baillet, M. 78n.1, 91n.49, 119, 119n.20, 156, 156n.9, 157, 160, 178n.20
Bardtke, H. 166n.54
Barthélemy, D. 78n.1, 89n.41,42, 91n.49, 221, 222
Bauchet, J.-M. P 154n.2
Baumgarten, A. 30n11, 33n.20
Baumgarten, J. M. xiv, 9nn.17,21, 29nn.7,8, 30n.10, 32n.15, 33n.19, 35n.28, 55n.60, 162n.36, 163n.40, 164n.44
Billerbeck, P. 60
Beckwith, R. T. 108n.28
Beer, G. 177n.14
Behm, J. 13n.34
Ben Shammai, H. 29n.6
Benoit, P. 6, 6n.8, 78n.1
Beyer, K. 181n.24, 182n.28, 185nn.37,40,41, 186n.43
Black, M. 176n.11

Blenkinsopp, J. 105n.22
Bonnani, G. 42n.21
Bradshaw, P. 165n.48, 171, 171n.66
Brin, G. 115n.7
Brooke, G. J. 9n.22, 112n.3, 116n.11, 194n.4, 196, 196n.9, 197n.13, 198, 206n.41, 207, 207n.47, 208n.51, 227n.29, 228n.30
Broshi, M. 42n.21, 45n.31, 202n.29, 214n.6
Bruce, F. F. 112n.3
Büchler, A. 29
Burrows, M. 78n.1, 89n.42
Carmignac, J. 193n.1, 246n.32
Carmy, I. 42n.21
Cavallin, H. C. C. 235n.3, 252n.40
Charlesworth, J. H. 21n.55, 23n.58, 50n.48, 155n.6
Chazon, E. G. 159n.24, 164, 164nn.42,43, 169n.61, 248n.34
Childs, B. S. 105n.22
Collins, J. J. xvii, 23n.58, 176nn.4,5,7,8, 177n.16, 179nn.21,22, 184n.34, 201n.26, 204n.37, 220.16
Collins, R. F. 12n.32
Cross, F. M. 18n.46, 38, 78n.1, 87n.30, 88 – 89n.39, 89n.42, 96, 97, 97n.7, 177n.16, 222nn.20,21, 223n.22

# INDEX OF MODERN AUTHORS 287

Davies, P. R. 194, 194n.2, 195, 195n.8, 204n.35
Davies, W. D. 204n.35, 209n.55
Davila, J. R. 85n.20
Denis, A.-M. 138n.3
Di Lella, A. A. 147n.11
Dimant, D. xvii, 33n.21, 107n.25, 112n.3, 118, 118n.17, 119, 119nn.18,19, 177n.14, 178n.18, 183n.32, 187n.47, 188nn.50,51, 189n.52, 197n.16
Dombrowski Hopkins, D. 166n.53
Driver, G. R. 184n.35
Duncan, J. A. 86n.25, 106n.23, 159n.26
Dupont-Sommer, A. 251n.39
Durkheim, E. 95, 95n.1
Eisenman, R. H. 185n.37, 208n.52, 215n.9, 233n.42
Elgvin, T. 120, 120n.22
Epstein, J. N. 32n.18
Erder, Y. 29n.6
Eshel, E. 86n.25, 118, 118n.16, 158n.20, 161n.34
Eshel, H. 158n.20
Fáierstein, M. 242n.23
Fishbane, M. 96, 96n.4, 195n.7
Fitzmyer, J. A. 3n.1, 23n.58, 35n.27, 78n.1, 186n.43, 207n.48, 235n.1, 242nn.23,24
Fleischer, E. 163n.39
Flint, P. W. 90nn.43,47, 91n.48
Flusser, D. 155n.6
Fraade, S. 52n.52
Frick, S. 95n.2
Fuller, R. E. 90n.45
Gabrion, H. 112n.3
García Martínez, F. 37n.1, 41, 41n.17, 46n.36, 78n.1, 182n.28, 186n.43, 194n.4, 195n.6, 199n.20, 236n.4
Geiger, A. 27, 35, 35n.26
Giddens, A. 98n.10
Ginzberg, L. 28, 28n.4, 29, 206n.42, 210n.56, 230, 230n.33
Glasson, T. F. 176n.6
Gnilka, J. 10n.24
Golb, N. 8n.14
Goldberg, A. 162n.35
Gooding, D. W. 89n.41
Greenberg, M. 132, 132n.43
Greenfield, J. C. 14n.38, 180n.23, 181n.24
Greenspahn, F. E. 20n.50
Grelot, P. 176n.10, 243n.26, 249n.36
Gross, M. D. 14n.37
Halivni, D. W. 53n.54
Hanson, P. 176n.3
Harrington, D. J. xvi, 139n.6
Hengel, M. 50n.48, 138n.5
Himmelfarb, M. 181n.25, 183n.33
Hoffman, L. 170n.64
Hollander, H. W. 181n.24
Holm-Nielsen, S. 154n.4, 160n.29, 166, 167n.55
Horgan M. P. 112n.3, 183n.31
Hultgård, A. 209n.54
Hunzinger, C.-H. 155
Hyatt, J. P. 167n.56
Ilg, N. 12n.32
Ivry, S. 21n.54
Ivy, S. 42n.21
Janzen, J. G. 90n.44
Jastram, N. 86n.24, 107n.23, 128n.39
Jaubert, A. 12n.32
Jeremias, G. 154n.4, 193n.1, 205n.40, 206n.42

Jeremias, J. 206n.42, 210n.56
Jonge, M. de 181n.24, 209n.53
Jungmann, J. A. 156n.10
Kapelrud, A. S. 12n.32
Kasowski, Ch. J. 14n.37
Kee, H. C. 10n.25, 11n.26
Kister, M. 34, 34n.22
Kittel, B. 160n.28
Knibb, M. 175n.2, 181n.23, 194, 194n.3, 197n.16, 206n.44
Kobelski, P. J. 234n.43
Koch, K. 178n.17
Kooij, A. van der 89n.39
Kraft, R. A. 78n.1
Kuhn, H.-W. 154nn.1,4, 167, 167n.57, 235n.2, 250n.37
Kvanvig, H. G. 176nn.4,9, 177n.14
Landsberger, B. 12n.30
Laurin, R. B. 246n.31
Lehmann, M. R. 55n.60
Le Moyne, J. 246n.31
Levine, B. A. 53n.55
Licht, J. 222, 222n.20, 225
Lichtheim, M. 144n.9
Lieberman, S. 29, 32n.18, 48n.44
Lim, T. H. 35n.25, 116n.11, 117n.14
Lindenberger, J. M. 184n.35
Liver, J. 209n.54
Lohfink, N. 14n.35, 101n.11, 104n.19
Lowy, S. 112n.3
Lust, J. 88n.33, 89n.41, 189n.54
Maier, J. 159n.25, 202, 202n.31
Mansoor, M. 160n.28
Mason, S. 33n.19
McKinnon, J. 165n.48
Mearns, C. L. 180n.23
Melamed, E. Z. 122n.23

Mendels, D. 50n.48
Milgrom, J. 43n.23, 46n.35, 53n.55
Milik, J. T. 14n.38, 18n.45, 29, 57, 78n.1, 89n.42, 90n.47, 117n.15, 119n.20, 164n.40, 176n.12, 177n.15, 180n.23, 181n.24, 182n.28, 185nn.38,39, 186n.44, 187, 187nn. 46,47, 188nn.48,49, 189n.55, 212, 213n.3, 215n.9, 221, 222, 224, 225, 230, 230n.34, 235n.1, 236n.4, 237n.7, 239n.14
Molin, G. 206n.42, 210n.56
Moore, G. F., 4n.4
Morawe, G. 154n.4
Moreno Hernández, A. 109n.29
Morrow, F. J., Jr. 89n.42
Muilenburg, J. 89n.42
Murphy-O'Connor, J. 154n.4, 204n.37, 237n.7
Nebe, G. W. 249n.35
Neugebauer, O. 176n.11
Neusner, J. 15n.39
Newsom, C. 107n.25, 138n.2, 157n.15, 161, 161n.33, 168, 168nn.59,60, 169, 169n.62
Nickelsburg, G.W.E. 235n.3, 246n.32, 249n.36
Nitzan, B. 158, 160, 160n.30
Olyan, S. 119
Patte, D. 112n.3
Paul, A. 236n.6, 239n.15, 241n.18
Ploeg, J. van der 112n.3, 161n.31, 165n.49
Pouilly, J. 237n.7
Prato, G. L. 149n.12
Puech, É. xviii, 31n.13, 154n.1, 158, 158n.22, 161n.31,

185nn.36,42, 208, 208n.52,
  220n.16, 222nn.20,21,
  237n.10, 238nn.11,12,
  241nn.19,20, 242n.22,
  243n.25, 251n.38, 252n.41,
  253n.42, 254n.46
Qimron, E. 10n.23, 22n.56, 30,
  30n.9, 40, 40n.14, 50, 54,
  54n.58, 57– 60, 62– 63, 66 –
  69, 72–73, 158n.19, 214n.6
Rabin, C. 28, 29n.5, 206n.45
Reeves, J. C. 177n.12, 187n.47
Reif, S. 162n.35
Rosen, D. 201n.28
Rost, L. 101n.11
Russell, D. S. 176n.5
Salvesen, A. 201n.28
Sanders, J. A. 78n.1, 84n.18,
  157nn.13,14, 165n.45, 179n.20
Sanderson, J. E. 78n.1,
  85 – 86n.21, 87n.25, 122n.24
Sandmel, S. 6n.10
Schechter, S. 27, 28, 28n.3, 29
Schiffman, L. H. xv, 30n.12,
  38n.6, 39n.11, 42n.22, 44n.28,
  45nn.31–33, 46nn.34,35,
  47nn.37,39,40, 52nn.51,53,
  53n.55, 54nn.57,59, 156n.12,
  159n.25, 165n.46, 166n.54,
  169, 169n.63, 199n.21, 213n.5,
  222, 222n.20
Schubert, K. 246n.30
Schürer, E. 112n.2
Schuller, E. M. xvii, 30,
  157nn.16,17, 158n.18,
  164n.41, 166n.50
Schwartz, D. R. 66, 66n.1,
  170n.65, 197, 197n.14
Schwartz, S. 33n.19
Segal, A. 14n.36
Shanks, H. 38n.7

Skehan, P. W. 78n.1, 85n.21,
  86 – 87n.25, 88n.35, 89n.42,
  90n.47, 122n.24, 147n.11
Starcky, J. 18n.45, 209n.55,
  238n.11, 241n.19
Stegemann, H. 22n.58, 47,
  47n.38, 53n.55, 54n.56, 61,
  107n.26, 126, 126n.37, 127,
  154n.1, 158, 158n.22, 168n.60,
  178n.17, 179nn.21,22,
  202n.31, 204n.37
Steudel, A. 163n.37, 199n.20
Stone, M. E. 14n.38, 118,
  118n.16, 175n.2, 179n.22,
  180n.23, 181n.24, 183n.32
Strack, H. L. 60
Strugnell, J. xv, xvi, 30n.9, 41,
  41n.18, 42, 42n.21, 54, 54n.58,
  107n.25, 109, 118n.17, 119,
  119nn.18,19, 123, 124, 139,
  154n.1, 156, 156n.12, 188n.50,
  232n.41, 240n.17
Sukenik, E. L. 78n.1, 89n.42,
  154, 155, 155n.5, 161n.32
Sussman, Y. 31, 32, 32nn.14,17,
  34, 34n.23, 35, 35n.24, 55n.60
Sutcliffe, E. F. 9n.18, 10n.24
Swete, H. B. 81n.9
Tabor, J. D. 233, 233n.42
Talmon, S. xiv, 4nn.3,5, 5n.6,
  6nn.7,9, 7n.12, 12n.29, 16n.41,
  18 –19n.46, 19nn.47,48,
  20 –21n.52, 21n.53, 96, 96n.6,
  101n.12, 123nn.28,29, 156,
  156n.11, 158n.18, 163,
  163n.38, 204n.36, 207n.50
Tanzer, S. J. 138n.4
Teeple, H. M. 205n.39
Then, R. 105n.21
Thompson, E. M. 80n.4
Thorion, Y. 20n.49

Tov, E. xvi, 39, 39n.10, 41, 41n.19, 44n.27, 78 –79n.1, 86n.23, 88n.36, 89nn.39,41, 90nn.44,46, 97, 97n.8, 102, 102n.13, 107, 107n.24, 111n.1, 115n.10, 119n.21, 120n.22, 123n.25, 125nn.32–34, 126nn.35,36, 127n.38, 134n.45, 137n.1, 139n.7, 159n.23
Trebolle Barrera, J. xii, 87nn.27,28,32, 89n.39, 103n.16
Trever, J. C. 78n.1, 89n.42
Ulrich, E. xv, 78n.1, 79n.2, 84n.19, 97, 106, 85n.21, 87nn.25,29,31, 88nn.36,37, 89n.39, 91n.49, 93n.52, 97n.9, 122n.24
Urbach, E. E. 20n.50, 32, 32n.18
VanderKam, J. C. xvii, 80n.6, 176n.9, 207n.49, 239n.14
Vaux, R. de 78n.1, 119n.20
Vermes, G. 10n.24, 81n.12, 112, 112n.2, 123n.30, 185n.36, 205n.39, 211n.1, 212n.2, 213n.4, 217n.14, 220, 223n.22, 232n.37
Wacholder, B. Z. 41, 41nn.16,18, 50, 50n.50, 140, 140n.8, 144, 144n.10, 187n.45, 195n.6, 214n.6, 215n.8, 217n.14, 218
Walters, S. D. 89n.40
Weber, M. 95, 95n.3, 101, 20n.52
Weinfeld, M. 49n.46, 159n.25, 165n.47, 167, 167n.56
Wenthe, D. O. 91n.50

White, S. A. 9n.22, 41, 41n.19, 42, 86n.25, 106n.23, 123 –24, 123n.25, 131n.42, 159n.26
Wieder, N. 29n.6, 205n.39, 210n.56, 241n.18
Wills, L. 46n.36, 184n.35
Wilson, A. M. 46n.36
Wilson, G. H. 90n.47
Wise, M. O. 43n.25, 46n.36, 115, 115nn.8,9, 185n.37, 195 –98, 195n.5, 196nn. 10,12, 197n.15, 198nn.18,19, 200 – 03, 200nn. 22–25, 201n.27, 202n.30, 203n.32, 204nn.35,37, 205nn.38,39, 208n.52, 215n.9, 233, 233n.42
Wölfi, W. 42n.21
Worrell, J. E. 138n.5
Woude, A. S. van der 205n. 39, 206, 206nn.43,45, 209n.54, 210n.56
Yadin, Y. 16n.40, 29, 37n.2, 38 – 40, 38nn.3,5, 39nn.8,9,12, 40nn.13,15, 42– 45, 42n.22, 43nn.24,26, 45nn.29,30,33, 46nn.34,35, 48 –51, 48nn.41– 43, 49n.45, 50n.49, 53 – 55, 53n.55, 195n.6, 198, 198n.17
Yardeni, A. 70, 158n.20
Zahavy, T. 165n.48
Zeitlin, S. 29
Zuckerman, B. 40

# Christianity and Judaism in Antiquity Series

1. ORIGEN OF ALEXANDRIA: HIS WORLD AND HIS LEGACY
   Edited by Charles Kannengiesser and William L. Petersen

2. THE BOOK OF RULES OF TYCONIUS: ITS PURPOSE AND INNER LOGIC
   Pamela Bright

3. GOSPEL TRADITIONS IN THE SECOND CENTURY: ORIGINS, RECENSIONS, TEXT, AND TRANSMISSION
   Edited by William L. Petersen

4. DE GRATIA: FAUSTUS OF RIEZ'S TREATISE ON GRACE AND ITS PLACE IN THE HISTORY OF THEOLOGY
   Thomas A. Smith

5. HEBREW BIBLE OR OLD TESTAMENT? STUDYING THE BIBLE IN JUDAISM AND CHRISTIANITY
   Edited by Roger Brooks and John J. Collins

6. THE EARLY EPISCOPAL CAREER OF ATHANASIUS OF ALEXANDRIA
   Duane W.-H. Arnold

7. EXEGESIS AND SPIRITUAL PEDAGOGY IN MAXIMUS THE CONFESSOR: AN INVESTIGATION OF THE QUAESTIONES AD THALASSIUM
   Paul M. Blowers

8. PLATONISM IN ANTIQUITY
   Edited by Stephen Gersh and Charles Kannengiesser

9. *De doctrina christiana*: A CLASSIC OF WESTERN CULTURE
   Edited by Dwayne W.H. Arnold and Pamela Bright

10. THE COMMUNITY OF THE RENEWED COVENANT: THE NOTRE DAME SYMPOSIUM ON THE DEAD SEA SCROLLS
    Edited by Eugene Ulrich and James VanderKam

www.ingramcontent.com/pod-product-compliance
Lightning Source LLC
Chambersburg PA
CBHW031251230426
43670CB00005B/130